The Single Market Review

IMPACT ON MANUFACTURING

PROCESSED FOODSTUFFS

The Single Market Review series

Subseries	**I —**	**Impact on manufacturing**
Volume:	1	Food, drink and tobacco processing machinery
	2	Pharmaceutical products
	3	Textiles and clothing
	4	Construction site equipment
	5	Chemicals
	6	Motor vehicles
	7	Processed foodstuffs
	8	Telecommunications equipment
Subseries	**II —**	**Impact on services**
Volume:	1	Insurance
	2	Air transport
	3	Credit institutions and banking
	4	Distribution
	5	Road freight transport
	6	Telecommunications: liberalized services
	7	Advertising
	8	Audio-visual services and production
	9	Single information market
	10	Single energy market
	11	Transport networks
Subseries	**III —**	**Dismantling of barriers**
Volume:	1	Technical barriers to trade
	2	Public procurement
	3	Customs and fiscal formalities at frontiers
	4	Industrial property rights
	5	Capital market liberalization
	6	Currency management costs
Subseries	**IV —**	**Impact on trade and investment**
Volume:	1	Foreign direct investment
	2	Trade patterns inside the single market
	3	Trade creation and trade diversion
	4	External access to European markets
Subseries	**V —**	**Impact on competition and scale effects**
Volume:	1	Price competition and price convergence
	2	Intangible investments
	3	Competition issues
	4	Economies of scale
Subseries	**VI —**	**Aggregate and regional impact**
Volume:	1	Regional growth and convergence
	2	The cases of Greece, Spain, Ireland and Portugal
	3	Trade, labour and capital flows: the less developed regions
	4	Employment, trade and labour costs in manufacturing
	5	Aggregate results of the single market programme

Results of the business survey

EUROPEAN COMMISSION

The Single Market Review

IMPACT ON MANUFACTURING

PROCESSED FOODSTUFFS

The Single Market Review

SUBSERIES I: VOLUME 7

OFFICE FOR OFFICIAL PUBLICATIONS
OF THE EUROPEAN COMMUNITIES

KOGAN PAGE . EARTHSCAN

This report is part of a series of 39 studies commissioned from independent consultants in the context of a major review of the Single Market. The 1996 Single Market Review responds to a 1992 Council of Ministers Resolution calling on the European Commission to present an overall analysis of the effectiveness of measures taken in creating the Single Market. This review, which assesses the progress made in implementing the Single Market Programme, was coordinated by the Directorate-General 'Internal Market and Financial Services' (DG XV) and the Directorate-General 'Economic and Financial Affairs' (DG II) of the European Commission.

This document was prepared for the European Commission

by

Bureau Européen de Recherches

It does not, however, express the Commission's official views. Whilst every reasonable effort has been made to provide accurate information in regard to the subject matter covered, the Consultants are not responsible for any remaining errors. All recommendations are made by the Consultants for the purpose of discussion. Neither the Commission nor the Consultants accept liability for the consequences of actions taken on the basis of the information contained herein.

The European Commission would like to express thanks to the external experts and representatives of firms and industry bodies for their contribution to the 1996 Single Market Review, and to this report in particular.

Office for Official Publications of the European Communities
2 rue Mercier, L-2985 Luxembourg
ISBN 92-827-8774-5   Catalogue number: C1-67-96-007-EN-C

Kogan Page . Earthscan
120 Pentonville Road, London N1 9JN
ISBN 0 7494 2311 0

Table of contents

List of tables

List of figures

List of abbreviations

ACF	Advisory Committee on Foodstuffs
ADI	Acceptable daily intake
AJVs	Alliances and Joint Ventures
BER	Bureau Européen de Recherches
bn	Billion
CAP	Common agricultural policy
CEECs	Central and Eastern European countries
CEN	Comité européen de normalisation
CIAA	Confederation of Food and Drink Industries of the EU
CPDA	Standing Committee on Foodstuffs
EMU	Economic and monetary union
EP	European Parliament
ERM	Exchange rate mechanism
EC	European Communities
ECU	European currency unit
EU	European Union
FAO	Food and Agriculture Organization of the United Nations
FDI	Foreign direct investment
GMOs	Genetically modified organisms
GVA	Gross value added
HACCP	Hazard Analysis and Critical Control Points
M&As	Mergers and acquisitions
MMC	Monopolies and Mergers Commission
mn	Million
NACE	General industrial classification of economic activities within the European Communities
NTBs	Non-tariff barriers
OECD	Organization for Economic Cooperation and Development
OJ	Official Journal of the European Communities
QUIDs	Quantitative ingredient declarations
R&D	Research and development
RCA	Revealed comparative advantage
SCF	Scientific Committee for Food
SM	Single market
SME	Small and medium-sized enterprises
SMP	Single market programme
VAT	Value-added tax

Acknowledgements

The project was directed by Conrad Caspari and Dr Maria Christodoulou (Bureau Européen de Recherches, Brussels) in collaboration with Dr Andrew Fearne (Wye College, University of London).

Other project members and country experts included: Rodolphe de Borchgrave (CADMOS, Brussels), Jessica Lewis-Bowen (CEAS, Wye), Andy Cunliffe (PROMAR International, Newbury), Alicia Langreo (SABORA, Madrid), Manuel Goulartt de Medeiros (AGRO-GES, Lisbon).

We would like to extend our thanks to the various food and drink trade associations in the Member States for their valuable input to this project as well as to all participants in the industry survey and the case studies.

1. Summary

This report on the effectiveness and impact of the single market programme (SMP) on the processed food and drinks sector presents the results from the four stages of the research undertaken.

The report is introduced by a brief overview of the salient features of the sector in terms of structure, technological intensity, market trends, employment, trade and output performance. For the specific product sectors covered directly by this study, 1993 figures indicate that a total of 33,000 firms generated output of some ECU 153 billion and employed 1.06 million persons. This represents some 35.7% of total production value and 45.9% of employment in the entire EU food and drinks industry. It should be noted that these sub-sectors tend to be in heavily branded and packaged food markets. These are generally more heavily concentrated than the food and drinks industry as a whole with a small number of large firms dominating EU production and trade.

Stage one of the study provides a descriptive analysis of the progress and implementation of the SMP to date and contains specific hypotheses designed to test the impact of legislation. The key feature of the SMP with regard to processed food and drink is the large volume of legislation which is specific to the sector (Chapter 2). Out of the 282 measures covered by the SMP, nearly 100 pertain directly or indirectly to the food industry. The launch of the SMP marked, for the food industry, the beginning of a new approach to food law harmonization based on horizontal rather than product-specific (vertical) measures. The basic framework legislation for these horizontal measures, as set out in the Commission's 1985 White Paper, has now largely been adopted. It should, however, be noted that a number of important detailed measures either have not yet been adopted/fully implemented (e.g. in the additives field) or have only been adopted recently (e.g. hygiene and food controls).

Stage two of the study provides a statistical analysis of secondary data designed to test and where appropriate substantiate the hypotheses established during stage one. Results from the primary data collection exercise undertaken in stage three in the form of an industry survey are also presented. Specific details of the analysis of the SMP impact on business strategy are largely based on five case studies carried out in stage four.

Before looking at the results of the study in detail, it is worth noting that the food and drinks sectors covered by this review indicated that, in spite of the very substantial progress made on the SMP legislation programme, in many instances they see the SMP as incomplete due to harmonized legislation which still needs to be adopted or fully implemented. In addition, there is a perception that new trade barriers may arise in future due to non-uniform implementation, interpretation and control mechanisms within the different Member States.

More generally the interview results obtained highlighted the need to place the SMP in perspective. While the initiative was strongly welcomed by companies, it was frequently noted that they were much more affected by factors either not related to the SMP at all (e.g. accession for Spain and Portugal, German unification, change in Central and Eastern Europe, raw material prices determined by the common agricultural policy, global market trends, stable consumption levels, geographical distance for certain markets such as Greece or Ireland) or only very indirectly related to the SMP (e.g. growing retailer concentration, general economic conditions, exchange rate volatility, fiscal barriers, socio-economic legislation on employment, advertising restrictions, environmental legislation, etc.). Thus, in most cases the SMP impact was perceived to have been indirect and/or additional to the above factors.

It is also important to distinguish between two kinds of impact. The SMP has had an impact both in terms of companies' general strategic response to the prospect of an enlarged market without trade barriers and more specifically in terms of particular adjustments made as certain items of legislation were adopted. The analysis shows that in many instances companies started to adjust their strategies fairly soon after the launch of the SMP, while the more specific legislation-induced adjustments occurred in line with the timing of the introduction of various items of SMP legislation. This means that a number of SMP effects are only just beginning to take place and others have not as yet started to occur.

The key results obtained from the study are as follows.

Market access: There is clear evidence that for most of the sectors under review (except pasta) not only has there been a consistent growth in trade, and particularly intra-EU trade, over the whole period under review (1978–94) but also that post-1986 the trend in this direction accelerated with an increase in the proportion of trade taking place within the EU (Section 4.2). These general findings from the statistical and time series analysis were reinforced by the industry survey and case studies. The industry survey in particular indicated that the SMP improved market access with 96 (out of 108) responses indicating that the SMP had either 'significantly' or 'to some extent' removed trade barriers.

While the above results confirm the hypothesis that there has been a post-1986 'Europeanization' process in the food and drinks industry, it should be noted that due to the nature of the products covered by this study (often high volume, low unit value products with distinct national/regional markets) overall trade is limited. Thus, only three product categories ('other foods', spirits and chocolate/confectionery), all of which have a favourable unit value/transport cost ratio, are classified as 'highly' traded goods with import penetration and export intensity ratios higher than 20%. This structural feature has remained stable throughout the 1978–94 period and this suggests that the SMP has accelerated rather than induced trade growth.

Production costs: The results of the study indicate that the SMP has significantly contributed to removing trade barriers and that this in turn has allowed for a number of short-term cost savings (Section 4.3). These cost reductions were noted all along the chain from production to marketing and distribution (and longer term from the rationalization of corporate structures). It was, however, noted that by and large the benefits of such savings tended to be seized by larger manufacturers more readily than smaller ones, particularly since the latter are increasingly being absorbed within corporations of growing magnitude. More generally it was noted both in the industry survey and in the case studies that the SMP had no impact on agricultural raw material costs, a significant element of production costs which is largely determined by the common agricultural policy.

Cross-border sales and marketing: The study results indicate that most food and drink sectors (except soft drinks/mineral water and beer) have intensified their trade activities and that this process accelerated post-1986 thus confirming the hypothesis of an SMP-induced 'Europeanization' of the industry (Section 4.4). The qualitative research did, however, indicate that vertical (product-specific) legislation was considerably less important than other factors (horizontal and other legislation, strong regional and local consumer preferences, global developments within the industry) in determining both trade and market growth.

More generally, the historically determined position of particular countries in production and trade appears not to have shifted significantly, i.e. those countries which were the predominant producers and traders generally continued to be so.

Scale and scope effects: The data analysis indicates that in five out of seven sectors reviewed the total number of enterprises fell in the 1978–93 period while production values increased suggesting an increase in scale of operation (Section 4.5). This is confirmed by industry survey results in which over half of the large firms interviewed indicated changes in the size and number of their plants. However, the study overall has provided only limited evidence that such plant and company rationalization was specifically SMP-induced. This is not surprising in a sector which has low technical economies of scale and where, therefore, the best strategy for expansion is through M&As and other alliances rather than an increase in the size of production units.

Foreign direct investment and location effects: There is strong evidence of extensive EU-wide cross-border merger and takeover activity in the processed food and drink sector, particularly post-1986 and until the early 1990s, which would be consistent with the impact hypothesized for the SMP (Section 4.6). It must be noted, however, that there are numerous reasons relating to corporate strategy that drive such activity, notably the need to counter increasing EU retailer concentration. Thus, the M&A trend is part of more global developments within the food industry which have occurred in parallel with the SMP. Nevertheless, by causing a 'Europeanization' of corporate thought processes and strategies, the SMP was considered to have helped to create the business environment for such activity. There is supporting evidence on this from the industry survey and case studies, with FDI increasing and a change in production locations seen as a direct result of the SMP.

Upstream/downstream linkages: One of the major drivers for the intense restructuring and alliance activity that has occurred in the food and drinks sector particularly over the last decade is the need to establish or consolidate supplier and customer relations in the face of increased retailer buying power (Section 4.7). The qualitative evidence indicates that the SMP indirectly contributed to this process by accelerating larger companies' moves to expand cross-border sourcing and rationalize their procurement and distribution operations although other factors were generally considered more important.

Changes in competition and market concentration: There is clear evidence that the level of concentration in the sector has increased substantially in the last decade, with the share of the three largest operators rising from 23% of the market in 1988 to 36% in 1991 and an even higher level now (Section 4.8). It is clear that these changes have in part resulted from companies repositioning themselves on a more comprehensive pan-European basis and that this has in part been a response to the SMP. Over half the companies interviewed felt that market entry conditions had become easier following the SMP although this view was not fully shared in the southern Member States.

In this context it should be noted that, in most of the product sectors reviewed, the market is dominated by a few powerful brands with an already established position maintained by high advertising expenditure and considerable R&D and product development budgets. This constitutes a significant barrier to entry as the costs of entry into new markets can be very high. This factor tends to diminish the trade and market liberalizing effects of the SMP, especially for SMEs who in any case tend to be squeezed between the increasing power of the multiple retailers and the larger brand manufacturers.

Productivity and competitiveness: The study provides positive quantitative evidence of increased investment for all sectors and some improvements in productivity and competitiveness in the industry post-1986 (Section 4.9). This result was confirmed by the industry survey, which shows that half the companies interviewed had recently seen changes in their R&D and product development strategies, and by some of the case study responses.

Employment: The hypotheses with regard to the SMP impact on employment which suggest that this will continue to decline are largely confirmed by the study, although the pattern between sectors and Member States has varied in response to specific changes such as German unification and EU accession for Spain and Portugal (Section 4.10).

Evolution of final prices: While the study results indicate continuous and significant price convergence over the period reviewed, for the most part there is only limited evidence of any direct linkage between the SMP and either price levels or the extent of price dispersion (Section 4.11). This is, however, hardly surprising given the aggregate nature of the data being analysed, exchange rate fluctuations and the fundamental role played by the increasing concentration on the retail side which offsets the ability of branded product producers to maintain prices.

Business strategy: The study has shown that the SMP has significantly influenced company strategies particularly in sectors with relatively highly traded goods (pasta, chocolate/confectionery, other foods, biscuits) (Chapter 5). Amongst larger firms the SMP was found to have increased the 'Europeanization' of procurement, intensified rationalization and restructuring within the industry, and caused companies to develop production and marketing strategies aimed at promoting a more consolidated range of products – so called 'Euro-brands' – identifiable EU-wide. More generally, the SMP appears to have encouraged managerial reorganization to capture the benefits of legislative harmonization as well as efforts to create a stronger EU-wide presence amongst larger companies, leaving SMEs to focus increasingly on niche product and regional or third-country markets.

2. Introduction

2.1. Objectives

The objectives of this study are twofold. First to identify what, if any, changes have occurred in the structure and performance of the food processing industry in the EUR-12 since the implementation of the single market programme (SMP); and second, to determine the extent to which these changes have been the result (either partly or uniquely) of the SMP legislation. More specifically, we are seeking to establish the nature (positive or negative) and strength (high or low) of causality with respect to the SMP legislation.

2.2. Methodology

Research was carried out in four stages. Stage one involved a descriptive analysis of the progress and implementation of SMP legislation to date and the generation of specific hypotheses regarding the impact of legislation on certain key aspects of the food processing sector. Stage two focused on a statistical analysis of secondary data, with the objective of substantiating and, where appropriate, testing the hypotheses identified in stage one. Stages three and four involved the generation of primary data, through an EU-wide survey of 78 food processing companies and detailed case studies of five companies with distinctly different experiences with regard to the impact of legislation and their response to the SMP in general. The results from the latter two stages of the study have been used to complete the testing of hypotheses with regard to the direct SMP impacts and shed light on those aspects which could only be elucidated by further qualitative examination.

2.2.1. Macroanalysis

The hypotheses generated in stage one of the legislation analysis represent the impacts which we might expect on a priori grounds given the legislation implemented to date, and are based on discussion with representatives from the trade and a review of the SMP literature.

The statistical macroanalysis undertaken in stage two covers the period 1978/79–1993/94 for each of the 12 Member States, and the data is aggregated to the 4-digit NACE classification level.[1] The tabulated data is presented per NACE code in a separate statistical appendix (Appendix D). The data is drawn from Eurostat (INDE, VISA and DEBA databases).

In order to identify the possible impact which the SMP may have already had on the industry, stepwise regression techniques were used to establish whether or not any (statistically significant) structural changes have taken place post-1986 and which would therefore point to potential SMP effects. This approach provided a suitable 'anti-monde' in which developments within the EU food and drinks industry were analysed prior to and after the SMP (1978–85 and 1986–93).

In addition to the analysis of the data for the EU, comparative data has been analysed, where available, for the USA. This has enabled us to determine whether any structural breaks

---

[1]   The sources used for the secondary data analysis are presented in Appendix D. A full description of the product coverage is presented in Appendix A.

identified for the EU may be considered unique to the EU and possibly due to the SMP, or whether they simply reflect global developments in the food processing industry.[2]

It should be noted that while the data for all of the variables examined (production, trade, GVA, investment, prices) is presented in Appendix D in both nominal and real terms, for the purposes of the structural break analysis the data has not been deflated. There are no a priori reasons for using deflated data for this purpose.

(a) The model to be estimated is not a structural one and is not specified with a view to establishing causality. Thus, we are not concerned about the existence or otherwise of inflationary forces *per se*.

(b) The process of deflating the time series introduces the risk of creating structural breaks for the 'wrong' reasons. The index of producer prices, which has been used to deflate some of the financial data in the descriptive statistics for the sector, is not a 'smooth' series and would almost certainly generate spurious structural breaks.

It should be stressed that while the time series analysis allows an examination of the type and direction of structural change over time, it is not used to derive a conclusion attributing causality to the SMP. Rather the purpose has been to examine the extent and direction of any significant change in the variables examined post-1986 (*vis-à-vis* the pre-1986 period) which point to the likelihood of an SMP influence. More specific issues of causality were investigated by the analysis of legislation, the literature review, and the industry survey and case studies.

With respect to trade data, in addition to the structural break analysis, two trade ratios were calculated: the import penetration ratio and the ratio of exports to imports (or trade ratio).

The overall empirical analysis and specific methodological issues are discussed and presented in Appendix C.1. Results of the statistical analysis are presented in Appendix D.

2.2.2. Microanalysis

This is composed of an industry survey and five case studies.

In the context of the overall methodology, the main objective of the industry survey has been to test and substantiate the statistical analysis and hypothesis testing of the macroanalysis with qualitative information and comments. In particular, the industry survey seeks to take the macroanalysis one step further by highlighting specific effects which can be directly linked to the SMP and which have taken place in the period 1985–95. A secondary objective has been to distinguish particular aspects of the incomplete SMP and outstanding barriers to food trade in the EU which are of relevance to the future of the industry.

With these objectives in mind, on the basis of a questionnaire developed by BER, we selected a sample of 78 companies for face-to-face interviews throughout the EU covering all the product sectors specified for this study. Both for company selection and for the finalization of the questionnaire we have had an input from national food and drink associations in the individual Member States. An in-depth, small scale, face-to-face interview-based survey was perceived as a

---

[2]   This issue is further discussed in the context of 'anti-monde' in Appendix C.1.

more reliable method of analysis than a large scale postal survey, and has yielded detailed, comprehensive and informed comments on the SMP's implications for businesses.

Appendix C.2 describes the sample selection and its representativeness in detail. In a varied sector such as the processed food and drinks industry, the aim has been to get a balanced sample that can adequately represent all product sectors and all Member States. In total the companies selected account for an important (up to 70% in some instances) share of national and EU markets (Appendix E, Figure E.0 and Table E.0). Although no overall figure can be given on the EU market share held by the total sample,[3] this includes most of the largest companies operating in the sectors under review.

Appendix C.3 briefly explains the case study framework. Summarized results of the industry survey are presented in Appendix E and of the case studies in Appendix F.

2.3. Overview of the sector

The EUR-12 food and drinks sector currently (1994) employs some 2.28 million or 11% of the EU industrial work-force and represents some 16% of industrial EU production value. France, Germany, the UK, Italy and Spain are the largest EU producers in terms of output value, while the sector is particularly important for the economy of Ireland, Denmark, Greece, Netherlands and Spain where it represents over 20% of national industrial production.

Product tradability is generally low: in 1994 only some 15% of production value was traded within the EU while a further 6.7% was exported outside the Union. Import penetration (extra-EU) is also quite low, averaging at less than 6% during the last decade.

A particular feature of the EUR-12 food and drinks industry which is consistently cited in relevant literature is the existence of a dual market structure. The sector is characterized by a small number of large companies which operate over a wide range of product sectors and geographical markets, and a large number of SMEs which tend to focus on niche product markets or regional/local geographical market segments. The emergence of this structure was already apparent in the early 1980s (OECD, 1983).

Within the EUR-12, the extent of convergence in the food and drinks sector has also been quite extensively examined. Irrespective of SMP effects, it has been argued that the market structures of food manufacturing industries in the EUR-12 have been converging due to similar competitive environments, foreign investment and trade, and the homogenization of consumer preferences (Shaw et al., 1989). Moreover, evidence of similar developments can be found in most food economies of high income countries (Connor et al., 1985), and particularly of the US (Uhl, 1991).

Technology intensiveness is rather low in this sector when compared with other consumer goods industries, such as pharmaceuticals, domestic electrical appliances, etc. Nonetheless, important variations exist between particular product industries and the further we move into high value-added, processed and branded goods the more technological development intensifies.

---

[3] Due to the wide variety of products and geographical markets covered.

On the demand side, food and drink represent the single largest item of expenditure in households' budgets although, over the years, there has been a significant shift towards higher value, added convenience, superior quality products (Stirling University, 1990). Despite a considerable convergence in consumer preferences, brought about by converging lifestyles and economic conditions (Blandford, 1984), national tastes and regional variations continue to persist and play an important role in purchasing patterns.

This study only focuses on a number of product sub-sectors within the industry, as follows: NACE 417: pasta; NACE 419: industrial baking (bread, biscuits, rusks, flour-based snacks); NACE 421: cocoa and sugar confectionery, ice cream; NACE 423: coffee, tea and other food; NACE 424: alcohol and spirits (not wine); NACE 427: brewing and malting; NACE 428: soft drinks and mineral waters (a detailed breakdown of the products covered is presented in Appendix A).

The sub-sectors selected concern products which have undergone a considerable degree of processing or value-adding activities (so-called second stage processed foods), so that the end product can be considered sufficiently remote from the raw material or agricultural origin. This selection reflects the particular relevance of the SMP to processed rather than fresh foods. It also assists in eliminating CAP-related effects which are particularly apparent in industries producing foods of a lesser degree of processing, such as dairy, meat, wine or prepared fruit and vegetables. The selected sectors' importance in terms of production, employment and exports is illustrated in Table 2.1.

Table 2.1.   Key data of the reviewed product sectors, 1993

	NACE code	Production value, mn ECU, (excl. VAT)	Number of firms *	Employment
Pasta	417	7,188	317	33,978
Baking	419	28,086	27,272	449,412
Chocolate etc.	421	23,824	1,180	158,407
Other foods	423	35,363	2,205	181,204
Spirits	424	13,150	461	31,946
Beer	427	27,713	616	117,986
Soft drinks	428	17,917	1,166	89,921
TOTAL		153,241	33,217	1,062,854
TOTAL food & drink		427,980	..	2,316,000
% covered by the study		35.7%	..	45.9%

* Only includes firms with >20 employees, except for Spain and Portugal.
Source: Eurostat (Appendix D).

Although, the sectors reviewed represent only some 36% of all food and drink production and some 46% of employment, they have a particularly strong presence in the branded and packaged food markets. These markets tend to be generally more heavily concentrated than the overall food and drink industry, with a small number of large firms heavily dominating EUR-12 production and trade (Shaw et al., 1989). As this suggests, the involvement of multinational groups and conglomerates is fairly pronounced in these industries as is product innovation and brand internationalization. For instance, all the large food multinationals have a strong presence in the chocolate and confectionery market.

Table 2.2 presents an overview of the competitive performance of some aspects of the sectors reviewed over the period 1986–93, by ranking them in terms of growth (real annual rates of change in value of output) and tradability (export intensity, intra-EU).

Table 2.2.   Export intensity vs. growth in EU food and drinks, 1986–93

Export intensity[2]	Growth in output[1]		
	LOW (<2.9%)	MEDIUM (3–4.5%)	HIGH (>4.6%)
LOW (<10%)	Beer (a: 0%, b: 4%)	Industrial baking (a: 4.3%, b: 7.1%) Pasta (a: 4%, b: 6.5%)	Soft drinks & mineral water (a: 5%, b: 4.6%)
HIGH (>10%)	Spirits (a: -0.2%, b: 15.1%)	All food and drinks (a: 3.1%, b: 13%)	Other foods (a: 5.6%, b: 11.9%) Chocolate etc. (a: 4.7%, b: 15%)

[1] Average annual rate of growth during the period 1986–93.
[2] Intra-EU export intensity, expressed as the percentage of EUR-12 production value that is exported within the EUR-12 (1986–93 average).
Source: BER based on Eurostat data.

In common with many consumer goods sectors, the overall food and drinks market has recorded considerable rates of growth during this period with certain market segments ranked among the fastest growing (chocolate and confectionery, soft drinks and mineral water, other foods). Strong demand for these products can be largely attributed to the faster growth in disposable incomes over the period under discussion (compared to the first half of the 1980s) and changes in household consumption patterns. On the other hand, the moderate to low growth sectors will reflect stagnant demand for these products especially in the beer and spirits sectors. It should be emphasized that the above rates include the effect of German reunification, which caused production of all food and drinks in Germany to grow at an average annual rate exceeding 10% after 1990 due to strong demand growth in the new *Länder*.

Export intensity (intra-EU), on the other hand, is generally low with the exception of spirits (among the slowest growing sectors), and chocolate confectionery and other foods (among the fastest growing sectors). The latter are thus most sensitive to EUR-12-wide economic conditions, changes in intra-EU demand trends and the competitive environment. For those product segments with moderate to fast rates of growth (industrial baking, pasta, soft drinks), a low export intensity implies that the strong output rise in the period 1986–93 was stimulated by demand developments within the national markets.

Figure 2.1 depicts the competitive position of the sectors examined in world markets on the basis of their average extra-EU export intensity and import penetration ratios during the period 1986–93.

Figure 2.1.   EU food and drinks industry: world competitive position

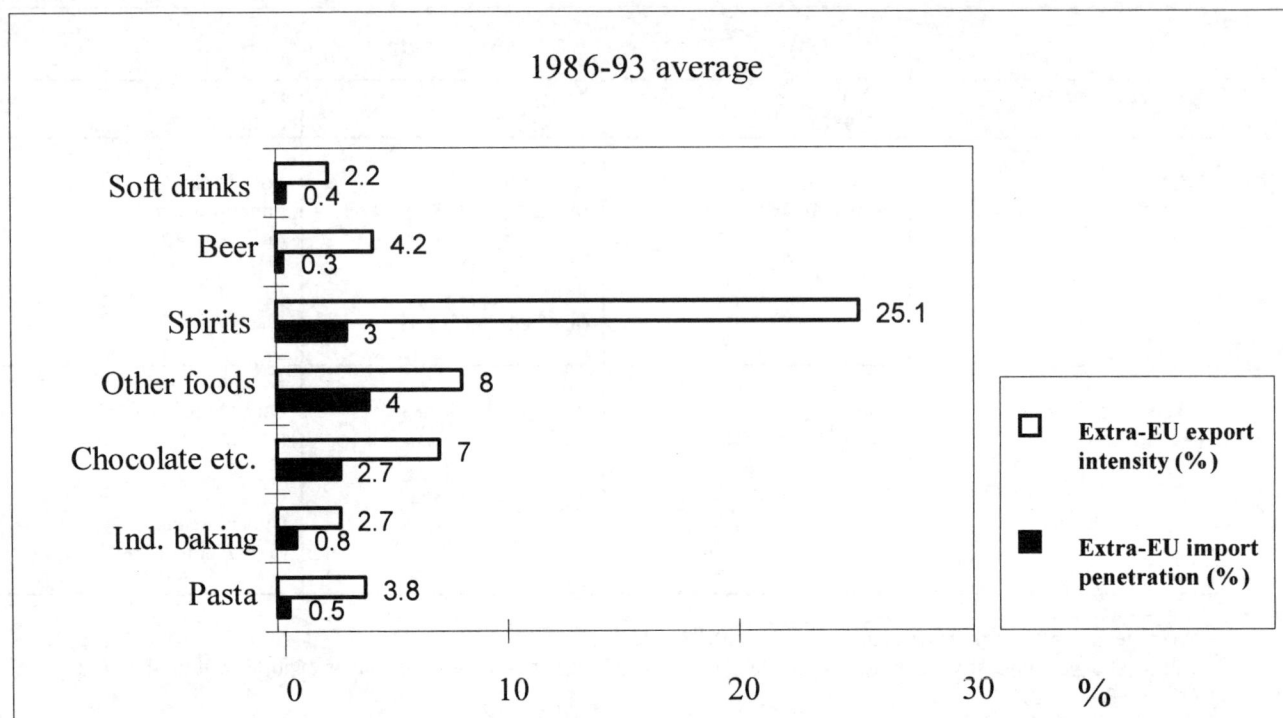

1986-93 average

Extra-EU export intensity (%)

Extra-EU import penetration (%)

Source: BER based on Eurostat data.

All of the industries examined, with the exception of spirits, display a low export orientation beyond the EUR-12, with less than 8% of production value exported to the rest of the world. Extra-EU import penetration is also low in all cases, with imports accounting for less than 4% of domestic consumption on average and falling to less than 1% for industrial baking, beer, pasta and soft drinks. It can thus be concluded that, with the exception of spirits, the sectors examined are largely shielded from world competition.

Finally, Table 2.3 rates the sectors reviewed on the basis of NTB presence and overall import penetration. As can be seen, most sectors, except chocolate, with a high level of NTBs (pasta, beer, soft drinks, mineral water) also indicate low levels of import penetration while conversely as would be expected a priori for the other foods and spirits category low levels of NTBs are associated with relatively high levels of import penetration.

Table 2.3.   Import penetration vs. NTBs in EU food and drinks, 1986–93

	Non-tariff barriers[1]		
Import penetration[2]	**LOW**	**MEDIUM**	**HIGH**
LOW (<10%)	Industrial baking (b: 7.9%)	No food or drink product in this category - more common with other consumer goods such as clothing	Pasta (b: 7.5%) Beer (b: 4.6%) Soft drinks & mineral water (b: 5.4%)
HIGH (>10%)	Other foods (b: 17.6%) Spirits (b: 22.1%)	As above	Chocolate etc. (b: 18.4%)

[1] NTB definition: based on a comparison of 174 product sectors, of which 113 are traded goods (Buigues et al., 1990). The main benchmark for the classification of sectors to low, medium, high impact has been the extent to which differences in standards or administrative and technical controls are an obstacle to market integration.

[2] Defined as the percentage of EUR-12 consumption that is imported from within and outside the EUR-12 (1986–93 average).

Source: BER based on Eurostat data.

An overview of the main features of each of the product sectors under review is provided in Appendix A.2.

2.4.   Report structure

Chapter 3 contains the analysis of the SMP legislation. The resulting hypotheses are then tested in Chapters 4 and 5 of the report.

More specifically, Chapter 4 presents in particular the impact of the single market on a number of factors associated with sectoral performance, incorporating the results of the macroanalysis and the industry survey. Chapter 5 is primarily concerned with the business strategy implications of the SMP.

In both Chapters 4 and 5, the hypotheses tested are presented at the beginning of each section. The results of the data analysis are then elaborated sector by sector. A discussion of the major trends over the period 1978/79 to 1993/94 is followed by a summary of the results from the structural break analysis (where applicable) and the industry survey and case studies. The main conclusions are drawn for the food and drink processing sector as a whole.

3. Legal and administrative measures taken to complete the single market

3.1. Barrier and measure definition

Contrary to some other sectors, there has never been a common policy in the processed food and drinks sector in the EU. Prior to the SMP, legislative efforts in this area aimed to ensure food security, public health and safety. Thus, the basis for the current EC food law framework and all measures relating to the food and drinks sector may be found in the overall industrial policy in the Community and in particular in the initiatives taken for the establishment of a single market after the publication of the 1985 White Paper. The liberalization and harmonization of procedures are laid down in some 282 measures of which about 100 directly or indirectly influence the food industry.

A list of these measures, both for food-specific and horizontal legislation, can be found in Table B.1 (Appendix B).[4] The methodology used for the definition of barriers and measures is in accordance with the White Paper classification of single market legislation. Thus, measures refer to the removal of technical, physical and fiscal barriers to the movement of goods, services and capital. It is in the particular area of technical barriers and the free movement of goods that a food-specific legislative programme was established by the White Paper. This sets out a list of urgent measures for which adoption was pursued in the period 1985–86, and a list of medium-term measures for adoption in the period 1987–92.

It should be noted that a number of industry initiatives for self-regulation are particularly important in the EU food and drinks sector. Examples of this would be voluntary standardization (particularly in the area of quality assurance with the EN 29000 series, distribution packaging, sampling and analysis methods), codes of practice and certification schemes.

3.2. Implementation of sector-specific measures

3.2.1. Nature of barriers

Sector-specific measures relate to barriers which impede the free movement of goods in the EU food and drinks market. Such barriers are erected by:

(a) differences in national regulations and industry standards;
(b) absence of relevant legislation in some countries;
(c) variations in interpretation of existing EC legislation.

The first and most thorough analysis of sector-specific barriers was provided by the 1988 Group Mac report *The Cost of non-Europe in the Foodstuffs Industry*. Some 218 barriers were identified in a number of fields in 10 product sectors all over the Community, including Spain and Portugal. Although the Group Mac project was carried out during the first phase of the White Paper's food-specific programme (1985–86), barriers were still present in the fields

---

[4]   Certain areas of legislation not explicitly stated in the White Paper, whether subsequently treated under the single market programme or not, in particular the removal of technical barriers relating to food and environmental issues, are also included in Table B.1, together with areas of food and related legislation in force prior to the launch of the single market programme.

covered by this programme as any relevant legislation adopted during this period had not yet been enforced. An advantage of the Group Mac work was the fact that it used the same sub-sector focus as the current study.

The barriers identified by the Group Mac provide invaluable background on the situation prior to the SMP. For the purposes of the current study, however, the barrier typology used is different from that followed by the Group Mac. In particular, barriers are reclassified under technical, physical and tax headings, in accordance with the definitions followed in the White Paper. Technical barriers are subdivided in a number of fields which are specific to food manufacturing and thus tie in with the development of legislation in this industry. The advantage of this approach is that it provides a direct basis for comparisons between food manufacturing and trading processes, types of barriers and areas of legislation.

Table B.2 (Appendix B) summarizes the results of this work on pre-SMP trade barriers and provides indications of where they applied as well as on the nature and frequency of such barriers.

The following observations may be made in relation to the pre-SMP position:

(a) the main type of barriers encountered in the food and drinks industry at the start of the SMP programme are technical;
(b) technical-type barriers are heavily concentrated in three fields: ingredients/processing aids (30% of cases); presentation and marketing, especially packaging (27%); traditional foods (17%);
(c) all sectors are equally affected by technical barriers; physical barriers touch on any product with meat/dairy/egg content (e.g. soups or baby food); tax barriers concern mainly excise duties on alcohol;
(d) similar barriers seem to exist across the EU; also, high, medium and low impact barriers seem to be equally spread across the EU;
(e) while most barriers relate to a specific product, in a number of cases a barrier applies across the whole range of food and drink products – such prominent cases are: UK: strict requirement on ingredient labelling; Italy: language detail on labelling; Spain: health registration and import licences necessary for all food products; Italy: samples of product needed for health controls; Greece: profit limit on imported product.

A wide range of justifications is used for the erection of a barrier. In most cases reference is made to public health and safety, but also consumer interests and fair trading (labelling, presentation and advertising), product image protection, quality control and, more recently, environmental concerns. In certain cases explicit reference is made to domestic or traditional manufacturer interests (e.g. traditional foods) and even the interests of the primary producer of the raw material if this has been significant for the country's agricultural economy (e.g. Italian requirement for the manufacture of pasta from durum wheat).

3.2.2. Analysis of measures

From a legislative point of view, the Community strategy for the elimination of barriers to cross-border operations in the food sector was largely determined by the White Paper on 'completing the internal market' (COM(85) 310 final) and a 1985 Communication on 'the internal market and the food industry' (COM(85) 603 final). While the former described the measures intended with a view to the smooth functioning of the SM by 1992, the latter lays down the particular approach to be taken in the food sector.

At the core of all Community effort in the foodstuffs sector has been the need to regulate only where necessary. Thus the 1985 Communication makes a clear distinction between 'matters which by their nature must continue to be the subject of legislation', and 'those whose characteristics are such that they do not need to be regulated' (point 7).

This has led to a combination of two instruments for the elimination of non-tariff barriers:

(a) legislative harmonization of rules pertaining to the foodstuffs sector following the 'new approach', based on Article 100a of the Treaty as inserted by the Single European Act;
(b) application of the principle of mutual recognition of national regulations and standards for matters which do not need to be regulated at a Community level, based on Articles 30 to 36 of the EC Treaty.

From an administrative point of view, under the Single European Act, more food legislation could be adopted by qualified majority voting under Article 100a instead of the unanimity originally required in the Council under Article 100 of the EC Treaty. In certain areas, the Commission has been empowered to adopt instruments for implementing the basic or 'framework' rules established by the Council. As a significant body of food legislation under the 'new approach' is composed of implementing rules, the delegation of power to the Commission simplified and accelerated the procedures.

Since the mid-1980s the Standing Committee on Foodstuffs (known by its French acronym CPDA or *Comité Permanent des Denrées Alimentaires*) has been central to the administration of this system since it provides a bridge for cooperation between the Commission and the Member States.

Legislative harmonization

In essence, the introduction of the single market programme, launched with the 1985 White Paper, marked the end of an approach to food law harmonization based on vertical (product-specific) measures. Instead, in line with Article 100a of the Single European Act, the SMP launches an approach based on horizontal legislation which primarily aims to address a number of social welfare objectives notably to ensure a high level of public health protection on nutritional, microbiological and toxicological issues, and adequate consumer information on the origin, nature, characteristics and prices of foodstuffs. These objectives are clearly stated in the Commission's 1985 Communication as follows:

> 'Community legislation on foodstuffs should be limited to provisions justified by the need to: protect public health; provide consumers with information and protection in matters other than health and ensure fair trading; provide for the necessary public controls' (p. 9).

Further targets for Community food legislation were set in the field of product quality and the associated geographical indications of origin and traditional foods. These objectives of a quality policy were set out in a 1988 Communication on 'the future of rural society' (COM(88) 501 final).

The above policy objectives have served to provide the framework for assessing what needs to be regulated at a Community level and the starting point for a number of food Directives.

Already in 1985, the White Paper had provided a list of food-specific legislation which needed to be harmonized at Community level. This was supplemented and clarified by the 1985 Communication and a further Communication on 'the free movement of foodstuffs within the Community', adopted in 1989. A complete list of such measures, including those laid down by the White Paper, the 1985 and 1989 Communications and those subsequently related to the SMP legislative activity in the period 1985 to date, is given in Table B.1 (Appendix B). These are composed of:

(a) horizontal measures, applicable throughout the food chain;
(b) vertical measures, applicable in particular sub-sectors of the food industry.

In the horizontal domain, the SMP initially concentrated on five so-called Framework Directives: control of food; food additives; materials and articles in contact with food; food for particular nutritional uses; and the labelling, advertising and presentation of foodstuffs. These are implemented through a number of specific Directives. In the field of veterinary legislation the legislative approach has been somewhat different with a proliferation of texts relating to hygiene and quality. Since the SMP approach is based on horizontal measures, no new vertical measures have been introduced since 1985, although harmonized rules have been adopted on some pre-1985 vertical measures, notably grain and similar products, fruit juices, coffee/chicory extracts, chocolate, honey, preserved milk, erucic acid. In the alcoholic drink sector specific rules have been laid down for wines and spirits.

According to Article 100b of the Single European Act the harmonization process was due to be completed by the end of 1992, with the Commission drawing up an inventory of national measures yet to be harmonized.

Table B.3 (Appendix B) briefly describes the main fields of SMP legislation and indicates the objectives pursued by harmonization in each field.

Mutual recognition

For those matters not yet harmonized in the technical field, national measures and the principle of 'mutual recognition' of such measures apply between Member States under the provisions of Articles 30 to 36 of the Treaty, which prohibit quantitative restrictions on imports and exports and all measures having equivalent effect. A benchmark year in this respect was 1989, when the Communication on 'the free movement of foodstuffs within the Community' (COM(89) 256 final) clarified the application of Articles 30 to 36 in the foodstuffs sector. Although Article 30 is open to interpretation on a case-by-case basis, it generally allows the circulation of goods when independent scientific evidence proves there is no danger to public health and/or the reasons for national restrictions are not justified. Reference to the case law of the Court of Justice (*Cassis de Dijon* and subsequent) may be made to ensure the free movement of foodstuffs.

It should be noted that the European Court of Justice has also defined examples where mutual recognition does not apply. Thus a 1995 ruling upheld Greek legislation requiring infant formulae to be sold only in pharmacies since it was considered that this did not impinge on cross-border trade. Similar judgements were made with respect to Belgian rules inhibiting the sales of spirits in cafés (Blesgen case). More generally the Court appears to argue that Article 30 of the Treaty applies to the characteristics of products rather than the conditions of sale.

National practices or rules contrary to Article 30 of the Treaty are most frequently found in the food and drinks industry. Governments frequently issue their own rules in this sector specifying the conditions food products should meet in order to be marketed, such as on labelling, packaging, composition, designation and identification, etc. These are intended to achieve domestic objectives set by the Member States, notably those relating to protection of health and the consumer, the environment and fairness in commercial transactions. Mutual recognition, based on case law, seeks to ensure that Member States may not prohibit the sale of imported products lawfully marketed in other Member States on the basis of national commercial rules. One of the main targets of this principle are those national rules that tie consumers to a given food product on the basis of its composition – the so-called 'recipe laws'.

Following the 1989 Communication, Member States were invited to examine national law and administrative practices and align them to the principles laid down by that Communication with a view to avoiding any potential barriers to intra-Community trade. Table B.4 (Appendix B) summarizes the principles that apply to particular fields of technical barriers. These are based on Court of Justice rulings on particular cases.

Particularly important from the SM perspective are the following.

(a) The principle of proportionality. This demands the adoption of measures that are least harmful to trade, in cases where a choice of measures is available.

(b) The fact that authorization procedures across the EU must conform to certain minimum requirements with regard to both the substance and the procedure itself. In assessing potential health risks, in particular, the findings of international scientific research must be taken into account (EC-CPDA, FAO-Codex Alimentarius, World Health Organization), as must technological change and results of tests/analyses/checks carried out in Member State of origin. Additional elements that may be taken into account are the traditional diet characteristics and eating habits of the importing country. Certain further provisions aim to guarantee that the procedures are user-friendly. Traders should have easy access to authorization procedures, and access to judicial review in case of rejection. Procedures should be complete within a maximum period of 90 days. Authorizations have general application, i.e. they cover all products fulfilling the conditions for authorization.

(c) In order to prevent the creation of new obstacles to the free movement of goods, Member States are encouraged to insert mutual recognition clauses in their national rules. These clauses concern mutual recognition in three fields: (i) national standards, rules and technical specifications; (ii) tests and certification carried out by national registered laboratories; (iii) conformity assessment procedures for the approval of national laboratories to carry out testing and certification.

The transparency of application of Article 30 is expected to be greatly enhanced in future by a recent Decision (adopted on 13 December 1995) of the European Parliament and the Council, which establishes a procedure for Member States to communicate any national measures derogating from the principle of free circulation within the single market (Decision 3052/95).

An additional instrument in the case of the absence of Community law is that envisaged by Directive 83/189/EEC on standards and technical regulations, as amended by Directive

88/182/EEC, which obliges Member States to communicate to the Commission information concerning technical regulations and standards adopted at a national level. As from 1 January 1989, the scope of this Directive was extended to foodstuffs. There are currently 60–80 such notifications of national technical regulations per year, and this has helped to prevent the emergence of trade barriers in this area.

3.2.3. Functioning

The following aspects of the functioning of SMP legislation are examined in this section: state of adoption of EU legislation; implementation, including transposition into national law (timing and correctness); application of the principle of mutual recognition; and SMP impacts on the food industry.

Adoption

As already indicated, the SMP philosophy has been to take a 'soft approach' to harmonizing legislation in the food industry. In most fields framework legislation paves the way for the gradual adoption of specific implementing rules and/or industry standards. The underlying aim has been to maintain respect for national practices, tastes and traditions while pursuing the objectives of the single market and allowing flexibility to accommodate technical progress. The latter is achieved through the establishment of 'positive lists' of authorized products, additives, other substances (e.g. contaminants). Procedures for authorization are uniform across the EU, as opposed to earlier practices. Both the initial authorizations and regular updates are subject to the approval of the Commission's Standing Committee on Foodstuffs, and are based on scientific evidence and/or detailed standard methods of analysis and tests.

Although framework legislation has now been adopted in all the five areas originally envisaged by the SMP, a significant volume of implementing legislation is still pending. This concerns the fields of: additives; materials and articles in contact with food; special nutritional foods; food labelling; and official food controls (Appendix B, Table B.3). In the case of the Additives Directive (89/107/EEC) adopted in 1989, the Directive lays down the basic rules and calls on the Commission to propose comprehensive rules, authorized lists, purity criteria and methods of analysis for particular categories of additives. Some of these items were only adopted in 1994 (colours, sweeteners) and in 1995 (other additives) while purity criteria are still pending (except for sweeteners, adopted in 1995). This significantly handicaps the SMP process, as, effectively, the means for enforcement of this body of legislation are still not fully in place.

In the remaining fields of the SMP for food, significant progress was made in the period up to 1989. In the period just after the White Paper, from 1985 to June 1989, some 45 of the proposed 100 measures touching on the food and drinks industry were adopted. Table 3.1 shows the state of adoption of the initial food law measures as contained in the Annex to the 1985 White Paper. Although a considerable number of measures were adopted by 1989, it should be noted that progress was considerably slower that had been originally envisaged in the White Paper.

Table 3.1.   State of adoption of the 1985 White Paper[1] measures: food law

	Field/measure	Expected		Actual
		Commission proposal	Council adoption	Council adoption
	Period 1985–86			
1	General Directive on food additives	1985	1986	1989
2	General Directive on materials and articles in contact with food	1985	1986	1989
3	General Directive on food for particular nutritional uses	1985	1986	1989
4	General Directive on food labelling	1985	1986	1986
5	General Directive on food inspection (official control of foodstuffs)	1986	1987	1989
6	Directive on sampling and analysis methods	1984	1985	1985
7	Directive on quick frozen foodstuffs	1984	1985	1989
8	Flavourings	1980	1985	1988
9	Extraction solvents	1983	1986	1988
10	Preservatives	1981	1985	1985
11	Emulsifiers	1984	1985	1985
12	Infant formulae	1984	1986	1991[2]
13	Cocoa and chocolate consolidation	1984	1986	dropped[3]
14	Coffee/chicory extracts	1984	1985	1985
15	Ingredient and alcoholic strength indications (amendment to Labelling Directive)	1982	1985	1986
16	Claims in the labelling of foods	1981	1985	dropped
17	Plastic materials in contact with food (simulants)	1984	1985	1985
18	Fruit juices etc.	1985	1986	1989
19	Fruit jams etc.	1985	1986	dropped
20	Consumer protection on price indication for foods	1984	1985	1988
	Period 1987–92			
21	Directive on food irradiation	1987	1988	pending
22	Novel foods[4] (Regulation)	..	..	pending
23	Nutritional labelling	1989	1990	1990
24	Adaptation of Directives to technical progress	1987–89	1988–90	largely pending

[1] COM(85) 310 final.

[2] Adopted as Commission Directive.

[3] Abandoned because of regulatory fat issue.

[4] The White Paper explicitly refers to 'new foodstuffs from biotechnology – release of GMOs', a proposal for which was first made in 1987 with expected adoption for 1988 and final adoption in 1990. The indicated 'Novel Foods' proposed Regulation was first submitted for consideration to the Council on 7 July 1992.

Sources: 1985 White Paper on Completing the Internal Market (COM(85) 310 final of 14.6.1985); Twelfth Annual Report on Monitoring the Application of Community Law (1994) (OJ C254 of 29.9.1995); BER update.

Implementation

For the harmonized legislation listed in part I of Table B.1 (Appendix B), the current state of play as regards national transposition and implementation was established by BER on the basis of an analysis of national legislation. Table B.5 (Appendix B) summarizes the results of this analysis.

The following points are of particular interest.

(a) The main body of the SMP legislation adopted so far has now been transposed in Member States.

(b) Certain variations in transposition and implementation exist between Member States. These arise from incorrect interpretation, maintenance of national standards and rules, different scope of national legislation, omissions.

(c) Generally speaking these variations are not deemed to be sufficient to cause significant barriers to trade on an EU-wide scale. The extent to which they are unlikely, in fact, to cause barriers to trade has been confirmed by further discussions between the consultants (BER) and the Commission.

(d) Certain items of legislation pose more problems in transposition than others. This is the case for the Labelling Directive (79/112/EEC and amendments), for Directive 85/572/EEC on materials and articles in contact with foods, for Directive 85/591/EEC on sampling and analysis methods and for Directive 93/5/EEC on scientific cooperation. In the case of the latter two the problem seems to be due to an ambiguity within the Directives themselves (see note on Table B.5).

(e) Vertical Directives are generally considered to be better transposed than horizontal legislation, and where problems arise these largely reflect certain countries' attempts to maintain national protection in sensitive sub-sectors (e.g. Greece: honey and fruit juices; Netherlands: fruit juices).

(f) A common problem with respect to the transposition practices of many countries is that this is done only by reference to the EC legislation (Denmark, Greece, Ireland, Luxembourg, Netherlands), i.e. without reproduction of the full text.

(g) Another common omission is the non-transposition of Annexes and of subsequent amendments to legislation (Greece, Netherlands, Spain).

Application of the principle of mutual recognition

The principle of mutual recognition of national commercial rules has played a key role in supplementing SMP legislation and eliminating technical barriers to trade in the food industry. It is in this sector that mutual recognition has been applied on the widest scale, especially after the 1989 Communication clarifying the use of Articles 30 to 36 of the Treaty in food trading. In 1994 alone, out of some 202 complaints received from EU economic operators some 35 related to the food and drinks sector, making it the industrial sector in which the greatest number of problems occurred (Figure 3.1). Germany and France, followed by Greece and the Netherlands, account for the largest number of complaints.

Apart from ensuring the free movement of food products as such, the principle of mutual recognition has played a key role in maintaining national diversity and the various traditions and habits of Member States, thus promoting an increase in product differentiation and the range of foods available throughout the Community. The effective application of mutual recognition means that the role of legislation in securing free movement of goods is minimized, so that eventually there is less need for fixed European food laws.

Table B.6 (Appendix B) gives some examples of where the application of existing principles formulated by case law have ensured mutual recognition and/or adjustment of national rules and practices, thus overcoming important barriers to food trading across Member States. By far the largest obstacle has been the requirement imposed by many Member States to undertake national authorization procedures prior to launching a product on the national market. This is designed to control either the composition of a product or the presence of certain additives, nutrients, vitamins, etc. This type of barrier persisted in 1994, posing one of the major obstacles to intra-Community trading (Report from the Commission to the Council and the EP: *The Single Market in 1994*, COM(95) 238 final of 15.6.1995). Member States are prohibited from using this type of barrier to imports of other EU products, although they may use other means, such as appropriate labelling, to notify their consumers of the differences between the various products.

As a complement to the application of the principle of mutual recognition, each year in cooperation with Member States the Commission carries out horizontal surveys of national rules in particular industry sub-sectors. One of the two such surveys carried out in 1994 concerned the marketing of baby milk.

Figure 3.1.   Complaints raised in the food sector (Arts. 30 to 36), 1994

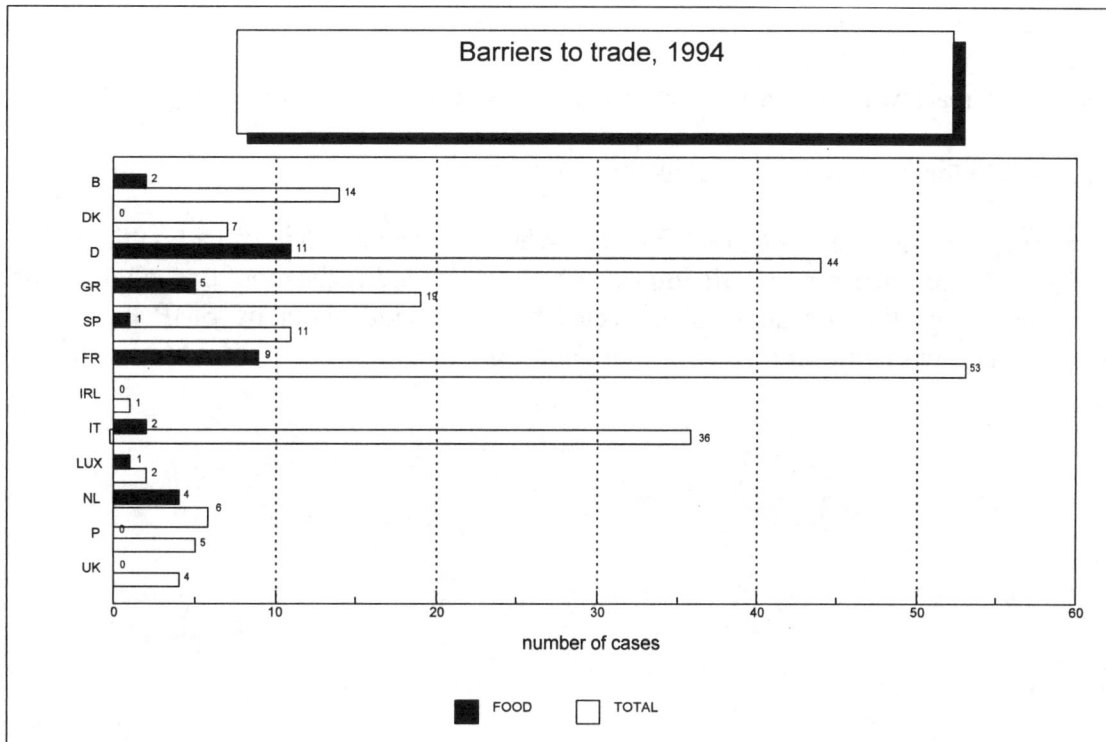

Barriers to trade, 1994

	FOOD	TOTAL
B	2	14
DK	0	7
D	11	44
GR	5	18
SP	1	11
FR	9	53
IRL	0	1
IT	2	36
LUX	1	2
NL	4	6
P	0	5
UK	0	4

number of cases

Source: BER.

SMP results

The above analysis indicates that to a significant extent food-specific legislation will not have affected industry to date. This is due to the following reasons.

(a) The most important and basic items of food legislation, including the five Framework Directives, were adopted in 1989 with implementation – partial or full – due in the early 1990s. Similarly, clarifications of the direction of food legislation and policy were only adopted in 1989 (COM(89) 256 on the SMP and food law).
(b) In the case of certain countries, further delays in transposition meant that legislation was introduced a year or two later than in the rest of the Community, therefore in the case of the five Framework Directives by 1992 or 1993.
(c) Detailed implementing rules that enforce the basic framework legislation have only recently started to be adopted. Thus, in most of the fields examined the system of EU-wide approvals and harmonized rules is not yet in place.

Nonetheless, the publication of the White Paper in 1985 and associated SMP awareness-raising activity in the Member States – on the initiative of the Commission, national authorities or industry professional organizations – are expected to have exerted a positive impact on industry attitudes and generated a response to the challenge of the SMP. Companies, particularly those most aware of the SMP, are expected to have reacted in the period 1985–92 to anticipated changes rather than to actual legislative change. These responses would have been based on concrete indications about the forthcoming changes as, by and large, the main aspirations and objectives of the new harmonized legislation had been formulated in the White Paper.

Typically this response should have been manifested in:

(a) upgrading of infrastructure;
(b) investment in new technology;
(c) increase in capacity to accommodate the scale economies that an enlarged market can offer;
(d) strategies of relocation, merger and takeover activity.

Apart from these general effects that the SMP as a whole is expected to have had on the EU food industry, Table 3.2 summarizes specific impacts of the SMP food legislation. In each of the areas examined, the change brought about or expected to be brought about by SMP legislation is described together with indications of importance and threats and opportunities arising for industry.

Table 3.2.   **Specific impact of SMP food legislation**

Field	Result of harmonization	Importance	Impact on industry	
			Opportunities	Threats
Food controls	Together with hygiene (below), this is probably the single most important field of food legislation with respect to elimination of trade barriers. Adopted in 1989, the Framework Directive paves the way for a harmonized system of controls, equivalence of inspection measures and the application of some European and international standards in this domain. Additional control measures were adopted in 1993 and enforced in 1995, with the application of common standards for testing laboratories (EN 45001–3) envisaged for November 1995.	High	If the system works effectively, it would ultimately remove the single most important barrier to trade. Application of the European standard quality control systems more cost-effective in larger scale of operations, thus inducing general economies of scale.	Because the application of the system depends on quality and efficiency of testing laboratory services, there could be location disadvantage and distortion of competition for companies based in countries with poor inspection systems. Equivalence of inspection standards is therefore a prerequisite for an effective removal of trade barriers.
Hygiene	Another important area of food legislation. Recently implemented (end of 1995), it will harmonize Member State rules applying to all stages of food processing, production and storage operations. The industry is responsible for ensuring prevention of health and hygiene risks through the concept of the HACCP and of voluntary industry guides to good practice. National provisions if higher than the EU may continue to apply.	High	Application of HACCP a stimulus for increasing scale of operation to obtain economies of scale. Correct implementation would eliminate risk of food scare, thus improving the 'image' of the food industry altogether.	HACCP largely prohibitive to SMEs and only applicable to minimum efficient size of operations. Flexibility of Directive through the application of voluntary industry guides adjusted to the type of operator could reduce the threat to SMEs.
Novel foods	All adopted and proposed legislation in this field now forms part of a Community strategy and a coherent policy for new food technology. This assists innovation, product development and R&D transfer. A barrier in intra-EU trade because of the existence of diverse national laws or an absence of rules is overcome. Should bring about transparency of rules and of licensing, patenting procedures. Public image of new foods improved altogether.	High	Important for new product development and product differentiation. Also improves EU industry competitiveness globally and vis-à-vis other technologically advanced countries, notably the US and Japan.	Complexity of application and approval procedures and associated increase in costs could well mean that SMEs are disadvantaged vis-à-vis large companies. In many ways, access of SMEs to primary R&D made more difficult.
Additives	A field with significant variations between Member States is now harmonized across the EU, except for additives in traditional foods. Industry (CIAA) view is that the latter exception could in some instances undermine the objective of the single market. However, a proposal that has recently come out in the field of traditional foods is expected to overcome this constraint. Additive rules tightened in general and subject to continuous scrutiny. Technical progress facilitated.	High	Trade facilitated. Cost savings arising from the fact a single authorization needed for additives traded in a range of countries.	Procedures of additive approval, if too long and cumbersome, could raise costs and act as a disincentive to product development.
Flavours	In certain countries (e.g., France, Italy) additive use is now permitted. Procedures for authorizing or banning flavouring substances made more transparent as well as stricter.	Medium	A boost to product differentiation.	Same as for additives.
Extraction solvents	Transparency and effectiveness of rules enhanced.	Low	Same as for additives.	Same as for additives.

Field	Result of harmonization	Importance	Impact on industry	
			Opportunities	Threats
Labelling	Detailed labelling made more widespread and rules made stricter.	High	Addresses major barrier to trade.	In the short term, increased labelling requirements may raise costs. In the medium to longer term, possibility of return to national language labelling could increase costs.
	Although role of national provisions was reduced, these are still important in terms of requirements and language on the label.		In the medium to longer term, possibilities of cost savings (production and distribution/logistics) from using same label across EU.	
Nutritional labelling	Common rules established. Clarification of nutritional claims made compulsory.	Medium	Could act as an incentive to product development and differentiation. Clarification of claims boosts product 'image'.	
Materials & articles in contact with food	Paves the way for harmonization in an extremely controversial area. However, system not actively in place yet (except for plastics).	High	Addresses major barrier to trade. Substantial cost savings as authorization needs to be given only once for products traded across the EU. Allows easy adjustment for technical progress, thus stimulating R&D.	As system is not in place yet, it is often the case that official approval procedures have to be taken in several countries, thus causing delays, undermining product development and raising costs.
Special nutrition foods	By and large national rules still apply, except in the area of infant formulae. Proposed legislation in this field will harmonize national rules. Revised proposal simplified by reducing the number of areas of application e.g. to baby foods and special diets. Proposal approved by the CPDA.	Medium	In many countries, adoption of harmonized rules will mean an opening of the market for this type of food.	
Health controls	This type of harmonization applies primarily to intra-EU trade with a view to the removal of physical border checks and other controls and replacement by uniform checks at origin. At the same time rules of hygienic compliance of premises and microbiological criteria and standards made stricter for most countries.	High	Important cost savings on transport and distribution costs. Rationalization of production structures. Required investment for updated technical equipment demands a larger scale of operations and can induce economies of scale.	Number of operators to fall and concentration in a smaller number of larger units. Effect will be different in the various Member States depending on previous level of advancement. A priori, southern countries should be expected to have higher adjustment costs and longer delays than countries of the north.
Excise duty for spirits	The harmonization does not concern the actual rates of duty. Although legislation in this field could potentially eliminate the single most important obstacle to trade in the spirit drinks sector, with the current legislation national differences in rates and payment and control procedures persist. Certain countries, for instance Denmark and Greece, apply significantly different rules than the rest of the EU.	High (spirits)	Terms of direct price competition can be improved. Altogether, intra-EU trade in spirits to be effectively liberalized.	As excise duties are a direct form of protection, their removal could in the short term cause problems to the domestic industry of the importing country. In the longer run, the structural adjustment that would be induced would be expected to lead to some rationalization of the importing country's domestic industry structures.

Source: BER analysis.

3.2.4. SMP impact: large companies vs. SMEs

The relevance of SMP legislation to SMEs is a particularly important concern for the food industry because of the presence of a large number of small and medium-sized enterprises in this sector, especially at the beginning of the period under review. From the outset the SMP made no special provisions to safeguard the position of SMEs or to differentiate in the legislative process between larger firms and SMEs. More recently, action in this domain has stemmed from concerns over the overall position of SMEs in the context of the single market and from the integrated programme in favour of the SMEs and the craft sector (COM(94) 207 final).

It can be argued that by its nature the single market is inherently bound to be more easily accessible to the larger companies in a given sector. Operators at all stages of the food chain need to be increasingly aware of a plethora of legislation not only in the field of food law but also relating more generally to the single market, the CAP, science and technology, competition, company law, transport policy, environmental policy, etc. Although rules have been harmonized across the EU, this does not necessarily imply they have been simplified. Monitoring this growing body of legislation and its implementation is increasingly proving to be a particularly difficult and costly task for SMEs. This observation has emerged clearly from our industry survey and has largely been confirmed by discussions with sector trade associations and in the case studies.

In this context, it should be emphasized that the extensive merger and acquisition activity that has taken place in the course of the last 10 years in the EU food market has meant that many national and smaller firms have merged with large multinational groups, many of which operate EU affairs and corporate offices in Brussels, to follow and influence EU policy and harmonization efforts.

Beyond issues of SME survival after the SMP, the impact of the SMP on SMEs in terms of facilitating intra-Community trade and improving the competitive environment would depend on:

(a) SME involvement in intra-Community trade;
(b) any secondary effects on the SME position resulting from changes in the terms of competition in domestic or local markets.

As was pointed out in the introduction, the structural characteristics of the EU food industry are such that a large number of small firms operate strictly within national borders and even at a more limited regional or local level. Although this will depend on the product sector and the opportunities for product differentiation and for realization of economies of scale, SME food companies generally tend to focus on the domestic market. A relatively small number of larger firms trade in neighbouring markets and a particularly small number of large concerns operate on a wider transnational scale and have, in the course of the last 10 years, set the scene for substantial EU-wide trade.

As SME involvement in intra-EU trade is limited by comparison to larger firms in the sector, the SMP will have been less relevant to them in terms of removing barriers to trade. Rather, the adjustment of national rules to the harmonized EC legislation has been most relevant for SMEs. The industry survey has shown that this type of impact has been particularly important for SMEs, especially in countries where the SMP was a driver for major rationalization in national food legislation and the decision-making processes relating to this.

In terms of competition, to the extent SMEs in a domestic market need to compete against new entrants of a multinational size, the upgrading of technical and infrastructure facilities and the complexity of the new procedures introduced by the SMP have been particularly challenging for the maintenance of SME market share in these markets. This issue is explored further in Chapter 4.

Certain items of the SMP food-specific legislation have been particularly difficult for SMEs. Higher quality standards, upgrading for technological development, EU-wide authorizations may all be less easily accessible to SMEs. In a few cases, this concern was incorporated in the drafting of legislation, thus exempting small operators from the rules or granting them longer derogation periods for a full adjustment to the new rules. This was the case, for instance, with the various Directives regarding the placing on the market of meat preparations, egg products and milk-based products (Appendix B, Table B.3).

Finally, a low degree of SME involvement in intra-EU trade and the trends of increasing competition and concentration in the single market seem to account for the low SME response to the introduction of the SMP. Our survey results have revealed that a smaller percentage of SMEs when compared to larger companies thought of the SMP as a challenge (38% of SMEs as opposed to 62% of larger firms).

3.3. Implementation of horizontal measures with an impact on the specific sector

Apart from food-specific legislation as such, a number of horizontal measures have impacted on the EU food and drinks industry. A list of such measures is given in part II of Table B.1. (Appendix B). These measures relate to the entire food chain and a number of issues related to technical, physical and fiscal barriers.

Table 3.3 presents the horizontal measures that are of primary importance for the food industry together with an indication of importance (ranging from low to high), a brief description of their objectives and likely impact on the EU food industry.

As can be seen, horizontal measures of relevance to the food industry cover not only the simplification of internal frontier formalities and customs checks, but also extend over a wide range of issues such as transport policy, industrial cooperation, company law, taxation, etc. At the time of the drawing up of the White Paper, industrial cooperation was still hampered by legal, fiscal and administrative barriers which gave rise to a whole series of laws in this area.

Table 3.3. Impact on the food industry of SMP horizontal legislation

Field/measure	Objectives	Impact on the food industry
Technical barriers		
[Food processing] Machinery [1] (D 89/392/EEC)	Harmonizes health and safety requirements for production, supply and use of food processing machinery, installations and related equipment. As this is a 'new approach' Directive harmonized rules are supplemented by European standards and technical specifications. Conforming machinery can receive the CE mark, following approval procedures adopted by the Council in 1993.	MEDIUM Food processors have traditionally set specific requirements for their suppliers of machinery and equipment. This Directive paves the way for harmonized basic health and safety standards in this area, therefore enabling food manufacturers to have a wider choice for procuring this material. Enhanced competition should improve price and quality of services rendered to the users of machinery – the food manufacturers.
Transport of goods (R (EEC) 1841/88, R (EEC) 4058/89, R (EEC) 4059/89, R (EEC) 4060/89)	R (EEC) 1841/88 aims to remove by 1993 any previous quantitative restrictions on intra-Community carriage of goods, thus creating a single market in this area. R (EEC) 4059/89 lays down rules, in this context, for non-EU resident carriers. A definitive cabotage system was subsequently introduced in July 1993 with a view to the total elimination of quotas. R (EEC) 4058/89 introduces common rules for the fixing of transport rates by free agreement between the parties concerned as a means of achieving a free transport system within the EU. R (EEC) 4060/89 removed border checks for inspection of vehicles/vessels involved in intra-EU transport of goods.	HIGH Gradual liberalization of transport services and consequent elimination of distortions to competition. Road haulage services improved and expected result would be cost savings and better timing in transport of foods intra-EU. This should have started to be felt in 1989, although the real impact is likely to have occurred after the introduction of the definitive cabotage in 1993.
Capital movements (D 88/361/EEC)	Aims to achieve liberalization of capital movements by 1993 – with derogations for Spain, Portugal, Greece and Ireland. These plans are somewhat undermined by the maintenance, by and large, of very diverse national systems of taxation.	LOW Could be beneficial to intra-EU trade, when system is effectively put into place.
Company law (D 89/666/EEC, D 89/667/EEC, D 90/604/EEC, D 90/605/EEC)	A number of Company Law Directives have been adopted in the context of the SMP with the aim of improving industrial cooperation, enhancing transparency over companies' affairs and facilitating the right of establishment across Member States. The ultimate goal would be that companies of one Member State establishing a branch in another should be subjected to the same company laws everywhere in the Community. First legislation in this field was adopted in 1968 covering companies which share capital. The cited Directives address questions regarding the opening of branches/subsidiaries by an EU company in other Member States, thus expanding on the possibilities offered by the SMP. The fields covered so far are company registration, internal mergers, one-man companies and company accounts. Harmonization in other fields of company law continues, e.g. 10th Directive on cross-border mergers, 13th Directive on takeover bids, Directive on the statute of a European company.	MEDIUM-HIGH The cited Directives should have a positive effect on the expansion of activity across the EU food industry to the extent they have achieved their goal of stimulating industrial cooperation. Increased requirements put on presentation of accounts but position of many food companies safeguarded by derogations for SMEs which were granted by D 89/667/EEC and D 90/605/EEC. Despite progress in this field, costs of merging are still quite high and procedures complex. Anticipated adoption of Directive on the statute of a European company is expected to resolve these constraints.

Field/measure	Objectives	Impact on the food industry
Trade marks (D 89/104/EEC, R (EEC) 40/94)	Aims to harmonize national legislation regarding trade marks thus eliminating distortions to competition and promoting the free movement of goods. The approximation of laws is not yet complete and only covers those provisions requested for the smooth functioning of the SM. Substantial transposition problems and delays have occurred in most Member States.	MEDIUM-HIGH Trade marks have been a sensitive area for some value-added branches of the food industry and are particularly important in the context of biotechnological innovations and additive/novel recipe technology. The cited legislation enhances protection at an EU-wide level while procedures become more transparent. Substantial cost savings can occur due to the fact that products only need to be registered and protected once in any Member State. While the new rules are of benefit to companies engaging in cross-border trade, the associated increase in legal fees and costs that have taken place in most EU countries (especially in the South) could be a disadvantage for SMEs operating locally or within domestic markets. Regarding biotechnology, specific legislation on the protection of copyright in this domain is currently in the pipeline.
Direct taxation (D 90/434/EEC, D 90/435/EEC, D 90/436/EEC)	Measures in this field aim to harmonize national systems of direct taxation with a view to facilitating industrial cross-border operations in the context of the SM. These seek to introduce rules that are neutral from the point of view of competition, so that transnational companies are no longer disadvantaged when compared to national companies. Also, a common tax system would avoid imposition of taxes in connection with mergers, transfers of companies, etc.	HIGH To the extent that improvement of the transparency and homogeneity of taxation rules has been achieved, this should be of benefit to the expansion of transnational food operations and should result in an increase in their productivity and competitiveness. Should also greatly enhance cross-border merger and acquisition activity.
Physical barriers Border controls on goods (R (EEC) 1900/85, R (EEC) 1901/85, R (EEC) 2726/90, R (EEC) 3330/91)	A long series of Regulations aiming to eliminate border controls and associated bottlenecks. The most important of them are basic R (EEC) 1900/85 and R (EEC) 1901/85 which sought to simplify procedures by the introduction of standard export and import documents, later consolidated in the SAD (Single Administrative Document). Subsequent supplementary legislation assured that the simplified system is in place by the scheduled date for the completion of the SM, i.e. by 1.1.1993. Other detailed rules have been adopted for transit procedures regarding non-EU goods (R (EEC) 2726/90), R (EEC) 3330/91 ensures that statistical documentation and procedures previously applying to their collection at the border point will continue after abolition of border controls (e.g. trade, industrial statistics, competition rules). In 1994 the removal of controls on goods was reported complete.[2]	HIGH Of potentially great benefit to the food industry. Cost savings on transport of goods and improvements in delivery times – subject to other constraints of the transport networks.

Field/measure	Objectives	Impact on the food industry
Tax barriers VAT/turnover taxes (D 91/680/EEC)	Legislation in this field adjusts VAT and turnover taxation system to the situation emerging post-1993 after the completion of the SM when fiscal controls within internal frontiers were abolished. Administrative and statistical formalities should be simplified as a result. Proposals for the definitive VAT regime, first submitted in 1987, are still pending. In the meantime, transitional measures apply until end of 1996.	Simplification of taxation system and overall removal of fiscal controls enhance trade and accrue cost savings which are of particular benefit to SMEs.

1. Scope of Directive extends over most industrial machinery, not just food processing.
2. Twelfth Annual Report on Monitoring the Application of Community Law, OJ C254, 29.9.1995.
Source: BER analysis.

3.4. Remaining legal and administrative obstacles and/or shortcomings

3.4.1. Obstacles

This section concentrates on outstanding barriers arising from the enforcement and transposition of harmonized legislation and from the persistence of non-harmonized legislation across the EU.

As a significant number of harmonized measures relating to foodstuffs have been adopted in the last few years, the SM legislative programme, as contained in the White Paper, is largely complete. According to the Commission report, *The Single Market in 1995* (European Commission, 1996), the majority have been transposed into national law.

Although the transposition of EC Directives into national legislation has been quite efficient in the case of food law, there are still a large number of infringements and, also, considerable difficulty with Member State failure to conform to Directives already transposed. Although the number of infringements for failure to comply are markedly lower than failures to notify (16 in the former case as compared to 85 in the latter in 1994), it is much more difficult and cumbersome for the Commission to deal with these cases. Most of the problems have occurred in the labelling field (Directive 79/112/EEC) where Member States seem to continue to impose a long list of indications in excess of what is required by the EC Directive. Although Directive 79/112/EEC allows the possibility of additional information on national labels, any such extra requirements imposed by Member States must be notified and approved by the Commission. Member States were found, however, to be taking unilateral measures without the Commission's prior approval.

As far as overall progress on harmonization is concerned, it is evident that, despite substantial progress, the remaining foodstuffs legislative programme on the basis of Article 100 of the Treaty is still quite large. It contains further implementing measures and supplementary legislation in the fields of hygiene, new foods, additives, flavours, processing aids, labelling, materials and articles in contact with food, nutritional foods, and a revision of vertical Directives. This is the case, for instance, with implementing legislation for the Framework Directive on additives, the forthcoming implementation of the Food Hygiene Directive (93/43/EEC) and for legislation supplementing the official control of foodstuffs (Directive 93/99/EEC).

Some of these measures are specifically listed as SMP-related, others not. Outstanding items of proposed legislation in all these fields, whether SMP-related or not, are indicated per item of legislation in Table B.1 (Appendix B), while a further description of the issues requiring harmonization is given in Table B.7 (Appendix B).

A number of these outstanding items have already been addressed by proposals which are now pending at some stage in the EU decision-making process. These are items of immediate concern to the EU food industry and their stage of advancement and potential impact are outlined in part I of Table B.8 (Appendix B). A further list of items which are likely to be addressed in the medium term are included in part II of Table B.8 (Appendix B). These issues account for the largest number of complaints currently received by the Commission relating to a lack of harmonization. There is also a clear demand by Member States for legislative action in these areas, following which some first consultation papers are to be launched by the Commission in the next few months.

3.4.2. Shortcomings

One of the major shortcomings of food legislation in general is considered to be the fact that it does not apply on the solid basis and principles of an EU food policy but rather aims to satisfy general social welfare objectives (food availability, product safety, quality control) and economic, trade and environmental considerations. This problem is to be addressed by a forthcoming Green Paper to be followed by a Framework Directive on food law. The objective is to consolidate all provisions regarding foods and to provide a coherent framework of the principles that need to underlie EC food legislation. A first draft of the Green Paper has been in preparation since June 1995 but is still in inter-service consultation within the Commission. The draft contains a series of uniform definitions on food manufacture, placing on the market, handling, labelling, additives and hygiene. Ambitious in its scope, the Directive aims to cover the whole of the food chain from the production of the raw material to primary and secondary processing, distribution and commercialization, and all sub-sectors of the food industry. At the time of writing, the completion of the draft is faced with two difficulties: provisions in the hygiene field, and incorporation of certain agricultural policy principles.

In the context of the single market the forthcoming Framework Directive on food law:

(a) would lay the groundwork for a gradual review of all adopted legislation in the light of the principles set by the Directive (this is expected to overcome problems of incoherence and inconsistency that currently exist between the various items of food legislation and thus consolidate EU food policy);

(b) places obligations on manufacturers and traders of food products and on Member States that aim to ensure the correct enforcement of food legislation, thus maximizing food safety and minimizing intra-Community trade barriers that could result from improper or incomplete implementation.

Finally, a particular complaint has frequently been expressed concerning the discriminatory application of public controls, both between and within Member States. This occurs where control is delegated to local and regional governments, and considerable differences arise in strictness of application or interpretation between control bodies. This shortcoming is expected to be alleviated by:

(a) the application of the principle of mutual recognition and related clauses to such cases of discrimination;

(b) the improvement of control and enforcement procedures through scientific cooperation between the various parties involved on the basis of Directive 93/5/EEC (in force since 1.6.1993), national control bodies on the basis of Directive 93/99/EEC (in force since 1.5.1995), and national laboratories on the basis of the EN 45000 series (to be introduced by 1.11.1998);

(c) the forthcoming establishment of a Commission 'Inspectorate', an independent body charged with the role of verifying the efficient and equivalent enforcement of legislation across the entire Community.

4. The impact of the single market on sectoral performance

4.1. Introduction

The hypotheses presented below represent the impacts anticipated a priori, given the analysis of legislation, BER's contacts with food industry and trade associations, a pre-survey with industry, and a review of the SMP literature. These hypotheses are tested in the secondary data analysis (statistical tables in Appendix D), the industry survey (Appendix E), and case studies (Appendix F).

4.2. Market access

4.2.1. General hypothesis

(a) The mere existence of the SMP (rather than specific legislation) has accelerated the process of 'Europeanization' in the food processing industry, which has resulted in an increase in the importance of intra-EU trade relative to extra-EU trade.

4.2.2. Specific hypotheses

(b) Elimination of border controls and simplification of export documentation will reduce intra-EU distribution costs and stimulate intra-EU trade.
(c) Harmonization of hygiene and inspection rules and of labelling requirements will stimulate intra-EU trade.

This section is concerned with the broad impact of the SMP on intra-EU trade. From the macroanalysis, it is not possible to isolate the specific impact of reduced distribution costs, harmonized health controls and labelling requirements (hypotheses (b) and (c)) on the development of intra-EU trade. The analysis of the trade data enables us to establish what, if any, evidence there is to support the general hypothesis that the SMP has encouraged intra-EU trade at the expense of extra-EU trade in processed food products (hypothesis (a)). In this context, it is important to emphasize from the outset that trade in the EU food and drinks industry has always been highly oriented to Community markets, as is clearly the case at the beginning of the period examined, when intra-EU flows in most cases already accounted for the bulk of both EU exports and imports with the world.

Overall, the trade analysis reveals significant growth in the level of real (deflated) total (intra-EU and extra-EU) exports during 1978–93 for most of the products reviewed (Table 4.1). In addition, an important increase in the balance of intra-EU relative to extra-EU exports seems to have occurred in all cases except for pasta, indicating a reorientation of export flows towards the EU. This reinforced the position of EU products in Community markets, especially for spirits and beer which tend to be mostly traded beyond EU borders. Despite the fact that these developments occurred in all of the sectors under review, wide variations in export patterns persist. These currently vary from an over 60% intra-EU share of exports in most cases to around 50% for beer and 35.6% for spirits.

Table 4.1.   Changes in export access for EU food and drinks, 1978–93

Change in intra-EU export focus[2]	Increase in total exports[1]		
	LOW (<5%)	MEDIUM (5–10%)	HIGH (>10%)
NEGATIVE			Pasta
POSITIVE LOW (<10%)			
POSITIVE MEDIUM (10–20%)	Chocolate/confectionery Spirits	Industrial baking	
POSITIVE HIGH (>20%)	Beer	Soft drinks/mineral water 'Other foods'	

[1] Real average annual % change in the value of total (intra-EU and extra-EU) exports.
[2] % change in relative importance of intra-EU to total exports.
Source: BER based on Eurostat data (Appendix D, Tables D.*.15 to D.*.17 and D.*.21).

The EUR-12 total export growth trend was repeated in every Member State, with few exceptions prior to the SMP (mainly southern Member States). Real average annual growth rates during the 1978–93 period varied considerably between sectors, from a high of 12.3% in the case of pasta to below 4% for beer, spirits and chocolate/confectionery products. The other sectors (industrial baking, 'other foods' and soft drinks/mineral water) are found in the middle between these two extremes. In most cases the rate of growth of intra-EU exports was even higher and this resulted, by the end of this period, in the above-mentioned increase in the relative importance of intra-EU to extra-EU exports.

A closer examination of the trend in intra-EU export focus within the 1978–93 period (Appendix D, Tables D.*.21 and Figures D.*.1) shows an acceleration in the relative importance of intra-EU to extra-EU flows after 1986 in the case of industrial baking, 'other foods' and beer. By contrast, extra-EU exports seem to be gaining more importance relative to intra-EU flows after 1986 in the case of confectionery, spirits and soft drinks/mineral water. The negative trend in the pasta intra-EU export focus occurs both prior to and after 1986.

On the import side, for all of the products under review, the EUR-12 as a whole sources the vast majority of its imports from within the EU. Only in the case of 'other foods', spirits and chocolate/confectionery has extra-EU product sourcing been somewhat more substantial, averaging at around 17–20% of the total value of imports over the period examined. Although the overall balance of intra-EU to extra-EU imports has changed little over time, it has substantially improved in the case of two out of these three relatively important extra-EU import products ('other foods' and chocolate/confectionery), thus further reducing the significance of extra-EU imports compared to the beginning of the period (Table 4.2). Even in those cases where the share of intra-EU imports appears to have deteriorated, the effect is only marginal. Thus the substantial change in total real imports that took place during 1978–93 was mainly fed from within the EU.

Table 4.2.   Changes in import sourcing for EU food and drinks, 1978–93

Change in intra-EU import focus[2]	Increase in total imports[1]		
	LOW (<5%)	**MEDIUM (5–10%)**	**HIGH (>10%)**
NEGATIVE (but marginal)		Industrial baking Beer	Pasta Mineral water/soft drinks
POSITIVE LOW (<10%)		Spirits	
POSITIVE MEDIUM (10–20%)	Chocolate/confectionery		
POSITIVE HIGH (>20%)		'Other foods'	

[1] Real average annual % change in the value of total (intra-EU and extra-EU) imports.
[2] % change in relative importance of intra-EU to total imports.
Source: BER based on Eurostat data (Appendix D, Tables D.12 to D.*.14 and D.*.20).

Looking more closely at the trend in intra-EU import focus within the 1978–93 period (Appendix D, Tables D.*.20 and Figures D.*.1), only in the case of confectionery has the rise in relative importance of intra-EU to extra-EU flows accelerated after 1986. For most products ('other foods' and all the drinks categories) there is a deterioration in the relative position of intra-EU imports after 1986. The moderate negative trend in the pasta and industrial baking intra-EU import focus is maintained throughout the period examined.

The above describes the overall EUR-12 developments and, as such, conceals certain important variations between Member States depending on the sector. Looking further at the situation by sector provides a better picture of these country patterns.

Pasta has been the most dynamic sector in terms of export growth. The sector was already highly oriented towards intra-EU markets in 1978 with 70% of exports destined intra-EU. By 1993 the situation had marginally changed: although intra-EU exports still accounted for nearly two-thirds of the total, there has been an increase in the extra-EU share, indicating that the export growth that took place in the course of this period was primarily extra-EU induced.

Italy, the principal pasta manufacturer, remains the dominant exporter, with a steady two-thirds market share of intra-EU exports and a share of world exports which rose from 65% in 1978 to 76% in 1993 (Appendix D, Figure D.1.2). France, Germany and Belgium, the only other Member States with significant exports, have maintained their position in the single market but lost share to Italy in world markets. Germany, France, the UK and Belgium are the main importers and have remained so throughout the period examined.

Industrial baking has witnessed an intensification of its export orientation, mainly intra-EU, during 1978–93. Intra-EU exports and imports already accounted for the bulk of trade in 1978 and this position was strengthened by 1993, with 73% of exports destined within the EU and 80% of imports being sourced from Community markets.

Germany, the UK, Benelux countries and France are currently the main exporters both within and outside the EU, as they were at the beginning of the period, although with some modifications in market shares held (Appendix D, Figure D.2.2). Italy has emerged as a significant new exporter due to the high export growth rates it has managed to achieve during this period (15.4% average annual rate of growth compared to 6.7% for the EUR-12). Of the main exporting Member States, the UK has reoriented towards the EU, while the Benelux countries seem to have increasingly turned their attention to world markets.

The **chocolate/confectionery** sectors have further intensified their strong export orientation over the course of 1978–93, mainly as a result of strengthened intra-EU trade flows. The share of intra-EU exports in total exports increased from 62% in 1978 to over two-thirds in 1993, and the growth in intra-EU imports share from 74% in 1978 to 85% in 1993 was even more substantial.

As might be expected, the main producers and consumers of chocolate/confectionery in the EUR-12 (Germany, France and the UK) join Belgium and the Netherlands in being the largest exporters both within and outside the EU (Appendix D, Figure D.3.2). Belgium is a relatively recent entry to this list. The Netherlands have lost substantial market share since 1978 when they used to have a third of the total EUR-12 export market, while the market share of other traditional exporters (Germany and Belgium) has expanded. The principal exporting countries are also the main importers and have remained so throughout the period examined.

'Other foods' is a sector which experienced substantial rates of export growth in the 1978–93 period, with even higher rates for intra-EU trade. This contributed to a significant rise in the intra-EU share of exports (from 50% in 1978 to 64% in 1993) and even higher for imports (from 56% in 1978 to 80% in 1993).

As with the other sectors, the dominant producers of these products (Germany and the UK) are also major exporters (Appendix D, Figure D.4.2). Together with France, Ireland and the Netherlands, these countries currently account for 69% of total EUR-12 exports. Germany, France and Ireland are particularly important traders within the EU, together realizing some 55% of all intra-EU exports. Ireland has emerged more recently on the EU export scene for these products, mainly at the expense of the UK and Dutch market shares.

Trade in **spirits** has increased modestly during the period. The intra-EU focus of exports is relatively weak, still accounting for only 36% of total exports although it has somewhat improved over the period. By contrast, the bulk of imports (86%) have always been sourced from within the EU.

France and the UK, the main EU producers of spirits, are also the principal traders, together accounting for 80% of EU exports (Appendix D, Figure D.5.2). This position has remained virtually unchanged over the period examined. However, there is an interesting distinction in the focus of their respective export markets, with a more even split (intra-EU 60:40 extra-EU) in UK exports compared to France, where the balance (80:20) has shifted more heavily in favour of third-country trade. Germany, France and Spain are currently the main importers, while the import shares of Italy and the UK have been reduced during the period examined.

Cross-border trade in **beer** is relatively limited and has remained so over the course of the period examined, reflecting the dominant consumer preferences for traditional and local or national brands. Moreover, the intra-EU share of the export trade is relatively modest, although somewhat improved from 40% in 1978 to over half by 1993.

All of the major brewers (Germany, the UK, the Netherlands, France and Belgium) are also the main exporters with relatively stable shares in both intra-EU and extra-EU markets during this period (Appendix D, Figure D.6.2). The UK, Germany and France also remain the main importers of beer throughout this period.

Over the period examined, the **soft drinks and mineral water** sectors have experienced considerable growth in export activity, albeit from a relatively low base which reflects the domestic orientation of the soft drinks markets and the production of global brands under licence in most Member States. The intra-EU focus has considerably improved in the case of exports (from around 48% in 1978 to around 68% in 1993) while intra-EU import shares have remained relatively constant at over 90% of the total.

France is by far the largest producer and exporter, accounting for one-third of total EUR-12 exports followed by Germany and the Benelux countries (Appendix D, Figure D.7.2). The UK had a more important export role back in 1978 but has lost market share. The main importers are Germany, Belgium and the Netherlands, although the importance of German imports has been somewhat reduced.

From a first examination of the development of trade during 1978–93, it seems that in most cases export growth and import patterns evolved differently in the pre-1986 as opposed to the post-1986 period, and this could point to a potential SMP influence on the trend. The extent to which significant changes in EU export and import patterns may have occurred after the launch of the SMP in 1986 has been examined in further detail by the structural break analysis (Table 4.3).

The key to interpreting the results of the structural break analysis is the degree of 'consistency' revealed. For this to occur, significant dummy variables have to occur exclusively after 1986 and the estimated coefficients should carry the same sign. On the other hand, if a significant positive break is followed by a significant negative break and the breaks occur both before and after 1986, this indicates an inherently unstable (volatile) time series from which little inference may be drawn with regard to possible policy-induced shifts over the specified time period.

The analysis identified consistent evidence of positive structural breaks in intra-EU trade, after 1986, for all of the sectors reviewed with the exception of soft drinks/mineral water. This indicates a significant growth in intra-EU flows which supports the above general hypothesis. There are, however, considerable variations by sector and between Member States.

In some cases the evidence is particularly strong, such as in the industrial baking, chocolate/confectionery and 'other foods' sectors, where the vast majority of Member States exhibit significant positive shifts towards intra-EU trade after 1986. In others, such as for pasta and spirits, there is evidence of significant breaks in both directions, pointing to intra-EU trade increases in some countries and reductions in others. In the case of pasta, Italy, the principal exporter and manufacturer, has two significant negative structural breaks, in 1984 and in 1989, but Germany, another major manufacturer, provides mixed indications although it has an overall positive trend over the period.

Table 4.3.   Results of the structural break analysis on trade (EUR-12)

NACE	Intra-EU trade						Extra-EU trade					
	Imports			Exports			Imports			Exports		
	+ ve	- ve	?	+ ve	- ve	?	+ ve	- ve	?	+ ve	- ve	?
417	*	*		*	*		*			*		
419	*			*				*			*	
421	*			*				*				*
423	*			*				*				*
424	*	*		*	*		*					*
427	*			*				*				*
428			*			*		*				*

Notes:
An asterisk in the first column (+ ve) indicates that there is consistent evidence of significant positive breaks in the data (i.e. increases in the value of the variable) for a number of Member States over the period after 1986.
An asterisk in the second column (- ve) indicates that there is consistent evidence of significant negative breaks in the data (i.e. reductions in the value of the variable) for a number of Member States over the period after 1986.
An asterisk in the third column (?) indicates that there is no consistent evidence of any significant structural breaks after 1986.
If asterisks have been placed in both of the first two columns (+ ve and - ve) this indicates consistent evidence of positive breaks in some countries and of negative breaks in others.
Source: BER based on Eurostat data.

The pattern identified for extra-EU trade was considerably less conclusive than that for intra-EU trade. Consistent positive structural breaks in extra-EU imports were identified in the case of two sectors (pasta, spirits), indicating a tendency for increased imports from outside the EU after 1986. In the case of pasta, this would mean that the recent growth in consumption throughout the EU has had a greater impact on imports from outside the EU than from within it. In the case of spirits, evidence of an increase in extra-EU imports is strong in every Member State and as this is also the case with intra-EU trade it demonstrates a marked increase in consumers' interest for a wider imported product range. On the other hand, evidence of trade diversion away from world markets to intra-EU trade was provided in the case of industrial baking imports.

As far as extra-EU exports are concerned, consistent evidence of structural breaks was identified in two sectors (pasta and industrial baking). In the case of pasta, this carried the positive sign implying a growth in extra-EU export activity. Given that this comes primarily from the major pasta manufacturers (Italy, Germany), the results demonstrate a concerted effort to penetrate third-country markets rather than focus on the single market. In the case of industrial baking, the post-1986 structural breaks carry a negative sign, reflecting significant downward trends in the Netherlands, the UK and Denmark, which may well indicate trade diversion effects towards the single market.

Although most sectors did not present any conclusive evidence of post-1986 shifts in extra-EU trade at an EUR-12 level, there are some cases where evidence of such shifts was provided at the level of the Member States. Thus, in the case of 'other foods', five Member States were found to have significantly increased their extra-EU exports and extra-EU imports after 1986, indicating that the structural shift in trade in this product reflects a general trend and cannot be attributable uniquely to the single market. In the case of chocolate/confectionery, there has been a significant positive shift, after 1986, in the level of extra-EU imports in most Member States. In the case of spirits, extra-EU exports have grown significantly in five Member States. Extra-EU exports and imports of beer have also significantly increased post-1986 in six and seven Member States respectively. Finally, extra-EU exports of mineral water have had a positive post-1986 shift in eight countries.

Except in the case of pasta, spirits and soft drinks/mineral water, the results of the structural break analysis for the EUR-12 market demonstrate a markedly different behaviour of intra-EU trade compared to extra-EU trade. It appears that the positive breaks identified in intra-EU data do not reflect a general structural shift in the level of exports, but a change in the market environment which is specific to internal trade. This statement, however, does not always hold at a Member State level, and the analysis has demonstrated a multitude of Member State and sector cases where the positive shifts in intra-EU trade post-1986 were accompanied by similar shifts in extra-EU trade activities suggesting more global developments.

In conclusion, the analysis of the trade data (macroanalysis and structural breaks) provides evidence which generally is in support of hypothesis (a), suggesting a post-1986 acceleration of the 'Europeanization' process in the EU food and drinks industry as manifested by an increase in intra-EU trade relative to extra-EU trade. Nonetheless, this evidence varies considerably depending on the product and level of aggregation (EUR-12 or Member State) and one can broadly distinguish between two groups of products: 'high impact' comprising industrial baking, chocolate and confectionery, 'other foods' and spirits; and 'low impact' comprising pasta, beer, soft drinks and mineral water. Further, the following observations may be made by sector.

Pasta. There is little evidence of any significant post-1986 impact on intra-EU trade. If anything, the analysis indicates that both the major pasta manufacturing countries (Italy, the Netherlands, France) as well as other Member States with an important pasta industry (Germany, Spain, Greece) have been developing third-country markets rather than focusing on the single market. Input costs are strongly affected by the support granted for durum wheat through the common agricultural policy (CAP), and the CAP reforms of the late 1980s and early 1990s, which resulted in downward pressure on support prices, may have enabled EU pasta manufacturers to compete more effectively in third-country markets. Internally, the dominance of Italian manufacturers with established branded products throughout the EU prior to 1986 would appear to have offset any trade liberalizing impacts which the SMP may have had on this sector, with the possible exception of Belgium, which has seen the emergence of significant pasta manufacturing industries focused almost exclusively on the EU market.

Industrial baking. Whilst not conclusive, there is some evidence of an increase in internal trade at the expense of third-country trade. In particular, whilst there would appear to have been an increase in both intra-EU and extra-EU exports over the period, there is a distinct difference in the import trade with EU imports taking an increasing share, at the expense of third-country imports, towards the end of the period.

Cocoa, chocolate and confectionery. The analysis reveals a steady increase in trade in general and intra-EU trade in particular over the entire period. There is strong evidence of a concerted attempt by manufacturers to develop the single market, with significant structural shifts in intra-EU exports apparent in most Member States after 1986. The growing penetration of intra-EU imports is reflected in significant structural shifts in intra-EU imports, although there is also evidence of a more widespread increase in third-country trade.

'Other foods'. Given the heterogeneity of products which comprise this sector, it is not surprising that the results of the data analysis are inconclusive. Moreover, without further disaggregation of the data it is impossible to identify the precise product categories in which growth in trade has occurred. There is clear evidence of a significant change in the structure of trade between Member States and with third countries, as evidenced by the growing penetration of intra-EU imports and the significant increase in intra-EU exports as a percentage of production. The time series analysis also provides evidence to support the trade-enhancing hypothesis of the SMP, but there is insufficient evidence to suggest that the single market has been the source of a unique structural change post-1986.

Alcohol and spirits. Developments in this sector are particularly interesting given the long established culture and tradition that is associated with so many of the leading brands. There is clear evidence of the growing importance of the single market, particularly in certain Member States, such as the UK and the Netherlands, and the results of the time series analysis were largely consistent with the general trends identified from the basic data.

Beer. The low levels of import penetration are evidence of a continuing consumer resistance to imported beers. However, niche markets for high quality imported beers have emerged in recent years and it may well be this development, rather than any market facilitating impacts of the SMP, that has been picked up by the time series analysis. The single market has grown in importance in those smaller Member States (i.e. the Netherlands, Belgium and Luxembourg, Denmark, Ireland) where beer exports make an important contribution to the balance of trade. However, there is insufficient evidence of a significant shift in the export trade, unique to the single market, which may be attributable to the SMP.

Soft drinks/mineral water. The analysis has revealed quite clearly the limited extent to which soft drinks manufacturers appear to have responded to the opportunities that the SMP has created. The limited penetration of intra-EU imports and the small share of intra-EU exports in production are indicative of the predominantly domestic focus adopted in this sector, which in turn is largely due to the localized structure of production, the dominance of a small number of global brands and the persistence of strong regional tastes.

The industry survey provides a general framework for interpreting the changes in market access resulting from the SMP. Aspects of the overall SMP impact, trade effects and market growth have been examined and the results point to an increasing Europeanization in the food and drinks industry which is in support of our hypotheses.

Evidence on the level of SMP achievement in removing trade barriers was overwhelming in most sectors. A total of 32 (out of 108) responses indicated that trade barriers were 'significantly removed', while a further 64 thought that barriers had been 'removed to some extent' (Appendix E, Figure E.5). Only in the beer and pasta sectors was there evidence of relatively more reservations as to the extent of barrier removal, although on balance most of the companies still felt that barriers had been 'removed to some extent'.

Related to this, a total of 75 (out of 106) responses on the overall contribution of the SMP impact indicated that this was 'positive', although a minority of 23 expressed 'indifference' towards the SMP (Appendix E, Figure E.6). There are no significant variations between sectors, although more 'indifference' was expressed by the beer and chocolate/confectionery industries than the other sectors. However, there are significant variations between size of operations. Five out of the 24 SMEs[5] viewed the overall impact of the SMP as 'negative', as opposed to only 4 out of the 50 large firms. Although in all Member States the majority of companies considered the SMP to have had a positive impact on their company, several companies in Portugal and Spain believed the impact was 'negative' (Appendix E, Table E.10).

Similarly, the majority of companies (41 out of 78) felt that the lifting of border controls was one of the most significant contributions of the SMP,[6] rating this at between 3–5 in terms of importance (on a scale of 1 to 7, 7 being the most important). There were no significant country or sector variations in this result, but SMEs seemed to attach more importance to the elimination of border controls than larger companies. A number of the larger multinational companies pointed out that considerable effort had already been made, prior to the SMP, to overcome problems of excessive paperwork and border control delays. Thus, the elimination of this obstacle by the SMP, although facultative, was not of such importance to them as it would have been to smaller operators.

Companies overall attached the greatest significance to the horizontal legislation introduced by the SMP, rating this at 7 (30 out of 78 companies). This view is shared by companies in all sectors, except in spirits. However, the results vary by size of operation and it seems that horizontal legislation is of more importance to larger companies than to SMEs, although this could really be a reflection of the generally greater familiarity larger companies had with the legislation.

Hygiene rules and labelling were the two fields of horizontal legislation most frequently mentioned, particularly among larger companies. Harmonization across the EU has allowed the use of common practices across the range of Member States in which the larger multinationals operate, thereby making possible substantial cost savings in raw material sourcing, production, marketing and distribution of final products.

The evidence of the importance of trade barrier removal is further substantiated by the fact that between 1985 and 1995 trade increased for just under three-fifths of the companies interviewed,

---

[5] It should be emphasized that the number of SMEs in the survey represent only a small fraction of SMEs in the sector.

[6] The others being 'horizontal legislation', 'vertical legislation' and 'other items of legislation'.

although fewer companies in the southern states claimed increases in trade (in particular Spain and Italy). Also, only half (four out of eight) of the companies in the spirits sector said their trade had increased between 1985–95. Companies were, however, very unsure as to the extent to which this increase in trade was linked to SMP effects beyond the direct benefits of the border control elimination. It should be noted that although for the majority (46 out of 78) of the companies interviewed the EU remained a trade priority in 1995 (Appendix E, Figure E.3), seven companies (industrial baking, chocolate, spirits and beer sectors) had reoriented their trade activities outside the EU. Also, intra-EU trade remained less of a priority for Greek, Portuguese and Spanish firms.

Less than half the companies interviewed saw market growth as having been induced by the SMP (either in terms of domestic or intra-EU markets) (Appendix E, Figure E.9). Results vary considerably between sectors. Only 4 out of the 11 brewing/malting companies and 6 out of the 19 baking companies said they had experienced market growth. In contrast, three-quarters of companies in the spirits sector said they had experienced market growth. No major variation between Member States on market growth was found, with the exception of Greece where all four companies interviewed experienced considerable market growth.

The case studies have provided mixed evidence of companies' reaction to the SMP in terms of new market opportunities. Variations in the findings have tended to be dependent on the sector of activity (Appendix F). For Whitbread (beer) and Danone (biscuits), the SMP was not perceived as a particular opportunity for market growth but this was largely attributed to the nature of the products which are not really tradable across borders (see also Section 4.3). In the case of Van Melle (confectionery) and Schöller (ice cream), the SMP has only facilitated and encouraged a process under way before the introduction of the SMP. No market expansion within the EU was recorded in the case of Grupo Gallo, and although the company expanded outside the EU in this period this was due to the general company philosophy and was not related to the SMP.

4.3. Production costs

4.3.1. General hypotheses

(a) In the short term, food and drinks companies would have seen an increase in production (and marketing) costs during an initial period of adjustment.
(b) These adjustment costs would have been more difficult to sustain for SMEs than for larger companies.
(c) Nonetheless, in certain cases the SMP may be expected to have resulted in cost savings.

The introduction of the SMP would have incurred certain adjustment costs both from the introduction of horizontal food-specific legislation (e.g. packaging, labelling and hygiene), and from other non-food-specific legislation (e.g. transport, border controls). It is important to note, however, that the varying timing of introduction of the different items of legislation means that companies have not adjusted as a one-off response to the SMP but rather have progressively adapted to the different items of legislation that were introduced over the period after 1986 and, effectively, to date.

This hypothesis has been difficult to test from the secondary information due to the absence of data on production costs. There is therefore little statistical evidence of the direct adjustment costs that the SMP would have entailed for the food industry. Due to companies' reluctance to release 'sensitive' information on production costs but also because, as stated above, any SMP-related changes were introduced progressively, the industry survey has not enabled a comprehensive review of the changes in production costs after the launch of the SMP. Nonetheless, overall the respondents to the survey indicated that, while highly dependent on the sector and scale of activity, the immediate impact of SMP on cost structure is small and not measurable.

A priori one would expect that relative to turnover the investment required has been more substantial for SMEs than for larger companies, although certain derogations (e.g. hygiene standards) aim to protect SMEs. In addition, for certain items of legislation, especially those introducing new technology, such as the hygiene legislation, HACCP systems and ISO 9000, larger companies had already started adjusting as an internal process in anticipation of the SMP and often quite independently of it.

This hypothesis was largely supported by the results of the industry survey. Thus, the SMP appears to have had no direct impact on production costs other than having accelerated a process the medium-larger manufacturers would have already undertaken, when adjusting their manufacturing practices to global technological breakthroughs. Most of the companies that participated in the industry survey did not consider such adjustment costs to be a direct consequence of the SMP, and even in the cases where such direct costs had occurred they seem to have been relatively easily absorbed.

Apart from production costs as such, the SMP has entailed quite substantial administrative costs associated with the monitoring and implementation of the new legislation. Although this would not have been as relevant to small-medium-sized enterprises, which in any case rely more on trade associations to retrieve this information, it has been of great importance for medium-large companies, especially those with more dynamic plans for expansion and growth across national borders.

On the other hand, certain items of the SMP legislation seem to have allowed substantial cost savings immediately after their introduction. The industry survey has provided concrete examples of such savings. For instance, the introduction of the new Cabotage Directive increased competition in the road haulage market and in Germany this resulted in a one-off reduction of up to 15–20% in transport costs. For a large German bakery goods manufacturer transport costs were reduced by 5–6% and these costs represent between 7–10% of turnover. More generally, adoption of the mutual recognition principle has avoided the repetition of lengthy and costly approval procedures for recipes, products, etc. at a national level for each market, resulting in considerable cost savings. Similarly, labelling harmonization has brought about a direct reduction in the amount of labelling required in the different Member States, although this saving would only be felt by companies trading across borders and there may well have been a cost increase for SMEs trading only within their national/regional markets. Pre-production costs (product development, R&D) also seem to have come down but this is a longer-term and indirect effect of increasing restructuring and rationalization of corporate organization and occurs uniquely among larger firms.

The case studies (Appendix F) have largely supported the results of the industry survey, indicating only marginal and non-measurable effects. In most cases, the SMP has served to accelerate developments already under way but the most important driver for the introduction of new technology and rationalization of sourcing, production, marketing and distribution has been increased competition and companies' response to the overall challenge of the SMP. In this context, the SMP may be seen as having had an indirect impact on production costs with its introduction inducing a dynamic response from certain larger companies wishing to expand further beyond national borders and compete for market position. For SMEs the effect has been only secondary and somewhat lagging by comparison with larger companies.

4.4. Cross-border sales and marketing

Building on the results on market access and in particular the hypothesis concerning the acceleration of the phenomenon of 'Europeanization' in the EU food and drinks industry, this section looks further into developments within particular product sectors and the likely impact of specific SMP legislation pertaining to these sectors. Specific hypotheses by sector are presented in Table 4.5.

From the analysis of trade data it is already clear that, in an environment of general trade growth which accelerated significantly after 1986, the product sectors reviewed have varied considerably in their development pattern.

In order to place the general growth in trade flows in the context of changes in the overall economy, import penetration and export intensity indices were computed for the sectors under review. The indices provide a relative measure of the food and drink industry's trade intensity by relating, in value terms, imports to consumption and exports to production respectively. This assists the interpretation of results in that a given export expansion will have different implications for trade-intensive sectors than for relatively less trade-intensive ones. Although exports may have grown considerably, the real impact on the production base will be limited if the sectors remain relatively non-export intensive, as is the case for soft drinks/mineral water. The same holds true for the relative value of imports to total consumption as reflected in the import penetration ratios.

Further, an increase in the value of exported production would suggest that manufacturers have expanded their production as a result of increased market opportunities: if this has occurred intra-EU it may well be related to an improvement in market conditions as a result of the SMP. Similarly, a growth in import penetration ratios within the EU suggests an expansion of EU consumer markets which was mainly covered by imports rather than an expansion of the local production base.

The results group the products reviewed into two categories: one with a relatively low trade intensity encompassing soft drinks/mineral water, pasta, beer and industrial baking; another with a distinctly higher trade intensity grouping together chocolate and confectionery, spirits and 'other foods' (Table 4.4).

Table 4.4.   Trade intensity in EU food and drinks, 1978 and 1993[1]

1978

Export intensity[3]	Import penetration[2]		
	LOW (<10%)	MEDIUM (10–20%)	HIGH (>20%)
LOW (<10%)	Pasta Industrial baking Soft drinks/mineral water Beer		
MEDIUM (10–20%)		Chocolate/confectionery 'Other foods'	
HIGH (>20%)		Spirits	

1993

Export intensity[3]	Import penetration[2]		
	LOW (<10%)	MEDIUM (10–20%)	HIGH (>20%)
LOW (<10%)	Soft drinks/mineral water Beer		
MEDIUM (10–20%)	Industrial baking Pasta		
HIGH (>20%)		Chocolate/confectionery	Spirits 'Other foods'

[1] Intra-EU and extra-EU.
[2] Imports as a % of consumption value.
[3] Exports as a % of production value.
Source: BER based on Eurostat data (Appendix D, Tables D.*.22 to D.*.25).

This characterization remains broadly valid throughout the period examined. In 1993 the situation is not markedly different from that in 1978, except that certain product sectors seem to have intensified their trade activities. Thus pasta and industrial baking products moved from a low export intensity position in 1978 to a medium one in 1993; 'other foods', spirits and chocolate/confectionery from a medium trade intensity in 1978 to a high one in 1993. The beer and mineral water/soft drinks sectors remain at the lowest scale of trade intensity, in spite of the considerable export growth for soft drinks during the period examined. The dynamism of export growth was in most cases the reason for the move by these sectors from a relatively weaker trading position in 1978 to a stronger one in 1993. While in some sectors this was mainly induced by the development of trade in the single market (chocolate/confectionery, industrial baking), in others this can be related to developments in both the single and world markets (pasta, 'other foods', spirits).

On the other hand, import penetration has generally grown very slowly, as is the case particularly in the beer and soft drinks/mineral water markets. Notable exceptions are chocolate/confectionery (from a 15.6% import penetration ratio in 1978 to 19.8% in 1993), 'other foods' (from 15.3% in 1978 to 20.4% in 1993) and spirits (from 11.8% in 1978 to 27.5% in 1993) where the substantial consumption growth during this period seems to have stimulated intra-EU trade and export orientation. This is also the case, but to a more modest degree and from a relatively low penetration base, for pasta and industrial baking.

The above describes the situation at an EUR-12 level and conceals variations between Member States. In most cases, the most export-intensive Member States are those with the largest manufacturing base and this picture has remained stable over the 1978–93 period. There are few instances of new countries emerging as major exporters in any of the product categories examined. By contrast, substantial changes seem to have occurred in the shares held by traditional exporters, with some reinforcing their market position and others losing a dominant position.

Similar variations exist on the import side, with the traditional importing countries maintaining their position and few changes in their share of imports, implying limited growth in the number of countries to which a product is marketed and sold.

From the findings of the industry survey and case studies, two reasons account for the above trends:

(a) cross-border trading and/or market penetration are made difficult because of persisting national preferences and/or the nature of the product, in particular high transport costs relative to the product's unit value (as is the case with beer, mineral water/soft drinks, industrial baking);
(b) the range of countries to which the product was distributed was already extensive prior to the SMP (as is the case with chocolate/confectionery and 'other foods').

Irrespective of the level of trade intensity, we note the significant increase in the share of trade accounted for by intra-EU trade and its growth in the 1978–93 period which further supports our hypothesis on the 'Europeanization' of the industry (Figure 4.1). In all cases (except for pasta), and especially in the more dynamic growth sectors (chocolate/confectionery, 'other foods', soft drinks/mineral water), the substantial improvements in trade flows which occurred during the 1978–93 period seem to have had an intra-EU orientation. It therefore follows that intensifying sectors have looked primarily within the EU to realize their trade expansion plans.

Figure 4.1.   Intra-EU focus of EU food and drinks trade intensity, 1978–93[1] (by NACE class)

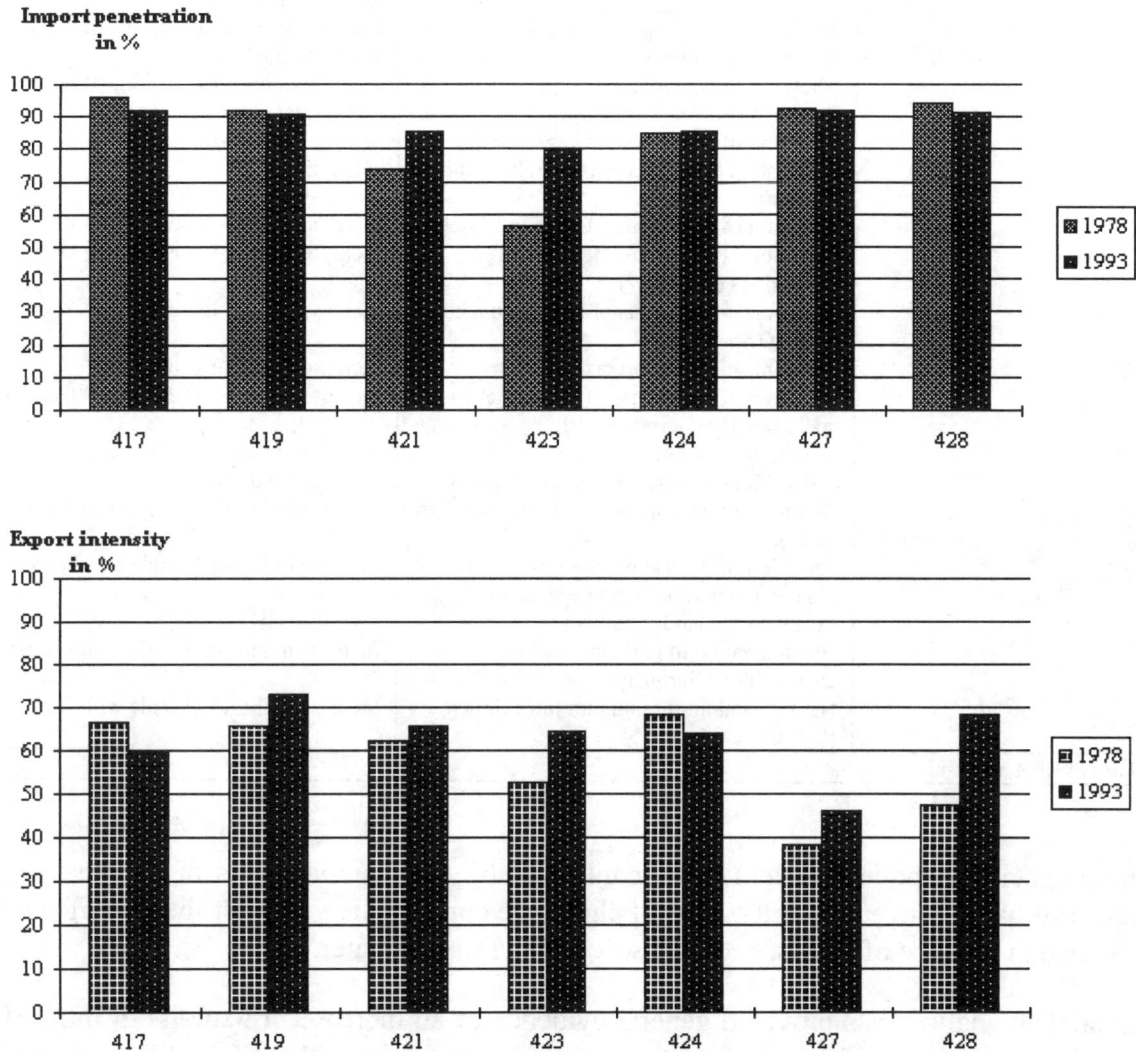

[1] Intra-EU import penetration as a % of total import penetration; extra-EU export intensity as a % of total export intensity.
Source: BER based on Eurostat data (Appendix D, Tables D.*.22 to D.*.25).

As the structural break analysis on trade has revealed, in a number of cases there are significant post-1986 changes in trade patterns suggesting a potential SMP impact. The validity of this general hypothesis has to be checked against particular developments within the main consumer and producer countries and specific legislation relating to the sectors reviewed.

Table 4.5 lists a number of specific hypotheses on an increase in cross-border operations as a result of such legislation. These relate to the removal of specific trade barriers either through the abolition of a previous national or EU-wide ban or through harmonization of national practices and restrictions. The hypothesized impact is then a trade-liberalizing effect in the region within which the restrictions previously applied.

Table 4.5.   Specific SMP legislation of potential impact on cross-border operations

Sector (NACE)	Legislation change	Expected impact
417	Abolition of purity law for production of pasta (Italy, France and Greece).	Increase in intra-EU trade and increase in intra-EU exports to these countries.
419	Abolition of ban on use of alginate (Italy).	Increase in intra-EU exports of biscuits and cakes to Italy.
	Abolition of controls over addition of vitamins and minerals (UK).	Increase in intra-EU exports of biscuits and snacks to the UK.
421	Abolition of ban on use of vegetable fats in ice cream (France, Germany).	Increase in intra-EU exports of ice cream to France and Germany.
	Abolition of ban on use of vegetable fat in chocolate (all EU except UK, Ireland and Denmark).	Increase in intra-EU trade in chocolate and confectionery.
424	Abolition of ban on use of amaranth (Italy).	Increase in intra-EU exports to Italy.
	Abolition of ban on use of artificial flavourings (Germany).	Increase in intra-EU exports to Germany.
	Harmonization of ethanol limits and alcohol content (Spain).	Increase in intra-EU exports to Spain.
427	Harmonization of wort taxes.	Increase in intra-EU trade.
	Abolition of ban on use of substitutes for malted barley (Germany).	Increase in intra-EU exports to Germany.
428	Abolition of ban on the use of aspartame and artificial sweeteners (France, Spain).	Increase in intra-EU exports of soft drinks to France and Spain.
	Abolition of the ban on the use of amaranth (Italy).	Increase in intra-EU exports of soft drinks to Italy.
	Abolition of the ban on the bulk transportation of mineral water (all EU except Netherlands and UK).	Increase in intra-EU trade in mineral water.
	Harmonization of national rules on composition (Germany).	Increase in intra-EU trade with Germany.
	Harmonization of minimum juice limits (Italy).	Increase in intra-EU trade with Italy.

Source: BER analysis.

These specific hypotheses seem to be confirmed by the macroanalysis in the case of pasta, industrial baking; rejected in the case of chocolate/confectionery; whilst there is inconclusive evidence in the case of spirits, beer and soft drinks/mineral water.

Pasta. The analysis has provided general evidence of an increase in trade, both intra-EU and extra-EU (together with a reorientation of trade away from the EU). Also, of the three countries for whom the removal of the pasta purity law poses the greatest threat in terms of substitution of imports for domestic production, post-1986 Italy has had significant positive shifts in intra-EU imports, whilst Greece saw a substantial trade surplus in 1978 deteriorate into a large deficit from 1988 onwards. Although the evidence is far from comprehensive, there are clear indications of changes in the balance and pattern of internal trade which are consistent with the hypothesized SMP impact.

Industrial baking. The above hypotheses suggest specific increases in intra-EU trade of biscuits and cakes to Italy and the UK as a result of the abolition of the bans on alginate and vitamins/minerals respectively.

From the macroanalysis it is clear that the real growth of intra-EU imports in Italy, which doubled from 2.8% in 1978 to 6.2% in 1993, is well above the average for the EUR-12. This is only exceeded by the UK, and the three new southern Member States, where there is a substantial increase, from the mid-1980s onwards, from the relatively low level of intra-EU imports in 1978. The structural break analysis also revealed significant positive shifts in the level of intra-EU imports in the UK in 1988 and in Italy in 1991.

There is thus considerable evidence, from the macroanalysis, to support the hypothesis that there has been a significant increase in the level of intra-EU imports, post-1986, in both Italy and the UK.

Chocolate/confectionery. It is difficult to test the two hypotheses specific to this sector due to the level of aggregation of the data and the lack of progress with the vertical legislation to which they refer. The trade analysis indicated a steady increase in trade in general and intra-EU trade in particular over the entire period. There is strong evidence of a concerted attempt by manufacturers to develop the single market, with significant structural shifts in intra-EU exports apparent in most Member States after 1986.

Looking specifically at the data for France and Germany, the two largest importers of intra-EU products, the value of intra-EU imports in both countries has increased in line with the overall increase in the EUR-12. However, whilst the share of intra-EU imports in total imports has fallen slightly in Germany, from 87% in 1978 to 80% in 1993, it has risen substantially in France, from 59% at the start of the period to 89% in 1993. The results of the structural break analysis were inconclusive, with mixed signs for shifts in intra-EU imports for Germany (a positive in 1989 followed by a negative in 1992) and a single negative shift for France in 1986, which is too early to have been influenced by the vertical legislation in this sector. Thus, whilst the secondary data analysis provides us with insufficient detailed information to test these product hypotheses properly, what evidence there is tends to oppose rather than support the hypothesized increased intra-EU imports in Germany and France.

Spirits. The trade analysis provided clear evidence of the growing importance of the single market, particularly in certain Member States, but the evidence is not sufficient to provide support for the specific SMP legislation-induced changes in trade postulated.

Beer. The trade analysis provided evidence of general consumer resistance to imported beers. However, the time series analysis did reveal significant structural breaks in the intra-EU trade data which might be attributable, at least in part, to the SMP and the Europeanization of the brewing industry (although again this would not relate specifically to the harmonization of wort taxes and excise duties which is still ongoing). The single market has clearly grown in importance in a number of the smaller Member States, including Denmark, where the share of beer exports in domestic production has increased over the period.

The evidence for Germany, in relation to the beer purity laws, is similarly inconclusive. Germany is the largest importer of beer produced in the EUR-12, yet the penetration rate is the second lowest in the EUR-12, after Denmark. However, in contrast with the Danish experience, there has been a marked decline in Germany's internal trade surplus and the structural break analysis revealed a significant positive shift in the level of intra-EU imports in 1991.

Soft drinks and mineral waters. The level of aggregation in the trade data makes it difficult to test the specific hypotheses relating to mineral water and fruit juice, and the data analysis undertaken revealed no patterns which would have confirmed them.

The industry survey does, however, provide evidence of the limited importance for cross-border trade of the vertical legislation in the sectors reviewed. For a start it is clear that only those specific products where vertical legislation existed or was introduced will be affected. In line with this only 34% of companies rated vertical legislation at 6–7 (on a scale of importance of 1 to 7, 7 being the most important) as opposed to 58% rating horizontal legislation at 6–7. It was also found that even in those sectors affected by specific legislation (e.g. chocolate) this was not always considered to pose a particular problem. Only the pasta, spirits and to a lesser extent the soft drinks sectors, attached equal importance to vertical and horizontal legislation. Also, SMEs tended to give vertical legislation lower importance ratings than larger companies.

The low tradability of beer, pasta and to a lesser degree mineral water/soft drinks is reflected in the survey results. Thus for these sectors the SMP contribution to barrier removal was generally characterized as limited and the overall impact of the SMP was generally viewed with indifference in contrast to the other sectors. In the case of beer and soft drinks/mineral water, this was attributed to the high transport costs relative to the products' unit value which restrict product tradability particularly over long distances. For beer, local transport costs generally amount to 3–4% of the product's wholesale price and longer distance transport may raise costs up to 20% of the wholesale price, making cross-border sales on a large scale prohibitively expensive.

Strong regional and local consumer tastes are another factor which contribute to the fragmentation of some food and drinks markets. Indeed this factor was emphasized as being a major and persisting impediment to market globalization in four out of the five case studies (Danone, biscuits; Whitbread, beer; Van Melle, confectionery; and to a lesser extent Schöller, ice cream) (Appendix F).

4.5. Scale and scope effects

4.5.1. General hypotheses

(a) Increased market integration has accelerated the process of rationalization and this would be manifested by a fall in the number of enterprises (and increased concentration of production structures).
(b) Average size of food manufacturing enterprises will rise, whilst the number of plants per firm will fall.

One of the aims of the SMP has been to create an enlarged free market allowing firms to capture all relevant economies of scale, thereby increasing the industry's efficiency and competitiveness in both EU and international markets. Technical economies of scale are, however, not important in most branches of the food industry. To a large extent their introduction is constrained by the nature of the products which tend to have high transportation costs in relation to unit value.

Where economies of scale exist, it seems that these were already largely captured prior to the introduction of the SMP. In a comparison of the ratio of market size to minimum efficient plant scale against market concentration ratios in the mid-1980s, Sutton (1991) demonstrates that for many of the product sectors reviewed (soups and prepared foods, soft drinks, beer), the size of the largest firms considerably exceeded the size necessary to achieve technical economies of scale. On the other hand it was noted that there was still scope for improvement in the mineral water, sugar confectionery and biscuit sectors, while the production of bread was seen as one of the most backward in terms of achievement of technical economies of scale. The pattern was similar across the EU (notably France, Germany, Italy and the UK) and in all cases more advanced than in the US.

In an industry with low economies of scale, limited scope for improvement and a slow overall growth in demand, one would expect that the SMP would have little impact on plant size as such. Rather the SMP would tend to exert its impact through a more general rationalization of the production structures which can come about by larger firms' strategies to capture market share and compete on a range of price and non-price elements (product differentiation, degree of innovation, marketing and distribution structures, promotion and advertising) which go beyond the simple achievement of technical economies of scale in the production process. These competitive benefits can be achieved through a company's 'external' expansion in the form of mergers, acquisitions, joint ventures and similar types of alliances rather than 'internal' growth in the size of production units.

Rationalization of production is a feature of technically developed and competitive markets and the EU food and drinks industry is no exception. Some of the largest and most technically advanced food manufacturers in the world are located within the EUR-12, having already established a strong presence at the beginning of the period under review. Unilever, BSN-Danone and Grand Metropolitan are currently ranked amongst the top 10 food manufacturers in the world, having an extensive number of production units throughout the EUR-12.

There is no published data on the number of production units per firm, but evidence on merger and other alliances in the EU food industry (both within and across national borders) demonstrates a massive wave of such activity in the run up to 1992,[7] suggesting that the number of units per enterprise should have been increased.

This trend is also captured by data on the number of enterprises whereby a fall may imply that they have merged under a smaller number of companies. In order for this assumption to hold, associated changes must have occurred in real production value,[8] so that a fall in the number of enterprises which is accompanied by an increase in production value denotes concentration of production in larger operations. It is important therefore to cross-check these two variables and a simple measure of average production per enterprise is used for this purpose.

In five out of the seven sectors under review (pasta, chocolate and confectionery, brewing, soft drinks and mineral water, alcoholic drinks) the total number of enterprises has fallen during the 1978–93 period (Appendix D, Tables D.*.1). The reduction was most marked in sectors dominated by global and large regional brands such as soft drinks, chocolate and beer, in all of which the number of enterprises has fallen by 40%, and spirits where the reduction was even more significant at 80%. Only the industrial baking industry presents a picture of relative structural stagnation, while the number of enterprises in the most diverse category of 'other food products' has actually increased, although by a modest 6%.

Apart from the above differences between sectors, the EUR-12 data conceals important differences between Member States. In order to seek an explanation for these variations the

---

[7]   This issue is also analysed under 'FDI and location effects' (Section 4.6).

[8]   Production value deflated by the producer price index to allow for change in the absolute level of prices.

results on the number of enterprises have been checked against total production value and average per enterprise, for each sector (Appendix D, Tables D.*.3 and D.*.4 respectively).

In the **pasta** sector, of the major producing countries (Italy, Netherlands and France) Italy is the only one to have reduced the number of enterprises, while numbers have increased substantially in the Netherlands. However, only in Italy can this be associated with efficiency improvements as, in real terms, total production value trebled during the period, while in Netherlands it actually fell. Some expansion in the size of operations was also found in France, where the total real value of production almost doubled during this period although the number of enterprises remained virtually unchanged. Since in the case of both Italy and France the increase in pasta production was translated into real export gains in this sector, while Dutch export intensity remained low, clearly the rationalization efforts of the former two countries can be an increase in EU export orientation. It therefore seems that the process of 'Europeanization' has been an important factor behind these developments.

In the **chocolate and sugar confectionery** industry, the fall in the number of EUR-12 enterprises seems to have come primarily from the notable reductions in Italy, Spain and Portugal (84%, 66% and 42% respectively) whilst there has been little change in the other Member States. However, production in real value terms has been increasing steadily in all Member States except Italy and Portugal, implying that while most countries have witnessed a healthy expansion of the sector and a concentration in larger operations, in the case of Italy and Portugal the reduction in the number of enterprises is associated with a complete cessation of production. To the extent that this has been brought about by a rapid substitution of globally branded confectionery products for domestic ones following the opening of the borders, the SMP may have had an (indirect) impact on these developments, although in Spain and Portugal this is most likely to have been the result of accession rather than the SMP.

In the **spirits** market, a substantial reduction in the number of enterprises occurred in every Member State except Greece. Spain experienced the largest reduction (80%), and in Germany, Italy, the Netherlands and the UK the number of businesses halved over the period. However, only in the case of Spain, France and Italy was this accompanied by a real production value increase suggesting an expansion in the scale of operations. In all other countries real production fell and the fall was most dramatic in the case of the UK and the Netherlands suggesting an overall contraction of the market.

In the **brewing** industry the fall in the number of enterprises that occurred throughout the EUR-12 mostly reflected closures of inefficient firms as it was accompanied by real production value reductions and no significant changes in the average size of the operations. The trend is common in all Member States, except France and Italy where a real rationalization seems to have taken place.

A sector which experienced considerable rationalization consistently throughout the EUR-12 is **soft drinks and mineral water**. The UK, Spain, France and the Netherlands in particular present strong evidence of expansion in the average size of operations throughout the period under review, making this sector one of the most dynamic in terms of structural change and scale effects.

In the remaining two sectors little or no significant change seems to have occurred in the number of enterprises. In the case of **industrial baking** this seems to be associated with a healthy expansion as production value has been increasing. This is evident particularly in the UK, one of the highest per capita consumers of industrial bread and biscuits, where there appears to be a proliferation of specialist bakeries producing branded products for selected, often niche markets towards the end of the period. Thus no real change in the average size of operations occurred in this sector, except in the case of Denmark, Italy and the UK. In the case of **'other foods'**, the sector seems to have undergone a period of significant growth with real increases in production value. The increase in the number of enterprises was modest enough to allow an expansion in the average size of the operations, throughout the EU Member States, with the notable exception of Portugal which seems to be moving out of this sector.

The pattern of rationalization in production structures has also varied over time, particularly between the 1978–85 and 1985–93 periods, and this is depicted by the structural break analysis on the number of enterprises (Table 4.6, first column) where the results demonstrate a significant fall in the number of manufacturers.

Table 4.6. **Results of the structural break analysis on industry structure (EUR-12)**

NACE	INDUSTRY STRUCTURE					
	Enterprises			Employment		
	+ ve	- ve	?	+ ve	- ve	?
417			*			*
419			*			*
421	*	*		*		
423			*	*		
424		*				*
427			*	*	*	
428		*				*

Notes:
An asterisk in the first column (+ ve) indicates that there is consistent evidence of significant positive breaks in the data (i.e. increases in the value of the variable) for a number of Member States over the period after 1986.
An asterisk in the second column (- ve) indicates that there is consistent evidence of significant negative breaks in the data (i.e. reductions in the value of the variable) for a number of Member States over the period after 1986.
An asterisk in the third column (?) indicates that there is no consistent evidence of any significant structural breaks after 1986.
If asterisks have been placed in both of the first two columns (+ ve and - ve) this indicates consistent evidence of positive breaks in some countries and of negative breaks in others.
Source: BER based on Eurostat data.

However, in most instances (e.g. the EUR-12 pasta and beer sectors and several national industries in the other sectors) significant negative structural breaks are accompanied by a longer-term declining trend, suggesting that rationalization was ongoing when the SMP was launched and therefore not SMP-induced. On the other hand, in some cases (chocolate and confectionery, spirits, and soft drinks and mineral water) rationalization has clearly been accelerated post-1985 suggesting a possible SMP impact.

Again significant variations in the results can be found among Member States.

In the **pasta** sector, although the evidence is not conclusive at an EUR-12 level, the identified positive trend in the Netherlands and the negative trend in Italy together with significant structural breaks after 1985 confirm our earlier observations on these two countries.

Despite the inconclusiveness of the results at an EUR-12 level in the **industrial baking** sector there are significant shifts in a number of cases indicating a change after 1986 in the number of enterprises: for instance, an increase in the number of Dutch and UK bread and biscuit manufacturers and closures in 1987 and 1988 respectively in Ireland and Portugal.

In the **chocolate and sugar confectionery** industry, there is a continuous long-term decline in six Member States but no significant structural breaks except in Spain and Portugal where the rate of decline is clearly accelerating after 1987; also, Italy and the Netherlands exhibit significant downturns in 1990.

In the **spirits** industry, significant negative structural breaks post-1986 were identified for Germany, Greece, France and Portugal, although in France and Portugal there seems to have been a longer-term declining trend throughout this period.

Brewing is an example of a sector where rationalization had been ongoing when the SMP was launched and there is no evidence to suggest the process was accelerated after 1985, except in Denmark. In the beer sector, significant negative breaks are identified in the UK, Spain, France and Belgium and, in the case of Spain and Belgium, these accompany longer-term declining trends.

Finally, in the **'other foods'** sector the absence of any distinct longer-term trends and the proliferation of significant structural breaks, up to and including 1986, indicate an unpredictable and volatile process of structural change not related to the SMP.

The industry survey revealed some, albeit limited, evidence of SMP-induced plant and company rationalization. Only around two-fifths of the companies interviewed saw changes in the number and size of their plants or their overall structure and these were in part directly attributed to the SMP (Appendix E, Figure E.13). Results vary according to company size. Over half of the large firms (26 out of 50) saw changes in size/number of plants, whereas less than a third (7 out of 24) of SMEs experienced such changes.

Further qualitative evidence from the industry survey points to the beneficial impact of the SMP on rationalizing production structures and companies' organization rather than inducing plant size effects as such, which is in support of our hypothesis on 'external' rather than 'internal' expansion. A large number of companies felt the SMP was promoting a more streamlined industry ownership structure that reduced the duplication of effort on R&D, marketing, finance, taxation, industrial relations, product mix and environmental strategy, while retaining a number of different brand and corporate identities.

Particularly for larger companies with cross-border operations, the harmonization of legislation and administrative procedures brought about by the SMP has allowed manufacturers to expand their production base, thus creating an opportunity for economies of scale. These manufacturers have been focusing and rationalizing their production lines while expanding their geographical base on a much larger scale thus reaching a new and substantial (corporate) competitive size.

Certain items of the SMP legislation were perceived to have had a particularly beneficial impact. Apart from the harmonization of labelling requirements mentioned above, the formalization of the mutual recognition principle in 1989 allowed companies in a number of sectors to move from having to comply with parallel recipes for the different markets to a greater uniformity of recipes.

This enabled the rationalization of production structures and the achievement of certain economies of scale.

Some of the case studies (Schöller, ice cream; Whitbread, beer; Grupo Gallo, pasta) have provided evidence of limited direct SMP effects on industry structure other than those resulting from the intensification of competition, an issue discussed in Section 4.7. Although substantial scale and scope changes were recorded in all of the case studies, these were not a result of the SMP but were primarily due to technological change and opportunities for the realization of economies of scale and/or global market trends (Appendix F). For certain sectors, however, constraints inherent in the production process (e.g. ice cream) have limited opportunities for scale expansion.

4.6. Foreign direct investment and location effects

4.6.1. General hypotheses

(a) Harmonization of company law will stimulate cross-border mergers and foreign direct investment (FDI).
(b) Harmonization of direct taxation will stimulate cross-border mergers and FDI.
(c) However, FDI is a market entry mode which is most commonly adopted when there are constraints on procurement or when local production and/or distribution costs provide competitive advantage. The improved market access associated with the SMP will improve access to inputs throughout the EU, and the lower distribution costs envisaged as a result of the SMP will reduce the need for FDI.

The most favoured form of transnational investment in the food and drinks industry seems to be through joint ventures and acquisitions of local companies rather than greenfield investment or 'softer' forms of expansion such as through subcontracting. These forms of FDI are typical in sectors with a relatively lower capital intensity, which are highly regulated and have a strong presence of SMEs. They allow firms to maintain some control over their investment but at a lesser cost than a greenfield investment and with a smaller risk than subcontracting or a licensing agreement.

Thus companies in the food and drink industry who engage in some form of FDI are *per se* seldom 'relocating' their activities. Rather they prefer to expand by reinforcing alliances with local operators, who can offer the advantages of established access to distribution networks and presence in the market, cultural proximity and a profound knowledge of the regulatory and trade environment. This is a common feature of transnational investment by EU, US and Japanese food and drink manufacturers. Larger food companies prefer to invest in wholly- or majority-owned subsidiaries in order to have a tighter control over product quality and maintain the standards associated with their brand names.

Joint ventures are a less frequent form of FDI than merger and acquisition and are usually set up with competitors or local producers to reduce risk or avoid market entry barriers, especially in 'difficult' markets. They are more common when improvements in the efficiency of transport and distribution systems are sought.

Although the level of merger and acquisition (M&A) activity varies across countries and sectors, a general trend towards an increasing number of M&As in the EU manufacturing industry has been observed after 1985. The food industry was no exception, with the number of mergers increasing from 22 in 1984/85 to 102 in 1989/90, although slowing down thereafter (Table 4.7). Indeed the second largest number of mergers occurred in this sector.

Although the majority of mergers still take place within national borders, between 1985 and the late 1980s there was a substantial increase in the proportion of cross-border (EU and international) operations. Among cross-border mergers there is a definite reorientation towards activity within the Community and a lessening of takeover efforts outside the EU.

Table 4.7.   Merger activity in the EU food industry (1984/85 – 1991/92)

		Share (%)		
	Total	National	Community	International
1984/85	22	90.9	4.6	4.6
1985/86	34	73.5	20.6	5.9
1986/87	52	75.0	21.1	3.9
1987/88	51	49.0	35.3	15.7
1988/89	76	46.1	35.5	18.4
1989/90	102	40.2	43.1	16.7
1990/91	71	41.0	36.5	22.5
1991/92	61	52.0	38.0	10.0

Source: BER based on Commission of the EC (Reports on competition policy).

The above trends clearly indicate a food industry response to the 1992 programme. Firms prepared themselves to take full advantage of the SMP challenges by reinforcing their position and expanding their Community basis, and completed this strategy before the completion of the SMP. Indeed the massive merger wave during the 1985–90 period was associated with a significant change in merger motivation.

A study carried out by the Commission in 1990 to examine motives for alliances in the EU manufacturing industry revealed that while in 1985 the main driver of merger activity was restructuring (29.9% of cases) followed by a need to expand (15.7%), by 1990 firms proceeded to mergers mainly in order to strengthen their market position (34.1%) and to continue expansion (2.3%). These two latter driving forces were particularly relevant in the EU food and drinks industry, where in 1990 some 39.2% of M&As were attributed to an effort to strengthen market position and 18.6% to an effort to expand. In particular the largest food and drink multinationals have increased their market share by acquiring rivals. Thus the vast majority of mergers occurred between firms with a combined turnover exceeding ECU 1 billion. Complementarity and synergy also rated high as a driver for M&As in the EU food and drinks industry (8.8%). Other factors, such as restructuring, diversification, integration, specialization, R&D, were of negligible importance. Alliances relating to R&D benefits are particularly limited in the EU food and drinks industry due to the low R&D intensity of the sector (*Panorama of EU industry 95/96*).

The importance of restructuring and expansion prior to 1992 is confirmed by the fact that the pace of M&As has slowed down since the early 1990s. According to data from the Commission, the total number of mergers in the food and drinks sector fell from 102 in 1989 to 61 in 1992. Data from another source (Seymour Cooke)[9] suggests that after reaching a record of 278 in 1992, M&As fell to 173 by 1994 (Table 4.8). This trend is common to every

---

[9]   Some divergence in the definition of M&A and in the year coverage between the different sources is possible.

EU Member State except the UK, which led in terms of the volume of M&A activity in the EU food and drinks industry. Although over this period the number of cross-border M&As fell as well, their proportion of total M&As was maintained at fairly high levels (43% of the total in 1994). Providing some global perspective, EU food and drinks M&As declined from around 60% of the world total in 1992 to well below 40% in 1993 and 1994.

Table 4.8. Food and drinks M&As by Member State (1992–94)

Country	Number of mergers and acquisitions[1]		
	1992	**1993**	**1994**
Bel./Lux.	10 (9)	4 (2)	9 (5)
Denmark	6 (7)	12 (6)	8 (1)
France	58 (14)	27 (15)	18 (11)
Germany	42 (14)	29 (14)	25 (9)
Greece	5 (4)	3 (2)	3 (2)
Ireland	15 (1)	4 (1)	2 (1)
Italy	34 (13)	16 (12)	11 (6)
Netherlands	19 (7)	16 (8)	12 (4)
Portugal	2 (2)	3 (3)	2 (1)
Spain	31 (17)	9 (9)	14 (11)
UK	56 (20)	73 (20)	69 (24)
EUR-12	278 (108)	196 (92)	173 (75)
Cross-border as % of total	39%	47%	43%
World	459	534	435
EUR-12 as % of world	60.6%	36.7%	39.8%

[1] Cross-border mergers and acquisitions are in parentheses.
Source: BER based on Seymour Cooke, *Mergers & Acquisitions Worldwide*, 1995.

This decline in M&As is explained, simply, by the increasing scarcity of commercially interesting takeover targets within the EU, after several years of frenetic M&A activity. The large majority of cross-border M&As were initiated and concluded by large-scale multinational firms. Within-country M&As were, more often, the result of activity by 'second order' firms, that is, nationally significant firms without a significant international presence.

Alliances and joint ventures (AJVs) completed in the EU food manufacturing sector follow a similar pattern of development. For the NACE codes of particular interest to this study, AJVs were particularly prevalent in the alcoholic beverage and soft drink sub-sectors, and the baking and milling sub-sector (Table 4.9).

Table 4.9.   Incidence of AJVs by major product category (1994/95)

Product	NACE	% of total European AJVs
Pasta and rice	417	-
Bakery and milling	419	10
Biscuits and snacks	419	4
Confectionery	421	3
Ice cream	421	4
Tea and coffee	423	-
Soups	423	1
Baby food	423	1
Alcoholic beverages	424 & 427	26
Soft drinks	428	10
Sub-total		59[1]
Total AJVs		100

[1] Major product areas accounting for the residual 41% were dairy products (17%), meat and meat products (6%), and sugar/sweeteners (5%).
Source: BER based on Seymour Cooke.

In general, the firms most active in AJVs were established international firms, and 5 of the top 10 are major players in international beer and/or alcoholic spirits markets (Table 4.10).

Table 4.10.   Top 10 European food and drinks firms most active in establishing AJVs (1994/95)

Rank	Company	EU AJVs as % of company's total AJV activity
1	Carlsberg	50
2	Tate & Lyle	62
3	Danone	62
4	Heineken	17
5	Allied-Domecq	46
6	Sodiaal	67
7	Interbrew	78
8	Hillsdown Holdings	56
9	United Biscuits	42
10	Nestlé	40

Source: BER based on Seymour Cooke.

In summary, the substantial structural changes that have been taking place in the European food manufacturing sector over the review period have reflected strategic moves by the principal firms (European- and American-owned) to: expand their businesses in a slow growth food market; defend their commercial interests against increasing retailer power; and acquire and build alliances with firms across Europe to take advantage of the evolving single market while, concomitantly, reducing the business expansion opportunities for their direct manufacturing competitors.

Within this dynamic economic environment, the hypotheses stated above – 'harmonization of company law and direct taxation will stimulate cross-border mergers and FDI' – clearly have some validity: they are facultative initiatives that help rather than hinder companies wishing to develop a pan-European presence and reap the benefits of an enlarged Single Market. These initiatives are important, but ancillary.

Evidence from our discussions with the trade associations and our industry survey suggests that in the food and drinks industry the primary considerations that influence whether a firm will seek to go one step further than exporting to other countries and expand its manufacturing presence past its domestic borders will include the following.

(a) **A firm's success in exporting and the growth potential of its current and prospective export markets**. Beer products provide a classic example of this. Initially, a brewing firm may elect to develop an export market through shipping the physical product to the market, perhaps using a specialist beer importer as the distributor in the export country. As export volume reaches a certain critical mass, the decision may be taken to widen distribution through an agreement with a brewery in the export country, leading to the establishment of a licensing agreement for this brewery to manufacture and distribute the exporters' beer products.

(b) **The physical nature of the product**. In essence, high volume, low value products are best produced close to the point of market, as transportation costs comprise a large proportion of total costs. Soft drinks provide a good case in point. The comprehensive international network established by Coca-Cola is based on the Atlanta-based 'mother' company shipping higher value syrup to its bottlers and distributors world-wide. High value alcoholic spirits, on the other hand, tend to be manufactured in a few, strategically located plants. In this case, the manufacturer may purchase alcoholic beverage firms in key export markets more for their distribution strength than for their manufacturing capacity.

(c) **For defensive strategic reasons**. In highly concentrated, mature domestic markets, firms may seek to purchase/invest in firms in current/prospective higher growth export markets as a defensive mechanism to preclude their major competitors 'stealing a march' on them in the export market. The ice cream market is a good example in this regard. Unilever and Nestlé are, frequently, the major participants in the ice cream markets of Europe and have both made defensive purchases in emerging European markets.

(d) **Local and/or regional taste**. There are relatively few food products that have pan-European appeal and, therefore, there is a requirement for an exporting firm to tailor its product to meet the particular needs of specific export markets. The biscuit sub-sector provides a useful example. The UK firm, United Biscuits, found that it did not have the understanding of local tastes in the Spanish market to service it effectively from the UK and, therefore, it was more commercially sensible to purchase an appropriate Spanish firm with a solid background in its domestic market. On the other hand, some luxury products are an exception to this rule: for instance, certain spirits have a more universal appeal making it more interesting for a firm to trade cross-border.

(e) **The corporate strategy of individual firms**. Some firms seek to market a relatively narrow range of products that have widespread appeal across national markets, whereas others may elect to have a country-specific range of products that are tailored to the very specific needs of local markets. For example, in chocolate-coated 'count line' products, Mars and Nestlé tend to adopt the former approach and, thereby, have centralized manufacturing facilities, whereas Cadbury often elects to follow the latter route – local manufacture, with local brand name and the Cadbury label understated.

(f) **Stability of currency and relationship of domestic currency to currencies in major export markets**. If the 'home' currency is pervasively strong against currencies in major export markets, then it will increase the incentive to establish a manufacturing base in the major export market to improve overall competitiveness. Conversely, in a country with an endemically weak currency, an import-based business might be better replaced by a domestic manufacturing facility, particularly for food and beverage products which are significantly price sensitive.

(g) **Investment incentives offered by national/regional authorities**. In EU countries that are characterized by relatively high levels of long-term unemployment, there are a plethora of national, regional and European investment incentive programmes designed to seduce the prospective investor. Particularly for capital intensive investments, the investing company will weigh up the pros and cons of accepting location-specific investment support.

(h) **Other market factors**, such as the slow rates of growth that generally characterize food and drinks markets, persisting trade barriers in the regulatory and quality fields and ability to access the established distribution networks and raw material sources in the country of location.

The above factors will determine the necessity and feasibility of FDI as an alternative to trade. One can assume that the improvement in market access conditions that the SMP has brought about, such as, for example, in the field of raw material sourcing, product transportation and distribution, and the removal of regulatory barriers, will reduce the need for FDI. The slow-down in M&A activity after 1992 could be pointing to such effects.

The survey has provided further evidence of relocation effects which are linked to the SMP. Nearly a third of the companies interviewed had seen geographical change in their production locations (Appendix E, Figure E.13). Six of them could confirm that this was a direct result of the SMP. Moreover, 30 companies (38% of the sample) had production units in countries other than the headquarters country in 1985. By 1995, this percentage had risen to 54% (42 companies).

Some striking evidence of relocation and FDI effects was provided by the case studies. The principal driver for this has been companies' plans to acquire prominent position in EU markets immediately after the opening of the single market. This has been, for instance, the case with Danone (biscuits) where the company, after 1986, swiftly moved to gain an EU-wide market presence, mostly through acquisition. Important relocation effects were also noted in the case of Van Melle (confectionery). Although the main driver has again been the response to the challenges of the single market, the strategy followed in this case has been to rationalize production structures by divesting from production locations in certain EU markets (Germany and the UK) in order to focus better the product range on harmonized products for sale across the EU. Finally, relocation effects within national borders were recorded in the case of Whitbread (beer), where the company cut down substantially the number of locations immediately after the SMP in an effort to rationalize on energy costs.

4.7. Upstream/downstream linkages

From the analysis of FDI it is clear that one of the major drivers for the M&A and alliance activity that took place in the EU food and drinks industry during the 1978–93 period was the need to establish and/or consolidate supplier/customer relations. Of the 237 AJVs reported for 1994/95, 30% involved some form of distribution agreement and a further 42% combined production/distribution agreements (Table 4.11). AJVs instigated by UK firms accounted for 24% of the total, followed by German (14%), French (12%) and Danish (11.5%) firms. These accounted for approximately one-third of world AJV activity.

The establishment of tight distribution linkages has been of extreme concern to EU food and drinks manufacturers during the last two decades. The extreme rise in supermarket chain and buying group bargaining power, increasing competition within the industry and the problem of obtaining retailer shelf space, as well as the structure of distribution networks and high transportation costs, have necessitated the tightening of food and drinks manufacturers' relations with their distributors. On the other hand, the introduction of technically advanced automated production systems and integrated product quality control have created the need to supervise closely raw material sourcing.

Table 4.11.   Type of AJVs in the EU food and drinks industry (1994/95)

	Total	Involving		
		Distribution	Production	Both
Bel./Lux.	11	3	-	8
Denmark	22	8	1	11
France	23	5	4	11
Germany	27	10	9	7
Greece	4	2	-	2
Ireland	17	3	5	9
Italy	14	7	2	5
Netherlands	8	1	1	6
Portugal	9	5	3	1
Spain	18	-	-	2
UK	45	13	8	19
EUR-12	191	57	33	81

Source: BER based on Seymour Cooke, *Alliances and Joint Ventures World-wide*, 1994/95.

Other types of forward/backward integration, such as by direct ownership, were prevalent in some of the sectors reviewed well before the SMP (e.g. pasta, ice cream, mineral water, industrial baking, spirits, beer). Again this is often due to the need to control the quality and availability of the raw material and/or distribution networks.

There is some evidence to support the idea that these developments may at least in part have been due to or accelerated by the SMP, although for the most part they seem to be the result of normal development patterns within the industry and the environment in which it operates. The industry survey revealed that a substantial number of companies (one-third of the companies interviewed) had changed their sourcing patterns but only five indicated that these shifts were a direct result of the SMP (Appendix E, Figure E.13). This relatively limited impact can also be attributed to the fact, noted by a large number of respondents, that for agricultural raw materials such as sugar, milk, grain, intra- and extra-EU sourcing is heavily influenced and often constrained by the common agricultural policy.

The industry survey did, however, provide some more qualitative evidence of a direct SMP impact on rationalizing upstream/downstream linkages and procurement structures, although only for larger companies. For instance, in the case of a large German confectioner, the SMP was reported to have exerted a direct influence on expanding the procurement of packaging material on an EU-wide basis. In the case of a multinational soft drinks manufacturer, the SMP directly resulted in the rationalization of canning lines with the entire production now taking place in a single unit in one Member State. Two large multinationals in the spirits sector have sought to centralize their control of distribution as well as procurement of some base raw materials, and this process was thought to be at least partially due to the SMP. Similarly a large UK alcoholic drinks manufacturer now owns 90% of its product distribution while 10 years ago the company had virtually no control over it.

In other cases, the SMP was thought to have accelerated rather than induced the process, with many multinationals further expanding their cross-border sourcing or rationalizing their procurement/distribution operations. Generally speaking, these larger manufacturers have increased market power to rationalize sourcing/distribution, reduce costs and consolidate their market position. More recently, smaller manufacturers have started using the same techniques to maintain a competitive edge within their national or regional markets.

Further qualitative evidence from the industry survey points to an increasing emphasis on FDI for most of the larger manufacturers. There are various drivers for this effort, which include: geographical expansion, further rationalization of production structures, improving flexibility in use of existing production sites, centralization of certain organizational activities (administrative, logistics, procurement, distribution, R&D, advertising, etc.). These developments are largely attributed to changes brought about by the SMP and are still in progress.

The findings from the case studies (Appendix F) largely confirm the results of the industry survey. No SMP-induced vertical integration effects were recorded for any of the companies studied, the reason being that other considerations were considered far more important than the SMP in determining company strategy on this issue. Such factors relate to the nature of the product and the need to form alliances that will secure supply and distribution. However, in two cases (Whitbread, beer; Schöller, ice cream) the companies moved away from previously tighter vertically integrated structures and, for at least one of the two (Whitbread), some indirect SMP effect was attributed to this move.

4.8. Competition and market concentration

4.8.1. General hypotheses

(a) Improved market access should stimulate intra-EU competition; this, *ceteris paribus*, would be manifested by an increase in the number of new entrants, lower prices and tighter profit margins (i.e. stimulate intra-EU competition).
(b) However, the scope for larger national or international companies to enter fragmented regional markets may result in increased concentration and this could counteract the effects suggested by (a).
(c) The longer-term impacts of the SMP on competition and concentration are likely to take several years to become established, as the larger manufacturers jockey for position in a market which is relatively static overall but which has some sectors (confectionery, pasta, ice cream, soft drinks) experiencing dynamic growth.

Enhancing competition in the single market has always been considered one of the primary effects of the SMP. By definition, the elimination of non-tariff barriers should improve conditions of access to other EU markets and shift the emphasis of competition from national to pan-European markets. Assuming that conditions of entry will have been made easier, this should result in lower prices and tighter profit margins.

On the other hand, new forms of entry barriers may have been erected if firms responded to the challenges of the 1992 programme by becoming more global, thus stimulating concentration. Indeed the SMP has been shown to have had some effect on the wave of M&As which took place in the EU food and drinks industry in the run up to 1992. Clearly this has resulted in a greater concentration of production in a smaller number of enterprises. Increased competition, whether price or non-price, seems to have resulted in the elimination of the most inefficient firms. Thus an increase in the concentration should have been brought about both by the growth of the larger firms and by the closure of smaller ones.

Evidence from concentration ratios (C ratios), i.e. of the market share held by the largest firms in the sector, demonstrates that the EU food and drinks industry experienced substantial increases in levels of concentration between 1987 and 1992 (Oustapassidis et al., 1995). This trend is common to all EU countries. Between Member States there are, however, wide variations in the levels of concentration with particularly high levels found in the UK, France and Greece and low levels in Germany.

The evolution of C ratios for the product sectors of specific interest to this study is presented in Table 4.12. National differences of data aggregation, both in the number of firms included in the C ratio and in the product coverage, make comparisons across countries and product sectors particularly cumbersome.[10]

Nonetheless, the available evidence suggests significant increases in concentration levels during the years 1987–92 in most cases. Greece is an exception but this is due to the particularly high concentration ratios already existing at the beginning of the period. Notable product exceptions, which experienced falls in the level of concentration, are industrial baking and ice cream. The increase in concentration in a number of Member States and sectors has been particularly significant, notably: in the UK confectionery market; French prepared foods, alcoholic beverages and soft drinks; and the German malt industry. A common feature of these product sectors is that they have experienced dynamic growth during the period examined, suggesting that companies' efforts to consolidate market power have been primarily induced by the 'attractiveness' of these markets.

---

[10]   Data on Italy and Spain were too weak for inclusion in Table 4.12. However, Table 4.13 incorporates current C-3 ratios on these two markets.

Table 4.12.   Evolution of C ratios in EU food and drinks markets, 1987–92

	UK 5-firm		France 4-firm		Germany 6-firm		Greece 4-firm		Portugal 4-firm	
	1987	1992	1987	1992	1987	1992	1987	1992	1990	1992
NACE 417 (pasta)			83.1				78.0	78.0	28.9	13.8
NACE 419	51.6	47.1								
Breads					15.6	15.8	84.0	79.0		
Biscuits and rusks							100	100		
NACE 421	63.2	70.3								
Sugar confectionery			60.1	62.0	39.7	45.7	74.0	75.0		
Chocolate			31.6	31.9	39.7	45.7	97.0	95.0		
Ice cream			69.5	51.4			100	96.0		
NACE 423									53.7	54.6
Coffee/tea/chicory			53.3	55.5	73.2	66.5	100	98.0		
Vinegar/sauces			58.3	67.0						
Diet foods/baby foods			65.6	73.9						
Breakfast cereals			74.3	92.0						
Soups			94.0	94.0						
Other prepared food			40.3	59.2			47.0	43.0		
NACE 424							71.0	65.0		
Ethyl alcohol					90.5	91.2				
Alcoholic beverages	65.4	57.0	27.8	46.9	48.0	52.2				
Fruit spirits			58.8	56.5						
NACE 427							100	100	98.9	99.9
Beer			90.5	88.7	18.9	21.6				
Malt	49.3	50.9			55.8	68.1				
NACE 428							92.0	77.0	47.9	49.5
Soft drinks	54.0	56.3	39.6	60.5						
Mineral water			82.6	79.3	25.3	25.6				
Average[1]	55.1	57.4	52.6	56.3	48.2	50.2	85.0	76.0	39.3	41.2

[1]   Average C ratio based on the specific product coverage in each country.
Sources: BER based on national statistical services; Oustapassidis et al. (1995).

In order to make some more meaningful comparisons of current concentration levels between Member States an attempt has been made to construct C-3 ratios, using Seymour Cooke data on market shares of the top three manufacturers as a source, for the countries and product segments available (Table 4.13). The results indicate a high degree of three-firm concentration throughout the EU with the top three manufacturers accounting for over 50% of output in most of the markets examined.

There are, nonetheless, wide variations in concentration across Member States, depending on the product. The example of the mineral water industry is the most marked with the top three suppliers in France and Ireland virtually dominating the market, while by contrast in Spain, Italy and to a lesser extent the UK their market shares are still fairly low. Soft drinks also present a far higher concentration in Ireland and Spain than in the UK. Other highly concentrated product markets, throughout the EU, are baby foods and coffee.

Table 4.13.   Top three manufacturers in EU food and drinks markets, 1993[1]

	UK	France	Germany	Italy	Spain	Ireland
(NACE 417)						
Dry pasta	70 *	48	62	52 *	57	65
(NACE 419)						
Biscuits	30 *	59	67	48 *		
(NACE 421)						
Chocolate/confectionery	76	83	57	50 *	81	85
Ice cream	58 *	56 *	88 *	80 *		
(NACE 423)						
Baby food	73	99	92 *		80	
Coffee (instant)	84	90			74	
(NACE 428)						
Mineral water	43	76		34 *	36 *	90
Soft drinks	50				80	70

[1] Figures marked with an asterisk are 1991.
Source: BER based on Seymour Cooke.

Using C-3=40% as a yardstick[11] to judge the extent to which market conditions can be characterized as 'competitive', i.e. implying an evidence of low entry barriers, we note that in the vast majority of country and product markets entry barriers were already particularly high even at the beginning of the period examined. Notable exceptions are biscuits (UK), mineral water (Italy and Spain), industrial bread (Germany), pasta (Portugal) and chocolate (France). This has major implications for the direction of price changes and competitiveness as will be discussed in the relevant sections of this report.

In recent years the already established polarization of the EU food market has been accentuated further. In 1992 the three largest food companies (Philip Morris, Nestlé, Unilever) accounted for over a third of the entire European food market (by sales value), while their market share only three years earlier was 23%.

In the product sectors under review, which are highly processed, added-value foods, the degree of polarization is even stronger. The leading manufacturers are, typically, multinational firms that have a strong European commercial presence and, generally, also a global presence. For instance, in the alcoholic drinks sector Allied-Domecq and Grand Metropolitan are major EU and world players, as is Heineken in beer. Excluding spirits and beer, only 13 firms are represented in the list of the top 20 EU brands (Table 4.14). Moreover, these 20 brands, which are specific to NACE codes 417, 419, 421, 423 and 428, account for 65% of the sales of the top 40 brands (all food and drinks). Four firms (Unilever, Nestlé, Coca-Cola and Kraft-Jacobs Suchard) account for 55% of the entries.

---

[11]   C-4=40% is commonly applied in industrial economics literature.

Table 4.14.   Top 20 European food and beverage brands, 1994[1]

Brand	Owner	Sector (NACE)	Sales (mn US$)
Coca-Cola	Coca-Cola	428	3,590
Barilla pasta	Barilla	417	1,105
Jacobs coffee	Kraft Jacobs Suchard	423	1,070
Nescafé	Nestlé	423	940
Langnese ice cream	Unilever	421	570
Fanta	Coca-Cola	428	550
Pepsi Cola	Pepsi Cola	428	525
Milka chocolate	Kraft Jacobs Suchard	421	505
Algida ice cream	Unilever	421	440
Knorr soups	CPC	423	415
Lavazza coffee	Lavazza	423	405
Douwe Egberts coffee	Sara Lee	423	395
Nutella spread	Ferrero	421	380
Kellogg's cornflakes	Kellogg's	423	375
Tchibo coffee	Tchibo	423	370
Motta ice cream	Nestlé	421	365
Mulino biscuits	Barilla	419	350
Ferrero Kinder chocolate	Ferrero	421	350
Mars bar	Mars	421	300
Walker's crisps	Pepsi Cola	423	285
Sprite	Coca-Cola	428	280
Top 20 (a)			13,565
Top 40 (all food & drinks)			20,985
Top 20 as % of Top 40			65%

[1] Examined product sectors only.
Source: BER based on Nielsen Europe.

The factors explaining the high levels of concentration and the more recent polarization in the EU food manufacturing sector are numerous, but the most important are as follows.

(a) A slowing of organic growth in the European market for manufactured food products explained, in part, by static population growth in the EU and low income elasticities (except for added-value, highly processed and/or luxury foods and drinks).

(b) Increasing concentration at the retail level across Europe, with substantial retail firms emerging, wielding massive buying power, means that manufacturers and retailers are competing aggressively for the attention of the food shopper. This is characterized as a struggle for retail shelf space and consumer 'mind space'. Manufacturers are recognizing that, in most EU markets, their products must be the number one or two national brand or they face a desisting threat from the retailer.

(c) In anticipation of trade liberalization within the EU and the establishment of the SMP, major firms have been rationalizing their product range to focus on core product areas, 'Euro-brands' and, through mergers, acquisitions, and the building of commercial alliances, repositioning their companies on a more comprehensive pan-European basis.

The survey provided further evidence of SMP-induced effects on competition and concentration. Half the companies interviewed felt that entry conditions had become 'easier' following the SMP, although seven companies mainly based in southern Member States believed entry was made 'harder' (Appendix E, Figure E.10). There were no major variations in the results between sectors or according to size. All the companies participating in the case studies indicated that the SMP has intensified the process of concentration in the markets and that competition has intensified (Appendix F).

These findings seem to be in full accordance with the conclusions of the DRI study based on a review of trade association attitudes (DRI, 1995a). According to this study the EU food and drinks federation (CIAA) has stressed the fact that the SMP has encouraged structural change in terms of M&A and AJV activity and increased competition, but that this was a trend already under way.[12]

4.9. Productivity and competitiveness

4.9.1. General hypotheses

(a) Harmonization of trademark legislation will encourage investment in technology and new product development.
(b) The stimulation of economies of scale and scope will in turn result in an acceleration in the growth of labour productivity.
(c) Improvements in resource use, productivity and innovation should increase EU competitiveness both in community and world markets.

The past decade has seen substantial changes in the level of investment. The analysis has already shown considerable rationalization in most sectors, with the number of businesses and the level of employment falling sharply in some Member States. In other sectors there has clearly been considerable market growth, which will have required (and facilitated) investment in additional, and in many cases more efficient, production capacity. However, one feature which is common to all sectors throughout the EU (and indeed the whole of Western Europe) is the rapid change in consumer tastes, preferences and purchasing behaviour, which has had a major influence on new product development and the investment of food manufacturers in the promotion (and defence) of their branded products.

In addition to changes in the absolute level of investment, changes would also be expected in the proportion of investment in gross value added at factor cost (GVA), which indicates the extent to which the value added generated in manufacturing is retained for investment purposes, whether it be in increased or upgraded capacity or new technology and product development. Also, in order to test whether the identified changes in investment behaviour are unique to the EU market or rather reflect global trends in food sectors, a parallel analysis of the above factors has been run for the US.

Although investment in real terms has increased throughout the food industry, there are substantial differences between sectors with regard to both the rate of investment growth and the level of investment intensity. 'Other foods', pasta and soft drinks/mineral water have had the highest investment growth during 1978–93. All of these sectors had relatively low levels of investment at the beginning of the period, although in the case of pasta and soft drinks/mineral water investment intensity when expressed as a proportion of GVA was relatively higher (Table 4.15). It is clear that, with the exception of spirits and pasta which remain relatively low investors, all the other sectors reviewed have intensified their investment activity during the period examined. Particularly striking are the examples of beer, 'other foods' and soft drinks/mineral water, all of which had become dynamic investors by 1993.

---

[12] It should be noted that overall the DRI study did not identify any substantial or direct SMP effects on the food and drinks industry's structure or performance.

Table 4.15.   Investment intensity in EU food and drinks, 1978 and 1993

1978

Investment/GVA (%)	Level of investment (bn ECU)[1]		
	LOW (<0.5 bn)	MEDIUM (0.5–1.5 bn)	HIGH (>1.5 bn)
LOW (<15%)	'Other foods' Spirits	Industrial baking Chocolate/confectionery	
MEDIUM (15–30%)	Pasta		Beer
HIGH (>30%)	Soft drinks/mineral water		

1993

Investment/GVA (%)	Level of investment (bn ECU)[1]		
	LOW (<0.5 bn)	MEDIUM (0.5–1.5 bn)	HIGH (>1.5 bn)
LOW (<15%)	Spirits		
MEDIUM (15–30%)	Pasta	Industrial baking Chocolate/confectionery	'Other foods'
HIGH (>30%)		Soft drinks/mineral water	Beer

[1] In real terms (1990=100).
Source: BER based on Eurostat data (Appendix D, Tables D.*.9 and D.*.10).

Again, the above analysis conceals substantial variations across Member States, with the main EU manufacturers usually realizing the highest investment expenditure during the period. For instance, Italy and the Netherlands but also Greece and Germany in the pasta sector; France, Germany and the UK in chocolate/confectionery; the UK, Germany, France and Italy in 'other foods'; France, Italy and Germany in spirits; Germany, France, Belgium and the Netherlands in beer; France, Germany, Italy, the UK and Belgium in soft drinks/mineral water. On the other hand, the importance of certain investors in some sectors has fallen, particularly among the smaller Member States, such as in Denmark and the Netherlands in the case of industrial baking; Denmark, the Netherlands, Ireland and Greece in chocolate/confectionery; the UK, the Netherlands, Denmark, Greece in spirits; the UK in beer. Overall, only in the soft drinks/mineral water, pasta and 'other foods' sectors has investment in real terms increased consistently throughout the EU.

There appears to be no clear link between evidence in the absolute levels of investment and the trend of investment as a proportion of GVA. While in some Member States the development of investment follows the direction of the trend in investment/GVA, in others it diverges considerably.

In comparison with the EU, in the US over the same period there has been a considerable increase in the real levels of investment in only two sectors (pasta and chocolate/confectionery). In most other sectors (industrial baking, 'other foods', soft drinks/mineral water and particularly spirits) US investment has grown at substantially lower rates than in the EU, while it has actually fallen in the beer sector. Also, the US seems to re-invest a much smaller proportion of its output value than the EU and has been doing so consistently throughout the period examined and in all of the sectors reviewed. These observations suggest that the pattern of investment behaviour was fairly unique to the EU food industry and does not reflect global industry trends.

To the extent that the SMP has accelerated the process of 'Europeanization' in the food manufacturing sector, we might expect the level of investment to have increased particularly post-1986. The analysis of the secondary data on investment at a sectoral level enables us to identify any significant trends or structural changes which may have occurred after 1986 and which may therefore point to SMP effects. The nature of this investment and the major reasons for it are examined in further detail in the industry survey and case studies.

The results of the structural breaks analysis undertaken identify significant and consistent positive breaks in investment (both in nominal terms and a percentage of gross value added) post-1986 in all of the seven sectors analysed (Table 4.16).

Table 4.16.   Results of the structural break analysis on performance (EUR-12)

NACE	Industry performance					
	Investment			Productivity[1]		
	+ ve	- ve	?	+ ve	- ve	?
417	*					*
419	*					*
421	*			*	*	
423	*			*		
424	*			*		
427	*			*	*	
428	*					*

[1] Gross value added per person employed.

Notes:

An asterisk in the first column (+ ve) indicates that there is consistent evidence of significant positive breaks in the data (i.e. increases in the value of the variable) for a number of Member States over the period after 1986.

An asterisk in the second column (- ve) indicates that there is consistent evidence of significant negative breaks in the data (i.e. reductions in the value of the variable) for a number of Member States over the period after 1986.

An asterisk in the third column (?) indicates that there is no consistent evidence of any significant structural breaks after 1986.

If asterisks have been placed in both of the first two columns (+ ve and - ve) this indicates consistent evidence of positive breaks in some countries and of negative breaks in others.

Source: BER based on Eurostat data.

Moreover, the results for the level of investment in the US reveal no significant trend nor any consistent structural breaks, thus suggesting there is no commonality in the behaviour of investment in the US and the EU.

Looking at variations between countries, the results broadly confirm the above view that investment growth has been most significant among the major manufacturers in each sector. It is therefore suggested that any likely effect of the SMP post-1986 would have been manifested in an acceleration of the investment activity among already established players in the EU market. The only countries listed above among the major investors in each sector but for which no significant post-1986 SMP effects have been identified are: Italy and the Netherlands in the pasta sector and the UK for which the downturn in investment seems to have already started prior to the SMP.

The arguments already made concerning the scale and scope effects of the SMP also apply to labour productivity. To gain some insight into the contribution that labour has made to the value of food manufacturing over the past 16 years, the trend of GVA per employee was examined. Clearly, this can rise (or fall) as a result of a change in a number of variables, most notably: the price of output; and changes in employment and the resulting physical output per labour/capital unit. In order to take the former factor into account, the evolution of the real (deflated) GVA through this period was also examined. While difficult to eliminate the latter factor, the trend in GVA per person has been checked against the development of employment. Thus, it is reasonable to assume that any significant changes in real GVA per person employed will be at least partly due to changes in labour productivity. Again, the analysis has also been undertaken for the US to shed some more light on the EU results.

A simple examination of the development of real GVA per person employed during this period reveals significant growth, which in most cases was accompanied by a reduction in employment levels suggesting real productivity improvements. 'Other foods' is the only sector where an increase in GVA per employee is accompanied by an increase in employment levels, suggesting that the GVA growth was induced by market growth rather than productivity improvements. Beer and spirits are among the sectors with the highest rates of GVA/employee growth and this is associated with high rates of employment decline in these sectors.

Nonetheless, country variations are important and the following points are worthy of comment: in the pasta sector, productivity improvements have been more considerable in France, Italy and the Netherlands than in Spain and Greece, the latter two having substantially lower returns throughout this period; Italy and the UK have had the higher rates of increase in labour productivity in the chocolate/confectionery industry. These were well ahead of all other Member States. While their labour force fell considerably during the period, Italy, Spain and the UK had substantially higher improvements than the rest of the EU in the spirits sector, although in the case of the southern Member States this was from a lower starting basis. In the UK in the beer sector, a threefold increase in the GVA per employee was accompanied by a threefold reduction in the number of employees, providing strong evidence of increases in productivity. In the soft drinks/mineral water sector the highest growth rates in GVA per employee occurred in the UK, France, Italy, Spain and Denmark. However, only in the case of the UK, Italy and Spain, where employment has proportionately fallen over the same period, can the GVA/employee growth be associated with real productivity gains.

US evidence demonstrates substantially higher returns but slower growth over the period and this, together with a fall in employment, is an observation common to all the sectors reviewed. The only exceptions where growth in US labour productivity was higher than in the EU are industrial baking and beer, where GVA per employee, starting from a higher base at the beginning of the period, grew at over double the EU rate.

Evidence from the structural break analysis on the post-1986 development of labour productivity is less conclusive than in the case of investment (Table 4.16). Unambiguous positive shifts have been identified only in the case of 'other foods' and spirits, while in the case of chocolate/confectionery and beer there is evidence of positive post-1986 shifts in some countries and of negative ones in others. There is little and inconsistent evidence of an increase in labour productivity post-1986 in the other three of the reviewed sectors (pasta, industrial baking and soft drinks/mineral water) at an EUR-12 level, although there is evidence of a positive shift in labour productivity for some Member States (Germany, the UK, Spain and Greece) in the soft drinks/mineral water sector. Indeed negative shifts in labour productivity post-1986 are identified in the case of: France, Italy, Belgium and Greece in pasta; Germany, France, Belgium and the UK in industrial baking; Italy and Belgium in beer. Again the US results bear no resemblance to the EU pattern of labour productivity, suggesting that whatever has occurred in the EU is unique to that market and not merely indicative of global trends.

Looking into the question of competitiveness we would note there are no absolute or unique measures[13] to provide an analysis of this issue. However, the fundamental issue of whether the SMP has contributed to the EU food industry becoming more competitive can be addressed by looking at the following question: the extent to which the SMP has influenced trade flows and the direction of this influence; and the impact of the SMP on foreign investment. Competitiveness can also be analysed at the level of a national economy, an individual sector, or a firm, and different measures are appropriate in each case.

Previous sections have demonstrated evidence of both an increase and a shift in intra-EU trade flows which are to some extent attributable to the SMP. Evidence on FDI and M&A activity also suggests a growing trend within the EU food and drinks industry which is attributed both to the evolving economic environment and to some restructuring in preparation for 1992. These trends have been reinforced by specific legislation relating to harmonization of company law and direct taxation. By these two counts, the food and drinks industry has become more competitive and this is partly due to the SMP.

Further evidence can be used to substantiate these conclusions.

Revealed comparative advantage (RCA), first developed by Balassa, has been applied as a measure of competitive performance for various industries and, recently, for sectors of the food industry (Winkelmann et al., 1995). The measure is calculated on the basis of trade (export data) and provides empirical evidence of a particular country's relative comparative advantage between sectors of the economy. It should be noted that the results cannot be used to compare between countries but only between product sectors within a specific country. This is due to the method of compilation of the RCA which relates it to the total size of a country's economy and can therefore give a biased picture when comparing across countries. This

---

[13]   A thorough discussion on this issues is provided by Pitts et al. (1995).

effectively means that for a given absolute level of trading in a certain product, smaller countries may exhibit substantially higher RCA scores than larger ones.

Table 4.17.   Most competitive food products by Member State, 1992 (a)

Country	Sector						
	417	419	421	423	424	427	428
France				Various (b) (17)	Alcohol (1) Spirits (c) (13)	Malt (8)	Mineral water (10)
Belgium			Ice cream (5) Chocolate (11)	Sauces (17)		Malt (10) 'Other' (d) (8)	
N'lands			Cocoa (3)	Soups (19)		Beer (14)	
Germany			Cocoa (17)	Coffee/tea (3) Honey (5) Cereal preps (7)		Beer (15)	
Italy	Pasta (1)			Vinegar (6) Yeast (20)	Alcohol (19)	Yeast (20)	
UK		Bread/ cakes (12)	Conf. (7) Chocolate (15)	Coffee/tea (14) Cereal preps (3)	Spirits (c) (2)	Malt (10) Other (d) (6)	
Ireland			Chocolate (10) Conf. (20)	Various (b) (2)	Spirits (c) (14)	Beer (15)	
Denmark		Bread/ cakes (20)	Ice cream (11) Conf. (18)	Cereal preps (2)		Beer (16)	
Spain			Ice cream (18) Conf. (20)	Spices (1) Honey (7) Soups (9)			
Greece			Ice cream (14)	Honey (16)			
Portugal				Soups (9) Yeast (5)		Yeast (5)	

(a)   RCA rate ranking indicated in brackets. Based on a comparison between 89 food and drink sectors.
(b)   Food preparations not elsewhere specified, including ready meals and soft drink concentrate.
(c)   Spirits, whisky and other alcoholic drinks (<80% volume).
(d)   Cider, perry, mead and mixtures thereof.
Source: BER based on analysis by Winkelmann et al. (1995).

Table 4.17 summarizes the RCA indices for those product sectors which exhibited the strongest performance in 1992, based on an examination of 89 agricultural and food product sectors throughout the EU. The index indicates the level of a country's trading performance in a given product relative to its overall trading performance. A score of 110, for instance, for a particular industry in a particular country would mean that its share of the world market was 10% higher than the country's share of total exports and the country has a (small) comparative advantage in that industry.

As can be seen the list includes a varied range of products and product categories in each Member State, with varying degrees of competitiveness. We note that 'other foods' and chocolate/confectionery appear to have a high degree of competitiveness, compared to most other food and drink sectors, in every single Member State. This is partly due to the extensive range of products that are covered by this category as is evident by a closer examination of Table 4.17. Indeed these products are the only ones which are competitive amongst all sectors examined in Spain, Greece, and Portugal. Beer appears highly competitive in every northern Member State, but not in Italy, Spain, Portugal or Greece. Pasta and mineral water are each competitive in only one country, Italy and France respectively. Similarly, industrial baking appears to be competitive only in the UK and Denmark, and spirits only in the UK, Ireland and France.

A time series examination of the RCA can also provide conclusions on the development of competitiveness of each country through time. A change in RCA may be due to actual changes in competitiveness of the products in question on international markets or, alternatively, may reflect changing competitiveness of other sectors of the economy. For the most part, RCA indices remained stable throughout the 1988–92 period, but a few notable exceptions of either an increase or a decrease emerged for some Member States (Table 4.18).

These results are broadly in accordance with the evidence from the other parts of this study.

France appears to be highly competitive in the mineral water and spirits sectors consistently throughout the 1988–92 period, while an emerging sector post-1988 is that of 'other food preparations' which includes a range of highly processed products and ready meals.

Belgium is most competitive in several of the sectors reviewed (ice cream, mineral water, malt, chocolate, sauces and jams) although it has lost some competitiveness post-1988 in the mineral water and ice cream markets.

The Netherlands are very competitive in the cocoa, beer and soups markets while, prior to 1988, the Dutch sugar confectionery industry also appeared to be highly competitive. There is little to suggest that this loss in competitiveness could be SMP-related, as all sugar-related industries have become less competitive over this period.

Germany appears most competitive in the coffee and tea, cocoa and beer markets. During the 1988–92 period, there is no significant change in competitiveness in these or indeed any of the industries reviewed.

Italy starts off with a major competitive advantage in the pasta industry throughout the period. The Italian food industry does not seem to be competitive in any of the other industries reviewed except for a few niche product markets.

Table 4.18.   Change of competitiveness in the EU food industry, 1988–92[1]

Country	Sectors where RCA increased			Sectors where RCA decreased		
	Product	Score 1988	Score 1992	Product	Score 1988	Score 1992
France	'Other' food preparations[2]	39	135			
Bel./Lux.				Mineral water	185	120
				Ice cream	436	233
Netherlands				Sugar confectionery	173	112
Germany				Food preparations based on cereals	190	141
Italy						
UK	Food preparations based on cereals	206	251			
Ireland	Beer	207	310	'Other' food preparations[2]	2394	1732
				Food preparations based on cereals	1029	818
Denmark	Sugar confectionery	327	403			
	Ice cream	462	719			
Spain	Spices	545	1244	Sugar confectionery	182	146
				Soups	373	265
Greece	Bread, pastry & cakes	20	44			
	'Other' food preparations[2]	11	25			
Portugal	Beer	33	73			

[1] Only the products reviewed in this study are mentioned.
[2] Food preparations not elsewhere specified, including ready meals and soft drink concentrate.
Source: BER based on analysis by Winkelmann et al. (1995).

The UK has a significant competitive advantage in most of the sectors reviewed: spirits, sugar confectionery, chocolate, bakery products, malt, coffee and tea. Moreover, it seems to have maintained competitiveness on export markets in all of these sectors. Cereal preparations (mainly cornflakes) are an emerging sector post-1988.

Ireland seems to follow closely the UK competitiveness pattern: food preparations (mainly soft drink concentrate), chocolate, spirits, beer and sugar confectionery feature amongst the most competitive sectors steadily throughout the 1988–92 period. An emerging sector post-1988 is that of beer. On the other hand the competitiveness of food preparations and cereal preparations (mainly cornflakes) seems to have been somewhat reduced, albeit from a particularly strong competitive position.

Denmark is also highly competitive in the ice cream, sugar confectionery, beer, baking products and cornflakes markets. The first two sectors witnessed marked improvements in competitiveness post-1988.

Spain, Greece and Portugal have very few processed products among the most competitive agricultural and food sectors. This largely reflects the continuing focus of these countries' export activity on primary and lightly processed agricultural products (fruit and vegetables, wine, nuts, etc.). Notable exceptions are spices, ice cream and sugar confectionery (Spain), ice cream and jams (Greece), soups (Portugal). The emergence, after 1988, of baking products and prepared foods (Greece) and of beer (Portugal) should also be noted although neither country has yet reached a competitive position for these products on international markets.

Although, with a few exceptions, no significant improvements in the competitiveness of the sectors examined was revealed, an important conclusion from the above analysis is that, overall, the balance of highly processed to less processed or raw material food product exports seems to have improved during the examined period for most Member States (Winkelmann et al., 1995). Thus, it can be said that after 1988 the shift of exports towards more added value foods demonstrates an overall gain in competitiveness for the EU food industry. This is particularly evident in France, Belgium, Germany, Italy and the Netherlands. The countries which witnessed small improvements in the processed/unprocessed ratio (Denmark and Ireland) or indeed deterioration (UK, Portugal) are those with particularly high ratios of processed to unprocessed food exports. Greece and Spain have traditionally focused on primary agricultural exports and seem to have continued doing so post-1988.

A less direct dimension of competitiveness is linked to product and process innovation. This distinguishes between innovation as a process and 'innovativeness' as a company attitude or strategy.[14] The launch of new products and/or services is widely regarded as an essential element of competition between firms and a key determinant of business performance. On the other hand, process innovations may reduce the cost and increase the efficiency of producing existing products, or enable the production of new ones.

In neo-classical economic theory, innovation is closely linked to technological change and research and development (R&D) statistics are often used to depict the level of technological development of an industry. By that definition, the food industry is classified as a low technology sector with one of the lowest R&D to sales ratios of any industrial sector. Fundamentally new innovations are scarce in food production. Empirical evidence suggests that few technological ruptures exist in the food industry although the ones which have occurred, mainly in the field of biotechnology and biological processes, have had considerable impact on competitive positioning. This is a common feature of both EU and non-EU food industries. Reported R&D to sales ratios as at the late 1980s in the EU are on average 0.5% for food and drink companies when compared to 12% for drugs, 8% for electronics and 4% for motor vehicles. Nonetheless, the period 1985–89 has seen some increase in these otherwise low ratios, with the notable exception of Germany (Table 4.19).

Table 4.19.   R&D to value-added ratios for food and drinks, %

	1985	1989
France	0.9	1.6
Germany	1.9	1.2
UK	0.9	1.0
Denmark	1.0	1.2

Source: BER based on European Commission (1992).

A different view on the issue of innovation is given in the marketing literature, which concentrates more on the non-technological aspects of innovation. It is argued that R&D does not guarantee innovative success unless technical intellectual property is adapted to the needs of the market. This relates to the market orientation of the company. Evidence suggests that this is particularly valid in the food industry, with high failure rates for new product

---

[14]   This issue is addressed in Section 5.2.

introductions, protracted penetration curves for new products and econometric analyses that show taste and habit changes for food to change very slowly. Investment into innovation and product development therefore proves to be not an easy key to success in the food and drinks industry.

A new framework for analysing innovation in the food sector which takes into account both the economic and the marketing views was developed recently, under the EU AAIR programme (Grunert et al., 1995). An important conclusion of this work is that there is no clear-cut relationship between innovation, as measured by R&D intensity, and business performance (neither in general nor in the food industry). This renders the analysis of R&D data alone insufficient for generating any important conclusions on industry competitiveness and points to the examination of innovativeness and market-orientation in company strategies as a supplementary means for testing business performance in the food and drinks industry.

The dynamics of the innovation process should also be taken into account. Following a model which hypothesizes that the rate of major innovations for both products and processes follows a general pattern over time, with high rates of R&D investment in the first phases and progressively diminishing thereafter (Utterback, 1994), it may be argued that the food industry has entered one of the latter phases where innovation appears in small, incremental steps. Indeed, Galizzi and Venturini (1994) argue that innovation in the food industry is less dependent on R&D expenditure than in other sectors, which is due to the incremental nature of innovation in this industry and the market opportunity for simple extensions of product lines and vertical product technology.

It is clear from the above arguments that the frequently cited incapacity of SMEs to innovate is far less important when looking at the food and drinks industry. Because of the nature of food production, SMEs are able to launch new products which are imitative rather than innovative, thus enabling them to maintain a competitive position in the market. Some barriers to innovation, in the real sense of the term, are however to be expected for SMEs because real innovation requires market research and tests, introductory advertising and other significant expenditure. It also requires a broad know-how base, extensive market intelligence, scientific knowledge, possibilities for financial support and sufficient information regarding legal regulations, all of which are more readily accessible to larger companies than to SMEs (although certain of these aspects may be attainable by vertical cooperation).

Some evidence of a change in productivity and competitiveness conditions, in support of the above hypotheses, is found in the survey results. Although the level of productivity gains has been impossible to establish quantitatively, an improvement in competitiveness was widely acknowledged among the participants and this was partly attributed to the broader effects of the SMP in terms of the widening of the market base and legislative/administrative harmonization. Also, over half of the companies interviewed (39 in number) had recently seen changes in their R&D and product development strategies (Appendix E, Figure E.13). Nine companies said these changes were a direct result of the SMP. There is a significant variation in the results according to company size. Two-thirds of the SMEs (16 out of 24) had changed their R&D strategies whereas only half of the larger firms had seen such changes, presumably because the latter had already started from an advanced R&D position pre-SMP. An increased R&D effort, to some extent due to the SMP, was also depicted by the case studies.

More generally, the case studies addressed the issue of the development of productivity and competitiveness. Although SMP effects were noted in all cases, the extent and type of influence is, once more, highly dependent on the sector (and country) of activity. Whitbread (beer), for instance, was highly critical of the effects of the SMP with respect to both capital and labour productivity, but this is largely due to specific national tax and other legislation on beer. In most other cases, productivity gains and an improvement in competitiveness were noted, some of which were directly attributed to the SMP. Reported examples of this effect derived from the introduction of the Additives and Labelling Directives which have allowed the use of uniform product recipes across the EU (Danone, biscuits; Schöller, ice cream; Van Melle, confectionery). Nonetheless, the measurable effect in quantitative terms was reported to be small if not marginal. It is also often difficult to separate this particular impact from other environmental factors such as technological improvement and internal company restructuring.

4.10. Employment

4.10.1. General hypotheses

(a) The SMP is unlikely to slow down the rate of employment decline in the food manufacturing sector as companies continue to seek cost advantages in a static market.
(b) The SMP may even result in a net loss of employment as small, specialized, regional manufacturers are squeezed out of the market through excessive adjustment costs (short term) and the longer-term squeeze on profit margins.

Employment has been falling during the 1978–93 period in all the sectors reviewed, except in pasta manufacturing and 'other foods' where it has actually marginally increased (less than 1% and about 2% respectively). Of all the seven sectors by far the largest employer continues to be industrial baking and to a large extent this reflects its fragmented structure. The fall in employment has been most dramatic in the spirits and beer sectors where it has fallen by 60% and 50% respectively, followed by chocolate/confectionery (over 30% reduction) and soft drinks/mineral water (14% reduction) (Appendix D, Tables D.*.2).

In most cases, the reduction in employment has been a common feature of all EU markets. There are notable exceptions in: the Netherlands and Greece in the pasta sector where an expansion of employment has actually been large enough to offset the downward trend in every other Member State, resulting in a net although marginal increase at EUR-12 level; Spain and Greece in industrial baking; Denmark in chocolate/confectionery; the Netherlands, Denmark, and to a lesser extent France and Belgium in soft drinks/mineral water. Also, in the 'other foods' sector the level of employment has increased in most Member States and particularly in Spain, Ireland, Denmark and France; exceptions have been the Netherlands, Belgium and the UK.

As with other variables, the structural break analysis attempted to examine whether developments post-1986 have been significantly different to the overall trend during this period. Results (Table 4.6 above) are fairly inconclusive suggesting no clear links between changes in employment levels (in any direction, positive or negative) and any likely post-SMP effects. Indeed only in the case of 'other foods' and chocolate/confectionery were significant and consistent shifts identified and these carry a positive sign suggesting market growth rather than rationalization of production structures.

In all other cases the lack of consistent structural shifts post-1986 and the existence of a longer-term declining trend in the data (particularly for spirits, chocolate/confectionery, beer) suggest no real post-SMP impact on employment, although an accelerating effect of already existing trends may have taken place. For instance, evidence of rationalization with a continuous decline in employment levels throughout the 1978–93 period is apparent in the spirits sector and seems to be clearly due to technical improvements in distilling and the rapid industrialization of the process over the last 20 years (with the most spectacular reduction in employment occurring in the UK where the work-force was reduced by 80% in total between 1978–93). Indeed the lack of any significant structural breaks in this sector post-1986 and the existence of negative trends throughout the 1978–93 period supports the view that the reduction in employment is a long-term process which started well before the introduction of the SMP. Very similar patterns were identified in the beer sector.

The inconclusiveness of the data in all other cases conceals important country variations. Thus consistent negative breaks post-1986, without longer-term trends, were identified in the case of: Portugal and Italy in the pasta sector; Spain and Portugal in alcohol/spirits. On the other hand, consistent positive breaks were identified in the case of: Germany, Spain and Greece in industrial baking; Belgium and Denmark in beer; France in soft drinks/mineral water.

The expansion of some of these sectors in some of the southern Member States post-1986 clearly indicates the dynamic development of the industry in these countries and a positive impact from their accession to the EU and improved access to the single market rather than direct SMP effects. However, Spain and Portugal seem also to have undergone considerable rationalization in some sectors (e.g. pasta) and, again, their accession to the EU seems most likely to have been the main driver for these developments.

Developments in southern Member States seem to be in marked contrast to the experience of most northern Member States and particularly the UK, France and Germany where a decline in the levels of employment in most sectors can be associated with efforts to rationalize production structures, via an expansion of the technological base and the closure of smaller inefficient production units. Again this reflects longer-term trends rather than post-1986 effects suggesting a priori a limited SMP impact.

The industry survey provided significant evidence of SMP-induced employment effects. Two-fifths of the companies interviewed saw changes in training/employment within their firms (Appendix E, Figure E.13). Seven companies specified that these changes are directly attributable to the SMP. Finally, a larger proportion of SMEs saw changes in training and employment (14 out of 24) than did larger companies.

4.11. Evolution of final prices

4.11.1. General hypotheses

(a) Improved market access, increased intra-EU trade and increased competition will result in a general reduction in consumer prices and a convergence of prices between Member States.
(b) The extent to which prices fall and/or converge will vary between sectors and will depend largely on the power and proliferation of brands.

In theory, the reduction of internal trade barriers should result in greater competition as the access for intra-EU imports is improved and the range of products offered to consumers is extended. However, the extent to which this results in a reduction in prices paid by consumers depends on three key factors: the degree of brand loyalty; the power of multiple retailers; and the pan-European pricing strategies adopted by the larger rapidly developing pan-European retail buying groups.

Standard neo-classical economics suggests that the existence of brand loyalty or consumer franchises reduces the price elasticity of demand and enables manufacturers and/or retailers to charge a premium for branded products, thus generating monopoly rents. Further, the ownership of a brand provides manufacturers with the power to set prices rather than take whatever is offered, as is the case with commodities or generic food products.

The power to set prices inevitably leads to price discrimination, as manufacturers seek to maximize returns on their brand investments. Thus, it is by no means inevitable that prices will either fall or converge as a result of an increase in internal trade. Indeed the increased penetration of branded goods which may result from improved market access would tend to slow down the process of price convergence and could well result in an increase in prices, at least for certain product categories, in the short term.

One important development which can act against and is therefore likely to reduce the ability of manufacturers to extend their price discrimination activities is the growing power and influence of the multiple retailers. Throughout Northern Europe and particularly in France, Germany and the UK, the power of multiple food retailers has increased substantially over the past decade, with own-label products challenging household brands for contested shelf space and retail buyers increasingly dictating terms on food standards, quality control, supply chain management and prices.

Table 4.20 illustrates the dominant position of the supermarket trade throughout Western Europe, as far as consumer purchases of packaged food products and soft drinks are concerned and Table 4.21 shows the market share of the top five food retailers in selected EU Member States, which confirms the fundamental role which retailers now play in determining range of products, availability and prices.

Table 4.20. Percentage of products purchased in different locations (average for Western Europe), 1992

	Supermarket	Hypermarket	Specialist store
Packaged food products	87	9	2
Soft drinks	81	10	6
Cheese	71	7	17
Fresh fruit and vegetables	48	5	31
Wine	48	5	36
Fresh meat	37	5	36
Fresh bread	28	2	67

Source: BER based on *Food Retailing and Distribution: Issues and Opportunities Around the World*, Food Marketing Institute (USA), The Coca-Cola Company, 1994.

Table 4.21.   Grocery market share of top five food retailers, 1992

	Market share (%)
Ireland	76
UK	61
France	52
Germany	52
Denmark	46
Belgium	45
Netherlands	33
Portugal	27
Spain	15
Italy	10

Source: BER based on *ISSO 1990, Food Retailing in Europe*, International Self-Service Organization, 1992.

To a large extent, the growth of retailer power has yielded considerable benefits to consumers, with sophisticated delivery systems and retail formats ensuring a rich product range of high quality food products. Moreover, the development of high quality own-label products at competitive prices has resulted in a reduction in retail price spreads and greater choice for the consumer. Table 4.22 shows the share of own-label products in selected countries, from which it is evident that in many Member States own-label products are no longer a minor category for the modern food retailer.

Table 4.22.   Percentage of sales of own-label products in supermarkets, 1992

	Percentage of grocery sales
UK	28
Germany	24
France	20
Belgium	18
Netherlands	17
USA	14

Source: BER based on Nielsen Europe.

Whilst the growth in the power of domestic food retailers has had an important impact on the choice and the price of food products, it is the emergence of pan-European buying groups that is most likely to result in greater price convergence between Member States. Table 4.23 shows the turnover of the nine largest pan-European buying groups in 1992, from which the bargaining power of these groups becomes readily apparent.

The aggregate turnover of these nine largest groups now exceeds one-third of the value of the total European food market and is fast approaching one-half. The largest of these groups, EMD, has an aggregate turnover slightly larger than the Unilever group, 25% larger than Nestlé and four times larger than the major French multinational, BSN (now Danone). The impact of these buying groups on the food market in general and food prices in particular is difficult to determine, not least because there is very little published data on retail food prices. However, it would seem reasonable to assume that such groups will seek to exploit scale economies and harmonize prices at levels which allow them to capture market share from their competitors. Thus, in the longer term, we might expect food prices to fall and converge across the EUR-12 to the extent that currency movements will allow, as a result of a fundamental shift in the balance of power between retailers and manufacturers and increased competition between retail chains.

Table 4.23.   The nine largest pan-European buying groups (1990–92)

	Combined turnover of members (bn ECU)
European Marketing Distribution (EMD)	56
Eurogroupe	55
Associated Marketing Services (AMS)	51
Deurobuying	48
Buying International Gedelfi Spar (BIGS)	43
Coopération Européenne de Marketing (CEM)	34
Di-Fra	16
Independent Distributors Association (IDA)	11
Interbuy	6
TOTAL	320

Source: BER based on Seymour Cooke/Coca-Cola Retailing Research Group.

In an attempt to identify what, if any, convergence there has been in pan-European food prices for the seven sectors covered by this study, pre- and post-SMP, we have undertaken an analysis of prices over the period 1978 to 1994. Pan-European data on prices for food products are compiled by Eurostat in the form of an index for both producer and consumer prices,[15] aggregated to the four-digit level of NACE classification.

The analysis is based on the DEBA producer price indices which give a trend and its direction, in the sense of convergence towards a lower or a higher level over time. The advantage over using the consumer price index is that the latter, for confidentiality reasons, only gives the relative position of national prices *vis-à-vis* the EU average at any given point in time. This implies that while the consumer price indices can be compared between any two points in time to show the extent of convergence, they can not be compared through time to show the direction of the convergence.

The results of the DRI study (DRI, 1995), based on the coefficients of variation in consumer price indices between the years 1980 and 1993 (Table 4.24), have demonstrated the following.

(a) Consumer price convergence has occurred to a significant extent in the drinks sector and to a lesser extent in the food sector, when comparing between 1980 and 1993 (prices excluding VAT – all drinks and all foods included[16]). This is an important development for the price of drinks, given that in 1980 this sector came second in terms of intensity of price dispersion of all the consumer goods sectors reviewed by DRI. In contrast, consumer price dispersion in the food sector was comparatively low both in 1980 and in 1993 (prices excluding VAT).

(b) As the DRI analysis distinguishes between three groups of countries depending on new Member State entry (EUR-6, EUR-9, EUR-12), it demonstrates that there has been rapid price convergence in the last three new Member States (Greece, Spain and Portugal) towards the EUR-9 average in 1993 in both the food and drink sectors (prices excluding taxes). The EUR-9 price convergence towards the EUR-6 has been by comparison much

---

[15]   Consumer prices: Eurostat. Producer prices: DEBA database.

[16]   Thus the product definition is somewhat broader in the DRI study than in the present one.

slower and less significant. This reflects the new Member States' increased economic integration following membership.

(c) Important conclusions may also be drawn on the level of dispersion of prices including taxes and of prices net of taxes (VAT). Comparing the coefficients of variation of prices including and excluding VAT at the beginning of the period, the differences in VAT rates across countries seem to have reduced the underlying price disparities both in the beverages and in the food sectors, although more strongly for food than for drinks. By 1993, price dispersion for prices net of VAT had diminished in both sectors more than that of prices including VAT.

(d) Comparing the overall trend of price dispersion (prices inclusive of taxes) over the 1980–85/1990–93 period, it seems that price convergence accelerated throughout these years between the EUR-9 and EUR-12 groups for both food and drink. However, in the food sector, price dispersion between the EUR-6 and EUR-9 groups increased in the 1985–90 period.

The existence of price convergence and its direction can point to the following conclusions.

(a) **Level and type of integration**. Integrated markets offer, under certain conditions, a greater possibility of demand transfer between suppliers on the basis of price net of 'other factors', such as transport costs, technical and language barriers and consumer preferences (European Commission, 1992). Economic theory tells us that a priori an increased cross-market substitution should be expected, to enhance price convergence for identical products between markets and also – due to increased competition – to drive prices to a lower level. However, these effects would be felt less in the food and drinks sector as 'other factors' in these markets are extremely important.

(b) **Product tradability**. A low level of price dispersion would imply high product tradability and vice versa.

(c) **Effects of integration**. Price convergence can result either from increased trade – following integration – or from the reorganization of the sector (e.g. structural change, production relocation, change in business strategy). A priori we would expect trade-induced price convergence to emerge more rapidly than that induced by sectoral reorganization. Also, the latter type of price convergence would tend to take place in products of a comparatively low tradability.

On the other hand, a lack of price convergence or indeed increased price divergence can be attributed to:

(a) the strong persistence of 'other factors' (point (a) directly above);
(b) the nature of competition shifting from price to non-price factors and the associated emergence of a dual structure, a characteristic of most food and drink markets, as the present study has demonstrated;
(c) increased pressure on food manufacturing from the growing power and scale of the distribution sector.

Table 4.24. Pattern of consumer price convergence for EU food and drinks, 1980–93

Convergence between 1980–93	Coefficient of variation, 1980		
	LOW	AVERAGE[1]	HIGH
SLOW	Jams, honey, syrups Pasta Products from potatoes Coffee and cocoa	Bread, cakes & biscuits	Spirits Confectionery Tea
AVERAGE[1]			Beer
STRONG	Soft drinks Spices, sauces, condiments		Mineral water Ice cream

[1] Average defined on the basis of movements within the entire food and drinks sector.
Source: DRI (1995) based on Eurostat data.

Our analysis of the evolution of producer prices over the 1978–93 period has concentrated on three indicators of price convergence – the standard deviation, the coefficient of variation (which presents the standard deviation as a percentage of the mean) and the range – calculated on the basis of the producer price index of each product sector (Annex D, Tables D.*.11). The results demonstrate that price convergence has been important and continuous throughout the period examined in all of the reviewed sectors, except in the case of spirits where the reduction in the dispersion of prices was neither significant nor sustained. On the other hand, price dispersion reaches its highest level in the 'other foods' category, once more reflecting the diversified nature of the products included in this classification. Price dispersion also remains particularly high in the case of spirits with a characteristic 70 point difference between the highest index number (171 in Greece) and the lowest (101 in Italy) in 1993.

Price volatility, as captured by the year-on-year percentage changes, has also declined significantly in most sectors and Member States. Exceptions, where price volatility remains particularly strong, are: chocolate/confectionery (particularly in the UK, Italy, Spain and Greece); 'other foods' (particularly Belgium and the UK); spirits (most countries except Germany, France, the Netherlands and Belgium post-1990); beer (most countries except Germany, France, Belgium and the Netherlands post-1990).

In many instances the evolution of prices highlights the importance of macroeconomic factors rather than any other effects. This may well be the case for the apparent correlation of price movements in depreciating versus appreciating currency countries, particularly towards the end of the period examined. For instance, the 20% reduction in nominal pasta prices in Italy and the substantial increases in Germany and the Netherlands over the last three years seems to reflect exchange rate movements; similarly the fall in Italian, Spanish and Portuguese prices for products of industrial baking and the rise in German and Dutch prices; the falling prices in Italy, the UK and Spain for spirits; Italian and Spanish falling prices for beer.

Bearing in mind the importance of exchange rate movements for any analysis of nominal price changes, the structural break analysis has sought to identify any significant changes in the data after the launch of the SMP (Table 4.25). The results do not point to any significant post-1986 effects on prices. Again, conclusions at an EUR-12 level conceal country patterns and in some cases an important post-1986 shift of prices has been identified. Such is the negative shift in Italy and Belgium in the pasta sector; a mixture of positive and negative breaks in a number of countries in industrial baking, which confirms the continuing price volatility in this sector; positive shifts in Dutch and Spanish prices and negative in French and Belgian in chocolate/confectionery; positive shifts in France, Germany and Greece in 'other foods'; and mixtures of negative/positive shifts in a number of countries in all of the other sectors.

Table 4.25.   Results of the structural break analysis on prices (EUR-12)

NACE	Output prices[1]		
	+ ve	- ve	?
417			*
419			*
421			*
423			*
424			*
427			*
428			*

[1] On the basis of the producer price index.
Notes:
An asterisk in the first column (+ ve) indicates that there is consistent evidence of significant positive breaks in the data (i.e. increases in the value of the variable) for a number of Member States over the period after 1986.
An asterisk in the second column (- ve) indicates that there is consistent evidence of significant negative breaks in the data (i.e. reductions in the value of the variable) for a number of Member States over the period after 1986.
An asterisk in the third column (?) indicates that there is no consistent evidence of any significant structural breaks after 1986.
If asterisks have been placed in both of the first two columns (+ ve and - ve) this indicates consistent evidence of positive breaks in some countries and of negative breaks in others.
Source: BER based on Eurostat data.

The above conclusions of our examination of producer prices seem to be confirmed by the DRI analysis of consumer prices, which confirm the existence of a price convergence over the 1980–93 period but at varying degrees between the different sectors and with a continuing high short-term price volatility for some sectors. Some more light is shed on some sectors which the DRI study has examined at a more disaggregated level, particularly for the more diversified product sectors. Thus, in the case of NACE 421 considerable convergence had occurred by 1993 in the prices of ice cream (one of the sectors with the highest price dispersion in 1980), but the prices of chocolate/confectionery maintained considerable divergence throughout this period; in the case of NACE 423, all products (except tea) seem to be characterized by low price dispersion at the beginning of the period with further convergence for spices, sauces and condiments but limited convergence of coffee prices; in the case of NACE 428, price convergence was intense throughout this period for both soft drinks and mineral water, although in the case of soft drinks this started from a lower price dispersion level at the beginning of the period.

Also of particular interest are results on spirit prices which confirm the continuing existence of some of the highest price divergences of all sectors, largely due to the persisting high levels of indirect tax disparities. By contrast, the growing convergence of prices in the beer sector seems to reflect some reduction in the distorting effect of VAT and excise duties after 1985.

The industry survey has provided some evidence of both a decrease in the level of market prices and a convergence between Member States. Although a large number of the companies interviewed felt that the SMP had had no impact on prices, two-fifths said that prices have decreased as a result of the SMP (Appendix E, Figure E.11). More companies in Portugal, Greece and Denmark reported decreases in market prices compared with other Member States. There are important variations on this result between sector of activity and it was mostly in the industrial baking, spirits and chocolate sector that a lowering of prices was revealed (Appendix E, Table E.26). By contrast, the beer, soft drinks/mineral water, 'other foods' and pasta sectors felt the SMP had a neutral effect on market prices.

Nearly a fifth of the companies also stated that price differentials had decreased as a result of the SMP, although a particularly high number of firms were unable to answer this question (Appendix E, Table E.27). It was generally felt, however, that prices have been aligning to those of the cheapest country.

It is important to note that nearly all of the respondents with cross-border (production or trading) operations emphasized that exchange rate volatility was a factor of far greater importance than any SMP-induced effects. Currency fluctuations cause 'disorderly' markets since they can create large price variations unrelated to the real product value and can render manufacturers in a strong currency zone particularly uncompetitive; for instance, this seems to currently be the case in Germany. Such issues can affect trading, production location, employment, etc. far more than the SMP.

Beyond the question of market prices, the survey addressed the question of the overall importance of the SMP for the consumer (whether of benefit or loss) in terms of consumer price and product choice. Again there is overwhelming evidence in support of the above hypotheses, with 53 (out of 109) responses indicating the impact of the SMP has been 'high' for the consumer and a further 27 indicating a 'medium' impact (Appendix E, Figure E.7). This reflects a strong belief that the SMP has lowered consumer prices and increased product choice. Only 8 (out of 106) responses believed that the changes introduced by the SMP have had a 'negative' impact for the consumer, although some 23 believed SMP effects are 'indifferent' (Appendix E, Figure E.8).

5. Business strategy [17]

5.1. Factors which determine corporate strategy

As outlined in the preceding sections, the impact of the SMP on factors which determine corporate strategy has been to accelerate or intensify rather than generate directly a process of structural change. In most instances, this process was dictated by the general macroeconomic conditions and a technological and business environment that brought about new functions and necessitated new forms of operation. Within this evolving environment, the prospect of an enlarged, unified market has given the impetus to faster and more dynamic adjustment.

In particular the following changes and SMP effects have been noted.

Production/investment

The removal of trade barriers has, in the long term, made possible the realization of economies of scale and cost savings along the production, marketing and distribution chain. The analysis demonstrated that these benefits in terms of cost savings were mainly seized by larger companies in the sector. This was due to the scale of investment required to compete and the fact that such companies were the major cross-border operators both pre- and post-SMP.

Entry barriers

Traditionally, barriers to entry in the food industry have not been as important as in other industries due to the relatively lower economies of scale in the production process, which meant that the optimal size of the firm was low and 'inviting' to the entry of new firms. Although economies of scale are still relatively low by comparison to other industries, these increased over the period examined when compared to their starting position pre-1985. This is not solely attributed to the SMP, however. Rather it has been brought about by a combination of new possibilities deriving from technological development and the increased potential for growth from the single market.

On the other hand, the threat of new entrants increases with an industry's 'attractiveness'. A number of variables determine 'attractiveness', such as the size of the market, the potential for expansion or development of niche markets, and past profitability in the sector. All of these factors have been positively influenced by the SMP, suggesting that the industry has become more 'attractive' to newcomers. This can lead, however, to reinforcing the position of existing competitors (through merger and acquisition activity) rather than to the entry of new businesses.

Buyer/supplier relationships

As already demonstrated, during the period examined and largely independently of the SMP, the food and beverages market has witnessed substantial increases in retail concentration and, consequently, retailer bargaining power. The emergence of powerful buyers and the reinforcement of their position has had enormous implications for the food and drinks industry. As competition for shelf space has increased, growing pressure has been put on manufacturer

---

[17] The theoretical framework used for the following analysis is based on the traditional structure conduct performance paradigm (SCP) (Porter, 1980, 1985).

selling prices and profit margins. The increasing presence of distributors' own-branded goods, manufactured exclusively under contractual agreements by SMEs of the food and drinks sector, has further intensified pressure on margins throughout the sector, and the restructuring process this is inducing is still far from complete.

On the other hand, the situation at the supply end (raw materials, components and various financial and business services) has not in most cases been significantly influenced by the SMP or changed to an extent that would have measurable impact for the food and drinks industry. This having been said, a large number of enterprises indicated they had 'Europeanized' their procurement strategy but in many instances they faced oligopolistic structures on the supply side, e.g. on packaging materials.

Competition

In addition to the increase in competition caused by the rising power of the distribution sector, competition has also intensified as a result of developments within the food and drinks industry itself, notably restructuring, intense M&A activity and the resulting increases in concentration which occurred particularly during the second half of the period examined (late 1980s and early 1990s). Again, these developments were largely due to the potential for growth, expansion and more substantial economies of scale that technological development made possible.

Product features

Apart from the broad macroeconomic factors outlined above, one must take into account the characteristics and nature of the product, which also impact on companies' strategic responses. In the case of the food and drinks industry the product's inherent constraints in terms of, on the supply side, high transport costs relative to the product's unit value, and, on the demand side, persisting strong national preferences, can hinder developments which the SMP should have facilitated.

Generally speaking the analysis has not revealed any particular Member State variations in SMP implications, other than those induced by:

(a) a country's existing comparative advantage in a particular sector, which provided a favourable background to further development after the SMP (i.e. the SMP has tended to reinforce pre-existing comparative advantage);

(b) the balance in the presence of SMEs compared to larger companies, which varies by country and sector of activity;

(c) geographical market proximity: certain markets which are geographically more distant from the 'heart' of Europe and where access is relatively more difficult (notably Greece, Portugal, Ireland, as well as peripheral regions of other Member States) have not been able to take full advantage of the opportunities created by the SMP;

(d) the accession of Spain and Portugal: this has been a special case where the SMP effect has been diluted by these countries' accession to the EU in 1986, i.e. at the same time as the launch of the SMP.

5.2. Nature of strategic responses

As is clear from the legislation analysis, companies seem to have addressed the SMP in two, fairly distinct, ways.

(a) First, they reacted to the prospect of the SMP as a whole in terms of the opening of borders, elimination of physical controls of goods and the potential of an expanded market. This, in many instances, generated a proactive approach to prepare for the perceived business challenges of the single market.

(b) Second, they have reacted to particular items of legislation from the SMP, such as the various items of horizontal or vertical food-specific legislation and/or product-specific Directives. This has been a more reactive approach, generating specific adjustments to the new legislation adopted/enforced.

The industry survey has provided evidence of the growing importance that EU companies attach to the SMP, although overall the SMP seems to have been more important in the food rather than in the drinks sector (Appendix E, Figure E.4). This attitude is largely due to the fact that the majority of companies that participated in the survey are currently involved in intra-EU trade.

Over half of the companies interviewed in the industry survey (42 out of 78) said they 'perceived the SMP as a challenge' (Appendix E, Figure E.12), especially in the smaller Member States. This perception was higher among companies in the pasta, soft drinks and 'other foods' sectors. A larger proportion of large firms when compared to SMEs thought the SMP has been a challenge, and this was mainly because they saw more opportunity for engaging in or expanding their trade activities.

In addition, an overwhelming majority of the companies interviewed (72 out of 78) indicated that the SMP had exerted some influence on company changes, although when specifically called on to identify a direct SMP impact only 41 out of the 78 companies were in a position to do so (Appendix E, Figure E.14). A direct SMP impact on company changes seems to have been felt more by companies in the pasta and 'other foods' sectors. There are significant country variations in this result, with the majority of companies in the south (Greece, Italy and Spain) but also in France indicating that the SMP has not had a direct impact on their changes.

The survey addressed various dimensions of companies' strategic decisions, such as internal structures and organization, employment, R&D, ancillary services (transport and logistics), marketing and distribution. Overall, only 31% of the changes mentioned were attributed directly to the SMP (Appendix E, Figure E.13). Although several aspects have been somewhat affected, most of the changes seem to have occurred in companies' internal organization (17.5%), transport/logistics (15.5%) and product lines (13.4%). These issues will be further examined below.

Apart from the industry survey, the issue of companies' strategic reaction to the SMP was addressed in further detail in five case studies.[18] Whilst detailed results of this work are presented in Appendix F, the following section includes some of the main conclusions relating to the broad business strategies that are being examined here.

[18] The case studies cover 5 out of the 7 sectors and 12 Member States under review. The companies involved are: Danone (biscuits – France); Schöller (ice cream – Germany); Van Melle (confectionery – Netherlands); Grupo Gallo (pasta – Spain); and Whitbread (brewing – UK). Period covered: 1985–95.

Internationalization

This refers either to the presence of production/distribution etc. facilities outside the headquarters country or cross-border trading activities or both. The vast majority of companies interviewed in the industry survey and the case studies fell under one of these definitions.

The strong relevance of the SMP to internationalization is reflected in the fact that nearly three-quarters of the companies that participated in the survey indicated that the SMP has had a medium to high importance for their operations, with only a quarter attaching a low importance to it. Furthermore, as would be expected, the SMP has been particularly important to companies involved in relatively more tradable goods (pasta, chocolate/confectionery, 'other foods', biscuits) and less important in sectors where product tradability has been lower (beverages and, to a lesser extent, industrial baking).

Further examples of the way the SMP has influenced companies' internationalization mentality were provided in the case studies.

In two cases (Van Melle and Danone, chocolate/confectionery and biscuits respectively), the companies created an international network of production activities within the EU. This took place around 1985 and specifically in anticipation of the opportunities the SMP would provide. Whilst in the case of Van Melle this was done through the company's organic growth, in the case of Danone it was through the acquisition of an already established group (General Biscuits). In one case (Grupo Gallo, pasta), the company expanded by establishing international divisions outside the EU (US and Canada) but it was not possible to establish whether this strategic move was primarily induced by the SMP or Spain's accession to the EU. In the remaining two cases (Whitbread and Schöller, brewing and ice cream respectively), no distinct internationalization strategies were adopted in response to the SMP although Schöller has greatly expanded its presence outside the EU (in Central and Eastern Europe).

Capacity adjustments

Adjustments in production capacity following the launch of the SMP could have occurred either in the positive direction, as a result of an expansion strategy (in geographical or product operations), or in the negative direction, as a result of rationalization and concentration in production activities. The choice of strategy depends on the product sector and its potential for growth but also on a company's individual philosophy and future aspirations. It also depends on the size of the firm, with larger corporations often employing aggressive expansion tactics, usually through M&As, while smaller corporations would tend to concentrate on more specific geographical and product markets.

The macroanalysis demonstrated that the restructuring which occurred in the EU food and drinks industry after 1986 resulted from intense expansion activity by the larger companies. The driving forces for this activity have been the overall developments in the industry, whereby companies merged in order to enlarge their scope of operations and exploit the economies of scale made possible by technological advance, but also as a way to defend themselves against the rising power of distribution and to consolidate vertical buyer/supplier relationships. The SMP seems to have intensified this process, as companies strategically repositioned in preparation for the single market. In this context SMEs either became the subject of larger companies' acquisitions, or maintained their corporate identity by focusing their activity in more 'niche' (geographical or product) markets, or served to supply the rising own-branded segment of retailers.

The case studies have provided examples of capacity adjustments in both directions. In two cases (Van Melle and Danone, chocolate/confectionery and biscuits respectively), total production capacity in the period 1985–95 increased by almost two-thirds. The tactics employed for achieving this have, however, varied. While in the case of Danone increased production capacity was sought through acquisitions of new plants along with rationalization of existing ones, in the case of Van Melle it was mainly through rationalization and restructuring. The SMP was considered to have played a key role in these strategic decisions.

In the remaining three cases (Schöller, Grupo Gallo and Whitbread, ice cream, pasta and brewing respectively), a strategy of cuts in production capacity was followed, with the closure of production plants and product refocusing. Except in the case of Schöller, the SMP impact on these decisions was, however, considered to be negligible. Instead the companies indicated that their actions were to be seen as a strategic response to developments within national markets.

Location decisions

Both the macroanalysis and the industry survey have demonstrated that the SMP has had very little impact on production location and relocation, either within or across national borders (excluding that relating to capacity adjustments and to the presence of a corporation in other markets through M&As and AJVs). Indeed, the industry survey has shown that the smallest number of changes in companies' strategic decisions related to those referring to the production location. Only six out of the 78 companies felt their location decisions were directly affected by the SMP, and in most cases this was a result of either capacity adjustments or M&As.

The case studies have largely supported this observation. Only in one case (Van Melle, chocolate/confectionery) was relocation said to have taken place as a direct consequence of the SMP. This formed part of a broader expansion strategy within the EU which necessitated rationalization (closure of poorly performing plants and concentration on others) and specialization of the product lines (which rendered the use of certain plants obsolete). No major SMP or otherwise determined relocation was reported in the other case studies.

Cost-cutting/rationalization

Although cost-cutting and rationalization can occur as a result of a number of strategic moves along the production, marketing and distribution chain, we refer here in particular to changes and restructuring in the production process.

At a macro-level the analysis has demonstrated that there was an extensive rationalization of the food and drink industry's production structures, which – in many instances – significantly accelerated post-SMP. Also, some 28 out of 78 companies in the industry survey noted changes in the number and size of their plants, although only in 5 cases was this attributed to the SMP alone.

Intense efforts to rationalize were revealed in all five case studies. The aim of these efforts was to increase competitiveness, although this was not always related to achieving cost savings but also to obtaining quality improvements (e.g. Danone, biscuits). The driving forces behind this development included increasing competition, both within the sector and *vis-à-vis* retailers, and a perceived need to gear up to exploit opportunities under the single market. As is indicated above, only in the case of Danone and Van Melle was such rationalization accompanied by an increase in production capacity. In all other cases, the rationalization resulted in cuts in production capacity.

Product range

It seems that one of the most significant effects of the SMP has related to the product range. According to the industry survey, the majority of companies (41 out of 78) changed their product lines in the period 1985–95 and 13 of these did so as a direct consequence of the SMP. While in some cases, the change has been in terms of an increase in product lines, in others it has been manifested as a cut and rationalization of the product range with specialization in particular lines.

The case studies have shed more light on the nature and motives for the change in the number of product lines. In all cases, companies have chosen to rationalize their product activities and specialize in particular product segments. This has formed part of a broader marketing strategy aimed at promoting a more consolidated range of products under 'Euro-brands', i.e. brands identifiable EU-wide.

Marketing strategies

This is another area in which significant adjustments took place during the 1985–95 period. From the industry survey, 32 out of the 78 companies indicated changes in their marketing strategies post-SMP, although only 7 companies were in a position to say that the SMP had a direct impact on this. The changes introduced usually included adaptations of the product range as well as EU-wide branding, advertising and marketing. These activities have been dictated by efforts to consolidate an EU-wide corporate presence and market share and to strengthen the manufacturers' position *vis-à-vis* the retail sector.

Further insight into companies' evolving marketing strategies under the SMP is provided in the case studies. In all cases (except Grupo Gallo, pasta) there has been a significant reorientation in marketing strategies. In some cases, this has centred around the promotion of Euro-brands alongside the maintenance of certain successful national brands. Danone and Van Melle (biscuits and chocolate/confectionery respectively) provide a good example of this strategy. Both companies have a portfolio of a few leading Euro-brands, horizontally promoted throughout the EU at competitive prices and subject to intense advertising, and a relatively larger number of national brands, promoted on a smaller scale and lesser intensity.

The SMP has had a vital role to play in the development of this strategy. It allowed a pan-European base for the development of uniform branding, promotion and advertising activities, while the general Europeanization process has also influenced consumer tastes and preferences towards more standard products with international appeal.

While such strategies have been possible for larger companies, smaller and medium-sized firms usually responded by cutting down the number of product lines, often resorting to niche products and geographically more restricted markets.

Vertical integration

The macroanalysis has shown that vertical integration, mainly driven by companies' efforts to consolidate supplier/buyer relations in an environment of increasing competition and rivalry for market dominance, has been fairly substantial in the EU food and drinks industry throughout the period examined. SMP effects, in this context, have been largely indirect: to the extent the SMP has influenced the level of competition and market concentration in the industry and its ancillary sectors (distribution, transportation, retailing, input sourcing), companies are expected to have responded by some form of forward or backward integration. Usually this was done through alliances and joint ventures and rarely through direct ownership.

The industry survey provided only very limited evidence of an SMP-induced increase in forward/backward integration. Only 5 out of the 78 companies indicated this had occurred, while 11 more companies embarked on a vertical integration strategy this was not said to be driven by the SMP.

It is interesting to note that for a significant number of smaller and medium-sized enterprises, becoming the subject of retailers' backward integration has been an important means of survival. These companies maintained or supplemented activity in their product sector by becoming the exclusive suppliers of own-branded goods for distributors' chains. With distributors' own brands expanding fast at the expense of branded products, this mode of operation is expected to gain further ground in future. This was the case for Grupo Gallo (pasta) with the company becoming the exclusive supplier of distributors' own brands: currently these account for 30% of Grupo Gallo's output.

In most instances the case studies have revealed neutral, or even negative, vertical integration effects. Three out of the five companies employ very little vertical integration and this strategy has not changed at all during the period examined. Of the other two, from the start of the period, Schöller (ice cream) in fact formed part of a vertically integrated structure (forward into product transport), and Whitbread (brewing) relied heavily on forward integration for the products' retailing and distribution. Today, both companies have moved away from these forward integrated structures (Schöller has in fact been taken over by its main raw material supplier) and have significantly relaxed their ties with ancillary services. In both cases the SMP has impacted indirectly: for Whitbread this is partially due to SMP effects on retail structures and for Schöller it is a result of a reorientation in marketing philosophy brought about by increased competition.

Transport logistics and product distribution are areas where companies particularly feel an increasing need to be active. A growing number of companies are therefore engaging in simple and more loose forms of vertical integration, such as distribution through affiliated companies (Van Melle is a good example). Also, they often try to maximize benefits by including other brands and products in the activity, such as transport and/or distribution of non-identical products with similar logistics/distribution requirements (e.g. fresh dairy or juices for an ice cream company). The industry survey provided many examples of such practices. The growing importance of transport and distribution logistics in a company's operation is reflected in the fact that some 25 of the 78 companies saw substantial changes in this domain over the 1985–95 period. Moreover, the SMP has had an important role to play in this, with 15 of the 25 companies that experienced a change identifying a direct SMP impact behind these developments.

Managerial organization

Under this heading, the industry survey and the case studies have addressed issues of structure and internal organization, i.e. issues at the core of a company's operational philosophy. According to the industry survey, both of these aspects have undergone substantial change in the period after the launch of the SMP, with some 29 out of the 78 companies indicating changes in their structure and 26 out of the 78 pointing to changes in internal organization. More importantly, 17 out of the 26 companies that had reformed their internal organization stated this was done specifically in response to the SMP.

All of the five companies participating in the case studies also experienced intense restructuring and managerial reorganization. In all instances this referred to more central coordination of certain operations such as administration, R&D and product development, sourcing and procurement, transport and distribution, marketing and promotion, and inter-plant logistics. It is clear that by doing so, larger corporations with transnational operations were able to rationalize and cost save on these activities. At the same time, the idea has been to maintain flexibility and autonomy in national and regional company cultures so that they are better able to respect and adapt to the environment in which they operate and develop own initiative. Examples of this policy have been Danone and Van Melle (biscuits and chocolate/confectionery respectively) and, to a lesser extent, Schöller (ice cream).

A common observation from all the case studies as well as the industry survey was the increasing need for EU policy monitoring that the SMP has created. Although advocating administrative and legislative simplification, the SMP has generated a large body of evolving legislation that requires close follow-up and analysis during the process of conception, development, adoption and implementation. Companies with international operations thus feel that, whilst eliminating national differences and trade barriers, the SMP still requires substantial monitoring at both an EU and a national level.

Responding to this need, larger companies have created their own EU affairs departments while medium-sized and smaller companies have usually added this function to a product development, marketing, export or public affairs department. Trade associations have also adjusted to the need in order to be in a better position to inform their members, while many of the larger companies have sought to be actively involved in legislation and policy as it develops, through participation in working and advisory groups. The time, cost and skill requirements of these new functions have clearly constituted a disadvantage for smaller companies which have been, in many instances, unable to follow developments as closely.

Employment

The impact of the SMP on companies' strategy regarding employment has been twofold: first on employee policy and numbers; second, on the skills required and training needs. While the SMP effect on the latter aspect has been clear and direct, with an increasing need for specialization and training to keep abreast of technological, legislative and market change, the SMP effect on the former aspect has been ambiguous and indirect.

The macroanalysis has suggested that during the period examined changes have taken place in both directions with both increases and reductions in the number of employees. Cost-cutting and rationalization and the closure of a substantial number of small firms (often of less than 20 employees) have been largely responsible for the reductions. On the other hand, medium-sized and larger corporations' expansion, especially in sectors of dynamic growth, have absorbed some of these reductions and have stimulated the demand for employment.

The industry survey and case studies have also provided examples in both directions. To the extent that the SMP has been responsible for rationalization and restructuring in the market, it can be said that the SMP may have had an (indirect) impact on employment. Thus, in the industry survey, 26 out of the 78 companies have indicated changes in employment and training strategies, but only for seven of the companies were these directly attributable to the SMP.

Innovation

The question of whether the SMP has stimulated innovation in the form of R&D and new product development was examined in all the different stages of the study. The macroanalysis revealed intense R&D and product development activity as companies sought to maintain and expand market share in an environment of increasing competition. Results from the industry survey showed that this was one of the most dynamic areas in the period 1985–95, with 30 out of the 78 companies indicating changes in their R&D and product development strategies and 9 of them attributing the change directly to the SMP.

Other aspects of a company's change in capacity to innovate as a result of the SMP come about indirectly, e.g. via investment in training or via efforts to integrate vertically or form alliances which suggest a willingness to innovate as they enlarge the know-how base necessary for this purpose.

The size of a company may also have an impact on its capacity to innovate, and the macroanalysis has suggested there may be support for the view that there is a higher degree of innovation amongst larger companies. Similarly, the product sector in which a firm operates will influence its innovativeness but arguments can be made pointing to a need for an increased effort to innovate for both fast growth and slow growth markets, depending on the company's motive.

The case studies have provided examples of companies' increased efforts to innovate and these were dictated either by a more general internationalization strategy (Van Melle, Danone, Whitbread: chocolate/confectionery, biscuits and brewing respectively), or by the need to safeguard current market share (Schöller, ice cream).

Competition avoidance

Broadly, the analysis undertaken has pointed to the following strategies which companies have employed with a view to avoiding competition:

(a) the development of business on a super-large scale which was made possible by the intense wave of M&As in the mid- to late 1980s: this had the added advantage of fortifying the manufacturers' position *vis-à-vis* growing retail power;
(b) vertical integration as a means of securing buyer/supplier relations;
(c) for medium-sized and larger firms, increasing specialization and focus in product range with EU-wide branding, promotion and marketing;
(d) for medium-sized and smaller firms, focus on niche product and regional or third-country markets.

The case studies provide examples of all of the above. Danone (biscuits) has followed a strategy combining internationalization and product specialization with Euro-branding, with limited vertical integration but more centralized sourcing and procurement. Van Melle (chocolate/confectionery) has employed a mix of Europeanization and product specialization (with Euro-branding) strategies. Grupo Gallo (pasta) has not adopted a particular strategy other than product specialization. Whitbread (brewing) has refocused within the UK market. Schöller (ice cream) has applied a strategy of product specialization (with Euro-branding) and market expansion, but has moved away from the tightly forward-integrated structures it had in the past.

In most cases, the SMP impact on competition avoidance was only additional, the primary driving forces being the broad restructuring of the industry and increasing rationalization and concentration during the period examined, along with growing retailer power.

APPENDIX A

Description of products included in the sectoral classifications and sector overview

A.1. Description of products included in the sectoral classifications

NACE Code 417   Spaghetti, macaroni and similar products

Spaghetti, macaroni and similar products, fresh or dried but not cooked

NACE Code 419   Products of bread and flour confectionery

Bread, bread rolls and other ordinary bakers' wares
Other bread and bread rolls
Other ordinary bakers' wares
Cakes and flour confectionery
Rusks
Products of biscuit making (including gingerbread and the like)

NACE Code 421   Cocoa, chocolate and sugar confectionery products

Cocoa products
Chocolate and chocolate goods
        Chocolate coatings
        Chocolate in tables or bars
        Other unfilled chocolate
        Chocolate confectionery and other filled chocolate goods
        Confectionery and other preparations of all kinds containing cocoa
Sugar confectionery
        Boiled sweets, caramels, toffees and the like
        Sugared almonds, pressed goods and pastilles
        Gums and liquorice confectionery
        Nougat, marzipan and the like
        Chewing gum
        Pastes and mass for making fondants and similar; liquorice extracts
        Other confectionery
        Artificial honey, whether or not mixed with natural honey
Ice cream
        Ice cream powder and other products for the preparation of ice cream
        Ice (sorbets, ice cream and other ices)

NACE Code 423   Other food products

Coffee and tea
        Unroasted coffee, free of caffeine
        Roasted coffee
        Extracts of coffee and similar preparations
        Residues from the processing of coffee
        Tea and maté

Products similar to tea (tisanes)

Extracts of tea and maté, and similar preparations

Mixtures of tea, milk powder and sugar

Residues from the processing of tea and maté

Roasted chicory and other coffee substitutes

Coffees from malt and other cereals

Other roasted coffee substitutes

Extracts and mixtures of coffee substitutes (whether or not mixed with coffee)

Vinegar, mustard and other condiments

Vinegar

Mustard flour; mustard

Vegetable extracts

Spices

Ice

Infants' food and dietetic foods

Powders or granules for making puddings, custards, table creams, etc.

Prepared flour for cakes and dry dough in powder form

Prepared baking powders

Baking additives and agents, pastry ingredients

Pudding powder and similar products

Soups, broths and sauces

Soups and broths

Seasonings for soups and broths, sauces, mayonnaise

Condensed condiments, peanut butter

Other foodstuffs

Preserved eggs in shell

Edible egg yolks

Edible eggs, not in shell

Edible ovalbumin

Albumins, inedible

Eggs not in shell, egg yolks, inedible

Prepared potatoes, but not frozen

Products (not frozen) from the processing of potatoes

Products with a basis of potatoes, frozen

Potatoes preserved in tins

Roasted and fried potatoes

Bees honey

Popcorn, puffed rice, cornflakes and similar products

Natural yeasts (other than brewers and bakers' yeasts and culture yeast); yeast extract

Other food preparations

NACE Code 424   Distilled, fermented ethyl alcohol; spirits and compounded spirits

Fermented ethyl alcohol, undenatured

Denatured ethyl alcohol, distilling dregs, fusel oil

Bakers' yeast from distilleries

Spirits from fermented vegetable products

Liqueurs, aperitifs and other spirits

NACE Code 427   Products of brewing and malting

Beer and its by-products
>   Beer in bottles or in cans
>   Beer in barrels and tanks
>   Brewery yeast
>   Brewers' dregs

Malt and its by-products
>   Malt and malt rootlets
>   Malting residues

NACE Code 428   Soft drinks and natural spa waters

Natural spring water, natural spa water from springs
Artificial spa waters; lemonade (other than fruit and vegetable juices)
>   Artificial spa waters; beverages for diabetics
>   Beverages with a basis of fruit juice
>   Lemonade and other soft drinks not based on fruit juice

A.2. Sector overview

From a review of the literature,[19] an investigation of the market[20] and the main economic indicators,[21] the following observations may be made for the individual sub-sectors.

A.2.1. Pasta (NACE 417)

This industry has recorded a steady expansion, in terms of real change in output, throughout the period examined, with a 4% average annual growth during 1986–93. The EU is the main world player in the pasta market, with total production well over 3 million tonnes, followed by the US (some 2 million tonnes).

Product tradability is relatively modest in terms of intra-EU trade, although the situation has improved during the review period. Italy is the main exporter of pasta to all other Member States. Extra-EU exports are particularly low at an average 3.7% of internal production over the 1986–93 period, and over 90% of the volumes exported come from Italy.

Due to traditional demand patterns, Italy is by far the most important producer and consumer of pasta, followed at a distance by France and Germany. Per capita consumption in Italy exceeds 30 kg per year, compared to all other EU countries where consumption is well below 10 kg (source: Consumer Europe, 1993). There would therefore be considerable potential for expansion of demand.

Both France and Italy lead technological development in this field via the development of new product lines and advanced processing methods. However, the French industry is considerably

---

[19]   Based on studies by BER and sister company PROMAR. Also, a comprehensive presentation of the industries is contained in the *Panorama of EU industry 1995/96* (European Commission, 1996).

[20]   Based on BER pre-survey of the market and meetings with the national food and drinks federations of the Member States.

[21]   A detailed analysis of these indicators and their evolution during the period under review is presented in Chapters 4 and 5.

more concentrated than that in Italy, where a number of SMEs still operate side by side with some of the largest food manufacturers in the EU.

A.2.2. Industrial baking (NACE 419)

This category encompasses five types of products: industrial bread-making, other bread-making, cakes, rusks and biscuits. This is one of the least industrialized of the sectors under review, still characterized by fragmented market structures and a comparatively large number of small, craft-bakery type firms, especially for the production of bread and patisserie products. While production increased slowly during the first part of the review period (i.e. prior to 1985), it expanded rapidly after 1985.

The movement of this production is mainly confined within national borders, with less than 7% traded on average across the EU. Similarly, the industry is not significantly export-oriented, with exports towards world markets at 3.7% of domestic production, while import penetration is negligible, accounting for less than 0.5% of domestic consumption (mainly coming from the US).

The UK, Germany, Spain, France and Italy are the main EU producers of industrial baking products, while some of the smaller Member States, Belgium, the Netherlands and Denmark, join the above countries with a significant share of intra-EU exports in this sector.

To a large extent, the apparent 'regionalization' of the market can be attributed to the particular product characteristics and associated heterogeneity in consumer preferences in each market. Apart from the qualitative differences in terms of product types, quality, presentation, modes of purchase, etc., there are also important quantitative variations in terms of per capita consumption volumes, especially for bread. In 1993, this ranged from 10 kg in Portugal to over 60 kg in France, Italy, Germany, Ireland and the Netherlands (source: Consumer Europe, 1993). Such, although less significant, variations also seem to exist for the other products of this category. Biscuits are a notable exception, where a certain qualitative standardization has occurred throughout the EU while per capita consumption volumes in the Member States converge at around 9 to 16 kg per person (Caobisco). It is in this latter category that the presence of large industrial firms is most pronounced.

The most important developments that have occurred in this industry, in the course of the period examined, are the emergence of an intensive new product development and the growing substitution of ordinary, 'baker's' bread by industrial bread. These innovations have been made possible by technological change and have been supported by a shift in consumer lifestyle and preferences. Such developments have generated an increasing interest for larger industrial groups, stimulating further development.

A.2.3. Chocolate/confectionery/ice cream (NACE 421)

This is a sector where the EU has a strong presence in world markets, compared to other industrialized countries such as the US or Japan. It should be emphasized that nearly 80% of EU chocolate and confectionery production (as well as the bulk of EU consumption) is realized by four countries: Germany, the UK, France and the Netherlands. Throughout the review period, production has been characterized by relatively strong growth, strongly stimulated by intra-EU and extra-EU trade.

The sector's tradability is particularly high, with an average 15% of the value of output exported within the EU and a further 7% to world markets over the 1986–93 period. By contrast, import penetration from extra-EU is limited, at an average 2.7% over the same period (coming mainly from the Central and Eastern European countries (CEECs)).

On the demand side, as this category encompasses very different products there are wide variation in terms of growth and change. A broad distinction can be made between 'leisure' products such as ice cream, and confectionery, the latter being regarded as more of a 'luxury' product. With health and diet considerations becoming an increasingly important concern for European consumers, the industry has dynamically turned to product innovation in order firstly to maintain and eventually to stimulate demand. Another reason why product innovation has paid off particularly well in this industry is that the product is largely subject to impulse-purchase, where novelties can play an important role. This is particularly the case in the confectionery product market, where the introduction of sugar-free products has led to a real growth in overall demand. Country variations in confectionery and chocolate consumption are important and, generally speaking, northern Europeans consume more of these products than southern Europeans (e.g. from over 13 kg per capita in Germany down to around 4 kg per capita in Italy – source: Caobisco, 1993). On the other hand, ice cream and to a lesser extent chocolate are subject to strong seasonal demand variations especially in southern Europe.

Similarly, market structure variations are markedly different both across the three product segments and between countries. The chocolate industry is characterized by strong concentration, with a few multinationals effectively controlling the bulk of the EU market. In the case of confectionery, however, a dual structure clearly prevails with a large number of SMEs operating strictly within their national borders, side by side with larger industrial interests. Both of these types of operator may also be found in the ice cream market together with a much larger number of 'craft' ice cream manufacturers in the south.

A.2.4. Other foods (NACE 423)

This category includes an extremely diversified range of products, which can be broadly classified in the following groups: hot beverages (coffee, tea and substitutes); vinegar; infant formulae and diet foods; soups/sauces; condiments; various food preparations. This translates into varied growth rates and developments within the group and the overall trends can be misleading in terms of the individual products. Generally speaking the most dynamic product segments are: hot beverages (except for tea); soups/sauces; condiments; baby food and diet foods. The main product in terms of value within this category is hot beverages, and the EU is a major player in the world coffee market led by Germany and Italy. Germany and the UK are by far the largest producers in value terms, followed by France, Italy and Spain.

The overall sector has recorded high rates of growth, with an average annual increase of 5.6% in terms of real output value during 1986–93. This is mainly attributed to the excellent performance of new market segments within the above product groups (e.g. ready soups).

Dependence on cross-border sales is fairly high, with some 11.9% of the production exported on average during 1986–93 towards other Member States and a further 8% outside the EU. Also, this is the sector with the most significant import penetration from non-EU origin countries (due to imports of coffee and tea), although this is quite low at a mere 4% of the internal value of consumption (1986–93 average) and has been decreasing through time.

Wide variations may also be found across Member States on the demand side and, once more, traditional preference patterns seem to persist despite some standardization in the consumption of certain new products. Tea is such a traditional product typically linked to Anglo-Saxon habits and with limited scope for expansion in the rest of the EU. Coffee is an expanding market with good potential in the southern Member States, where consumption is still low by comparison with the north. Soup consumption is particularly high in the UK, Belgium and the Netherlands but shows weak rates of growth in the south. Germany comes first in the consumption (and production) of condiments, followed mostly by northern Member States, and again a fairly limited interest from the south.

A common feature of all product groups within this category is the strong involvement of multinationals and this accounts for the fairly concentrated structures of the sector. Brand competition seems to be the single most important success factor in these markets, especially for hot beverages, soups and condiments, hence the emphasis on promotion and advertising. A particular reason for the presence of some of the largest multinationals in the coffee sector is the investment required for fairly sophisticated technology. On the other hand, despite the extensive product range, product innovation is considered relatively limited.

A.2.5. Alcohol and spirits (NACE 424)

This category encompasses two groups of product. one of which, ethyl alcohol, is of direct agricultural origin. The other, spirits, can be considered more as a second stage processed product and the one at the focus of this study. Three main types of product are included in the spirits group: whisky; vodka, rum, gin and eaux-de-vie; punch, liquors and other spirits. In total these account for about a quarter of the alcoholic drinks market.

This is a sector strongly affected by specific taxation and vertical legislation regarding the promotion and distribution of products, which can vary substantially across Member States. The UK and France account for 65% of EU production by volume, followed by Germany (14%), Spain (8.2%) and Italy (6.4%). The sector suffered from a fall in production in the early 1980s which slowed down and eventually stopped in the late 1980s with marginal increases thereafter. Thus the average annual rate of change during the 1986–93 period was negative, at -0.2%. Much of the recovery that took place after 1988 can be attributed to technological improvements, which led to new products or bottling methods.

Product tradability is particularly high. The EU is the world leader in exports of alcoholic drinks and these exports mainly consist of whisky and eaux-de-vie. The US and Japan are the two main destinations, absorbing over 40% of EU exports. In particular, the share of Japan as an importer of EU products has increased. On the other hand, the EU is also a significant importer of world spirits, the main origins of which are the US, the Caribbean and the CEECs. The US share of EU imports has increased substantially over the period examined. Both export intensity and import penetration (extra-EU) are particularly high during the period under review, at respective average rates of 25.1% and 3%.

EU demand for spirits varies considerably per country, in terms of both product type and levels of consumption. In terms of the latter, while average per capita consumption in the EU is currently estimated at just below 6 litres, the Greek figure is highest with 14 litres, with the lowest that of Italy at 3 litres. These figures are counterbalanced by the consumption of substitute drinks, notably wine and beer.

Market structure is extremely concentrated in this sector. Six multinational firms account for over 40% of the production and these operate side by side with a large number of small, specialist manufacturers found in more niche regional or product markets. This pattern is particularly pronounced in the UK and France and in the case of more international products such as whisky, rum and gin. On the other hand, the German, Italian and Greek markets are still relatively fragmented, although the entry of large multinational groups, through the acquisition of successful local firms in these markets, has recently changed the picture. Competition between international brands is particularly fierce and merger and acquisition activity intense.

The nature of the market is the main reason for the presence of a wide range of products, presentations and brands. With the involvement of multinational firms certain of these products have acquired an increasingly international character. Nonetheless, demand has proven difficult to stimulate in some countries, due to economic factors such as the general recession and the increase in taxes and excise duties, notably in the UK. Thus, in Italy and the UK demand has fallen in recent years. By contrast, it has increased in Germany (partly due to reunification), Spain (partly due to the country's accession to the EU which resulted in the lifting of trading and duty restrictions) and France.

An important and more recent development is the sale of spirits from supermarket and large retail chains as opposed to the specialized, licensed retailers that have been typically associated with the distribution of this product.

A.2.6. Brewing and malting (NACE 427)

As opposed to malting, which can be considered a direct output from the agricultural sector, brewing is more a second stage processing method and, as such, is at the focus of this study. The sector encompasses a wide range of products, notably of low and high fermentation, of different alcohol content down to the most recent launch of non-alcoholic and light beer, and of different malt content.

The EU and the US are the most important markets in the international beer economy, but both are regarded as having reached their full growth potential since the late 1980s. Within the EU, northern EU countries have been historically the main producers and consumers of beer as well as of malt. Germany and the UK alone account for over half of total EU beer production by volume. These countries, followed by France, have, at least with regard to the more traditional type of product, become saturated since the mid-1980s. Thus, in the last 10 years, both beer production and consumption have stagnated in real value terms in these countries.

Wide variations in per capita consumption may be found across Member States, with Germany leading (144 lit/head), followed by Denmark and the Netherlands, and Italy at the lowest end (23 lit/head) (Consumer Europe, 1994). A reason for this disparity is competition in low consumer countries from other alcoholic drinks, mainly wine, a traditional product of the south.

Product tradability is rather low and this is partly due to the strong, regional character of the product. Apart from a few, international brands widely traded across borders throughout the EU, over 95% of products is consumed within national markets. Extra-EU trade is not significant representing less than 10% of total trade.

A characteristic of the EU beer market, largely due to the high production costs, is the increasing involvement of multinational firms. Linked to this, merger and acquisition activity intensified in the late 1980s to early 1990s. This has created a difficult situation for smaller producers who are increasingly confined to regional and/or niche product segments. This is a sector representing one of the highest closure rates in the food and drink industry. Only Germany, Belgium and the UK maintain a relatively higher number of breweries, largely reflecting the specialization and fragmentation of the market.

More recent trends are shaping the market. These are the increasing importance of international brands, under-licence production of smaller breweries, and exclusive import and distribution contracts.

A.2.7. Soft drinks and mineral water (NACE 428)

Both markets have seen remarkable rates of growth throughout the period examined. In particular, the mineral water industry has been in continuous expansion during the last decade. Further potential for growth exists for both markets due to the current low intake of mineral water in certain EU countries (e.g. the UK) and the proliferation of new products in the case of soft drinks.

Trade is largely confined within the EU and extra-EU product tradability in terms of import penetration and export intensity is not significant. The extra-EU trade balance is positive and has remained so throughout this period.

Market growth has been largely due to the launch of new products and methods of packaging (e.g. plastic and cans as opposed to glass bottles) and has increased mineral water and soft drink consumption at the expense of alcoholic drinks. Particularly successful have been 'light' and fruit-based soft drinks and sparkling waters and, more generally, products associated with a healthy diet.

Per capita consumption of soft drinks is highest in the UK (over 100 litres), followed by Germany, the Netherlands and Spain. Italy leads in mineral water consumption per capita (115 litres), followed by Germany and France (source: Consumer Europe, 1993). Seasonal variations in consumption tend to reverse the above order as in southern Member States both soft drink and mineral water consumption increase significantly during the summer months.

With regard to mineral water, a development which has opened new possibilities in the market has been their presentation in plastic rather than glass bottles and the launch of sparkling as opposed to still waters. These two factors have contributed significantly to the strong expansion of the market. While the strong rates of expansion in the soft drinks market have been largely brought about by the presence of multinationals and their advanced marketing, promotion and distribution methods, the growth of the mineral water industry has been largely due to the existence of many different types and sources of water. This fragmented, strongly regional supply structure has obstructed the internationalization of the market, although since the mid-1980s the presence of multinationals through takeover of profitable national SMEs has increased as the sector exhibits rapid rates of growth. Thus multinational firms play an increasingly important role in the mineral water industry, approaching the more concentrated structures found in the soft drinks industry where competition has been particularly fierce.

Today, two large multinational groups control over 35% of the EU mineral water market. France is one of the most concentrated markets where these two groups have a nearly 70% share. The Italian market is also rather concentrated. In most other countries structures are still rather fragmented. In the soft drinks sector the largest two firms control over 45% of production, although one of these (Coca-Cola) is largely an owner of brands rather than a manufacturer.

APPENDIX B

Analysis of legislation

Table B.1.   List of SMP legislation

Items in bold: measures which form part of single market programme (White Paper including subsequent additions).

Column definition: A: entry into force;   B: date until which non-conforming products are allowed to circulate in the market.

Abbreviations: D: Council Directive; Dec: Commission Decision; R: Council Regulation; COM(..): Commission proposal.

I.1.   Sector specific – Removal of technical barriers

I.1.a.   Free movement of goods - sectoral approximation: foodstuffs

		Date entry into force A	B	Number of amendments	Last amendment	Comments: legislation in the field prior to the White Paper; subsequent amendments
GENERAL PROVISIONS – INSTITUTIONS						
Dec 69/414	Standing Committee for Foodstuffs (CPDA).					Role of CPDA amplified in the context of D 85/591 regarding sampling and analysis for food inspection.
Dec 74/234	Scientific Committee for Food (SCF).	26.11.1980		1	Dec 86/241	Composition and role of SCF redefined by Dec 95/273.
Dec 80/1073	Advisory Committee on Foodstuffs (ACF).					Repeals Commission Decision 75/420 which first established ACF.
D 93/5/EEC	Assistance and cooperation with scientific examination for questions relating to food.					Concerns cooperation between Member States and the Commission, through the involvement of CPDA.
CONTROL OF FOODSTUFFS						
D 85/591/EEC	**Sampling and analysis methods.**					**Introduces common methods of analysis.**
D 89/397/EEC	**Official controls of foodstuffs.**	01.06.1993	20.06.1991	1	D 93/99	**D 93/99 introduces additional measures by 01.05.1995 and harmonized standards for laboratories (EN 45000 series) by 01.11.1998.**
D 92/59/EEC	General product safety.	29.06.1994				Supplements original D 85/374 on product liability.
R (EEC) 315/93	Contaminants in food.	01.03.1993				Maximum tolerance levels to be established.
D 93/43	Hygiene of foodstuffs.	14.12.1995				Defines common rules to apply to food production (application of HACCP and the EN 29000 series).
Proposed legislation:						
..	Equivalence of control measures.					Proposal currently drafted on the basis of Article 100b of the Treaty, as amended by the Single Act.
PROCESSING METHODS						
D 89/108/EEC	**General rules on all quick frozen foodstuffs.**	10.07.1990	10.01.1991			**Implementing legislation: D 92/1; D 92/2.**
	Novel foods, ingredients and processing methods: For GMOs (genetically modified organisms) see section II.1 on 'Horizontal – Technical barriers'.					

	Description	Date entry into force A	B	Number of amendments	Last amendment	Comments: legislation in the field prior to the White Paper; subsequent amendments
Proposed legislation:						
COM(92) 295	**Regulation on novel foods and novel food ingredients.**			1	COM(93) 631	Amendment concerns approval procedures. Proposal in second reading in EP. Amendments on labelling.
COM(88) 654	**Harmonizing provisions concerning the irradiation of foodstuffs.**			1	COM(89) 576	Parliament completed first reading. Dossier blocked in the Council.
INGREDIENTS/PROCESSING AIDS						
D 89/107/EEC	**Framework Directive which provides a basis on which lists of authorized additives and the conditions for their use may be drawn up.**	28.12.1990	28.12.1991	1	D 94/34	Framework Directive replaces and consolidates a number of other legislation, see list below. D 94/34 deals with the issue of additives in 'traditional foods'.
Implementing measures:						
D 94/35/EEC	Sweeteners for use in foodstuffs.	31.12.1995	30.06.1996			Partially replaces D 62/2645. Supplemented by D 95/45 laying down specific purity criteria for colours.
D 94/36/EEC	Colours for use in foodstuffs.	31.12.1995	30.06.1996			
D 95/2/EEC	Additives other than colours and sweeteners.	25.09.1996	25.03.1997			Replaced Directives 64/54, 70/357, 74/329 and 83/463.
D 95/31/EEC	Purity criteria for sweeteners.	01.07.1996				
Directives prior to Framework Directive 89/107/EEC:						
D 62/2645/EEC	Colouring matters for use in foodstuffs.	26.10.1963		8	D 81/712	Repealed by D 94/36.
D 70/357/EEC	Antioxidants in foodstuffs.					Repealed by D 95/2.
D 74/329/EEC	Emulsifiers, stabilizers, thickeners & gelling agents for use in foodstuffs.					Repealed by D 95/2.
D 85/585/EEC	**Purity criteria for preservatives.**	31.12.1986		3	D 92/4	Amends D 64/54. To be partially replaced by D 95/2.
D 86/102/EEC	**Purity criteria for emulsifiers, stabilizers, thickeners and gelling agents.**	26.03.1987				Amends 78/663. To be partially replaced by D 95/2.
D 78/664/EEC	Purity criteria for antioxidants.	01.02.1980		1	D 82/712	In the context of D 95/2 to be repealed by future legislation.
D 81/712/EEC	Methods of analysis to verify purity of certain additives.	20.02.1983				In the context of D 95/2 to be repealed by future legislation.
Proposed legislation:						
COM(95) 126	Amendment to D 94/34/EEC with regard to additives in traditional foods (maintenance of national laws, prohibiting the use of certain additives).					Submitted to Commission 19.04.1995.
..	Purity criteria miscellaneous additives.					Anticipated adoption 1996, but 700 pages long and will take some time to get through.
..	Amendment to D 95/2/EEC. Draft Commission Directive laying down specific criteria of purity of colours.					To repeal D 65/66, D 78/663, D 78/664 and D 81/712.
..	Regulation laying down procedure for flavouring substances used in foodstuffs.					Adopted 25 June 1996.
D 88/388/EEC	**Framework Directive on flavours used in foodstuffs and on their source materials.**	22.06.1990	22.06.1991	1	D 91/71	D 91/71 supplements D 88/388 and introduces labelling requirements for flavours. D 91/71 deadlines: A: 30.06.1992 B: 01.01.1994.

		Date entry into force A	B	Number of amendments	Last amendment	Comments: legislation in the field prior to the White Paper; subsequent amendments
Proposed legislation: II/3490/91 Rev.3	Proposal for a Commission Directive on additives and other substances necessary for the storage and the use of flavouring.					Currently in consultation of national experts.
D 88/344/EEC	Extraction solvents used in the production of foodstuffs and food ingredients.	13.06.1991		2	D 94/52	
Proposed legislation (other fields): ...	Processing aids and enzymes.					Proposal to be drafted.
...	Fortification with vitamins and minerals.					Proposal to be drafted.
...	Dietary supplements.					Proposal to be drafted.
PRESENTATION AND MARKETING Labelling: D 79/112/EEC	Framework Directive on labelling, presentation and advertising of foodstuffs.	22.12.1980	22.12.1982			First harmonized legislation in this field.
D 86/197/EEC	Labelling, presentation and advertising of foodstuffs.	01.05.1988	01.05.1989	3	D 93/102	Amends D 79/112. Defines alcoholic strength volume.
D 89/395/EEC	Labelling, presentation and advertising of foodstuffs.	20.12.1990	20.06.1992			Amends D 79/112. Extends scope and 'use-by date'.
D 89/396/EEC	Identifying the lot number of foodstuffs (lot and batch marking).	20.06.1990	01.07.1992	2	D 92/11	
D 90/496/EEC	Nutrition labelling.	01.04.1992	01.10.1993	1	D 96/21	Amendment (sweeteners) adopted February 1996.
D 94/54/EEC	Compulsory indication on labelling of certain foodstuffs other than those provided for in D 79/112/EEC.	01.01.1997				
Proposed legislation: SEC(89)2151	Codified version of D 79/112/EEC.					Current draft abandoned. Blocked at Council level, will not be advanced before modifications to D 79/112 finalized.
COM(91) 561	Amending D 79/112/EEC - QUID, language of labelling, products consisting of single ingredients, sales denomination & mandatory mentions in labelling.			1	COM(94) 24	Currently in discussions between EP, Commission and Council. New procedure (pre-conciliation).
EN/SPC/94	Proposal on the use of claims relating to foodstuffs					Currently in inter-service discussions.
Advertising & claims: D 84/450/EEC	Directive concerning misleading advertising.	01.10.1986				
Proposed legislation: SPA/62/Orig-Fr/Rev.1	Directive on the use of claims relating to foodstuffs.					Proposed Directive abandoned. Commission considering revision under Labelling Directive (D 79/112) and Misleading Advertising Directive (D 84/450).
Materials & articles in contact with foodstuffs: D 89/109/EEC	Framework Directive which paves the way for the adoption of specific Directive on particular types of material and articles in contact with foodstuffs.	10.07.1990	10.01.1992			Repeals original D 76/893.

	Date entry into force A	B	Number of amendments	Last amendment	Comments: legislation in the field prior to the White Paper; subsequent amendments
Implementing measures:					
D 85/572/EEC	**Basic rules for migration testing of plastic materials & articles in contact with foodstuffs.** A: 01.01.1991	**01.01.1993**	**2**	**D 93/8**	**Amends D 82/711.**
D 90/218/EEC	Specific Directive on plastic materials and articles in contact with food. A: 31.12.1990		3	D 95/3	D 95/3, with effect from 01.01.1996, partially replaces D 85/572 on plastic material migration testing in line with the Framework D 89/109.
D 93/10/EEC	Specific Directive on regenerated cellulose film. A: 01.01.1994	01.01.1995	1	D 93/11	Amends and repeals original D 83/229 in line with the Framework D 89/109.
Directives prior to Framework Directive D 89/109/EEC:					
Vinyl chloride:					
D 78/142/EEC	Permissible levels. A: 26.11.1979				
D 81/432/EEC	Method of analysis for determination of VC present in foods. A: 01.10.1982				
D 82/711/EEC	Definition of plastic materials and articles.				
Regenerated cellulose film:					
D 83/229/EEC	Directive on regenerated cellulose film. A: 01.01.1986		1	D 92/15	Lists substances whose use is authorized in manufacture of cellulose film.
Ceramics:					
D 84/500/EEC	Analysis methods and limits for migration. A: 17.10.1987	18.10.1989			
Rubber teats and soothers:					
D 93/11/EEC	Release of N-nitrosamines and N-nitrosarable substances. A: 01.04.1994	01.04.1995			
Proposed legislation:					
III/5382/94 Rev.4	Amends migration testing for plastic materials.				Adoption has been postponed.
Packaging (environmental considerations):					
D 85/339/EEC	Directive on production, marketing, use, recycling and refilling of liquid containers. A: 03.07.1987				
D 94/62/EEC	Directive on packaging and packaging waste.				General field of application, not just food.
FOODSTUFFS FOR PARTICULAR NUTRITIONAL PURPOSES					
D 89/398/EEC	**Framework Directive on foodstuffs intended for particular nutritional uses.** A: 16.05.1990	**16.05.1991**			**Repeals D 77/94.**
Implementing measures:					
D 91/321/EEC	**Infant formulae.** A: 01.12.1992	**01.06.1994**	1	**D 96/4**	**Lays down essential requirements on production, labelling and marketing in line with Framework D 89/398. Modification adopted 16 February 1996.** Adopted 16 February 1996.
D 96/5/EEC	Directive on processed cereal-based foods and baby foods for infants and young children.				Adopted 16 February 1996.
D 96/8/EEC	Directive on foods intended for weight control diets.				Adopted 16 February 1996.
Proposed legislation:					
COM(94) 97	Amends D 89/398/EEC to limit the foodstuff categories it relates to.		1	COM(94) 600	Adoption expected in 1996.

		Date entry into force A	B	Number of amendments	Last amendment	Comments: legislation in the field prior to the White Paper; subsequent amendments
TRADITIONAL FOODS - FOOD QUALITY						
R (EEC) 2081/92	Geographical indication and designations of origin (includes non-Annex II products).	24.07.1993		1	R 2037/93	R 2037/93 lays down detailed rules.
R (EEC) 2082/92	Certificates of specific character (includes non-Annex II products).	24.07.1993		1	R 1848/93	R 1848/93 lays down detailed rules. Amended by R 2515/94 introducing a Community symbol of specificity.
Proposed legislation:						
III/3308/91	Quality instruments for the food industry.					Draft DG III Communication currently blocked at inter-service consultations.
VERTICAL LEGISLATION: SPECIFIC FOODS						
R (EEC) 1411/71	Production and marketing of fresh milk and milk products.					Supplemented by D 79/1067 on methods of analysis for preserved milk, D 83/417 on caseins and caseinates, and subsequent legislation.
D 73/241/EEC	Basic Directive on rules and definition for cocoa and chocolate products as regards their composition and manufacturing specifications and names.	01.08.1974		9	D 89/344	
D 73/437/EEC	Basic Directive which defines categories of sugar.	13.12.1975				
D 74/409/EEC	Basic Directive which defines the term 'honey' and describes the main types according to both origin and mode of presentation.	23.07.1976				
D 76/621/EEC	Basic Directive on maximum levels of erucic acid in fats & oils.	01.07.1977		1	D 80/891	D 80/891 introduced methods of analysis.
D 79/786/EEC	Methods for verification of the composition of certain categories of sugar.					
D 88/593 /EEC	**Basic Directive on fruit jams, jellies, marmalades and sweetened chestnut puree.**	**31.12.1989**	**01.01.1991**			**Amends basic D 79/693.**
R (EEC) 2991/94	Marketing standards for spreadable fats.	01.01.1996				
Proposed legislation:						
COM(95) 722	**Draft proposals for Directives relating to: fruit jams, jellies, marmalades and sweetened chestnut puree; cocoa and chocolate products; sugars and honey.**					**Adopted 17 April 1996.** EC Commission undertook to rationalize seven of the vertical Directives in the area of foodstuffs.
VERTICAL LEGISLATION: BEVERAGES						
D 93/45/EEC	Production of nectar with no added sugars or honey.	31.12.1993				
D 89/394/EEC	**Fruit juices and certain similar products.**	**14.06.1990**	**14.06.1991**			**Amends for a third time D 75/726. Repealed by D 93/77, a codified version of D 75/726 and its subsequent amendments.**
D 80/777/EEC	Exploitation and marketing of waters recognized as natural mineral waters.	17.07.1982	17.01.1984	1	D 80/1276	
D 85/573/EEC	**Defines and regulates coffee extracts and chicory extracts.**	**01.01.1987**	**01.07.1988**	**2**	**D 85/573**	**Amends D 77/436.**

		Date entry into force A	B	Number of amendments	Last amendment	Comments: legislation in the field prior to the White Paper; subsequent amendments
R (EEC) 1576/89	**General rules on definition, description and presentation of spirit drinks.**	**15.06.1989** Full impl: **15.12.1989**	15.12.1991	2	R 3378/94	Implementing measures: Art. 1(3): R 2009/92, Art. 1(4): R 1014/90 with effect from 01.05.1990 & R 3773/89 with effect from 15.12.1989.
R (EEC) 1601/91	General rules on the definition, description and presentation of aromatized wines, aromatized wine-based drinks and aromatized wine product cocktails.	17.12.1991		2	R 122/94	Implementing measures R 3664/91 with effect from 17.12.1991 & R 2009/92 with effect from 17.06.1992.
Proposed legislation: COM(94) 423	Amendment of D 80/777/EEC: update technical provisions.					Common position reached in December 1995. Final adoption expected summer 1996.

I.1.b. Free movement of goods – sectoral approximation: other items

		Date entry into force	Number of amendments	Last amendment	Comments: legislation in the field prior to the White Paper; subsequent amendments
GOOD LABORATORY PRACTICE					
D 87/18/EEC	Harmonization of laws, regulations and administrative provisions relating to the application of good laboratory practice.	30.06.1988			
D 88/320/EEC	**Inspection and verification of good laboratory practices.**	**01.01.1989**	1	D 90/18	**Based on mutual recognition of test results. Annexes to this Directive replaced by D 90/18, with effect from 01.07.1990.**
D 90/679/EEC	**Worker health and safety - biological agents.**				**Supplemented by D 91/322.**
PROCESSING METHODS	(Novel foods, ingredients etc.):				
D 90/219/EEC	**GMOs (genetically modified organisms).**	23.10.1991	1	D 94/51	**Supplemented by Dec 91/590.**
D 90/220/EEC	**Release into the environment of GMOs.**	23.10.1991	1	D 94/15	Paves the way for application of European (CEN) standards on biotechnology.
...	Commission Strategy Paper: 'Promoting the Competitive Environment for Industrial Activities based on Biotechnology'.	April 1991			
PRICES					
D 88/315/EEC	**Consumer protection in the indication of the prices of foodstuffs.**	07.06.1990			**Amendment to D 79/581.**
Proposed legislation: COM(94) 431	Amending D 79/581/EEC to prolong transition period for application of unit pricing.				Commission adopted proposal on 12.07.1995 (NB: impact on small shops).

I.2. Sector specific – Removal of physical barriers

I.2.a. Control on goods

	Date entry into force	Number of amendments	Last amendment	Comments: Legislation in this field prior to the White Paper; subsequent amendments
VETERINARY AND PLANT HEALTH CONTROLS				
Potentially all health controls affect the food industry but only legislation directly relevant to the study's product subsections included.				
D 88/657/EEC Health requirements for mince meat and preparations.	01.01.1992			Amends previous legislation (since 1964). Supplemented by D 88/658.
D 89/437/EEC Hygiene and health problems affecting the placing on the market of egg products.	31.12.1991	2	D 91/684	
D 92/5/EEC Health conditions for meat products (covers non-Annex II preparations).	01.01.1993			Amends basic D 77/99 for technical progress and extends scope to intra-EC trade. Supplemented by specific legislation on meat products for industrial use.
D 92/46/EEC Health rules for the production and placing on the market of raw milk, heat-treated milk and milk based products.	01.01.1994	2	D 94/71	Repeals D 85/397 on heat-treated milk (transposed from 1.1.1989). Derogation of Article 2 §2 by D 92/47.
R (EEC) 2092/91 Organic production of agricultural products and indications referring to products and foodstuffs.	22.07.1991 Full impl.: 22.07.1992	6	R 529/95	Implementing legislation: R 94/93, R 3457/92 and R 207/93.
Proposed legislation:				
COM(93) 60 Regulation on marketing standards for certain milk and non-milk fats and fats composed of animal and plant products.				To be adopted in 1995. Awaiting opinion from the European Parliament.
COM(93) 558 Amends R (EEC) 2092/91 with regards to labelling provisions and technical improvements.				
4932/VI/95 Draft proposal for a Regulation on organic animal production.				Products with >70% organic ingredient to be labelled as 'organic' instead of previous 95% minimum requirement. Commission intends to adopt proposal in July 1995.
8972/VI/93 Draft document clarifying concept of milk-based products.				Aims to overcome problem of interpretation between Member States.
COM(95) 185 Amends D 92/5/EEC on hygiene, transport and production of prepared foods containing meat.				Gone to European Parliament reading.

I.3.   Sector specific – Removal of tax barriers

EXCISE DUTIES	Date entry into force	Number of amendments	Last amendment	Comments: legislation in the field prior to the White Paper; subsequent amendments
D 92/83/EEC	**01.01.1993**			
Harmonization of structures of excise duties on alcohol and alcoholic beverages.				
D 92/84/EEC	01.01.1993			
Approximation of rates of excise duty on alcohol and alcoholic beverages.				
R (EEC) 3199/93	23.11.1993			
Mutual recognition of procedures for the complete denaturing of alcohol for the purposes of exemption from excise duty.				

II.1. Horizontal – Removal of technical barriers

	Date entry into force	Number of amendments	Last amendment	Comments: legislation in the field prior to the White Paper; subsequent amendments
FREE MOVEMENT OF GOODS: NEW APPROACH DIRECTIVES				
D 89/392/EEC	Directive relating to machinery - contains detailed health and safety requirements for agri-foodstuffs machinery.	01.01.1992	3	D 91/368	Amended by 91/368 with effect from 1.1.1992.
D 94/62/EEC	Packaging and packaging waste.	30.06.1996			Repeals D 85/339.
COMMON MARKET IN SERVICES: Transport				
R (EEC) 1841/88	Carriage of goods by road between Member States.	01.07.1988 Full impl: 01.07.1993	4	R 881/92	Amends R 3164/76 by revising country haulage quotas with a view to their gradual abolition. Definitive cabotage system was adopted in 1993.
R (EEC) 4058/89	Fixing of rates for carriage of goods by road between Member States.	01.01.1990			Replaces basic R 3568/83 which expired 31.12.1989. Supplementing R 1841/88 above.
R (EEC) 4059/89	Inland cabotage: non-resident carriers operating national road haulage services within Member States.	01.07.1990 Full impl: 01.01.1993	2	R 3118/93	Implementing legislation: Dec 92/258. Definitive cabotage system was adopted in 1993.
R (EEC) 4060/89	Elimination of controls at frontiers of Member States in road & inland waterway transport.	01.07.1990	2	R 3356/91	Concerns technical inspection and checks of vehicles/vessels.
CAPITAL MOVEMENTS				
D 88/361/EEC - to be updated	Liberalization of capital movements (implementation of Article 67 of the Treaty).	01.07.1990 Full impl: 01.01.1993			Repeals D 60/921 and D 72/156 and all their subsequent amendments. Derogations until end of 1992 for GR, IRL, E and P as regards short-term capital movement, and for B and L as regards the two-tier foreign exchange market.
INDUSTRIAL COOPERATION: COMPANY LAW				
D 89/666/EEC	Disclosure requirements in respect of branches opened in Member States by certain types of company governed by the law of another State (11th Company Law Directive)	01.01.1992			Amends D 68/151, D 78/600 and D 83/349 (1st, 4th and 7th Directive).
D 89/667/EEC	12th Company Law Directive on single-member private limited-liability companies.	01.01.1992			
D 90/604/EEC	Annual accounts of certain types of companies - exemptions for small and medium-sized companies.	01.01.1993			Amends D 78/600 and D 83/349.
D 90/605/EEC	Scope of D 78/600/EEC and D 83/349/EEC (4th and 7th Company Law Directives).	01.01.1993			Amends D 78/600 and D 83/349.
Proposed:				
COM(88) 823	13th Directive on company law concerning takeover and other bids.		1	COM(90) 416	EP first reading completed.
COM(89) 268	Directive complementing the statute of European company (employee involvement).				EP first reading completed.
COM(91) 174	Regulation on the statute of a European company.				EP first reading completed.
INDUSTRIAL COOPERATION: INTELLECTUAL PROPERTY - Trade marks				
D 89/104/EEC	First Council Directive relating to trade marks.	31.12.1992	1	Dec 92/10	Proposal first presented prior to White Paper, in 1980.
R (EEC) 40/94	Community trade mark.	15.03.1994	1	R 3288/94	As above.

		Date entry into force	Number of amendments	Last amendment	Comments: legislation in the field prior to the White Paper; subsequent amendments
Proposed legislation: COM(85) 844 COM(88) 496	Implementing rules for R (EEC) 40/94. Legal protection of biotechnological inventions.		2	COM(92) 245	Proposal sent to European Parliament. Proposal before Council for adoption.
INDUSTRIAL COOPERATION: DIRECT TAXATION					
D 90/434/EEC	Common system of taxation: mergers, divisions and contributions of assets, shares for companies of different Member States.	01.01.1992			**Derogation for P until 01.01.1993 as regards transfers of assets and exchange of shares.**
D 90/435/EEC	Common system of taxation for parent companies and their subsidiaries.	01.01.1992			**Derogation for GR for charging corporation tax on distributed profits; derogations for D until mid-1996 and for P until approximately the year 2000.**
Convention 90/436	Convention on the elimination of double taxation - adjustment of profits of associated companies.				
Proposed legislation: COM(93) 293	Amends D 90/435/EEC to extend its scope and eliminate double taxation; amends D 90/434/EEC to extend its scope.				19.04.1994 Parliament approved Commission's proposal subject to certain amendments. Unanimity vote required.
COM(84) 404	Directive to harmonize laws on Member States relating to tax arrangements for the carry over of losses of undertakings. COM(90) 595 proposes implementing rules.		1	COM(85) 319	**Unanimity vote required. Adoption expected in 1995.**

II.2.   Horizontal - Removal of physical barriers

		Date entry into force	Number of amendments	Last amendment	Comments: legislation in the field prior to the White Paper; subsequent amendments
CONTROL ON GOODS					
R (EEC) 1900/85 R (EEC) 1901/85	Community export and import declaration forms: Single Administrative Document (SAD).	01.01.1988	3	R 717/91	**Related proposals were first submitted prior to the SMP, in 1982. The cited Regulations amend basic R 2102/77. The SAD was essentially introduced by R 717/91 (implemented on 01.01.1993).**
R (EEC) 2726/90	Customs controls and formalities: Community transit (simplification procedures).	01.01.1993	1	R 1214/92	**Repeals basic R 222/77 and subsequent modifications. Implementing legislation: R 1214/92. Supplemented by R 719/91 on TIR and ATA carnets as transit documents. Implementing legislation: R 2453/92 and R 2713/92.**
R (EEC) 3648/91	Abolition of customs formalities at internal frontier crossings: methods of using the 302 form.	01.02.1992			**Repeals R 3690/86 (TIR Convention - implemented 01.07.1987) & R 428/88 (common border posts - implemented 01.07.1989).**
R (EEC) 3330/91	Statistics relating to the trading of goods between Member States.	19.11.1991 Full impl: 01.01.1993	2	R 3046/92	**Repeals R 2954/85 and R 1736/75. Implementing legislation: R 2256/92 & R 3046/92.**

II.3. Horizontal – Removal of tax barriers

	Date entry into force	No. of amendments	Last amendment	Comments: legislation in the field prior to the White Paper; subsequent amendments.
VAU VAT **D 91/680/EEC** Supplementing the common system of value-added tax and amending D 77/388/EEC with a view to the abolition of fiscal frontiers.	01.01.1993			**D 77/388 is the 6th Directive on harmonization of turnover tax laws (repealing all previous, the first being D 67/227) and introduces a common VAT system. This Directive amends D 77/388 but also the effects of D 69/169; D 74/651; D 83/182 and D 83/183.**
Proposed legislation: COM(92) 215 Directive on harmonization of laws concerning turnover taxes.				Partially amends 77/388. Adoption expected in 1995. Unanimity vote required.
COM(87) 322 Directive introducing the definitive VAT regime (removal of fiscal frontiers).				Amends D 77/388. Adoption expected in 1996. Unanimity vote required.
COM(86) 444 Amends D 77/388/EEC to include a common VAT scheme applicable to small and medium-sized businesses.		1	COM(87) 524	**Partially amends D 77/388.** Proposal before Council for adoption. Unanimity vote required.
EXCISE DUTIES **D 92/12/EEC** General arrangements for products subject to excise duty: holding and movement of such products.	01.01.1993	2	D 94/74	**Directive amends the effect of D 69/169; D 74/651; D 83/183 and D 68/297.** Implementing legislation: R 2719/91; R 3649/92 on a simplified accompanying document for the movement of the goods.

Table B.2. Food-specific barriers: situation in 1985

Field	% of total[1]	Barrier	Examples — Sector	Examples — Country	Effect
TECHNICAL BARRIERS Barriers of this type pertain throughout the food production and marketing chain and include a diverse range of issues, such as the use of ingredients, controls on product health and safety, packaging and labelling requirements, restrictions on product denominations and the use of generic names, and specific rules on certain products (e.g. chocolate, alcohol).					
CONTROL OF FOODSTUFFS This category includes barriers associated with the control of products for commercialization in a Member State, such as import licences, health registration, product testing and various inspections.					
Health inspections	10%	All food products must undergo health inspection before entry to the country.	All	Spain	Imported product costs increased. Delays caused.
TOTAL	10%				
PROCESSING METHODS This refers mostly to new methods of production, new products or new ingredients.					
Irradiation	2%	Different countries apply different rules.	All	All	Complete lack of harmonization increases producer costs.
TOTAL	2%				
INGREDIENTS/PROCESSING AIDS Restrictions in this field generally prohibit trade and use of a product containing certain ingredients such as additives, processing aids, etc. In particular, the food industry faces barriers in the following areas:					
Sweeteners	7%	Aspartame and all artificial sweeteners not allowed.	'Diet' soft drinks	France, Spain	Diet segment of the soft drinks market cannot exist.
Colours	8%	Colouring agent 'amaranth' (E123) prohibited.	Soft drinks and spirits	Italy	Imports of certain products prohibited.
Flavours	3%	Artificial flavouring prohibited.	Spirits	Germany	Imports restricted or recipe change necessitated.
Other additives	7%	Alginate not allowed.	Biscuits and cakes	Italy	Imports restricted. Foreign manufacturers forced to change recipes.
Vitamins and minerals	2%	Addition of vitamins and minerals in foods prohibited, unless special authorization given.	Biscuits and snacks	UK	Imports restricted. Foreign manufacturers may change recipes.
TOTAL	27%				
PRESENTATION AND MARKETING Restrictions in this field touch on the packaging, labelling and even transport and marketing of products.					
Labelling	7%	Long list of label requirements (beyond scope of Labelling Directive 79/112/EEC).	All	Spain	Undermines uniformity of labelling rules as laid down by D 79/112. Manufacturer costs increased.
Advertising and claims	2%	Strict rules on label information which is perceived as linked to product advertising.	All	Spain	Restrictions on imports, especially in certain sectors.
Packaging	10%	Cans not allowed. Strict reuse laws on glass bottles.	Soft drinks, mineral water and beer	Denmark	Distribution costs increased. Need for packaging differentiation for foreign manufacturers exporting to Denmark.
Packaging and transport	3%	Bulk transport prohibited. 1980 Directive inhibits transport. Bottling to take place at source. UK and NL have derogation.	Mineral water	All countries but NL and UK	Restricts consumption of spring water.
Materials and articles in contact with food	3%	Characteristics of containers coming in contact with food different in the various Member States.	Biscuits, confectionery	Italy	Costly controls undertaken by importers to check product suitability.
TOTAL	25%				

Field	% of total[1]	Sector	Barrier	Examples	
				Country	Effect
TRADITIONAL FOODS					
Restrictions refer to traditional methods of producing, presenting and even marketing a product which are specific to a country. Product denominations have also been included in this category. These are cases where the use of generic names may be prohibited if the product does not conform to certain content requirements.					
Purity laws	3%	Beer	Malted barley may not be substituted in beer production by other products. Other countries allow substitution at maximum limits which are set differently in each country.	Germany, Greece	Imports less than 1% of the German market and production highly fragmented with large number of small breweries in place.
Product denominations	7%	Pasta	Only durum wheat may be used in production of pasta, unless if product is exported.	Italy, France, Greece	Durum wheat producers protected. Imports restricted. Price/quality competition limited.
		Ice cream	Prohibits use of vegetable fats in ice cream.	France, Germany	Restricts use of generic name ice cream. Production costs higher if only animal fat used.
Minimum contents	5%	Soft drinks	Minimum juice content limits exist.	Italy	Limited product choice, higher product prices. Foreign manufacturers must change recipes.
TOTAL	15%				
VERTICAL LEGISLATION					
Restrictions refer to description, production and ingredients of particular products.					
Alcohol	8%	Spirits	Sets maximum ethanol limits lower in Spain than in other countries. Also, various import controls associated with alcohol content in spirits on the grounds of consumer health or protection of national markets.	Spain	Imports of specific liquors restricted.
TOTAL	8%				
TOTAL TECHNICAL	87%				
PHYSICAL BARRIERS					
This includes various plant health and veterinary controls which cover the processed foods sectors, including rules on toxic residues.					
TOTAL	3%				
TAX BARRIERS					
Barriers of this type include fiscal discrimination, especially regarding taxes and excise duties in the alcohol drinks sector, as well as variations in excise taxes between countries and close substitute products. Eco-taxes and related environmental taxes are excluded.					
Beer and alcohol	5%	Beer	Wort taxes (based on fermentation volumes) are used. System differs between countries and certain levy excise tax on finished product rather than wort tax.	Five countries	Tax discrimination caused unfair competition between domestic and foreign manufacturers.
Other	5%	Biscuits and confectionery	Certain ingredients contained in these products, such as sugar and cocoa are taxed according to content percentage.	Italy	No direct discrimination between foreign and domestic producers, but importers must declare product composition in detail.
TOTAL	10%				
GRAND TOTAL	100%				

[1] Based on the total 218 measures of the Group Mac work. However, barrier typology has been adjusted to conform to the typology followed in the present study.

Source: BER based on Group Mac (1988).

Table B.3. Harmonized food-specific legislation (Articles 100a and 100b following the Single European Act)

REMOVAL OF TECHNICAL BARRIERS: FOOD & DRINKS

HORIZONTAL

Field	SM legislation	Details
Food controls & hygiene	D 89/397/EEC	Background: No prior common rules. Objectives: The cited Framework Directive aims to lay down and harmonize the general principles governing controls to verify food compliance with EC legislation and in particular the four Framework Directives listed below. Thus, it covers controls over the entire food production process from raw materials to additives and ingredients, labelling and presentation, processing methods and materials and articles in contact with food. Regular controls as well as on-the-spot inspections are envisaged on this and Member States are requested to submit yearly reports on the Directive's implementation and cases of infringement on the basis of which annual programmes of coordinated EU-wide inspections are prepared. To guarantee the equivalence of inspection standards between the food inspectors and laboratories involved in each Member State, supplementary measures were adopted by D 93/99/EEC (European testing standards EN 45001-3 series). Also, the provisions of D 89/397/EEC are supplemented by the 1985 Directive on sampling and analysis methods for the monitoring of foods (D 85/591/EEC), the 1993 Food Hygiene Directive (D 93/43/EEC), and the 1993 Regulation on the monitoring of contaminants in food production (R (EEC) 315/93) which relates with further legislation on good manufacturing practices (D 88/230/EEC). Particularly important is the 1993 Food Hygiene Directive which promotes producer responsibility through the HACCP concept (Hazard Analysis and Critical Control Points) and the related European quality assurance standard (EN 29000 series). Exemptions: Specific national provisions can be maintained/introduced, provided these are not less stringent than the EC rules and do not constitute a barrier to trade.
Novel foods	COM(93) 631	Background: No prior common rules. Objectives: This field concerns advances in food technology in general. The proposed Regulation on novel foods aims at the approximation of rules and administrative procedures. It stipulates that all novel products, whether ingredients, semi-finished, finished, or manufacturing procedures should be subjected to a safety and nutritional assessment and requires notification to the Commission in some cases depending on the novelty. Finally, the proposed irradiation Directive aims to harmonize EC rules. It defines the use of the method (in particular, it specifies this is not a substitute for good hygiene) and 11 categories of products to which it could apply and requires the certification of establishments carrying out this treatment. The list of foodstuffs that should be allowed to undergo irradiation is at the centre of the debate and the EP wants this to be limited to herbs and spices. Exemptions: Novel food ingredients that fall within the definition of food additives/solvents etc. not covered by the novel food Regulation. GMOs (genetically modified organisms) covered by separate, horizontal, non-food specific legislation (D 90/219/EEC and D 90/220/EEC).
Additives	D 89/107/EEC	Background: EC legislation on particular additives exists since 1962 (colours), 1970 (antioxidants), 1964 (preservatives), 1970 (emulsifiers etc.). The latter two in particular formed part of the original SMP (D 85/585/EEC and D 86/102/EEC). In all other areas, including sweeteners, national laws apply. Objectives: The cited Framework Directive of 1989 aims to harmonize existing national rules and to set a coherent approach for future EC legislation regarding all types of additives. Following the Framework, three detailed Directives were adopted on sweeteners (1994), colours (1994) and the catch-all on other additives (1995). Purity criteria were adopted for sweeteners in 1995 and more criteria are to be adopted for colours and the other additives. To allow for technical progress a 'positive list' of authorized additives has been drawn up and will be regularly updated, based on scientific evidence, toxicological testing and evaluation. To be approved, additives must specify the foods in which they will be used, the 'need' for such use, and the ADI (acceptable daily intake) level. Strict rules also cover aspects of additive labelling and packaging. Exemptions: Flavourings (D 88/388/EEC), extraction solvents (D 88/344/EEC), processing aids/enzymes (need for proposal being considered), vitamins/minerals added in food (proposal envisaged) dealt with by separate legislation. For additives used in traditional foods, national rules maintained. Limited derogations for additives used in certain traditional foods.
Flavours	D 88/388/EEC	Background: No prior common rules. Objectives: Harmonizes national provisions and procedures for approval or prohibition of flavourings across the EU. Sets common maximum limits on presence of such substances in foodstuffs. Proposed Regulation for setting up positive list at Community level. Adopted 25 June 1996. Exemptions: None.
Extraction solvents	D 88/344/EEC	Background: No prior common rules. Objectives: Harmonizes national provisions across the EU. Single list of permitted solvents established as well as purity criteria and conditions of use. Exemptions: Solvents used in food additives, vitamins, etc. covered by that specific legislation.

Field	SM legislation	Details
Labelling	D 86/197/EEC D 89/395/EEC D 91/72/EEC D 93/102/EEC D 94/54/EEC	Background: Harmonized labelling rules for food sold to the ultimate consumer have applied throughout the EC since 1979 (Framework D 79/112/EEC). Objectives: The cited Directives aim to improve D 79/112/EEC in the context of the single market. All principles of D 79/112/EEC retained and extended also to catering foods. 'Use-by date' introduced for perishable foods. Indication of irradiated treatment made compulsory. Main ingredient lists required. Alcoholic strength (for >1.2% volume) needs to be indicated. Exemptions: Specific rules on aspects of labelling not covered by this Directive may still be dealt with by national provisions (e.g. product names and description). Labelling of mineral water (D 80/777/EEC) and foods for nutritional purposes (D 89/398/EEC) is covered by older vertical legislation specific to these and other fields (fruit juices, jams, jellies, chocolate).
Nutrition labelling	D 90/496/EEC	Background: No prior common rules. Objectives: Aims to introduce harmonized and compulsory nutrition labelling rules to foods with specific nutritional claims (e.g. 'sugar-free', 'low-fat', 'high fibre'). Two lists of nutrients established with differing requirements: labelling is compulsory for the first list (proteins, fats, carbohydrates and energy value), and optional for the second list (sugar, saturated fat, dietary fibre) unless specific claim is being made. Exemptions: Mineral waters covered by D 80/777/EEC, food supplements to be covered by specific legislation (currently in draft form).
Materials and articles in contact with foods	D 89/109/EEC	Background: Harmonized EC rules exist for specific materials and articles since 1976. Objectives: The cited Framework Directive harmonizes rules further across the EU and consolidates the approach to be taken for all legislation in this field and all types of materials (plastics, cellulose, ceramics, metal, rubber, etc.). Establishes general principles for the development of a series of 10 specific Directives. For each type of material, a 'positive' list of authorized materials needs to be established, as well as purity standards, conditions of use, migration limits (especially controversial for plastics), compliance control and methods of analysis. Legislation prior to the Framework D 89/109/EEC to be used as a basis in many of these areas. Exemptions: Member States retain some discretionary powers and may grant derogations, under certain conditions, for two years maximum.
Special nutrition foods	D 89/398/EEC	Background: No prior common rules. Objectives: The cited Framework Directive aims to harmonize rules on foods for special nutritional purposes by setting common standards on the nature, raw materials and composition of products, hygiene requirements, additives, labelling and presentation, and methods of analysis. All of these aspects are to be determined in a series of specific Directives for the following categories of food: infant formulae (D 91/321/EEC), foods for diabetics, medical foods (proposals to be drafted). Purity criteria are also to be set. Exemptions: None. Categories of foods for which specific Directives are to be drawn up have been revised and are subject to further revisions.

VERTICAL

Field	SM legislation	Details
Food	D 88/593/EEC	Background: Common EC rules existed in a number of sub-sectors since the early 1970s. Objectives: The cited Directive is the first vertical food Directive which was revised in line with the objectives of the single market. This concerns the fruit jam sector. A further number of product Directives are to be revised and rationalized in the short future. Exemptions: Only food products covered by vertical Directives are: fruit jams etc., fats/oils (erucic acid), cocoa and chocolate, sugars and honey. An objective of food legislation after the White Paper has been that vertical Directives should be kept to a minimum.
Drinks	D 89/394/EEC D 85/573/EEC R (EEC) 1576/89	Background: Common EC rules existed in a number of sub-sectors since the mid-1970s. Objectives: The cited Directives have been revised after the SMP. They concern respectively fruit juices, coffee and chicory extracts, and spirit drinks. Exemptions: Only other drink products covered by vertical Directives are: nectars, natural mineral waters, aromatized wines. An objective of food legislation after the White Paper has been that vertical Directives should be kept to a minimum.

REMOVAL OF PHYSICAL BARRIERS

Field	SM legislation	Details
Health controls		There is a wide range of rules governing health controls and hygiene, e.g. for meat preparations, milk-based product, etc. A detailed list of these can be found in Appendix B. The application of this legislation is for sectors outside the scope of this study and is therefore not further examined in detail. We do, however, examine the legislation concerning official controls and hygiene of foods and related legislation which are classified as technical barriers.

REMOVAL OF TAX BARRIERS

Field	SM legislation	Details
Excise duties	D 92/83/EEC	Background: No previous common rules. Objectives: Apply to spirit drinks. The cited Directive aims to harmonize the structure of excise duties and subsequent legislation deals with the actual approximation of rates. Exemptions: None.

Source: BER analysis.

Table B.4.   Principles underlying mutual recognition (Articles 30 to 36 of the Treaty)

Field	Principle applying
General barriers	Accepted on the following grounds: (a) protection of consumers, fair trading, environmental protection; (b) fit for the objective; (c) hindering trade the least of all measures with equivalent effect (principle of proportionality). Where necessary and justified authorization procedures may be followed to determine, on the basis of scientific evidence, the validity of arguments used against importation of a product.
Labelling	Laid down by Directive 79/112/EEC & subsequent amendments. Certain details, in particular trade name of product, supplemented by national provisions. Case law applies, and improvements in labelling legislation envisaged.
Marketing (trade name)	Generic sales names may not be reserved to national products solely on the grounds that these are produced: (a) in a given territory; (b) from specific raw materials; (c) with specific concentration of characteristic ingredients. Trade descriptions (indicated on the label) may be the same across Member States, provided these can be understood by consumers. A 1995 Court of Justice[1] ruling underlined the above by rejecting a German effort to preclude the use of the term 'sauce béarnaise' on a product although it had an ingredient list. Certain issues (e.g. language on label) dealt with by D 79/112/EEC on labelling & subsequent amendments. In particular, a 1993 Communication clarifies the use of language in the marketing of foodstuffs, by interpreting Article 30 of the Treaty and Article 14 of D 79/112/EEC (COM(93) 532 final, 10.11.1993).
Packaging	Specific packaging cannot be reserved to national products solely because they: (a) display certain characteristics; (b) originate in a given area. Products marketed in their country of origin in a given package should generally be accepted in the same form of packaging in other Member States. National restrictions that apply to food packaging for environmental reasons, in particular those regarding containers for liquid foods, are judged in the spirit of the relevant Directive 85/339/EEC.
Pre-packaged ranges	Legal basis: Directives 75/106/EEC (liquids) and 80/232/EEC (other foods) and subsequent amendments. Certain aspects not covered by above legislation dealt with by case law.
Additives	Prior to harmonization in this field as established by Framework Directive 89/107/EEC and implementing Directives (adopted in 1994 and 1995) and lists of approved additives, principles of case law extensively used to limit trade barriers of different national provisions. Thus, foods containing additives authorized in Member State of manufacture must be allowed to circulate in importing Member State: (a) if scientific evidence demonstrates these do not pose a danger to public health; (b) if these meet a genuine need, particularly of a technological nature. Exceptionally, an import restriction may be allowed if it is judged that the ADI (acceptable daily intake) is exceeded.
Other fields	In the absence of Community legislation, the Court has ruled that the same principles as those in the case of additives should apply. Thus, if national restrictions are justified on health policy grounds, the legitimacy of the justification must be demonstrated.

[1] Case C-51/94 *Commission v Germany* [1995] ECR I-3599.
Sources: Communication on the free movement of foodstuffs within the Community (COM(89) 256); European Commission, *The Community Internal Market*, 1993 report.

Table B.5.   Member State implementation of EC food legislation: key points

Country	Key points
Denmark	• Three Directives not implemented (scientific cooperation; sampling and analysis methods; vinyl chloride analysis). • Some Orders give the National Food Agency provisions to derogate from the terms of the Order. • Language in labelling may cause barriers to trade. • A number of Directives adopted by reference only. • Scope of Fruit Jam Directive made wider. • Deviations in flavourings legislation could lead to distortions in trade.
Germany	• Of 44 Directives, 38 have been transposed correctly (with only minor deviations), 3 can be criticized as not being correctly transposed and 3 have not been implemented (scientific cooperation; infant formulae; sampling and analysis methods). • Some legislation over-restrictive by comparison with EC rules. • Methods of sampling/analysis regulations are printed in the Official Collection (*Bundesgesetzblatt*). It is questioned if publication in the Official Collection represents the correct legal framework, as these methods can be altered at any time without any need for proper legislation.
Greece	• Five Directives not implemented (infant formulae; fruit juices; regenerated cellulose film; sampling and analysis methods; honey). • There has been delay in the transposition of most Directives which could have created barriers to trade. • Labelling provisions state that information must not be given by measures other than words, which differs from the Labelling Directive. • Greek legislation occasionally does not reproduce the annexes to the Directive (just implemented by reference). • Many amendments not implemented.
Italy	• Two Directives not implemented (scientific cooperation and sampling) and five partially implemented (foodstuffs for particular nutritional use, coffee, chocolate, fruit jams, honey) • There has been a delay in transposition of 80 % of the Directives. • Many amendments to Directives not implemented. • Broader scope of Chocolate Directive. • Materials in Contact Directive could lead to distortions in trade.
Ireland	• Three Directives not implemented (scientific cooperation; sampling and analysis methods; quick frozen foods), one Directive only partially implemented. Question of compliance arises for most legislation which has been adopted. • Some annexes implemented by reference only. • Omissions in implementing legislation on material and articles in contact with foods might distort trade.
Luxembourg	• One Directive not implemented (scientific cooperation) and two Directives partially implemented (additives; sampling and analysis methods). • Language labelling requirements could lead to a barrier in trade. • Some legislation implemented by reference only. • Scope of legislation on materials and articles in contact with foods and on coffee wider than Directive. • Within cocoa and honey legislation, there are additional rules to ensure consumer protection but this should not have an impact on trade. • Some other errors in transposition but unlikely to pose a barrier to trade.
Netherlands	• Three Directives not implemented (scientific cooperation; sampling and analysis methods; coffee) and two not specifically implemented (materials and articles in contact with foodstuffs; fruit juices). • Some legislation implemented by reference only. • A number of omissions which could lead to distortions in trade. • Coffee and fruit juice implementing legislation broader than Directive. • Labelling Directive made too complex. • Frequent failure to lay down labelling requirements. • A number of product Directives implemented by reference only.
Spain	• Two Directives not implemented (scientific cooperation; erucic acid). • Delay in transpositions. • Not all amendments to Directives implemented. • Legislation on material and articles in contact with foods too confusing. • Scope of sugar and jams legislation broader than the corresponding Directives. • Not as many Directives included in the study as for the other countries.
UK	• Of the 43 Directives examined, specific implementing legislation has been adopted for all but 4 (scientific cooperation; infant formulae; sampling and analysis methods; nectar). Questions of compliance arise for almost all of the legislation that has been adopted. • No provisions within regulation requiring labelling particulars to be given in a language easily understandable to purchasers. • Many wording differences which mean the scope of UK regulations is narrower than Directives.

Notes: With regard to scientific cooperation, Art. 7 of Directive 93/5/EEC calls for the adoption of laws, regulations and administrative provisions where necessary. It is reasonable to assume that the countries that have not implemented any legislation feel it is not necessary. With regards to sampling and analysis, Directive 85/591/EEC does not establish provisions that clearly require implementation.
Source: BER analysis.

Table B.6.   Examples of application of mutual recognition, post-1989

Field	Principle applying	Barrier/outcome
General	Excess requirements on imports not accepted for products lawfully manufactured and marketed in country of origin, unless based on grounds of public health protection, fair trading, environmental protection.	Spain – all foods: Spanish authorities required official health certificate from the country of origin that products had been lawfully manufactured and that their consumption presented no health risks. Outcome: Spain had to repeal this requirement, as products lawfully marketed in country of origin.
Food composition	Import restrictions on products not complying to national composition laws not accepted, unless based on grounds of public health protection, fair trading, environmental protection.	Italy – bread: An Italian rule stated that bread sold in Italy should have specific characteristics/properties and thus restricted imports into Italy of bread not conforming to this specific composition. Outcome: The rule was altered, through the introduction of appropriate labelling, to allow the sale of non-conforming bread in Italy.
Marketing (trade name)	Generic trade names may not be reserved to national products. Trade descriptions (on the label) may be the same across Member States, provided these can be understood by consumers.	Germany – beer: Although import of beer under this generic name into Germany is no longer prohibited after the 1984 case and related Court of Justice judgment on the German purity law, imported products were still requested to indicate their ingredients on the label. Outcome: Germany has to alter its rules on ingredient indication on the label as this was found to discriminate against products not complying with the national recipe. Portugal – chocolate: According to Portuguese rules, chocolate products containing vegetable oils and fats other than cocoa butter as a total or partial substitute for the latter must be labelled as 'artificial chocolate'. Outcome: Portuguese authorities repealed the rules and adopted a Decree stipulating a change of name only for products containing >5% vegetable oils and fats other than cocoa butter. France – meat products: Various imported meat products were not allowed to be marketed in France under names such as 'saucisse', 'terrine', 'pâté' as their composition did not comply with French rules. Outcome: France had to repeal these rules as found to protect the national recipe and to discriminate against imported products. Netherlands – fruit drinks: According to Dutch law fruit lemonades need to contain at least 10% fruit in order to bear the name 'authentic lemonade'. Outcome: Imports of lemonade from other Member States can no longer be prohibited on the basis of this requirement.
Labelling	Laid down by Directive 79/112/EEC & subsequent amendments. Certain details, in particular trade name of product, supplemented by national provisions.	France – pasta: Italian pasta manufacturers have developed a method that makes it possible to market fresh pasta with a use-by date of up to 120 days. Import of this product into France was restricted by a French rule that 'fresh' product shelf-life cannot exceed 42 days. Outcome: Imports into France of 'fresh' Italian pasta now authorized, subject to appropriate labelling on the product.
Additives	Foods containing additives authorized in Member State of manufacture must be allowed to circulate in importing Member State, unless scientific evidence proves there are reasons of public health.	Italy – salami: An Italian rule prohibited the use of the additive monosodium glutamate in uncooked meat, thus restricting imports of salami and raw ham into Italy. Outcome: The use of monosodium glutamate was found to pose no problems to public health and import restrictions were removed. France – confectionery: France banned the use of sorbic acid in milk chocolate fillings and restricted imports of products that contained this substance. Outcome: The use of sorbic acid was found to present no health risk and products containing it were allowed to enter the French market in future. Germany – syrups: Germany prohibited the importation and marketing of syrups containing tartrazine (E 102). Outcome: The ban had to be lifted as not justified on health grounds by scientific evidence.

Sources: European Commission, The Community Internal Market, 1993 report, Report from the Commission to the Council and the EP, The Single Market in 1994 (COM(95) 238 final of 15.6.1995).

Table B.7.   Outstanding issues in SM food legislation

Field	Issues	Reference
REMOVAL OF TECHNICAL BARRIERS: FOOD		
HORIZONTAL		
Food controls & hygiene	<u>Official controls</u>: Further proposals currently being prepared on the equivalence of control measures taken by the various Member States and designated laboratories for the official inspections.	Framework D 89/397/EEC
	<u>Hygiene Directive</u> Voluntary industry guides to good hygiene practice are to be developed to assist manufacturers with compliance with the Directive. Also 'European guides to good hygiene practice' are to be developed.	D 93/43/EEC
	<u>Contaminants Regulation</u>: Maximum tolerance limits to be established in the form of a regularly updated non-exhaustive Community list.	R (EEC) 315/93
Novel foods	<u>GMOs</u>: CEN standards in the process of being formulated, based on the mandates granted to CEN in 1992 by the Commission. <u>Novel foods</u>: Adoption pending.	April 1991 Commission strategy on biotechnology
	<u>Food irradiation</u>: Adoption pending - a very limited number of foods to be covered anyway.	
Additives	Purity criteria soon to be adopted for colours and miscellaneous additives. Methods of analysis to be established in some cases and the procedure for taking samples for analysis. When the entire system is put in place, then the additive legislation will effectively be operational. Criteria for inclusion in the list and maintenance of Additives used in traditional foods: national laws to be maintained for a list of traditional products. Criteria for inclusion in the list and maintenance of national prohibitions currently proposed.	Framework D 89/107/EEC
Flavours	Specific purity criteria and methods of analysis to be adopted. Further legislation to be proposed in this field.	Framework D 88/388/EEC
Extraction solvents	Specific purity criteria and methods of analysis to be adopted.	D 88/344/EEC
Labelling	Community provisions to be adopted to supplement existing rules, particularly in the field of quantitative ingredient labelling (QUIDs) where rules are to be made stricter regarding nature and characteristics of products.	Framework D 79/112/EEC (1989 consolidated version)
	Implementing measures of a technical nature to be adopted by the Commission. Use of claims in foodstuffs pending. Language issue of labelling pending.	
Nutritional labelling	None.	
Materials & articles in contact with food	Only implementing legislation so far adopted is on migration testing of plastic materials and on regenerated cellulose film. A significant number of implementing legislation still to be drafted. Until this is adopted, previous rules apply which although harmonized in some cases are mostly outdated and not in the spirit of the SMP. Even in the area of plastic materials, certain lists of authorized substances (latest amendment in 1995) are still not complete and in these cases national rules apply.	Framework D 89/109/EEC
Special nutrition foods	Only implementing legislation so far adopted is on infant formulae. Long list of subjects awaiting the drafting of specific legislation and purity criteria also need to be set. Until these are adopted, national rules apply and a truly harmonized market is not yet in place.	Framework D 89/398/EEC
VERTICAL		
Foods	Clarifications, update to technical progress and further harmonization to be introduced by proposed Directives on: fruit jams, erucic acid, preserved milk, cocoa and chocolate, and sugars and honey. In view of demand for legislative simplification, some or all of these may be dropped.	
Drinks	<u>Mineral Waters Directive</u> to be updated for technical progress. Further arrangements to be introduced concerning the transport of spirits.	D 80/77/EEC
REMOVAL OF PHYSICAL BARRIERS		
Health controls	Further harmonization concerning production and commercialization of prepared meals containing meat.	D 92/5/EEC
	Concept of milk-based products to be clarified.	D 92/46/EEC

Source: BER analysis.

Table B.8. State of advancement with outstanding technical issues in SM food legislation

Field	State of advancement	Likely impact
I. Pending proposals		
Labelling (Quantitative Ingredient Declarations - QUIDs)	This proposal has just been discussed by the EP. Intention to adopt by the end of 1995. Pre-conciliation in 1996.	Manufacturers will have to give the quantity of an ingredient used if this appears in the name of the product or is associated with that name by the consumer or is emphasized on the label. Key question is sale denomination (Article 5 of existing Directive). Another important issue is whether likely to move to national language labelling of ingredients, because the proposal stipulates that foods should be labelled in a language 'easily understood' by the consumer. Labelling of alcoholic drinks has been left out of the proposal.
Novel foods	Adoption process is progressing despite the fact that this is a very controversial issue. Key issue is how novel foods should be labelled.	The proposal covers foods, ingredients and manufacturing processes which are novel in that they have not so far been used for human consumption. This includes GMOs (genetically modified organisms), modified molecular structures etc. Examples: genetically modified yeast in bread or in beer, novel fat replacer, etc. These technologies are rather new (for instance, the Food Advisory Committee in the UK has been discussing them since 1988).
Food irradiation	Deadlocked for some time now. Some progress expected by end of 1995.	Two Directives are being proposed: one on general guidelines and the other on a list of foods which may be irradiated.
Flavours	A list of authorized flavours will be established progressively.	So far, the proposal suggests that Member States should establish the list of flavours currently used in their territory and these national lists will then be scrutinized by the Standing Committee for Foods (CPDA). The main disagreement is between Member States on how the list will be established. In particular, there is disagreement over using a so-called 'accelerated' procedure for approving chemically derived flavourings; this procedure would mean that such flavours could be approved/rejected without prior toxicological tests.
Unit pricing	A proposal for this will shortly be discussed by the EP.	Unit pricing demands that product prices are indicated per unit of content (e.g. per kg or per lit) as well as per pack (e.g. per 100 g pack or 1.5 lit bottle). This is meant to protect consumer interests as it allows easy comparison of prices between homogeneous or close substitute products. To some extent, product substitution towards cheaper alternatives may take place. Overall, there are no adverse implications of the proposed legislation for the food and drink industry. However, the rules relating in particular to prescribed ranges could be restrictive in that product differentiation, as sought by differences in processing or packaging, may be discouraged.
Traditional foods	Proposal being discussed in the EP.	This would allow Member States to put in a list a number of foods and drinks which are considered as 'traditional' because of the specificity of their ingredients or of their processing methods.
Chocolate (Vertical Directive)	This is intended to revise D 73/241/EEC. Adopted in April 1996.	Key issue is that only cocoa-derived products may be used for the manufacture of articles sold under the designation 'chocolate' (thus excluding use of vegetable fats). Another issue is the amount of cocoa in milk chocolate. Both issues are particularly important for British chocolate.
Coffee and chicory extracts (Vertical Directive) Mineral water (Vertical Directive)	Intended to revise D 79/1066/EEC. At the moment this is in draft form and is not treated as an urgent item. Common position now reached.	This covers labelling rules, bottling rules, definitions of what is 'mineral water', what is 'spring water'. Key issue of dispute is question of whether producers should be allowed to use ozone enriched air to remove iron and other particles. The European Parliament is considering allowing the continued use of ozone but requiring the removal of the word 'natural' from the label if this is used.

Table B.8.   (continued)

II. Possible future proposals

Food processing aids Enzymes	Consultation paper to be launched. No agreement yet on how products which are used in manufacturing processes (e.g. natrium in water, baking powder) should be used/labelled. No draft proposal as yet on this subject. There is a view that enzymes can be considered as ingredients or as additives or as processing aids and depending on the classification they could therefore go under the legislation pertaining to either of these sectors. A scientific cooperation task launched in the summer of 1995 set out to examine the conditions of use of vitamins in food and the results of this work could form the basis for an important proposal in this area.
Vitamins in food	At present there is no agreement among the scientists as to what should be the daily intakes and therefore no agreement as to how added vitamins should be labelled. Serious opposition from many Member States, particularly Italy where vitamin addition in food is totally prohibited.
Dietary supplements	No draft proposal as yet. Approach taken is similar to that for vitamins in food.
Claims (food)	Initially this was a separate proposal but completely abandoned. Plans now are to incorporate it either in the Labelling Directive or in the Misleading Advertising Directive.

Source: BER analysis.

APPENDIX C

Methodology

C.1. Macroanalysis

In order to determine the existence and nature of structural change over time, a series of multiple regression equations have been estimated which incorporate a simple trend variable (to account for any systematic trends in the time series), a lagged dependent variable (to remove any serial correlation) and a number of dummy variables (to pick up any structural breaks in the time series).[22] Thus, the basic model is:

$$Y_t = a + b_1(T) + b_2(Y_{t-1}) + \sum_{i=1}^{k} g_i(D_{i,t}) + e_t$$

where:

Y_t = Dependent variable
a = Constant
T = Deterministic time trend
Y_{t-1} = Dependent variable lagged one period
D_i = Dummy variable in time period i (D_i = 0 before t<i and 1 after t>i)
e_t = Stochastic error term

The number of dummy variables included in the model is determined by an interactive (stepwise) procedure which eliminates those explanatory variables which are not statistically significant (as determined by appropriate t-tests and F-tests). Thus, 11 dummy variables are constructed for the period 1982–92 and the stepwise procedure selects only those which are statistically significant. The model selected by this procedure enables us to identify the extent to which statistically significant shifts have occurred pre- and post-SMP legislation (beginning in 1986), as it will include only those dummy variables which are associated with statistically significant shocks (structural breaks in the data).

It is important to note that we are not able to draw any inferences with regard to causality from the secondary data analysis alone. The data available are highly aggregated and only covers a limited number of variables and, more importantly, whilst the 'Europeanization' impact of the SMP may reveal itself in the published data, much of the key vertical legislation, which is sector specific, has only recently been implemented or has still to be agreed and would therefore not be reflected in the data to 1994. Moreover, the macroeconomic environments in several Member States have been subject to considerable 'shocks', which are likely to have had a far greater impact on corporate strategy and trade flows than the SMP.

---

[22]   For a review of the literature on recursive tests under structural breaks, see Bhaskara Rao (1994). The approach adopted here is similar, conceptually, to that explained by Pierron, P., 1994, in Bhaskara Rao (op. cit.).

The full accession of Greece in 1986 and Spain and Portugal in 1991 is likely to have been the dominant factor in the Mediterranean region. The unification of East and West Germany has undoubtedly had a profound impact on the German economy and the focus of food manufacturers in both the East and the West of the new Federal Republic. And finally, the currency crisis in 1992/93, which followed the collapse of the Exchange Rate Mechanism (ERM), created havoc on the European currency markets which will inevitably have had a considerable impact on the pattern of internal trade.

The time series analysis enables us to infer whether or not any (statistically) significant changes have occurred in the data post-1986, but the question of causality can only be addressed by raising the appropriate issues with representative food processing businesses, in stages three and four of the study. Moreover, to the extent that the impact of certain legislation has yet to be seen, the survey and case study analyses will provide important insights into longer-term future impacts of the SMP on the food processing industry.

The results of the structural break analysis are summarized in tabular form. Estimated coefficients are presented along with their associated t-statistics, the coefficient of multiple determination (R^2) and Durbin-Watson statistics. However, it is important to note that the purpose of the analysis is to establish the existence and nature (positive or negative) of structural breaks in the time series. Thus, we are not interested in the 'goodness of fit' or explanatory power of the estimated equations, but we need to pay particular attention to the specification of selected equations (i.e. the statistical significance of selected variables) and the sign of the estimated coefficients.

Where dummy variables have been selected by the stepwise regression procedure a negative sign implies a significant reduction in the value of the dependent variable, whilst a positive coefficient implies the opposite. Where more than one dummy variable has been selected, we need to consider their relative statistical significance, as indicated by the respective t-statistics. The absence of dummy variables in selected equations implies that the time series is free from any (statistically significant) structural breaks.

For the analysis of the trade data, in addition to the structural break analysis described above, two trade ratios were calculated – the import penetration ratio and the ratio of exports to imports (or trade ratio).

The penetration ratio gives an indication of the importance of imports in domestic consumption and is calculated as follows:

$$\text{Import penetration ratio} = 100 \quad x \quad \frac{\text{value of imports}}{\text{value of domestic consumption}}$$

The resulting ratio will lie between zero (indicating no imports in domestic consumption) and 100 (indicating all of domestic consumption is imported).

The trade ratio, first used by Balassa (1966), is simply a measure of the relative importance of imports and exports and is calculated as follows:

Trade ratio = $$\frac{\text{value of exports - value of imports}}{\text{value of exports + value of imports}}$$

The resulting ratio will lie between +1 (indicating imports are zero) and -1 (indicating exports are zero) with zero reflecting a balance of trade.

Beyond a comparison of the situation before and after the SMP, in considering how to address the issue of 'anti-monde' a detailed review has been undertaken of the possibility of taking a geographical non-EU comparator. On closer examination, none of the other markets examined (EFTA and the US) proved to be fully appropriate for this purpose. In the case of EFTA, cross-border trade in food and drink products is not really significant. With respect to the US, this already constituted a fully integrated market to provide a suitable 'anti-monde'. Nonetheless, US data have been analysed in some cases to establish whether these paralleled developments in the EU, which could therefore be considered as part of more global trends affecting the industry.

Both the results of the structural break analysis and the ratios calculated are presented, sector by sector, in a statistical appendix (Appendix D).

C.2. Industry survey

C.2.1. The sampling frame

Our sample has been drawn primarily from trade association lists which were kindly supplied by the national food and drinks associations of most of the individual Member States. A cross-reference with other lists of companies was made, as follows:

(a) *Annuaire de l'Agro-Alimentaire DIC-AGRI*, Editions EPS, Paris, 1995 (lists of French and European companies, by product sector);
(b) *The European Food Trade Directory*, Newman Books Ltd, London, 1995 (Vol I: UK, Vol II: Continental Europe);
(c) PROMAR (BER sister company) in-house food and drink company databases. PROMAR specializes in market research and strategic reviews of the food and drink sector and, as such, keeps an extensive database of companies, including SMEs, operating in the sector;
(d) List of major companies in each sector derived from macroanalysis (including Seymour Cooke M&A database).

C.2.2. The sampling methodology

Taking into account the objectives of the industry survey, our sampling methodology has been to construct a balanced sample, including companies from all countries and sectors of activity, so that no country or sector would be under-represented. We have therefore covered a total of 12 countries across five product groups.

C.2.3. The sample size

A total of 78 companies. Appendix E contains the results of the industry survey and more detailed information on the spread of the sample (in terms of country location, NACE code, size and market presence).

C.2.4. Sample representativeness

The question of the representativeness of the sample cannot, in our view, be addressed solely in terms of the statistical significance of the sample. With a total sample of 78 companies, our aim has been to get a balanced sample that represents all countries and sectors concerned. In this context we would point out that the selected companies account for fairly substantial market shares in the sectors in which they operate. While this may reflect a bias towards larger companies, this has been accepted as the right procedure to follow in view of some initial contacts with smaller companies, a trial pre-survey and consultations with the food and drinks associations, all of which demonstrated that:

(a) SMEs and in particular smaller companies largely lack real understanding of SMP issues; and/or

(b) SMEs and in particular smaller companies lack interest in the SMP and would have provided a poor response overall.

The above lack of understanding/interest/response can be attributed to a number of factors, notably low SME awareness of SMP issues, lack of resource availability and also – most importantly – the fact that in the sectors examined (processed, packaged, high value-added foods and drinks) the bulk of production and cross-border trade has always been conducted by a relatively limited number of relatively large, including multinational, companies.

C.2.5. Response

Response has been 100% (except for some specific questions relating to unit cost data).

C.2.6. Type of questionnaire

All interviews have been carried out face to face at senior management level within each company, on the basis of a standard questionnaire developed by BER. The design of the questions covers a span of 10 years, i.e. the entire period from 1985 to 1995.

C.3. Case studies

The final stage of the study has involved detailed case studies of five food processing companies, the purpose of which has been to provide further information on the specific aspects of SMP implementation and impact which have required a higher level of involvement and cooperation on the part of the respondents. In particular, the issues connected with business strategy which have required detailed qualitative information, the question of cost data, and the impact of the vertical legislation which in most cases has had a higher (and more complex) technical component have been examined in detail.

The selection of companies for the case study analysis has been determined by:

(a) the results of the survey, which have highlighted the fundamental issues as well as those which justify more profound examination;

(b) the willingness of candidate firms to participate in the exercise.

The companies selected are sufficiently heterogeneous in terms of size, product range, geographical presence (production and sales) and strategic focus, in order to draw some useful conclusions. In particular, the purpose of the analysis has been to provide important evidence in support (or refutation) of the hypotheses regarding business strategy and those relating to the vertical legislation. The case studies have also been a more appropriate means of establishing the likely future impact of existing SMP legislation and, more importantly, the significance of the legislation which has yet to be agreed.

All case studies have involved discussions with senior personnel in key decision-making positions (procurement, production, logistics, sales, marketing and corporate strategy).

Appendix F presents the individual case studies.

APPENDIX D

Results of macroanalysis (secondary data)

Data sources

Data have been collected and analysed for the period 1978–93 (1978–94 for trade data) for each EUR-12 Member State, aggregated to the four-digit NACE classification level.

The main source for the secondary data analysis is Eurostat. The EUR-12 data on the key structural and performance variables are drawn from the INDE database. The comparable data for the USA is drawn from the VISA database and the EUR-12 trade data is drawn from the DEBA database. All value data are expressed in million ECU. The producer price index has been used for the deflation of the data.

Data on market shares and concentration are notoriously difficult to obtain. For the purposes of this study information has been drawn from a wide range of sources, including: Mintel (*ad hoc* market reports), Economist Intelligence Unit (*Marketing in Europe*), Euromonitor and Europanel (*ad hoc* market reports), Seymour Cooke (annual reports on mergers and acquisitions) and *ad hoc* single and multi-client sectoral studies by PROMAR International and BER.

Seymour Cooke is now established as the leading source for data on mergers and acquisitions in the food industry and their annual reports are the main source of information on cross-border mergers and acquisitions, partnerships and alliances in the EUR-12 after 1989.

Contents

(Tables numbered in same sequence in each product sector.)

Notes:

Data exclude eastern *Länder*. Totals are not always exact due to rounding.

D.1.   NACE 417

4170   **Manufacture of pasta (spaghetti, macaroni, etc.)**

Table D.1.1.   Number of enterprises

Country	1978	1986	1993	Country share (%)			Total change (%)		
				1978	1986	1993	78/86	86/93	78/93
FRG	19	18	19	5.1%	5.4%	6.0%	-5.3%	6.0%	0.4%
France	19	16	18	5.1%	4.8%	5.6%	-15.8%	11.0%	-6.5%
Italy	161	122	95	43.5%	36.3%	29.9%	-24.2%	-22.2%	-41.0%
Netherlands	84	98	104	22.7%	29.1%	32.7%	16.8%	5.9%	23.6%
Belgium	6	5	5	1.5%	1.4%	1.7%	-15.8%	11.0%	-6.5%
Spain	44	50	57	11.9%	14.9%	17.9%	13.7%	13.7%	29.2%
Greece	16	14	13	4.3%	4.3%	4.1%	-10.0%	-9.7%	-18.7%
Portugal	22	13	7	5.9%	3.9%	2.1%	-40.3%	-47.9%	-68.9%
EUR-12	370	336	317	100.0%	100.0%	100.0%	-9.2%	-5.6%	-14.3%

Table D.1.2.   Number of persons employed, excluding home workers

Country	1978	1986	1993	Country share (%)			Total change (%)		
				1978	1986	1993	78/86	86/93	78/93
FRG	4424	2327	1793	13.1%	6.9%	5.3%	-47.4%	-22.9%	-59.5%
France	4003	3349	3286	11.9%	9.9%	9.7%	-16.3%	-1.9%	-17.9%
Italy	11732	12064	10051	34.7%	35.7%	29.6%	2.8%	-16.7%	-14.3%
Netherlands	8732	12304	15595	25.9%	36.4%	45.9%	40.9%	26.7%	78.6%
Belgium	875	732	718	2.6%	2.2%	2.1%	-16.3%	-1.9%	-17.9%
Spain	1398	934	707	4.1%	2.8%	2.1%	-33.2%	-24.3%	-49.4%
Greece	1090	1341	1560	3.2%	4.0%	4.6%	23.0%	16.3%	43.1%
Portugal	1508	755	268	4.5%	2.2%	0.8%	-49.9%	-64.6%	-82.3%
EUR-12	33762	33806	33978	100.0%	100.0%	100.0%	0.1%	0.5%	0.6%
USA	9278	8211	8139						

Table D.1.3. Production value, excluding VAT

Country	Actual			Deflated			Country share (%)			Real average annual change (%)		
	1978	1986	1993	1978	1986	1993	1978	1986	1993	78/86	86/93	78/93
FRG	245	259	350	344	274	322	6.8%	4.4%	4.9%	-2.1	4.0	0.7
France	309	570	857	447	589	860	8.5%	9.7%	11.9%	3.8	5.6	4.6
Italy	786	2381	3116	1262	2566	3466	21.7%	40.7%	43.3%	9.6	4.9	7.4
Netherlands	2046	2319	2404	2735	2403	2118	56.4%	39.6%	33.4%	-1.5	-1.7	-1.6
Belgium	115	122	165	187	137	152	3.2%	2.1%	2.3%	-3.1	2.9	-0.3
Spain	77	88	109	142	108	109	2.1%	1.5%	1.5%	-2.8	0.6	-1.2
Greece	26	60	113	52	73	107	0.7%	1.0%	1.6%	4.7	6.0	5.3
Portugal	22	57	76	53	70	56	0.6%	1.0%	1.1%	4.4	-2.9	1.0
EUR-12	3627	5857	7188	5222	6220	7190	100.0%	100.0%	100.0%	2.3	2.1	2.2
USA	694	1476	1751	1327	1486							1.7

Table D.1.4. Production value per enterprise

Country	Actual			Deflated		
	1978	1986	1993	1978	1986	1993
FRG	12.9	14.4	18.4	18.1	15.2	16.9
France	16.3	35.6	48.2	23.5	36.8	48.4
Italy	4.9	19.5	32.8	7.8	21.0	36.5
Netherlands	24.4	23.7	23.2	32.6	24.5	20.4
Belgium	20.2	25.4	30.9	32.8	28.5	28.6
Spain	1.8	1.8	1.9	3.2	2.2	1.9
Greece	1.7	4.2	8.7	3.3	5.1	8.2
Portugal	1.0	4.4	11.2	2.4	5.4	8.2
EUR-12	9.8	17.4	22.6	14.1	18.5	22.6

Table D.1.5. Consumption value

Country	Actual			Deflated			Country share (%)			Real average annual change (%)		
	1978	1986	1993	1978	1986	1993	1978	1986	1993	78/86	86/93	78/93
FRG	265	322	502	352	323	419	7.4%	5.6%	7.3%	-0.4	4.7	2.0
France	325	633	951	646	617	758	9.0%	11.0%	13.9%	-0.4	3.0	1.2
Italy	712	2072	2421	1885	1957	1574	19.8%	36.1%	35.3%	0.8	-2.7	-0.9
Netherlands	2048	2329	2419	2796	2324	2110	56.9%	40.5%	35.3%	-2.2	-1.3	-1.8
Bel. & Lux.	121	126	157	189	125	130	3.4%	2.2%	2.3%	-4.5	2.0	-1.5
UK	8	46	89	16	44	60	0.2%	0.8%	1.3%	15.8	4.8	10.7
Ireland	1	4	10	1	3	8	0.0%	0.1%	0.1%	18.7	18.0	18.4
Denmark	2	6	9	3	6	7	0.0%	0.1%	0.1%	12.0	3.6	8.1
Spain	76	90	100	180	82	62	2.1%	1.6%	1.5%	-8.9	-3.5	-6.4
Greece	22	58	116	84	47	33	0.6%	1.0%	1.7%	-6.8	-4.8	-5.8
Portugal	21	57	82	85	51	37	0.6%	1.0%	1.2%	-5.2	-4.2	-4.7
EUR-12	3601	5743	6856	6238	5581	5198	100.0%	100.0%	100.0%	-1.3	-1.0	-1.2

Table D.1.6. Labour costs

Country	Actual			Deflated			Country share (%)		
	1978	1986	1993	1978	1986	1993	1978	1986	1993
FRG	73	58	62	102	61	57	13.7%	7.3%	5.8%
France	72	88	119	104	91	119	13.5%	11.1%	11.2%
Italy	170	298	406	273	321	451	32.0%	37.3%	38.3%
Netherlands	172	317	407	230	329	358	32.3%	39.7%	38.4%
Belgium	16	20	22	26	22	21	3.1%	2.4%	2.1%
Spain	17	13	16	32	16	16	3.2%	1.7%	1.5%
Greece			25			24			2.4%
Portugal	11	5	3	27	6	2	2.1%	0.6%	0.2%
EUR-12	531	799	1059	794	846	1048	100.0%	100.0%	100.0%
EU (average)	76	114	132	99	106	131			

Table D.1.7. Gross value added at factor cost

Country	Actual			Deflated			Country share (%)			Real average annual change (%)		
	1978	1986	1993	1978	1986	1993	1978	1986	1993	78/86	86/93	78/93
FRG	73	69	77	102	73	71	14.5%	5.6%	4.3%	-2.5	1.7	-0.5
France	72	156	215	103	161	216	14.2%	12.6%	12.0%	6.1	4.3	5.3
Italy	137	439	616	219	473	685	27.1%	35.5%	34.3%	10.4	6.2	8.5
Netherlands	161	494	785	216	512	692	32.1%	40.0%	43.8%	11.6	4.5	8.3
Belgium	14	30	41	22	33	38	2.7%	2.4%	2.3%	5.4	1.9	3.8
Spain	27	27	27	49	33	27	5.3%	2.2%	1.5%	-4.5	-2.6	-3.6
Greece	21	21	32	41	25	31	4.1%	1.7%	1.8%	-5.4	3.1	-1.4
EUR-12	503	1236	1794	753	1312	1760	100.0%	100.0%	100.0%	7.3	4.4	6.0
USA	320	805	975		724	828					2.0	3.5

Table D.1.8. Gross value added per person employed (in 000 ECU)

Country	Actual			Deflated		
	1978	1986	1993	1978	1986	1993
FRG	16.5	29.7	43.1	23.1	31.4	39.7
France	17.9	46.5	65.5	25.9	48.1	65.8
Italy	11.6	36.4	61.2	18.7	39.2	68.1
Netherlands	18.5	40.2	50.4	24.7	41.6	44.4
Belgium	15.5	40.5	57.0	25.2	45.4	52.7
Spain	19.1	29.1	38.5	35.2	35.6	38.5
Greece	18.9	15.6	20.7	37.2	18.9	19.7
EU (average)	16.9	34.0	48.1	27.1	37.2	47.0
USA	34.4	98.1	119.8		88.2	101.7

Table D.1.9. Investment

Country	Actual			Deflated			Country share (%)		
	1978	1986	1993	1978	1986	1993	1978	1986	1993
FRG	7	19	19	10	20	18	9.2%	7.4%	6.6%
France	10	24	27	15	25	27	12.6%	9.4%	9.3%
Italy	18	116	140	29	125	156	22.6%	45.5%	47.9%
Netherlands	45	94	97	59	97	85	55.6%	36.7%	33.1%
Greece		3	9		0	19		1.0%	3.1%
EUR-12	80	256	292	114	268	305	100.0%	100.0%	100.0%
EU (average)	20	51	58	28	67	61			
USA	17	45			40				

Table D.1.10. Proportion of investments in gross value added at factor cost (in %)

Country	1978	1979	1980	1981	1982	1983	1984	1985	1986	1987	1988	1989	1990	1991	1992	1993
FRG	10.1	11.0	14.3	17.3	9.7	23.4	16.3	19.8	27.4	16.1	27.0	24.1	17.8	20.9	30.7	24.9
France	14.1	15.5	15.1	14.9	17.1	13.0	16.1	18.1	15.4	12.9	15.9	29.8	16.1	14.4	12.9	12.6
Italy	13.3	21.5	20.4	20.9	23.3	24.0	27.2	24.3	26.5	22.5	29.7	19.7	23.6	20.2	23.1	22.7
Netherlands	27.6	15.7	17.0	17.4	11.4	23.3	15.5	15.9	19.0	18.0	16.5	14.3	15.0	14.2	13.0	12.3
Greece	17.6	10.0	10.8	11.1	7.3	14.8	9.9	10.1	12.1	11.5	20.6	20.4	23.8	30.0	26.9	28.2
EU (average)	16.5	14.8	15.5	16.3	13.7	19.7	17.0	17.7	20.1	16.2	21.9	21.6	19.3	19.9	21.3	20.2
USA	5.2	9.7	10.1	10.3	8.8	6.5	4.6	5.1	5.6	5.3	5.3	6.6	6.8	11.4	9.1	

Table D.1.11. Producer price index

Country	1978	1979	1980	1981	1982	1983	1984	1985	1986	1987	1988	1989	1990	1991	1992	1993
FRG	71.3	74.5	77.0	81.2	89.1	95.2	97.0	91.8	94.5	95.4	102.9	102.2	100.0	98.9	102.0	108.6
France	69.1	71.7	68.7	75.1	78.8	83.2	87.4	94.6	96.7	95.0	93.1	95.2	100.0	100.1	98.8	99.6
Italy	62.3	65.6	68.8	66.6	71.9	80.1	86.4	88.6	92.8	93.4	92.1	98.0	100.0	101.7	99.8	89.9
Netherlands	74.8	75.8	76.0	77.1	86.8	91.0	91.4	92.2	96.5	98.3	98.4	98.3	100.0	103.2	106.6	113.5
Bel. & Lux.	61.7	65.0	69.2	71.7	73.9	77.0	78.2	82.5	89.1	95.7	96.7	97.3	100.0	101.0	105.3	108.2
Spain	54.3	65.2	64.3	70.6	77.1	71.5	79.2	83.7	81.8	83.5	87.9	95.5	100.0	108.8	108.3	100.0
Greece	50.8	47.7	54.9	66.2	73.2	74.2	80.3	84.9	82.8	80.4	83.0	90.7	100.0	108.8	107.0	105.2
Portugal	40.8	42.1	47.3	57.6	65.2	63.7	70.0	82.0	81.5	82.0	80.1	86.3	100.0	121.5	140.3	136.0
USA							140.3	145.7	111.2	98.3	102.4	114.0	100.0	103.6	103.3	117.8

Table D.1.12. Total imports (million ECU)

Country	Actual			Deflated			Country share (%)			Real average annual change (%)		
	1978	1986	1993	1978	1986	1993	1978	1986	1993	78/86	86/93	78/93
FRG	25.8	82.6	180	36.2	87.4	165.7	29.5%	27.3%	30.6%	11.8	11.3	11.5
France	25.3	93	143.9	36.6	96.2	144.5	29.0%	30.8%	24.5%	13.0	6.1	9.8
Italy	0.5	0.6	4.7	0.8	0.6	5.2	0.6%	0.2%	0.8%	2.5	36.7	18.5
Netherlands	7.9	22.3	36.5	10.6	23.1	32.2	9.0%	7.4%	6.2%	11.0	5.0	8.2
Bel. & Lux.	10.5	30.8	59.4	17.0	34.6	54.9	12.0%	10.2%	10.1%	9.6	7.7	8.7
UK	11.4	53.2	107	23.0	61.3	98.3	13.0%	17.6%	18.2%	13.6	7.3	10.7
Ireland	1.2	4.9	10.1	1.7	5.1	10.1	1.4%	1.6%	1.7%	16.4	10.6	13.7
Denmark	1.9	6.7	16.5	2.7	6.9	16.6	2.2%	2.2%	2.8%	13.0	14.0	13.5
Spain	1.6	3.9	10.5	2.8	4.3	9.9	1.9%	1.3%	1.8%	421.4	15.8	232.1
Greece	1.1	3.3	12.4	2.2	3.9	11.8	1.3%	1.1%	2.1%	16.4	18.3	17.3
Portugal	0.1	0.5	6.8	0.2	0.6	4.9	0.1%	0.2%	1.2%	18.5	38.5	27.8
Total EUR-12	87.4	302.3	588	134.0	323.9	554.1	100.0%	100.0%	100.0%	11.7	8.4	10.2

Table D.1.13. Intra-EU imports (million ECU)

Country	Actual			Deflated			Country share (%)			Real average annual change (%)		
	1978	1986	1993	1978	1986	1993	1978	1986	1993	78/86	86/93	78/93
FRG	24.4	73.8	159.3	34.2	78.1	146.7	29.8%	26.4%	29.7%	11.0	11.4	11.2
France	24.1	87.6	136.8	34.9	90.6	137.3	29.4%	31.4%	25.5%	12.9	6.3	9.8
Italy	0.3	0.5	4.1	0.5	0.5	4.6	0.4%	0.2%	0.8%	11.9	39.8	24.9
Netherlands	7.1	19	31.2	9.5	19.7	27.5	8.7%	6.8%	5.8%	10.4	5.2	8.0
Bel. & Lux.	10.2	30.2	57.4	16.5	33.9	53.0	12.5%	10.8%	10.7%	9.7	7.5	8.7
UK	10.2	49.1	93.4	20.6	56.6	85.8	12.5%	17.6%	17.4%	14.0	6.6	10.6
Ireland	1.2	4.9	9.8	1.7	5.1	9.8	1.5%	1.8%	1.8%	16.5	10.1	13.5
Denmark	1.6	6.3	16.1	2.3	6.5	16.2	2.0%	2.3%	3.0%	14.5	14.7	14.6
Spain	1.5	3.5	9.9	2.8	4.3	9.9	1.9%	1.3%	1.8%	421.4	15.8	232.1
Greece	1.1	3.2	12.4	2.2	3.9	11.8	1.4%	1.1%	2.3%	16.4	18.3	17.3
Portugal	0.1	0.5	6.7	0.2	0.6	4.9	0.1%	0.2%	1.2%	18.5	38.5	27.8
Intra-EUR-12	81.9	279.1	537.1	125.5	299.7	507.5	100.0%	100.0%	100.0%	11.6	8.3	10.0

Table D.1.14. Extra-EU imports (million ECU)

Country	Actual			Deflated			Country share (%)			Real average annual change (%)		
	1978	1986	1993	1978	1986	1993	1978	1986	1993	78/86	86/93	78/93
FRG	1.3	8.8	20.7	1.8	9.3	19.1	24.1%	38.1%	40.7%	23.4	11.4	17.8
France	1.3	5.3	7.1	1.9	5.5	7.1	24.1%	22.9%	14.0%	15.6	4.0	10.2
Italy	0.2	0.1	0.6	0.3	0.1	0.7	3.7%	0.4%	1.2%	-19.6	45.7	10.8
Netherlands	0.8	3.2	5.3	1.1	3.3	4.7	14.8%	13.9%	10.4%	19.0	5.6	12.8
Bel. & Lux.	0.3	0.6	2.1	0.5	0.7	1.9	5.6%	2.6%	4.1%	15.7	23.6	19.4
UK	1.2	4.0	13.6	2.4	4.6	12.5	22.2%	17.3%	26.8%	15.5	15.6	15.6
Ireland	0.0	0.0	0.3	0.0	0.0	0.3	0.0%	0.0%	0.6%	0.0	21.6	10.1
Denmark	0.2	0.4	0.5	0.3	0.4	0.5	3.7%	1.7%	1.0%	10.8	10.8	10.8
Spain	0.1	0.4	0.6	0.2	0.5	0.6	1.9%	1.7%	1.2%	-2.1	6.4	1.8
Greece	0.0	0.0	0.0	0.0	0.0	0.0	0.0%	0.0%	0.0%	0.0	0.0	0.0
Portugal	0.0	0.0	0.0	0.0	0.0	0.0	0.0%	0.0%	0.0%	0.0	-14.3	-6.7
Extra-EUR-12	5.4	23.1	50.8	8.5	24.4	47.4	100.0%	100.0%	100.0%	15.9	10.2	13.2

Table D.1.15. Total exports (million ECU)

Country	Actual			Deflated			Country share (%)			Real average annual change (%)		
	1978	1986	1993	1978	1986	1993	1978	1986	1993	78/86	86/93	78/93
FRG	6.1	19.4	27.9	8.6	20.5	25.7	5.4%	4.7%	3.0%	12.3	5.1	8.9
France	9.1	29.4	49.0	13.2	30.4	49.2	8.0%	7.1%	5.3%	11.4	7.6	9.6
Italy	74.9	309.6	699.8	120.2	333.6	778.4	66.0%	74.5%	75.8%	15.1	13.0	14.1
Netherlands	5.5	12.6	21.3	7.4	13.1	18.8	4.8%	3.0%	2.3%	8.3	6.5	7.5
Bel. & Lux.	4.9	26.3	67.1	7.9	29.5	62.0	4.3%	6.3%	7.3%	19.2	12.2	16.0
UK	3.2	7.4	18.3	6.5	8.5	16.8	2.8%	1.8%	2.0%	4.7	11.1	7.7
Ireland	0.7	1.3	0.1	1.0	1.3	0.1	0.6%	0.3%	0.0%	10.3	39.7	24.0
Denmark	0.3	0.7	7.7	0.4	0.7	7.7	0.3%	0.2%	0.8%	28.5	50.3	38.7
Spain	2.4	2.4	19.1	4.5	2.9	19.1	2.2%	0.6%	2.1%	23.0	31.2	26.8
Greece	5.5	5.5	9.0	10.7	6.6	8.6	4.8%	1.3%	1.0%	-4.0	9.3	2.2
Portugal	0.9	0.5	1.2	2.3	0.6	0.9	0.8%	0.1%	0.1%	17.6	11.4	14.7
Total EUR-12	113.5	415.5	922.8	182.7	447.9	987.3	100.0%	100.0%	100.0%	12.6	12.0	12.3

Table D.1.16. Intra-EU exports (million ECU)

Country	Actual			Deflated			Country share (%)			Real average annual change (%)		
	1978	1986	1993	1978	1986	1993	1978	1986	1993	78/86	86/93	78/93
FRG	4.0	14.2	16.9	5.6	15.0	15.6	5.0%	5.3%	3.0%	11.2	5.1	8.6
France	4.4	17.9	31.1	6.4	18.5	31.2	5.5%	6.6%	5.5%	16.4	4.0	11.0
Italy	55.2	189.5	396.8	88.6	204.2	441.4	69.6%	70.3%	70.0%	8.6	12.0	10.0
Netherlands	4.1	9.8	17.0	5.5	10.2	15.0	5.2%	3.6%	3.0%	7.1	8.2	7.6
Bel. & Lux.	4.8	25.6	64.8	7.8	28.7	59.9	6.1%	9.5%	11.4%	17.0	11.9	14.8
UK	2.0	6.5	16.9	4.0	7.5	15.5	2.5%	2.4%	3.0%	11.6	6.0	9.2
Ireland	0.7	1.3	2.5	1.0	1.3	2.5	0.9%	0.5%	0.4%	6.3	59.9	29.3
Denmark	0.1	0.3	5.6	0.1	0.3	5.6	0.1%	0.1%	1.0%	6.5	76.4	36.5
Spain	0.9	0.0	11.5	1.7	0.0	11.5	1.2%	0.0%	2.0%	-17.4	82.1	25.2
Greece	3.1	3.9	3.3	6.0	4.7	3.1	3.9%	1.4%	0.6%	1.2	-4.8	-1.3
Portugal	0.0	0.1	0.2	0.0	0.1	0.1	0.0%	0.0%	0.0%	-13.7	16.0	-1.0
Intra-EUR-12	79.3	269.4	566.6	126.8	290.6	601.5	100.0%	100.0%	100.0%	8.8	10.8	9.7

Table D.1.17. Extra-EU exports (million ECU)

Country	Actual			Deflated			Country share (%)			Real average annual change (%)		
	1978	1986	1993	1978	1986	1993	1978	1986	1993	78/86	86/93	78/93
FRG	2.1	5.2	11	2.9	5.5	10.1	6.2%	3.6%	3.1%	8.8	13.4	10.8
France	4.7	11.4	17.8	6.8	11.8	17.9	13.9%	7.9%	5.0%	6.2	5.6	5.9
Italy	19.7	118.9	303	31.6	128.1	337.0	58.3%	82.1%	85.1%	20.6	17.6	19.3
Netherlands	1.5	2.7	4.3	2.0	2.8	3.8	4.4%	1.9%	1.2%	6.3	5.9	6.1
Bel. & Lux.	0.1	0.6	2.3	0.2	0.7	2.1	0.3%	0.4%	0.6%	21.6	24.4	22.8
UK	1.2	0.8	1.4	2.4	0.9	1.3	3.6%	0.6%	0.4%	-9.6	10.5	-1.0
Ireland	0.0	0.0	0.0	0.0	0.0	0.0	0.0%	0.0%	0.0%	0.0	0.0	0.0
Denmark	0.1	0.4	2.1	0.1	0.4	2.1	0.3%	0.3%	0.6%	35.0	42.6	38.3
Spain	1.2	2.4	7.6	2.1	2.9	7.6	3.5%	1.7%	2.1%	41.5	15.2	30.2
Greece	2.3	1.6	5.7	4.6	1.9	5.4	6.9%	1.1%	1.6%	-7.4	31.6	9.3
Portugal	0.9	0.3	1.1	2.2	0.4	0.8	2.6%	0.2%	0.3%	38.6	9.0	25.9
Extra-EUR-12	33.8	144.8	356.2	55.0	155.5	388.2	100.0%	100.0%	100.0%	14.2	16.2	15.0

Table D.1.18. Trade ratio (extra-EU)

Country	1978	1979	1980	1981	1982	1983	1984	1985	1986	1987	1988	1989	1990	1991	1992	1993
FRG	0.24	0.23	0.21	-0.02	0.00	0.03	0.07	-0.12	-0.26	-0.24	-0.23	-0.28	-0.26	-0.29	-0.04	-0.31
France	0.57	0.55	0.59	0.53	0.53	0.45	0.35	0.34	0.37	0.42	0.47	0.48	0.45	0.46	0.50	0.43
Italy	0.98	0.99	1.00	1.00	1.00	1.00	1.00	1.00	1.00	1.00	1.00	1.00	1.00	1.00	1.00	1.00
Netherlands	0.30	0.04	0.21	0.12	0.25	0.17	0.06	-0.12	-0.08	-0.05	0.01	-0.06	0.03	0.03	-0.06	-0.10
Bel. & Lux.	-0.50	-0.43	-1.00	-1.00	-0.33	-0.60	-0.67	-0.45	0.00	0.00	0.33	0.00	0.13	-0.07	-0.06	0.05
UK	0.00	-0.40	-0.30	-0.30	-0.42	-0.50	-0.60	-0.74	-0.67	-0.69	-0.65	-0.70	-0.56	-0.75	-0.79	-0.81
Ireland	0.00	0.00	0.00	0.00	0.00	0.00	0.00	0.00	0.00	0.00	0.00	-1.00	0.00	-1.00	-1.00	-1.00
Denmark	-0.33	-0.33	-0.33	-0.33	-0.67	-0.20	-0.43	0.00	0.00	0.40	-0.33	0.25	0.50	0.69	0.65	0.62
Spain	0.84	0.85	0.86	0.82	0.86	0.71	1.00	1.00	0.71	0.66	0.71	0.65	0.75	0.79	0.83	0.85
Greece	1.00	1.00	1.00	1.00	1.00	1.00	1.00	1.00	1.00	1.00	1.00	1.00	1.00	1.00	1.00	1.00
Portugal	1.00	1.00	1.00	1.00	1.00	1.00	1.00	1.00	1.00	1.00	1.00	1.00	1.00	0.89	1.00	1.00
EUR-12	0.72	0.66	0.71	0.75	0.79	0.73	0.75	0.72	0.72	0.72	0.74	0.77	0.76	0.78	0.81	0.75

Table D.1.19. Trade ratio (intra-EU)

Country	1978	1979	1980	1981	1982	1983	1984	1985	1986	1987	1988	1989	1990	1991	1992	1993
FRG	-0.72	-0.70	-0.74	-0.72	-0.73	-0.73	-0.72	-0.64	-0.68	-0.74	-0.78	-0.80	-0.76	-0.77	-0.85	-0.81
France	-0.69	-0.66	-0.69	-0.66	-0.66	-0.55	-0.57	-0.64	-0.66	-0.60	-0.64	-0.64	-0.63	-0.65	-0.62	-0.63
Italy	0.99	0.98	0.99	0.99	1.00	1.00	0.99	0.99	0.99	1.00	0.99	0.99	0.99	0.99	0.98	0.98
Netherlands	-0.27	-0.25	-0.39	-0.43	-0.51	-0.41	-0.47	-0.37	-0.32	-0.37	-0.25	-0.25	-0.21	-0.34	-0.27	-0.29
Bel. & Lux.	-0.36	-0.32	-0.36	-0.39	-0.44	-0.25	-0.21	-0.17	-0.08	0.00	-0.01	0.05	0.09	0.10	0.15	0.06
UK	-0.67	-0.61	-0.51	-0.71	-0.68	-0.73	-0.73	-0.76	-0.77	-0.68	-0.68	-0.71	-0.71	-0.69	-0.69	-0.69
Ireland	-0.26	-0.38	-0.47	-0.66	-0.53	-0.79	-0.75	-0.67	-0.58	-0.65	-0.02	0.04	-0.04	-0.22	-0.39	-0.59
Denmark	-0.88	-0.58	-0.42	-0.81	-1.00	-1.00	-0.96	-0.93	-0.91	-0.93	-0.86	-0.69	-0.73	-0.63	-0.50	-0.48
Spain	-0.24	-0.19	-0.22	-0.33	-0.06	-0.80	-1.00	-1.00	-1.00	-0.90	-0.82	-0.57	-0.54	-0.41	-0.30	0.07
Greece	0.46	0.45	0.57	0.42	0.40	0.52	0.37	0.28	0.10	0.15	-0.21	-0.47	-0.55	-0.67	-0.68	-0.58
Portugal	-1.00	-1.00	0.00	-1.00	-1.00	-0.33	-0.33	-1.00	-0.67	-0.71	-0.85	-0.91	-0.93	-0.90	-0.96	-0.94
EUR-12	-0.02	0.06	-0.01	-0.05	-0.05	-0.06	-0.02	0.00	-0.02	-0.02	-0.01	-0.01	-0.02	-0.04	-0.04	0.03

Table D.1.20. Intra-EU imports as % of total

Country	1978	1979	1980	1981	1982	1983	1984	1985	1986	1987	1988	1989	1990	1991	1992	1993
FRG	94.6	93.9	93.6	92.2	92.6	91.6	89.6	88.4	89.3	90.0	92.0	92.4	93.4	93.4	92.9	88.5
France	95.3	94.3	95.1	93.7	94.1	93.0	91.4	93.0	94.2	95.0	95.4	95.2	95.5	95.3	95.5	95.1
Italy	60.0	75.0	75.0	75.0	50.0	50.0	66.7	71.4	83.3	71.4	80.0	85.7	82.4	84.6	93.6	87.2
Netherlands	89.9	88.0	91.1	88.1	88.8	83.7	83.9	79.7	85.2	87.5	87.6	89.1	90.0	90.6	89.6	85.5
Bel. & Lux.	97.1	96.2	98.0	98.5	99.1	97.8	98.1	97.2	98.1	97.5	98.3	97.5	97.4	95.8	96.4	96.6
UK	89.5	81.8	83.4	88.8	88.3	89.9	89.6	87.1	92.3	92.0	90.4	91.6	91.9	91.0	90.1	87.3
Ireland	100.0	100.0	100.0	100.0	97.1	100.0	100.0	97.8	100.0	100.0	100.0	98.3	98.6	98.8	97.8	97.0
Denmark	84.2	82.6	81.5	80.6	86.1	90.0	91.4	90.2	94.0	95.1	95.7	96.6	97.9	98.8	97.9	97.6
Spain	93.9	94.1	93.3	94.1	94.7	90.0	100.0	100.0	89.7	89.4	87.9	82.5	88.2	90.6	92.0	94.3
Greece	100.0	100.0	100.0	100.0	100.0	94.1	100.0	96.7	97.0	97.1	100.0	98.4	98.8	99.1	100.0	100.0
Portugal	90.0	75.0	100.0	100.0	50.0	66.7	66.7	100.0	100.0	85.7	100.0	100.0	96.3	100.0	97.8	98.5
EUR-12	93.7	91.8	92.7	92.5	92.8	91.9	91.0	90.1	92.3	92.6	93.2	93.4	94.1	93.9	93.5	91.3

Table D.1.21. Intra-EU exports as % of total

Country	1978	1979	1980	1981	1982	1983	1984	1985	1986	1987	1988	1989	1990	1991	1992	1993
FRG	65.6	63.4	57.8	67.7	66.7	61.7	54.7	68.2	73.2	68.5	70.3	70.3	76.2	76.7	53.7	60.6
France	48.4	49.6	48.4	49.0	50.6	59.8	58.2	59.0	60.9	65.8	63.0	60.9	64.4	61.4	62.9	63.5
Italy	73.7	74.9	70.5	59.6	54.7	58.9	54.9	54.8	61.2	62.7	63.0	59.4	62.3	58.8	53.3	56.7
Netherlands	74.5	79.1	73.1	71.6	60.0	59.5	63.6	69.7	77.8	77.9	80.3	84.5	84.8	81.9	84.7	79.8
Bel. & Lux.	98.0	97.1	100.0	98.9	97.6	98.5	98.8	98.5	97.3	97.5	96.9	97.7	97.1	97.0	97.6	96.6
UK	62.5	72.1	75.0	71.2	78.3	79.4	83.3	84.7	87.8	91.4	88.7	90.6	86.9	92.6	92.8	92.3
Ireland	100.0	100.0	100.0	100.0	100.0	100.0	100.0	100.0	100.0	100.0	100.0	100.0	100.0	100.0	100.0	100.0
Denmark	33.3	66.7	75.0	42.9	0.0	0.0	25.0	25.0	42.9	27.3	70.0	77.8	78.6	77.6	76.5	72.7
Spain	38.2	41.8	36.0	36.4	50.0	11.8	0.0	0.0	0.0	9.1	12.5	23.6	26.5	31.7	36.4	60.2
Greece	56.2	57.2	47.8	61.7	59.7	68.5	70.7	71.2	70.9	70.3	75.0	52.3	56.1	42.0	38.3	36.7
Portugal	0.0	0.0	0.0	0.0	0.0	4.8	7.7	0.0	20.0	14.3	11.1	12.5	11.1	10.0	6.3	16.7
EUR-12	69.8	71.9	68.2	61.3	57.3	61.5	58.3	59.2	64.8	66.4	66.9	63.9	67.4	64.1	58.7	61.4

Table D.1.22. Import penetration ratios (extra-EU)

Country	1978	1979	1980	1981	1982	1983	1984	1985	1986	1987	1988	1989	1990	1991	1992	1993
FRG	0.5	0.9	1.0	1.3	1.3	1.7	2.2	2.7	2.7	2.8	2.5	2.6	2.5	2.3	3.1	4.1
France	0.4	0.5	0.4	0.6	0.6	0.8	1.0	1.0	0.8	0.8	0.6	0.7	0.7	0.7	0.7	0.7
Italy	0.0	0.0	0.0	0.0	0.0	0.0	0.0	0.0	0.0	0.0	0.0	0.0	0.0	0.0	0.0	0.0
Netherlands	0.0	0.1	0.1	0.1	0.1	0.1	0.1	0.2	0.1	0.1	0.1	0.1	0.1	0.1	0.2	0.0
Bel. & Lux.	0.2	0.5	0.2	0.2	0.2	0.3	0.4	0.7	0.5	0.5	0.4	0.7	1.0	1.3	1.3	1.3
UK	14.6	25.2	25.2	14.2	14.3	12.3	12.2	15.0	8.7	9.8	11.8	10.0	9.8	10.9	12.0	15.3
Ireland	0.0	0.0	0.0	0.0	0.0	0.0	0.0	0.0	0.0	0.0	0.0	3.3	0.0	3.3	3.8	3.0
Denmark	12.5	19.4	26.7	20.7	14.7	8.1	9.3	9.4	6.7	4.2	4.8	3.3	1.7	1.6	3.6	5.7
Spain	0.1	0.1	0.1	0.1	0.1	0.3	0.0	0.0	0.4	0.6	0.5	0.9	0.7	0.7	0.9	0.6
Greece	0.0	0.0	0.0	0.0	0.0	0.0	0.0	0.0	0.0	0.0	0.0	0.0	0.0	0.0	0.0	0.0
Portugal	0.0	0.0	0.0	0.0	0.0	0.0	0.0	0.0	0.0	0.0	0.0	0.0	0.0	0.1	0.0	0.0
EUR-12	0.1	0.2	0.2	0.3	0.3	0.3	0.4	0.5	0.4	0.4	0.4	0.5	0.5	0.6	0.6	0.7

Table D.1.23. Import penetration ratios (intra-EU)

Country	1978	1979	1980	1981	1982	1983	1984	1985	1986	1987	1988	1989	1990	1991	1992	1993
FRG	9.2	14.3	15.0	16.4	17.0	18.5	18.8	20.6	22.9	25.4	29.6	32.5	36.0	33.0	40.2	31.7
France	7.4	7.7	7.9	8.9	10.0	10.3	11.4	12.6	13.8	14.6	13.8	13.1	15.1	14.8	15.1	14.4
Italy	0.0	0.1	0.0	0.0	0.0	0.0	0.0	0.0	0.0	0.0	0.0	0.1	0.1	0.1	0.2	0.2
Netherlands	0.3	0.4	0.5	0.6	0.6	0.5	0.6	0.7	0.8	1.0	1.1	1.1	1.2	1.2	1.4	1.3
Bel. & Lux.	8.4	13.9	15.4	18.1	18.2	19.0	20.1	23.4	23.9	23.8	27.8	28.7	36.8	29.2	36.1	36.5
UK	124.4	113.5	131.5	112.2	112.1	109.2	107.6	101.1	107.2	113.6	112.2	110.3	112.3	111.4	109.6	105.3
Ireland	240.0	180.0	155.6	125.9	137.5	113.5	116.7	121.6	136.1	127.0	176.7	193.3	236.7	270.0	171.7	98.0
Denmark	100.0	122.6	146.7	100.0	91.2	97.3	98.1	103.8	105.0	109.9	107.1	125.6	121.2	138.5	169.4	183.0
Spain	2.0	2.0	1.5	1.7	2.2	2.4	0.1	0.1	3.9	6.3	4.7	4.6	6.2	6.9	10.0	9.9
Greece	5.1	4.8	1.9	4.3	4.4	3.4	3.6	5.1	5.5	4.7	4.8	7.2	8.1	9.3	9.9	10.7
Portugal	0.5	0.4	0.5	0.3	0.2	0.5	0.4	0.5	0.9	1.1	2.1	3.9	3.8	5.2	5.9	8.2
EUR-12	2.3	2.6	2.8	3.3	3.6	3.7	3.8	4.3	4.9	5.4	5.8	6.6	7.8	8.5	8.9	7.8

Note: In the case of the UK, Ireland and Denmark, domestic consumption appears to exceed the value of EU imports in most years.

Table D.1.24. Intra-EU exports as a % of production

Country	1978	1979	1980	1981	1982	1983	1984	1985	1986	1987	1988	1989	1990	1991	1992	1993
FRG	1.6	2.9	2.6	3.2	3.1	3.4	3.6	5.5	5.5	4.9	5.1	5.1	7.1	6.0	5.2	4.8
France	1.4	1.7	1.5	1.9	2.2	3.2	3.3	3.1	3.1	4.1	3.4	3.2	3.8	3.5	4.0	3.6
Italy	7.0	8.0	6.7	6.7	7.2	6.1	6.2	7.1	8.0	8.4	9.2	11.3	12.4	13.9	12.6	12.7
Netherlands	0.2	0.3	0.2	0.2	0.2	0.2	0.2	0.3	0.4	0.5	0.6	0.7	0.8	0.6	0.8	0.7
Bel. & Lux.	4.2	7.8	7.9	8.9	7.9	12.5	14.1	18.0	21.0	24.0	27.4	30.8	40.7	33.7	43.2	39.3
Spain	1.2	1.4	1.0	0.9	2.0	0.3	0.0	0.0	0.0	0.3	0.5	1.3	1.9	2.8	5.2	10.6
Greece	11.6	10.8	6.3	9.5	9.2	9.5	7.2	8.5	6.5	6.1	3.2	2.7	2.5	1.9	2.0	2.9
Portugal	0.0	0.0	0.0	0.0	0.0	0.2	0.2	0.0	0.2	0.2	0.2	0.2	0.2	0.3	0.1	0.3
EUR-12	2.2	2.9	2.7	3.0	3.2	3.2	3.6	4.2	4.6	5.1	5.6	6.3	7.3	7.6	7.9	7.9

Table D.1.25. Extra-EU exports as a % of production

Country	1978	1979	1980	1981	1982	1983	1984	1985	1986	1987	1988	1989	1990	1991	1992	1993
FRG	0.9	1.6	1.8	1.5	1.5	2.1	3.0	2.6	2.0	2.2	2.2	2.1	2.2	1.8	4.5	3.1
France	1.5	1.7	1.6	2.0	2.1	2.1	2.3	2.1	2.0	2.1	2.0	2.0	2.1	2.2	2.3	2.1
Italy	2.5	2.7	2.7	4.5	5.9	4.2	5.1	5.8	5.0	5.0	5.4	7.7	7.5	9.7	11.1	9.7
Netherlands	0.1	0.1	0.1	0.1	0.1	0.1	0.1	0.1	0.1	0.1	0.2	0.1	0.1	0.1	0.1	0.2
Bel. & Lux.	0.1	0.2	0.0	0.0	0.1	0.1	0.1	0.3	0.5	0.5	0.8	0.7	1.2	1.1	1.1	1.4
Spain	1.5	1.5	1.4	1.1	1.6	1.6	0.7	0.6	2.7	3.2	3.2	4.1	5.1	6.1	9.0	7.0
Greece	8.8	7.8	6.9	5.6	6.0	4.4	3.0	3.3	2.7	2.6	1.1	2.2	1.8	2.6	2.8	5.1
Portugal	4.1	3.0	5.7	1.8	1.0	4.5	2.4	0.9	0.5	1.1	1.4	1.1	1.2	2.6	2.1	1.4
EUR-12	1.1	1.2	1.3	2.0	2.5	2.1	2.6	2.9	2.5	2.6	2.8	3.5	3.5	4.3	5.7	5.4

Figure D.1.1. Intra/extra- EU exports

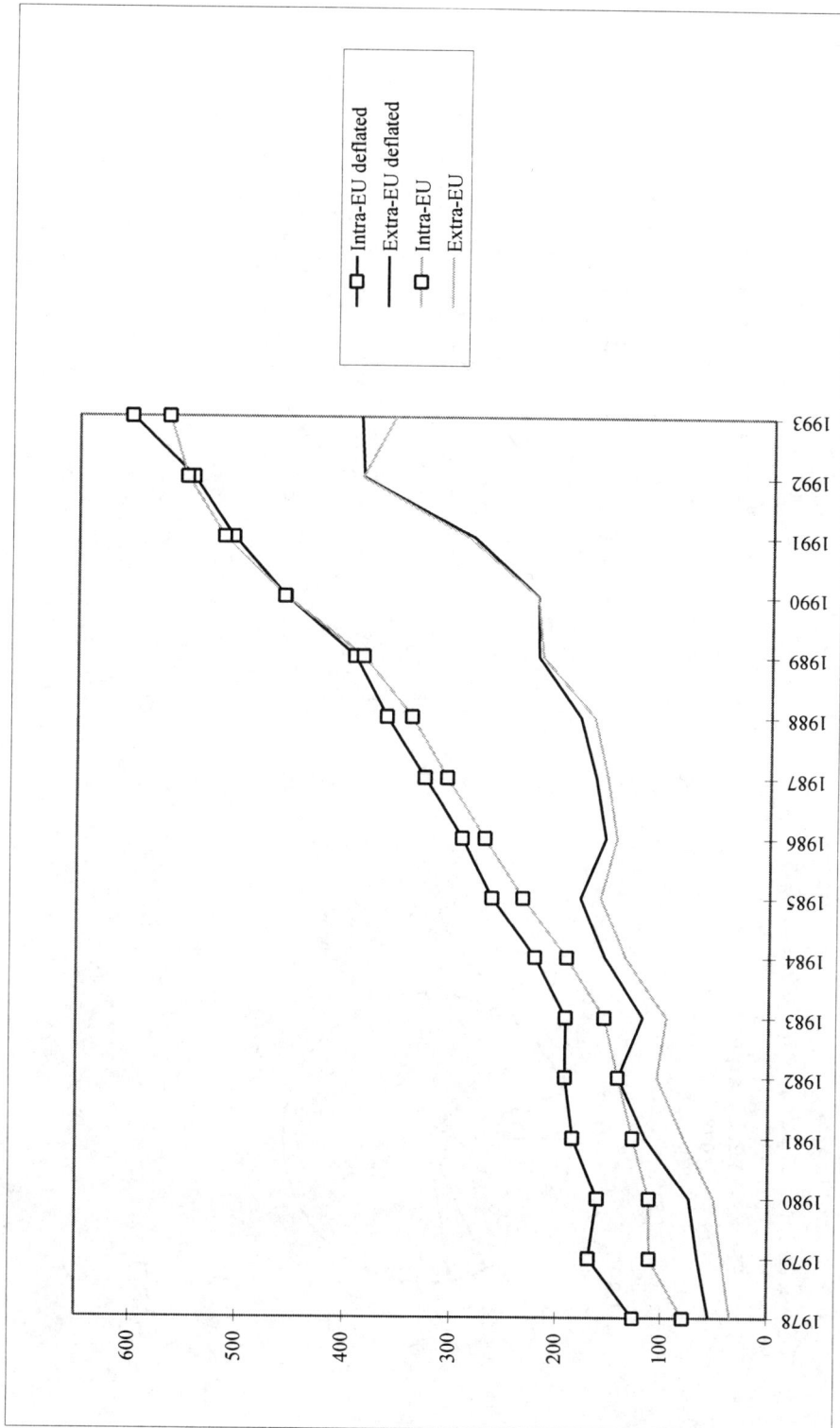

Note: 1978, 1979 are estimated figures (estimated for Spain, Portugal and Greece).

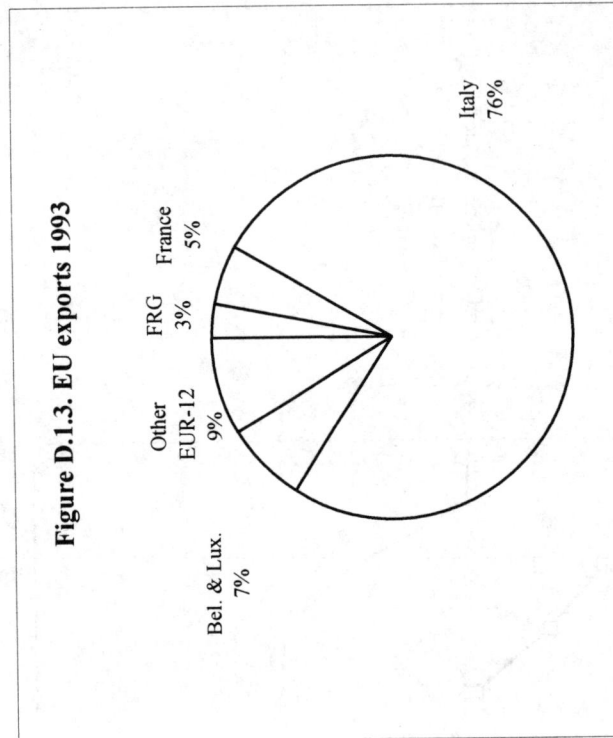

Figure D.1.3. EU exports 1993

Italy 76%
France 5%
FRG 3%
Other EUR-12 9%
Bel. & Lux. 7%

Figure D.1.2. EU exports 1978

Italy 65%
France 8%
FRG 5%
Other EUR-12 18%
Bel. & Lux. 4%

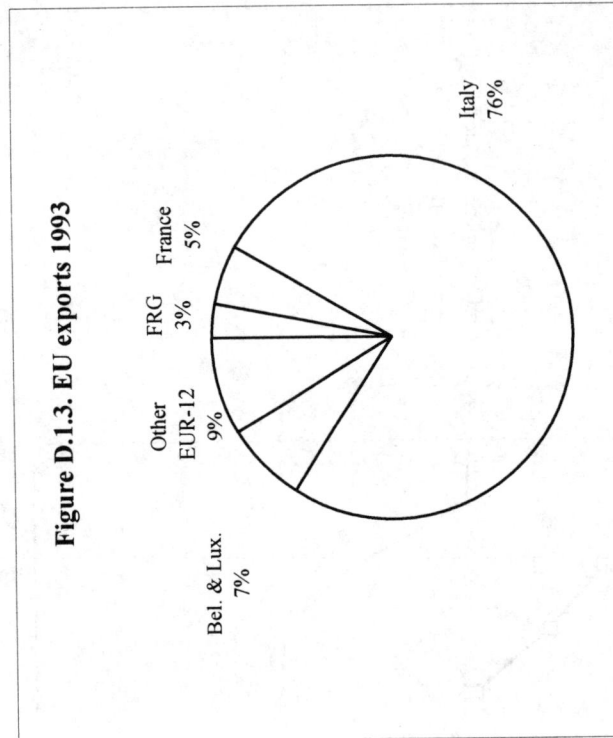

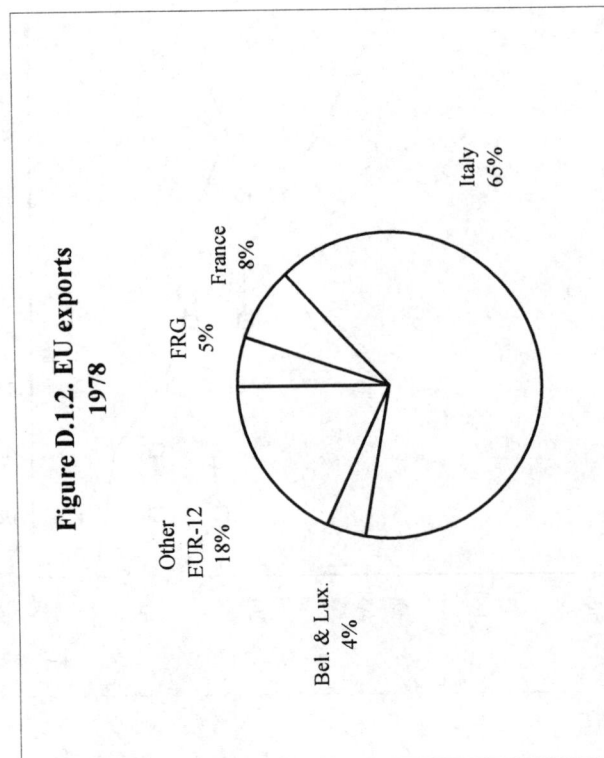

Note: Intra- and extra-EU exports.

D.2. NACE 419

4190 Industrial baking (bread and flour confectionery)

Table D.2.1. Number of enterprises

Country	1978	1986	1993	Country share (%)			Total change (%)		
				1978	1986	1993	78/86	86/93	78/93
FRG	769	887	1184	2.8%	3.3%	4.3%	15.3%	33.5%	54.0%
France	282	327	389	1.0%	1.2%	1.4%	16.0%	18.9%	37.9%
Italy	192	206	252	0.7%	0.8%	0.9%	7.3%	22.4%	31.3%
Netherlands	229	238	280	0.8%	0.9%	1.0%	3.9%	17.5%	22.1%
Belgium	110	98	141	0.4%	0.4%	0.5%	-10.9%	44.3%	28.6%
Luxembourg	11	9	11	0.0%	0.0%	0.0%	-18.2%	23.0%	0.6%
UK	580	564	659	2.1%	2.1%	2.4%	-2.8%	16.8%	13.6%
Ireland	73	76	53	0.3%	0.3%	0.2%	4.1%	-30.7%	-27.9%
Denmark	49	33	24	0.2%	0.1%	0.1%	-32.7%	-27.2%	-51.0%
Spain	22439	22516	22510	82.7%	83.1%	82.5%	0.3%	0.0%	0.3%
Greece	46	50	52	0.2%	0.2%	0.2%	6.9%	5.6%	12.9%
Portugal	2343	2094	1717	8.6%	7.7%	6.3%	-10.6%	-18.0%	-26.7%
EUR-12	27123	27098	27272	100.0%	100.0%	100.0%	-0.1%	0.6%	0.5%

Table D.2.2. Number of persons employed, excluding home workers

Country	1978	1986	1993	Country share (%)			Total change (%)		
				1978	1986	1993	78/86	86/93	78/93
FRG	69156	79884	108753	15.2%	19.7%	24.2%	15.5%	36.1%	57.3%
France	31323	33269	35179	6.9%	8.2%	7.8%	6.2%	5.7%	12.3%
Italy	25034	19202	17243	5.5%	4.7%	3.8%	-23.3%	-10.2%	-31.1%
Netherlands	18044	14848	17661	4.0%	3.7%	3.9%	-17.7%	18.9%	-2.1%
Belgium	9223	9130	10324	2.0%	2.3%	2.3%	-1.0%	13.1%	11.9%
Luxembourg	410	520	687	0.1%	0.1%	0.2%	26.8%	32.2%	67.6%
UK	170779	121421	128783	37.5%	30.0%	28.7%	-28.9%	6.1%	-24.6%
Ireland	7566	5822	3581	1.7%	1.4%	0.8%	-23.1%	-38.5%	-52.7%
Denmark	3505	3401	3627	0.8%	0.8%	0.8%	-3.0%	6.6%	3.5%
Spain	90272	89994	98964	19.8%	22.2%	22.0%	-0.3%	10.0%	9.6%
Greece	2274	3048	3724	0.5%	0.8%	0.8%	34.0%	22.2%	63.8%
Portugal	27743	24359	20885	6.1%	6.0%	4.6%	-12.2%	-14.3%	-24.7%
EUR-12	455328	404898	449412	100.0%	100.0%	100.0%	-11.1%	11.0%	-1.3%
USA	267894	242839	261306				-9.4%	7.6%	-2.5%

Table D.2.3. Production value, excluding VAT

Country	Actual			Deflated			Country share (%)			Real average annual change (%)		
	1978	1986	1993	1978	1986	1993	1978	1986	1993	78/86	86/93	78/93
FRG	1975	3443	5643	3052	3702	4848	21.0%	19.8%	20.1%	2.5	4.4	3.4
France	999	2323	3637	1776	2622	3202	10.6%	13.4%	12.9%	5.1	3.0	4.1
Italy	856	1812	2933	1685	1995	3192	9.1%	10.4%	10.4%	2.6	7.3	4.8
Netherlands	671	992	1389	1086	1046	1218	7.2%	5.7%	4.9%	-0.3	2.3	0.9
Belgium	324	539	754	561	593	673	3.5%	3.1%	2.7%	0.8	1.9	1.3
Luxembourg	15	20	37	26	22	33	0.2%	0.1%	0.1%	-0.2	6.6	2.9
UK	2795	4712	8224	5647	5428	7552	29.8%	27.2%	29.3%	-0.5	5.0	2.1
Ireland	146	254	210	245	254	203	1.6%	1.5%	0.7%	0.7	-3.0	-1.0
Denmark	137	321	444	243	362	391	1.5%	1.8%	1.6%	5.3	1.5	3.5
Spain	1225	2517	4228	2876	3252	4117	13.1%	14.5%	15.1%	2.1	3.6	2.8
Greece	41	95	193	71	115	153	0.4%	0.6%	0.7%	6.4	4.4	5.5
Portugal	199	318	393	488	390	289	2.1%	1.8%	1.4%	-2.4	-3.9	-3.1
EUR-12	9382	17343	28086	17756	19780	25871	100.0%	100.0%	100.0%	1.4	4.0	2.6
USA	13277	28324	34492		26422	29058						

Table D.2.4. Production value per enterprise

Country	Actual			Deflated		
	1978	1986	1993	1978	1986	1993
FRG	2.6	3.9	4.8	4.0	4.2	4.1
France	3.5	7.1	9.4	6.3	8.0	8.2
Italy	4.5	8.8	11.6	8.8	9.7	12.7
Netherlands	2.9	4.2	5.0	4.7	4.4	4.4
Belgium	2.9	5.5	5.3	5.1	6.0	4.8
Luxembourg	1.4	2.2	3.4	2.3	2.4	3.0
UK	4.8	8.4	12.5	9.7	9.6	11.5
Ireland	2.0	3.3	4.0	3.4	3.3	3.9
Denmark	2.8	9.7	18.5	5.0	11.0	16.3
Spain	0.1	0.1	0.2	0.1	0.1	0.2
Greece	0.9	1.9	3.7	1.5	2.3	2.9
Portugal	0.1	0.2	0.2	0.2	0.2	0.2
EUR-12	0.3	0.6	1.0	0.7	0.7	0.9

Table D.2.5.   Consumption value

Country	Actual			Deflated			Country share (%)			Real average annual change (%)		
	1978	1986	1993	1978	1986	1993	1978	1986	1993	78/86	86/93	78/93
FRG	2018	3330	5477	2680	3335	4570	21.9%	19.7%	20.1%	2.9	5.0	3.8
France	1026	2532	3781	2038	2467	3011	11.2%	15.0%	13.9%	2.5	3.0	2.7
Italy	857	1767	2769	2270	1669	1800	9.3%	10.4%	10.2%	-3.3	1.5	-1.1
Netherlands	591	821	1113	806	819	971	6.4%	4.8%	4.1%	0.5	2.6	1.5
Bel. & Lux.	304	466	632	476	460	524	3.3%	2.8%	2.3%	109.3	2.0	59.2
UK	2693	4632	8042	5099	4479	5408	29.3%	27.4%	29.6%	-1.5	3.3	0.7
Ireland	157	289	279	375	278	220	1.7%	1.7%	1.0%	-3.4	-3.2	-3.3
Denmark	103	171	268	185	164	209	1.1%	1.0%	1.0%	-0.4	3.8	1.6
Spain	1215	2510	4215	2865	2307	2624	13.2%	14.8%	15.5%	-2.3	2.0	-0.3
Greece	35	92	199	131	75	56	0.4%	0.5%	0.7%	-6.7	-3.7	-5.3
Portugal	199	316	418	822	283	190	2.2%	1.9%	1.5%	-12.1	-5.5	-9.0
EUR-12	9197	16926	27192	17748	16337	19584	100.0%	100.0%	100.0%	-1.0	2.8	0.8

Table D.2.6.   Labour costs

Country	Actual			Deflated			Country share (%)		
	1978	1986	1993	1978	1986	1993	1978	1986	1993
FRG	664	1145	1924	1026	1231	1653	24.4%	17.0%	20.3%
France	305	660	925	542	745	814	11.2%	9.8%	9.8%
Italy	219	378	589	431	417	641	8.0%	5.6%	6.2%
Netherlands	213	298	395	344	314	346	7.8%	4.4%	4.2%
Belgium	115	169	226	200	185	202	4.2%	2.5%	2.4%
Luxembourg	4	7	15	7	7	13	0.1%	0.1%	0.2%
UK	789	1299	2106	1595	1497	1934	29.0%	19.3%	22.3%
Ireland	46	79	47	77	79	46	1.7%	1.2%	0.5%
Denmark	43	70	99	76	79	87	1.6%	1.0%	1.0%
Spain	273	561	1017	641	725	991	10.0%	8.4%	10.8%
Greece			45			36			0.5%
Portugal	52	66	79	128	81	58	1.9%	1.0%	0.8%
EU (average)	499	833	1414	5065	5361	6821	100.0%	100.0%	100.0%
EUR-12	2722	6719	9461	7043	7347	8814	100.0%	100.0%	100.0%

Table D.2.7. Gross value added at factor cost

Country	Actual			Deflated			Country share (%)			Real average annual change (%)		
	1978	1986	1993	1978	1986	1993	1978	1986	1993	78/86	86/93	78/93
FRG	856	1467	2529	1323	1578	2173	23.4%	22.0%	22.2%	2.3	5.3	3.7
France	382	896	1299	679	1012	1144	10.4%	13.4%	11.4%	5.2	1.8	3.6
Italy	288	556	865	566	612	942	7.9%	8.3%	7.6%	1.3	6.7	3.8
Netherlands	267	367	537	432	387	471	7.3%	5.5%	4.7%	-1.2	3.0	0.8
Belgium	143	236	324	248	260	290	3.9%	3.5%	2.8%	0.8	1.6	1.2
Luxembourg	6	9	21	11	10	19	0.2%	0.1%	0.2%	0.7	8.9	4.5
UK	1130	1902	3476	2283	2191	3192	30.9%	28.5%	30.5%	-0.5	5.8	2.4
Ireland			79			76			0.7%		-1.7	-1.7
Denmark	51	101	240	91	114	212	1.4%	1.5%	2.1%	3.2	9.4	6.1
Spain	533	1132	1944	1251	1463	1893	14.6%	17.0%	17.1%	2.8	3.9	3.3
Greece			66			52			0.6%		7.1	7.1
EUR-12	3656	6667	11382	6885	7627	10463	100.0%	100.0%	100.0%	1.3	4.8	2.9
USA	7079	17157	20889		16005	17598						

Table D.2.8. Gross value added per person employed (in 000 ECU)

Country	Actual			Deflated		
	1978	1986	1993	1978	1986	1993
FRG	12.4	18.4	24.1	19.1	19.8	20.0
France	12.2	26.9	37.6	21.7	30.4	32.5
Italy	11.5	28.9	45.7	22.6	31.9	54.6
Netherlands	14.8	24.7	30.3	23.9	26.1	26.7
Belgium	15.5	25.9	29.6	26.9	28.5	28.1
Luxembourg	15.5	18.0	25.0	26.6	19.9	27.0
UK	6.6	15.7	25.4	13.4	18.0	24.8
Ireland			26.8			21.3
Denmark	14.7	29.6	58.7	26.1	33.5	58.3
Spain	5.1	12.6	20.0	13.9	16.3	19.1
Greece			18.2			14.0
EU (average)	8.2	16.8	-55.0	15.5	19.3	23.7
USA	26.4	70.7	79.9		65.9	67.3

Table D.2.9. Investment

Country	Actual 1978	Actual 1986	Actual 1993	Deflated 1978	Deflated 1986	Deflated 1993	Country share (%) 1978	Country share (%) 1986	Country share (%) 1993
FRG	102	183	367	158	197	315	4.3%	6.6%	10.8%
France	49	127	204	87	143	180	2.1%	4.6%	6.0%
Italy	31	98	178	61	108	194	1.3%	3.5%	5.2%
Netherlands	53	68	90	86	72	79	2.2%	2.5%	2.6%
Belgium	13	24	65	23	26	58	0.5%	0.9%	1.9%
Luxembourg	1	2	5	2	2	5	0.0%	0.1%	0.2%
UK	125	223	442	253	257	405	5.3%	8.1%	13.0%
Ireland	7	12	9	11	12	9	0.3%	0.4%	0.3%
Denmark	13	43	34	23	48	30	0.6%	1.5%	1.0%
Greece			20			16			0.6%
EUR-12	2373	2765	3407	705	864	1290	100.0%	100.0%	100.0%
USA	398	785			733				

Table D.2.10. Proportion of investments in gross value added at factor cost (in %)

Country	1978	1979	1980	1981	1982	1983	1984	1985	1986	1987	1988	1989	1990	1991	1992	1993
FRG	11.9	11.5	11.0	11.1	10.7	10.9	10.2	11.1	12.5	13.3	13.7	13.4	12.4	15.2	16.3	14.5
France	12.9	14.4	13.6	11.3	11.2	10.2	13.9	12.9	14.1	17.6	14.0	15.2	14.7	16.7	15.6	15.7
Italy	10.7	15.3	15.3	16.8	13.5	20.1	21.5	20.3	17.6	23.9	24.7	17.9	18.4	18.0	20.5	20.6
Netherlands	20.0	20.3	13.7	11.6	13.6	12.1	20.1	18.8	18.5	14.5	14.4	17.8	16.7	17.8	16.7	16.7
Belgium	9.1	9.2	9.3	10.2	9.7	9.4	9.3	9.1	10.0	11.1	13.1	15.1	16.4	17.8	19.0	20.1
Luxembourg	15.9	9.1	20.8	19.0	9.0	7.2	12.0	9.1	18.1	27.2	8.9	34.5	17.1	23.8	24.5	25.0
UK	11.1	10.1	9.8	9.3	8.2	9.2	12.0	11.2	11.7	12.4	13.3	14.1	12.1	11.1	12.6	12.7
Ireland											11.8	18.1	9.1	12.0	11.7	11.4
Denmark	25.7	17.0	26.7	14.4	20.2	24.0	24.6	25.0	42.5	31.0	26.5	16.8	13.7	16.5	13.7	14.3
Greece										17.4	18.9	21.2	26.8	28.2	29.4	30.6
EU (average)	14.7	13.4	15.0	13.0	12.0	12.9	15.4	14.7	18.1	18.7	15.9	18.4	15.7	17.7	18.0	18.2
USA	5.6	5.3	4.8	4.2	5.0	4.0	5.4	5.0	4.6	5.1	4.7	4.8	5.4	5.7	5.1	

Table D.2.11. Producer price index

Country	1978	1979	1980	1981	1982	1983	1984	1985	1986	1987	1988	1989	1990	1991	1992	1993
FRG	64.7	67.4	69.1	71.6	78.3	83.6	85.9	88.1	93.0	95.6	96.3	97.0	100.0	104.2	110.5	116.4
France	56.2	59.9	60.9	67.0	70.6	74.4	79.0	85.0	88.6	89.7	91.6	95.1	100.0	102.4	107.9	113.6
Italy	50.8	54.8	58.9	58.6	65.5	74.1	81.8	86.6	90.8	90.9	91.5	96.3	100.0	102.5	102.0	91.9
Netherlands	61.8	64.4	67.5	72.0	81.7	85.5	88.2	89.8	94.8	97.5	97.5	98.1	100.0	102.4	107.3	114.1
Bel. & Lux.	57.7	61.3	65.8	69.5	67.9	71.6	80.6	87.2	90.9	93.3	94.5	96.3	100.0	103.6	106.8	111.9
UK	49.5	55.7	69.0	80.0	83.6	83.7	88.0	93.0	86.8	85.8	96.5	99.9	100.0	109.3	109.3	108.9
Ireland	59.8	63.1	63.8	71.7	80.0	82.2	86.5	91.1	99.9	99.7	100.8	95.9	100.0	103.9	108.6	103.2
Denmark	56.2	59.9	60.9	67.0	70.6	74.4	79.0	85.0	88.6	89.7	91.6	95.1	100.0	102.4	107.9	113.6
Spain	42.6	52.3	54.5	60.5	65.8	63.7	73.6	80.7	77.4	80.2	85.8	93.7	100.0	106.6	109.0	102.7
Greece	57.5	58.3	63.8	76.7	82.1	80.3	84.4	88.4	83.0	81.9	84.9	93.4	100.0	105.6	120.3	126.4
Portugal	40.8	42.1	47.3	57.6	65.2	63.7	70.0	82.0	81.5	82.0	80.1	86.3	100.0	121.5	140.3	136.0
USA							126.4	135.3	107.2	93.6	97.1	111.1	100.0	106.4	104.8	118.7

Table D.2.12. Total imports (million ECU)

Country	Actual			Deflated			Country share (%)			Real average annual change (%)		
	1978	1986	1993	1978	1986	1993	1978	1986	1993	78/86	86/93	78/93
FRG	137.2	235.0	496.2	212.1	252.7	426.3	30.8%	18.7%	21.3%	2.4	8.2	5.1
France	98.2	408.5	590.2	174.6	461.1	519.5	22.1%	32.5%	25.3%	13.1	1.8	7.8
Italy	25.8	97.2	187.1	50.8	107.0	203.6	5.8%	7.7%	8.0%	11.3	9.7	10.6
Netherlands	45.8	116.2	191.5	74.1	122.6	167.8	10.3%	9.2%	8.2%	6.8	5.2	6.0
Bel. & Lux.	64.7	144.1	224.2	112.2	158.5	200.4	14.5%	11.5%	9.6%	4.5	3.6	4.1
UK	26.6	119.3	288.9	53.7	137.4	265.3	6.0%	9.5%	12.4%	13.4	10.6	12.1
Ireland	21.4	60.0	115.3	35.8	60.1	111.7	4.8%	4.8%	4.9%	7.6	9.4	8.4
Denmark	18.5	45.2	62.9	32.9	51.0	55.4	4.2%	3.6%	2.7%	5.8	1.2	3.7
Spain	4.0	24.6	107.2	9.4	31.8	104.4	0.9%	2.0%	4.6%	109.3	19.5	67.4
Greece	1.9	5.2	28.7	3.2	6.3	22.7	0.4%	0.4%	1.2%	20.7	25.4	22.9
Portugal	1.2	1.2	37.6	3.0	1.5	27.6	0.3%	0.1%	1.6%	9.3	64.8	35.2
Total EUR-12	445.3	1256.9	2329.8	761.8	1389.9	2104.7	100.0%	100.0%	100.0%	7.9	6.3	7.1

Table D.2.13. Intra-EU imports (million ECU)

Country	Actual			Deflated			Country share (%)			Real average annual change (%)		
	1978	1986	1993	1978	1986	1993	1978	1986	1993	78/86	86/93	78/93
FRG	115.7	187.3	411.5	178.8	201.4	353.5	28.6%	16.6%	19.6%	1.6	9.0	5.1
France	95.4	375.0	551.0	169.6	423.3	485.0	23.6%	33.3%	26.2%	12.3	2.1	7.5
Italy	24.0	88.9	172.2	47.3	97.9	187.4	5.9%	7.9%	8.2%	11.2	9.8	10.5
Netherlands	42.4	105.9	171.4	68.6	111.7	150.2	10.5%	9.4%	8.2%	6.5	5.0	5.8
Bel. & Lux.	62.9	139.8	218.4	109.0	153.8	195.2	15.6%	12.4%	10.4%	4.5	3.7	4.1
UK	23.6	107.3	249.9	47.7	123.6	229.5	5.8%	9.5%	11.9%	13.9	10.1	12.1
Ireland	21.1	59.4	113.7	35.3	59.5	110.2	5.2%	5.3%	5.4%	7.7	9.3	8.5
Denmark	12.2	33.7	47.5	21.7	38.0	41.8	3.0%	3.0%	2.3%	7.6	1.4	4.7
Spain	3.8	23.7	103.8	8.9	30.6	101.1	0.9%	2.1%	4.9%	115.5	19.7	70.8
Greece	1.8	4.8	25.9	3.1	5.8	20.5	0.4%	0.4%	1.2%	21.9	23.8	22.8
Portugal	1.1	1.2	36.7	2.8	1.5	27.0	0.3%	0.1%	1.7%	12.0	63.9	36.2
Intra-EUR-12	404.0	1127.5	2102.0	692.8	1247.0	1901.3	100.0%	100.0%	100.0%	7.7	6.4	7.1

Table D.2.14. Extra-EU imports (million ECU)

Country	Actual			Deflated			Country share (%)			Real average annual change (%)		
	1978	1986	1993	1978	1986	1993	1978	1986	1993	78/86	86/93	78/93
FRG	21.5	47.7	84.7	33.2	36.5	72.8	52.3%	36.9%	37.2%	6.5	5.3	5.9
France	2.9	33.4	39.1	5.2	8.3	34.4	7.1%	25.8%	17.2%	29.3	-0.5	15.4
Italy	1.8	8.3	14.9	3.5	4.4	16.2	4.4%	6.4%	6.5%	15.1	11.1	13.2
Netherlands	3.3	10.3	20.1	5.3	9.0	17.6	8.0%	8.0%	8.8%	14.4	7.4	11.2
Bel. & Lux.	1.8	4.3	5.8	3.1	3.9	5.2	4.4%	3.3%	2.5%	7.3	2.6	5.1
UK	3.0	11.9	39.0	6.1	7.0	35.8	7.3%	9.2%	17.1%	12.0	14.8	13.3
Ireland	0.3	0.5	1.6	0.5	0.5	1.6	0.7%	0.4%	0.7%	3.5	21.2	11.7
Denmark	6.3	11.4	15.4	11.2	10.5	13.6	15.3%	8.8%	6.8%	2.0	1.1	1.6
Spain	0.1	0.8	3.4	0.3	0.3	3.3	0.3%	0.6%	1.5%	94.1	24.7	61.7
Greece	0.1	0.3	2.7	0.1	0.2	2.1	0.2%	0.2%	1.2%	18.4	56.3	36.1
Portugal	0.0	0.0	0.9	0.0	0.0	0.7	0.0%	0.0%	0.4%	0.0	19.8	9.3
Extra-EUR-12	41.1	129.4	227.7	68.5	80.6	203.2	100.0%	100.0%	100.0%	9.9	5.3	7.8

Table D.2.15 Total exports (million ECU)

Country	Actual			Deflated			Country share (%)			Real average annual change (%)		
	1978	1986	1993	1978	1986	1993	1978	1986	1993	78/86	86/93	78/93
FRG	93.9	347.3	662.8	145.1	373.4	569.4	14.9%	20.7%	20.6%	12.6	6.5	9.8
France	71.5	199.2	446.3	127.1	224.8	392.9	11.3%	11.9%	13.8%	7.7	8.4	8.0
Italy	24.5	142.2	351.8	48.3	156.6	382.8	3.9%	8.5%	10.9%	16.9	13.8	15.4
Netherlands	126.1	287.3	467.5	204.0	303.1	409.7	20.0%	17.2%	14.5%	5.2	4.5	4.9
Bel. & Lux.	99.2	236.1	383.3	172.0	259.7	342.5	15.7%	14.1%	11.9%	5.4	4.1	4.8
UK	128.8	199.2	471.2	260.2	229.5	432.7	20.4%	11.9%	14.6%	-1.4	9.6	3.7
Ireland	10.5	24.9	45.9	17.6	24.9	44.5	1.7%	1.5%	1.4%	5.0	12.3	8.4
Denmark	52.5	195.3	239.0	93.3	220.4	210.4	8.3%	11.7%	7.4%	11.7	-0.2	6.1
Spain	13.8	31.3	120.5	32.4	40.4	117.3	2.2%	1.9%	3.7%	14.0	17.9	15.8
Greece	8.4	8.9	23.1	14.5	10.7	18.3	1.3%	0.5%	0.7%	-3.1	12.7	4.3
Portugal	1.4	2.5	12.5	3.3	3.1	9.2	0.2%	0.1%	0.4%	5.3	24.5	14.2
Total EUR-12	630.5	1674.6	3224.1	1118.0	1846.8	2929.7	100.0%	100.0%	100.0%	6.5	6.8	6.7

Table D.2.16. Intra-EU exports (million ECU)

Country	Actual			Deflated			Country share (%)			Real average annual change (%)		
	1978	1986	1993	1978	1986	1993	1978	1986	1993	78/86	86/93	78/93
FRG	57.6	248.8	465.4	89.0	267.5	399.8	14.1%	22.0%	19.8%	14.8	6.7	11.0
France	50.0	142.8	357.7	88.9	161.2	314.9	12.2%	12.6%	15.2%	8.3	10.3	9.2
Italy	14.4	100.8	239.0	28.4	111.0	260.1	3.5%	8.9%	10.2%	20.3	13.1	17.0
Netherlands	112.6	240.1	398.6	182.2	253.3	349.3	27.6%	21.3%	17.0%	4.3	4.9	4.6
Bel. & Lux.	92.3	209.4	324.0	160.0	230.4	289.5	22.6%	18.5%	13.8%	4.7	3.4	4.1
UK	56.6	105.9	325.1	114.3	122.0	298.5	13.9%	9.4%	13.8%	1.1	13.8	7.0
Ireland	9.0	23.1	44.5	15.1	23.1	43.1	2.2%	2.0%	1.9%	5.8	13.4	9.4
Denmark	12.9	53.3	119.0	22.9	60.2	104.8	3.2%	4.7%	5.1%	14.6	8.8	11.9
Spain	2.8	3.4	62.4	6.5	4.4	60.8	0.7%	0.3%	2.7%	15.8	54.8	34.0
Greece	0.1	1.3	5.2	0.1	1.6	4.1	0.0%	0.1%	0.2%	59.9	20.8	41.6
Portugal	0.1	0.4	8.0	0.2	0.5	5.9	0.0%	0.0%	0.3%	-0.9	47.7	21.8
Intra-EUR-12	408.3	1129.7	2348.9	707.7	1235.1	2130.8	100.0%	100.0%	100.0%	7.2	8.1	7.7

Table D.2.17. Extra-EU exports (million ECU)

Country	Actual			Deflated			Country share (%)			Real average annual change (%)		
	1978	1986	1993	1978	1986	1993	1978	1986	1993	78/86	86/93	78/93
FRG	36.2	98.4	197.5	56.0	56.4	169.7	16.4%	18.1%	22.6%	8.4	7.6	8.0
France	21.5	55.9	88.6	38.2	43.4	78.0	9.7%	10.3%	10.1%	6.6	3.4	5.1
Italy	10.1	41.0	112.8	19.9	26.3	122.7	4.6%	7.6%	12.9%	12.3	15.9	14.0
Netherlands	12.6	45.9	68.9	20.4	19.3	60.4	5.7%	8.5%	7.9%	12.4	3.8	8.4
Bel. & Lux.	6.9	26.6	59.4	12.0	12.2	53.1	3.1%	4.9%	6.8%	15.0	10.7	13.0
UK	72.2	93.2	146.1	145.9	126.8	134.2	32.6%	17.2%	16.7%	-3.3	3.4	-0.2
Ireland	1.5	1.7	1.4	2.5	1.9	1.4	0.7%	0.3%	0.2%	9.1	-2.4	3.8
Denmark	39.7	142.0	120.1	70.6	73.2	105.7	17.9%	26.2%	13.7%	11.3	-5.2	3.6
Spain	11.0	27.8	58.1	25.8	22.4	56.6	5.0%	5.1%	6.6%	17.1	7.3	12.5
Greece	8.3	7.5	17.9	14.4	14.0	14.2	3.7%	1.4%	2.0%	-5.3	16.3	4.8
Portugal	1.2	2.0	4.5	3.1	2.9	3.3	0.6%	0.4%	0.5%	5.1	14.3	9.4
Extra-EUR-12	221.2	542.8	875.1	408.6	398.7	799.2	100.0%	100.0%	100.0%	5.3	4.3	4.8

Table D.2.18. Trade ratio (extra-EU)

Country	1978	1979	1980	1981	1982	1983	1984	1985	1986	1987	1988	1989	1990	1991	1992	1993
FRG	0.25	0.21	0.29	0.29	0.35	0.43	0.42	0.47	0.35	0.36	0.34	0.38	0.38	0.44	0.40	0.40
France	0.76	0.68	0.68	0.65	0.60	0.59	0.52	0.35	0.25	0.15	0.15	0.17	0.28	0.38	0.35	0.39
Italy	0.70	0.71	0.69	0.73	0.61	0.70	0.75	0.75	0.66	0.54	0.46	0.54	0.61	0.62	0.69	0.77
Netherlands	0.58	0.36	0.45	0.50	0.64	0.73	0.78	0.72	0.63	0.58	0.52	0.48	0.52	0.53	0.47	0.55
Bel. & Lux.	0.59	0.52	0.64	0.66	0.74	0.82	0.86	0.81	0.72	0.59	0.55	0.71	0.71	0.72	0.76	0.82
UK	0.92	0.90	0.83	0.85	0.85	0.83	0.80	0.82	0.77	0.74	0.73	0.71	0.70	0.65	0.62	0.58
Ireland	0.67	0.60	0.50	0.68	0.29	0.33	0.47	0.48	0.55	0.26	0.37	0.30	0.22	0.00	-0.19	-0.07
Denmark	0.73	0.75	0.77	0.78	0.80	0.81	0.85	0.85	0.85	0.83	0.80	0.82	0.82	0.82	0.81	0.77
Spain	0.98	0.98	0.98	0.98	0.97	0.96	0.97	0.98	0.94	0.94	0.88	0.82	0.78	0.84	0.84	0.89
Greece	0.98	0.98	1.00	0.98	0.95	0.98	0.95	0.91	0.92	0.83	0.41	0.07	0.00	0.60	0.67	0.74
Portugal	1.00	1.00	1.00	1.00	1.00	1.00	1.00	1.00	1.00	1.00	0.89	0.91	0.87	0.80	0.69	0.67
EUR-12	0.69	0.64	0.66	0.67	0.68	0.71	0.71	0.70	0.61	0.55	0.52	0.54	0.55	0.58	0.57	0.59

Table D.2.19. Trade ratio (intra-EU)

Country	1978	1979	1980	1981	1982	1983	1984	1985	1986	1987	1988	1989	1990	1991	1992	1993
FRG	-0.34	-0.31	-0.29	-0.22	-0.10	-0.05	-0.02	0.06	0.14	0.17	0.11	0.24	0.18	0.11	0.03	0.06
France	-0.31	-0.25	-0.21	-0.19	-0.31	-0.35	-0.37	-0.37	-0.45	-0.46	-0.40	-0.42	-0.37	-0.36	-0.27	-0.21
Italy	-0.25	-0.18	-0.33	-0.37	-0.19	-0.10	0.04	-0.03	0.06	0.13	0.11	0.08	0.11	0.08	0.09	0.16
Netherlands	0.45	0.44	0.44	0.46	0.47	0.42	0.39	0.37	0.39	0.36	0.36	0.38	0.37	0.38	0.34	0.40
Bel. & Lux.	0.19	0.16	0.17	0.15	0.13	0.20	0.20	0.21	0.20	0.19	0.21	0.21	0.23	0.22	0.17	0.19
UK	0.41	0.44	0.33	0.08	-0.01	0.00	-0.01	0.02	-0.01	0.06	0.00	-0.07	-0.06	-0.08	-0.06	0.13
Ireland	-0.40	-0.47	-0.57	-0.55	-0.51	-0.49	-0.47	-0.47	-0.44	-0.57	-0.55	-0.52	-0.62	-0.66	-0.48	-0.44
Denmark	0.03	0.24	0.36	0.49	0.51	0.45	0.36	0.30	0.23	0.18	0.17	0.17	0.27	0.38	0.43	0.43
Spain	-0.15	-0.19	-0.39	0.07	-0.32	-0.29	-0.44	-0.26	-0.75	-0.81	-0.68	-0.64	-0.68	-0.49	-0.50	-0.25
Greece	-0.92	-0.88	-1.00	-0.91	-0.84	-0.43	-0.75	-0.78	-0.57	-0.47	-0.60	-0.73	-0.74	-0.74	-0.71	-0.67
Portugal	-0.89	-0.81	0.00	-1.00	-0.43	-0.33	-0.25	-0.25	-0.50	-0.70	-0.80	-0.87	-0.84	-0.84	-0.81	-0.64
EUR-12	0.01	0.02	0.01	0.00	0.00	0.01	0.00	0.01	0.00	0.01	-0.01	0.00	0.01	-0.01	-0.01	0.06

Table D.2.20. Intra-EU imports as % of total

Country	1978	1979	1980	1981	1982	1983	1984	1985	1986	1987	1988	1989	1990	1991	1992	1993
FRG	84.3	83.9	85.6	84.1	83.2	84.5	84.1	84.0	79.7	80.8	83.0	81.3	82.6	84.6	85.7	82.9
France	97.1	95.3	95.3	95.2	94.7	94.7	94.3	92.3	91.8	90.4	90.5	90.3	92.2	93.2	93.5	93.4
Italy	93.0	92.5	93.1	93.5	90.6	91.9	92.9	93.7	91.5	87.9	85.3	86.1	88.8	89.5	91.3	92.0
Netherlands	92.6	89.4	91.5	90.9	92.5	94.7	95.0	92.7	91.1	91.5	90.9	90.1	91.4	91.0	91.3	89.5
Bel. & Lux.	97.2	96.6	96.5	96.5	96.6	97.0	97.9	97.7	97.0	96.1	95.9	96.8	96.3	96.9	97.2	97.4
UK	88.7	87.8	84.4	90.0	91.5	90.6	89.6	89.6	89.9	89.5	90.0	90.0	90.0	89.9	90.0	86.5
Ireland	98.6	99.0	99.0	99.0	99.0	99.2	99.1	99.0	99.0	99.0	99.1	99.0	99.0	98.5	98.1	98.6
Denmark	65.9	67.3	68.5	65.7	65.0	65.6	70.7	70.4	74.6	76.8	77.4	78.7	79.0	79.0	79.2	75.5
Spain	95.0	95.0	95.3	94.6	94.9	90.5	96.6	91.7	96.3	97.1	96.6	93.8	93.8	95.7	96.0	96.8
Greece	94.0	94.2	90.0	95.7	94.4	93.8	96.9	94.7	92.3	93.0	88.1	78.4	79.1	90.1	89.5	90.2
Portugal	91.8	90.6	87.5	94.4	83.3	100.0	100.0	100.0	100.0	96.6	96.5	98.6	99.0	98.2	98.0	97.6
EUR-12	90.7	89.9	90.7	90.7	90.7	91.2	91.4	90.8	89.7	89.2	89.4	89.0	89.9	90.9	91.4	90.2

Table D.2.21. Intra-EU exports as % of total

Country	1978	1979	1980	1981	1982	1983	1984	1985	1986	1987	1988	1989	1990	1991	1992	1993
FRG	61.3	64.0	64.7	65.0	66.2	66.2	67.5	67.9	71.6	74.0	65.4	76.2	75.1	72.8	73.3	70.2
France	69.9	69.9	72.1	73.9	70.5	68.8	70.3	72.4	71.7	72.1	75.0	72.7	75.2	74.5	80.0	80.1
Italy	58.8	58.6	55.1	49.8	60.8	61.3	66.0	66.7	70.9	73.5	72.4	68.3	70.8	70.1	69.5	67.9
Netherlands	89.3	90.1	90.6	89.5	87.9	86.7	84.3	81.6	83.6	85.6	86.9	87.3	87.6	86.8	88.4	85.3
Bel. & Lux.	93.0	92.7	89.4	88.5	84.4	82.3	83.5	87.3	88.7	90.5	91.6	89.1	87.7	89.0	86.9	84.5
UK	43.9	50.5	49.5	46.2	46.4	47.4	47.9	47.8	53.2	58.7	58.8	56.8	59.2	61.8	65.1	69.0
Ireland	85.7	90.5	92.0	87.2	94.5	96.6	94.0	92.2	92.8	93.3	94.4	94.9	93.4	93.1	96.6	96.9
Denmark	24.6	32.6	38.0	41.2	38.9	34.0	29.8	25.6	27.3	30.7	35.3	33.8	39.6	45.3	50.5	49.8
Spain	20.2	17.9	12.9	30.5	11.9	11.7	12.5	9.4	10.9	11.6	24.7	24.7	25.9	39.3	41.6	51.8
Greece	0.9	1.6	0.0	1.1	3.8	12.6	9.8	9.5	14.6	30.2	42.9	33.0	36.1	25.3	22.6	22.5
Portugal	4.9	7.3	6.3	0.0	14.3	18.2	12.5	13.6	16.0	22.7	20.5	17.9	37.0	35.3	48.6	64.0
EUR-12	64.8	66.7	66.9	66.0	65.1	64.2	64.6	64.2	67.5	70.7	70.2	70.9	72.3	72.2	73.8	72.9

Table D.2.22. Import penetration ratios (extra-EU)

Country	1978	1979	1980	1981	1982	1983	1984	1985	1986	1987	1988	1989	1990	1991	1992	1993
FRG	1.1	1.1	0.9	1.1	1.1	1.0	1.1	1.1	1.4	1.4	1.3	1.3	1.3	1.2	1.4	1.5
France	0.3	0.4	0.4	0.5	0.6	0.6	0.8	1.1	1.3	1.6	1.5	1.5	1.2	1.0	1.1	1.0
Italy	0.2	0.2	0.2	0.3	0.4	0.3	0.3	0.4	0.5	0.7	1.0	0.8	0.7	0.7	0.6	0.5
Netherlands	0.6	0.9	0.8	0.9	0.7	0.5	0.5	0.9	1.3	1.2	1.3	1.4	1.4	1.5	1.8	1.8
Bel. & Lux.	0.6	0.7	0.9	0.9	0.9	0.8	0.6	0.7	0.9	1.2	1.0	0.8	1.1	1.0	1.0	0.9
UK	0.1	0.1	0.2	0.2	0.2	0.2	0.3	0.3	0.3	0.3	0.3	0.3	0.3	0.3	0.4	0.5
Ireland	0.2	0.2	0.1	0.2	0.2	0.1	0.2	0.2	0.2	0.3	0.2	0.3	0.3	0.5	0.8	0.6
Denmark	6.1	6.2	7.0	6.3	7.6	8.2	8.5	9.1	6.7	6.7	6.1	5.2	4.2	4.2	4.2	5.7
Spain	0.0	0.0	0.0	0.0	0.0	0.0	0.0	0.0	0.0	0.0	0.1	0.1	0.1	0.1	0.1	0.1
Greece	0.2	0.2	0.0	0.2	0.3	0.1	0.3	0.5	0.3	0.6	1.1	3.6	4.0	1.7	1.7	1.4
Portugal	0.0	0.0	0.0	0.0	0.0	0.0	0.0	0.0	0.0	0.0	0.1	0.1	0.1	0.1	0.2	0.2
EUR-12	0.4	0.5	0.4	0.5	0.5	0.5	0.5	0.6	0.8	0.8	0.8	0.8	0.8	0.7	0.8	0.8

Table D.2.23. Import penetration ratios (intra-EU)

Country	1978	1979	1980	1981	1982	1983	1984	1985	1986	1987	1988	1989	1990	1991	1992	1993
FRG	5.7	5.9	5.6	6.0	5.5	5.3	5.7	5.6	5.6	5.9	6.4	5.7	6.1	6.6	8.4	7.5
France	9.3	9.0	8.9	9.3	10.4	11.3	12.8	13.3	14.8	14.8	14.2	14.3	14.5	14.1	15.4	14.6
Italy	2.8	2.9	3.2	3.8	4.2	3.9	3.3	5.3	5.0	5.3	5.6	5.2	5.5	5.9	6.6	6.2
Netherlands	7.2	7.5	8.9	9.0	8.2	8.8	10.5	11.4	12.9	13.1	13.3	13.2	14.4	14.9	18.4	15.4
Bel. & Lux.	20.7	20.9	23.5	25.4	26.5	26.7	26.1	28.8	30.0	29.4	26.0	26.2	28.1	32.0	35.0	34.6
UK	0.9	0.9	1.1	1.7	2.0	2.1	2.2	2.2	2.3	2.2	2.4	2.7	2.9	3.1	3.9	3.1
Ireland	13.4	15.5	17.4	20.1	20.0	21.3	20.7	21.3	20.6	24.0	26.8	29.7	30.4	34.7	39.4	40.7
Denmark	11.9	12.7	15.1	12.1	14.0	15.6	20.8	21.6	19.8	22.1	21.0	19.2	16.0	15.6	16.1	17.7
Spain	0.3	0.3	0.2	0.2	0.2	0.2	0.1	0.1	0.9	1.3	1.6	1.5	1.7	2.1	2.8	2.5
Greece	5.1	5.2	1.9	4.0	5.3	4.4	7.8	8.2	5.2	8.3	8.5	13.2	15.3	15.4	15.1	13.0
Portugal	0.6	0.5	0.4	0.7	0.2	0.1	0.2	0.2	0.4	0.9	2.6	4.2	5.2	7.2	8.5	8.8
EUR-12	4.4	4.4	4.3	4.7	4.9	5.2	5.6	6.1	6.7	6.9	6.7	6.5	6.9	7.1	8.5	7.7

Table D.2.24. Intra-EU exports as a % of production

Country	1978	1979	1980	1981	1982	1983	1984	1985	1986	1987	1988	1989	1990	1991	1992	1993
FRG	2.9	3.1	3.1	3.9	4.5	4.8	5.4	6.2	7.2	8.1	7.5	8.9	8.3	8.0	8.8	8.2
France	5.0	5.5	5.9	6.4	5.7	5.7	6.2	6.5	6.1	6.0	6.6	6.3	7.1	7.1	9.4	9.8
Italy	1.7	2.0	1.6	1.8	2.8	3.2	3.5	4.9	5.6	6.7	6.8	6.0	6.7	6.7	7.6	8.1
Netherlands	16.8	16.9	19.9	20.6	19.4	18.6	20.3	21.1	24.2	23.5	24.0	24.6	26.1	27.4	30.5	28.7
Bel. & Lux.	27.3	26.4	29.5	30.6	30.5	33.1	32.7	36.5	37.5	36.8	34.2	34.1	36.8	40.6	40.9	41.0
UK	2.0	2.3	2.1	1.9	1.9	2.1	2.1	2.3	2.2	2.5	2.4	2.3	2.6	2.6	3.4	4.0
Ireland	6.2	6.2	5.4	6.8	7.6	8.5	8.5	8.9	9.1	7.9	9.5	11.7	9.3	9.9	18.8	21.2
Denmark	9.4	14.3	19.9	21.2	22.8	20.8	20.3	17.7	16.6	18.3	18.9	17.4	18.7	22.0	25.4	26.8
Spain	0.2	0.2	0.1	0.2	0.1	0.1	0.0	0.1	0.1	0.1	0.3	0.3	0.3	0.7	0.9	1.5
Greece	0.2	0.3	0.0	0.2	0.4	1.6	1.1	1.0	1.4	3.0	2.2	2.3	2.6	2.5	2.7	2.7
Portugal	0.0	0.0	0.1	0.0	0.1	0.1	0.1	0.1	0.1	0.2	0.3	0.3	0.5	0.7	0.9	2.0
EUR-12	4.4	4.5	4.4	4.6	4.8	5.1	5.5	6.0	6.5	6.8	6.4	6.4	6.8	6.9	8.2	8.4

Table D.2.25. Extra-EU exports as a % of production

Country	1978	1979	1980	1981	1982	1983	1984	1985	1986	1987	1988	1989	1990	1991	1992	1993
FRG	1.8	1.8	1.7	2.1	2.3	2.4	2.6	2.9	2.9	2.8	2.5	2.8	2.8	3.0	3.2	3.5
France	2.2	2.3	2.3	2.3	2.4	2.6	2.6	2.5	2.4	2.3	2.2	2.3	2.3	2.4	2.3	2.4
Italy	1.2	1.4	1.3	1.8	1.7	1.9	1.8	2.4	2.3	2.4	2.5	2.7	2.8	2.9	3.3	3.8
Netherlands	1.9	1.7	1.9	2.3	2.5	2.7	3.7	4.7	4.6	3.8	3.5	3.5	3.6	4.0	4.0	5.0
Bel. & Lux.	2.0	2.1	3.5	3.9	5.6	7.1	6.5	5.3	4.8	3.9	3.1	4.2	5.1	5.0	6.2	7.5
UK	2.6	2.2	2.1	2.2	2.2	2.3	2.3	2.5	2.0	1.7	1.7	1.8	1.8	1.6	1.8	1.8
Ireland	1.0	0.7	0.5	1.0	0.4	0.3	0.5	0.7	0.7	0.5	0.6	0.6	0.6	0.7	0.7	0.7
Denmark	29.0	29.7	32.5	30.2	35.8	40.4	47.6	51.5	44.3	41.1	34.7	34.0	28.4	26.7	24.9	27.0
Spain	0.9	0.8	0.6	0.4	0.6	0.8	0.3	0.5	1.1	1.0	0.9	1.0	0.9	1.1	1.3	1.4
Greece	20.2	17.0	13.9	14.8	11.3	10.9	10.0	9.6	7.9	6.7	2.9	4.7	4.6	7.3	9.2	9.3
Portugal	0.6	0.6	0.7	0.4	0.5	0.3	0.7	0.6	0.6	0.5	1.1	1.4	0.8	1.2	1.0	1.1
EUR-12	2.3	2.2	2.1	2.3	2.5	2.8	3.0	3.3	3.1	2.8	2.4	2.6	2.6	2.7	2.9	3.1

Figure D.2.1. Intra/extra-EU exports

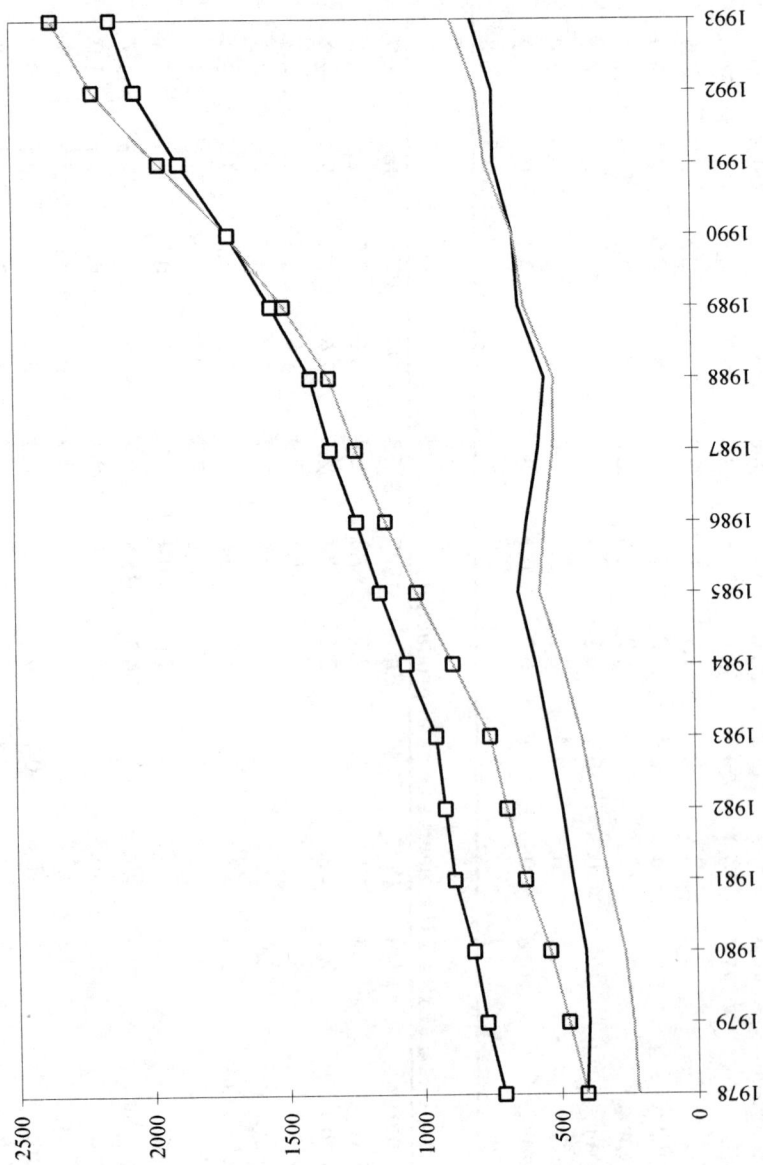

Legend:
- Intra-EU(12) deflated
- Extra-EU(12) deflated
- INTRA-EU(12)
- EXTRA-EU(12)

Note: 1978, 1979 are estimated figures (estimates for Spain, Greece and Portugal).

Figure D.2.2. EU exports 1978

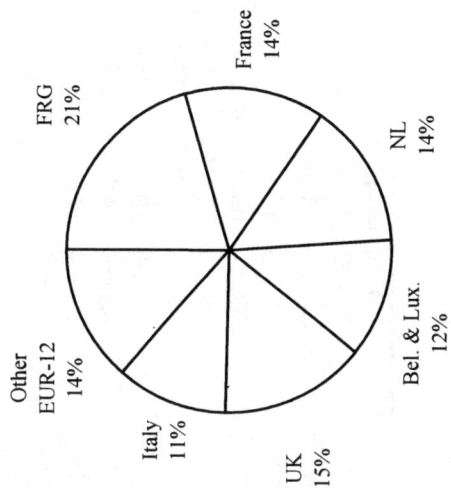

Figure D.2.3. EU exports 1993

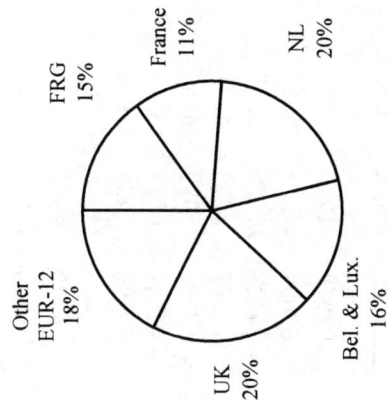

Note: Intra- and extra-EU exports.

D.3. NACE 421

4210 Manufacture of cocoa, chocolate and sugar confectionery

Table D.3.1. Number of enterprises

Country	1978	1986	1993	Country share (%)			Total change (%)		
				1978	1986	1993	78/86	86/93	78/93
FRG	148	143	141	7.3%	9.3%	12.0%	-3.4%	-1.3%	-4.6%
France	155	127	124	7.6%	8.3%	10.5%	-18.1%	-2.7%	-20.3%
Italy	102	19	17	5.0%	1.2%	1.5%	-81.4%	-9.9%	-83.2%
Netherlands	55	47	41	2.7%	3.1%	3.5%	-14.5%	-12.6%	-25.3%
Belgium	51	53	57	2.5%	3.5%	4.8%	3.9%	7.7%	11.9%
UK	127	129	121	6.3%	8.4%	10.3%	1.6%	-5.9%	-4.4%
Ireland	22	14	11	1.1%	0.9%	0.9%	-36.4%	-20.2%	-49.2%
Denmark	27	27	28	1.3%	1.8%	2.3%	0.0%	2.0%	2.0%
Spain	1203	864	538	59.3%	56.4%	45.5%	-28.2%	-37.8%	-55.3%
Greece			33			2.8%			
Portugal	140	109	69	6.9%	7.1%	5.9%	-21.9%	-36.4%	-50.3%
EUR-12	2030	1532	1180	100.0%	100.0%	100.0%	-24.5%	-23.0%	-41.9%

Table D.3.2. Number of persons employed, excluding home workers

Country	1978	1986	1993	Country share (%)			Total change (%)		
				1978	1986	1993	78/86	86/93	78/93
FRG	53009	44213	45817	22.9%	26.8%	28.9%	-16.6%	3.6%	-13.6%
France	34123	27586	23258	14.7%	16.8%	14.7%	-19.2%	-15.7%	-31.8%
Italy	26397	2902	5291	11.4%	1.8%	3.3%	-89.0%	82.3%	-80.0%
Netherlands	7793	7080	6969	3.4%	4.3%	4.4%	-9.1%	-1.6%	-10.6%
Belgium	7467	6915	6579	3.2%	4.2%	4.2%	-7.4%	-4.9%	-11.9%
UK	69992	46456	41916	30.2%	28.2%	26.5%	-33.6%	-9.8%	-40.1%
Ireland	7466	5556	3552	3.2%	3.4%	2.2%	-25.6%	-36.1%	-52.4%
Denmark	4479	5978	6250	1.9%	3.6%	3.9%	33.5%	4.5%	39.5%
Spain	16276	14675	13709	7.0%	8.9%	8.7%	-9.8%	-6.6%	-15.8%
Greece			3263			2.1%			
Portugal	4558	3329	1803	2.0%	2.0%	1.1%	-27.0%	-45.8%	-60.4%
EUR-12	231560	164690	158407	100.0%	100.0%	100.0%	-28.9%	-3.8%	-31.6%
USA	56734	56395	61610				-0.6%	9.2%	8.6%

Table D.3.3. Production value, excluding VAT

Country	Actual 1978	Actual 1986	Actual 1993	Deflated 1978	Deflated 1986	Deflated 1993	Country share (%) 1978	Country share (%) 1986	Country share (%) 1993	Real average annual change (%) 78/86	Real average annual change (%) 86/93	Real average annual change (%) 78/93
FRG	3263	5145	7131	4271	5034	6460	28.7%	29.4%	29.9%	2.3	3.9	3.0
France	2066	3523	4618	3290	3662	4069	18.2%	20.1%	19.4%	1.6	1.7	1.6
Italy	1194	418	1039	1915	437	1115	10.5%	2.4%	4.4%	-8.0	19.6	4.9
Netherlands	916	1517	1732	1333	1602	1549	8.1%	8.7%	7.3%	2.5	-0.4	1.1
Belgium	439	912	1109	614	911	969	3.9%	5.2%	4.7%	5.2	1.1	3.3
UK	2224	3665	4851	3822	3814	4651	19.6%	20.9%	20.4%	0.1	3.4	1.6
Ireland	307	474	580	440	496	553	2.7%	2.7%	2.4%	1.9	1.7	1.8
Denmark	203	559	807	322	581	711	1.8%	3.2%	3.4%	7.8	3.0	5.6
Spain	625	1060	1605	1230	1252	1691	5.5%	6.1%	6.7%	0.4	4.8	2.5
Greece	67	160	266	92	157	223	0.6%	0.9%	1.1%	8.5	5.5	7.1
Portugal	60	84	86	148	103	63	0.5%	0.5%	0.4%	-3.2	-6.5	-4.8
EUR-12	11364	17517	23824	17477	18049	22055	100.0%	100.0%	100.0%	0.5	3.0	1.7
USA	5191	11028	12959	9167		11328				1.4	3.2	2.8

Table D.3.4. Production value per enterprise

Country	Actual 1978	Actual 1986	Actual 1993	Deflated 1978	Deflated 1986	Deflated 1993
FRG	22.0	36.0	50.5	28.9	35.2	45.8
France	13.3	27.7	37.4	21.2	28.8	32.9
Italy	11.7	22.0	60.7	18.8	23.0	65.1
Netherlands	16.7	32.3	42.2	24.2	34.1	37.7
Belgium	8.6	17.2	19.4	12.0	17.2	17.0
UK	17.5	28.4	40.0	30.1	29.6	38.3
Ireland	14.0	33.9	51.9	20.0	35.4	49.5
Denmark	7.5	20.7	29.3	11.9	21.5	25.8
Spain	0.5	1.2	3.0	1.0	1.4	3.1
Greece			7.9			6.7
Portugal	0.4	0.8	1.2	1.1	0.9	0.9
EUR-12	5.6	11.4	20.2	8.6	11.8	18.7

Table D.3.5. Consumption value

Country	Actual			Deflated			Country share (%)			Real average annual change (%)		
	1978	1986	1993	1978	1986	1993	1978	1986	1993	78/86	86/93	78/93
FRG	3344	5051	7021	4441	5058	5858	30.3%	30.1%	31.6%	1.8	2.5	2.1
France	2243	3765	4690	4458	3667	3735	20.3%	22.4%	21.1%	-2.3	0.4	-1.0
Italy	1163	414	883	3080	391	574	10.5%	2.5%	4.0%	-13.6	11.1	-2.1
Netherlands	458	759	954	625	758	833	4.1%	4.5%	4.3%	2.6	2.0	2.3
Bel. & Lux.	468	756	624	733	747	517	4.2%	4.5%	2.8%	97.4	-4.5	49.9
UK	2204	3836	4814	4173	3710	3238	20.0%	22.8%	21.7%	-1.4	-1.6	-1.5
Ireland	254	421	512	606	405	404	2.3%	2.5%	2.3%	-4.6	0.5	-2.2
Denmark	203	531	721	365	512	562	1.8%	3.2%	3.2%	4.9	1.4	3.2
Spain	563	989	1522	1327	909	948	5.1%	5.9%	6.9%	-4.2	1.1	-1.8
Greece	78	173	291	295	141	83	0.7%	1.0%	1.3%	-8.3	-7.1	-7.7
Portugal	68	99	172	280	89	78	0.6%	0.6%	0.8%	-12.2	-1.8	-7.4
EUR-12	11045	16794	22203	20384	16387	16828	100.0%	100.0%	100.0%	-2.6	0.5	-1.2

Table D.3.6. Labour costs

Country	Actual			Deflated			Country share (%)		
	1978	1986	1993	1978	1986	1993	1978	1986	1993
FRG	596	871	1235	780	852	1119	28.7%	28.6%	29.8%
France	388	663	854	617	689	753	18.7%	21.8%	20.6%
Italy	255	64	46	408	67	50	12.3%	2.1%	1.1%
Netherlands	116	181	240	169	191	214	5.6%	5.9%	5.8%
Belgium	101	136	171	141	136	150	4.9%	4.5%	4.1%
UK	398	706	950	683	735	911	19.2%	23.2%	22.9%
Ireland	56	121	138	80	126	131	2.7%	4.0%	3.3%
Denmark	58	125	179	93	130	157	2.8%	4.1%	4.3%
Spain	95	165	268	186	195	282	4.6%	5.4%	6.5%
Greece			49			41			1.2%
Portugal	13	14	14	32	18	10	0.6%	0.5%	0.3%
EU (average)	136	234	357	319	314	347			
EUR-12	2075	3046	4143	3191	3139	3818	100.0%	100.0%	100.0%

Table D.3.7.   Gross value added at factor cost

Country	Actual			Deflated			Country share (%)			Real average annual change (%)		
	1978	1986	1993	1978	1986	1993	1978	1986	1993	78/86	86/93	78/93
FRG	836	1216	1769	1095	1190	1602	27.4%	25.6%	24.9%	1.3	4.8	3.0
France	535	1062	1447	851	1104	1275	17.5%	22.4%	20.4%	3.8	2.1	3.1
Italy	367	133	151	589	139	162	12.0%	2.8%	2.1%	-6.0	8.9	1.0
Netherlands	158	278	430	230	293	385	5.2%	5.9%	6.1%	3.5	4.1	3.8
Belgium	139	206	280	193	206	245	4.5%	4.3%	4.0%	1.2	2.9	2.0
UK	680	1251	1797	1169	1301	1723	22.3%	26.4%	25.3%	1.5	4.5	2.9
Ireland			214			204			3.0%		2.6	2.6
Denmark	73	198	348	116	206	306	2.4%	4.2%	4.9%	8.1	6.7	7.4
Spain	263	403	599	517	476	631	8.6%	8.5%	8.4%	-0.8	4.7	1.8
Greece			58			49			0.8%		2.2	2.2
EUR-12	3050	4745	7091	4760	4914	6580	100.0%	100.0%	100.0%	0.6	4.4	2.4
USA	1930	4701	6456	1930	3908	5644				3.9	5.9	5.4

Table D.3.8.   Gross value added per person employed (in 000 ECU)

Country	Actual			Deflated		
	1978	1986	1993	1978	1986	1993
FRG	15.8	27.5	38.6	20.7	26.9	35.0
France	15.7	38.5	62.2	25.0	40.0	54.8
Italy	13.9	45.8	28.5	22.3	47.9	30.5
Netherlands	20.2	39.2	61.7	29.5	41.4	55.2
Belgium	18.5	29.8	42.6	25.9	29.7	37.3
UK	9.7	26.9	42.9	16.7	28.0	41.1
Ireland			60.2			57.4
Denmark	16.2	33.1	55.6	25.8	34.4	49.0
Spain	16.1	27.5	43.7	31.8	32.4	46.0
Greece			17.8			14.9
EUR-12	13.2	28.8	44.8	20.6	29.8	41.5
USA	34.0	83.4	104.8		69.3	91.6

Table D.3.9. Investment

Country	Actual 1978	Actual 1986	Actual 1993	Deflated 1978	Deflated 1986	Deflated 1993	Country share (%) 1978	Country share (%) 1986	Country share (%) 1993
FRG	117	198	347	153	193	314	28.5%	28.7%	30.2%
France	57	153	227	90	159	200	13.8%	22.2%	19.8%
Italy	38	29	51	60	30	55	9.1%	4.2%	4.5%
Netherlands	25	69	62	37	73	56	6.1%	10.0%	5.4%
Belgium	27	30	82	38	30	71	6.6%	4.3%	7.1%
UK	108	165	289	185	172	277	26.2%	23.9%	25.2%
Ireland	19	19	27	28	20	26	4.7%	2.8%	2.3%
Denmark	20	27	45	32	28	40	4.9%	3.9%	3.9%
Greece			17			14			1.5%
EUR-12	411	689	1147	623	705	1053	100.0%	100.0%	100.0%
EU (average)	51	86	127	78	88	117			
USA	121	342			284				

Table D.3.10. Proportion of investments in gross value added at factor cost (in %)

Country	1978	1979	1980	1981	1982	1983	1984	1985	1986	1987	1988	1989	1990	1991	1992	1993
FRG	14.0	15.9	15.1	14.5	13.9	15.5	13.5	14.2	16.2	12.7	16.2	17.8	21.3	22.6	19.5	19.6
France	10.6	9.9	10.2	9.1	10.6	12.3	13.7	15.6	14.4	11.5	13.9	14.3	14.7	16.7	15.5	15.7
Italy	10.2	11.6	14.9	12.9	10.8	29.5	34.5	17.3	21.8	18.5	17.1	11.1	31.8	30.5	30.3	33.9
Netherlands	15.9	22.3	11.1	11.1	13.8	27.5	14.4	21.7	24.8	14.5	15.5	12.0	8.8	17.0	14.6	14.5
Belgium	19.7	14.3	11.2	11.9	12.8	11.6	14.1	12.3	14.5	18.8	30.1	36.3	50.6	27.5	28.3	29.1
UK	15.8	15.6	13.5	13.7	17.2	16.8	15.1	15.3	13.2	13.4	13.5	15.5	17.5	17.7	16.0	16.1
Ireland											16.6	14.1	14.9	13.3	12.9	12.5
Denmark	27.5	16.9	14.6	13.9	12.9	13.9	18.8	17.0	13.6	12.7	13.8	10.3	13.8	14.9	16.8	12.9
Greece										44.1	33.6	33.1	23.1	39.4	30.1	29.0
EU (average)	16.3	15.2	12.9	12.4	13.1	18.2	17.7	16.2	16.9	18.3	18.9	18.3	21.8	22.2	20.5	20.4
USA	6.3	5.4	6.3	5.2	6.4	6.4	6.6	5.4	7.3	6.6	6.5	7.7	7.4	7.2	9.2	

Table D.3.11. Producer price index

Country	1978	1979	1980	1981	1982	1983	1984	1985	1986	1987	1988	1989	1990	1991	1992	1993
FRG	76.4	77.2	78.7	80.1	87.0	93.0	96.1	98.7	102.2	103.0	101.1	99.5	100.0	101.5	105.0	110.4
France	62.8	66.1	65.6	71.5	75.5	77.6	84.0	90.6	96.2	96.6	95.6	96.9	100.0	103.1	107.4	113.5
Italy	62.3	65.7	69.1	67.7	71.3	78.1	87.2	92.7	95.6	95.4	94.0	98.5	100.0	103.9	103.6	93.2
Netherlands	68.7	68.2	68.0	69.5	77.3	83.1	88.8	90.9	94.7	95.9	95.7	97.5	100.0	102.3	106.2	111.8
Bel. & Lux.	71.6	74.3	75.9	77.6	75.2	80.5	93.2	100.4	100.1	98.3	96.9	97.4	100.0	104.0	108.5	114.4
UK	58.2	66.5	81.3	94.9	96.7	96.1	99.6	105.2	96.1	94.2	100.3	101.6	100.0	107.4	106.3	104.3
Ireland	69.8	72.5	66.7	75.0	83.6	85.9	90.5	95.2	95.7	91.8	95.6	97.0	100.0	102.8	105.4	104.8
Denmark	62.8	66.1	65.6	71.5	75.5	77.6	84.0	90.6	96.2	96.6	95.6	96.9	100.0	103.1	107.4	113.5
Spain	50.8	58.9	59.4	63.1	68.3	66.9	79.7	86.2	84.7	85.3	90.0	96.8	100.0	102.1	103.7	94.9
Greece	72.2	63.9	64.6	75.3	82.3	90.5	99.3	103.7	101.6	88.1	90.3	95.2	100.0	106.3	111.6	119.2
Portugal	40.8	42.1	47.3	57.6	65.2	63.7	70.0	82.0	81.5	82.0	80.1	86.3	100.0	121.5	140.3	136.0
USA							147.2	153.4	120.3	104.0	101.3	112.5	100.0	105.9	101.3	114.4

Table D.3.12. Total imports (million ECU)

Country	Actual			Deflated			Country share (%)			Real average annual change (%)		
	1978	1986	1993	1978	1986	1993	1978	1986	1993	78/86	86/93	78/93
FRG	408.3	674.7	945.9	534.4	660.2	856.8	23.7%	22.3%	21.5%	3.2	4.4	3.8
France	383.5	618.1	891.3	610.7	642.5	785.3	22.3%	20.4%	20.3%	1.0	3.0	1.9
Italy	77.5	226.3	292.7	124.3	236.7	314.1	4.5%	7.5%	6.7%	9.4	4.2	7.0
Netherlands	216.5	342.0	537.0	315.1	361.1	480.3	12.6%	11.3%	12.2%	3.0	5.0	3.9
Bel. & Lux.	176.8	273.6	393.9	246.9	273.3	344.3	10.3%	9.0%	9.0%	1.5	3.5	2.4
UK	319.7	584.4	654.6	549.3	608.1	627.6	18.6%	19.3%	14.9%	2.6	0.6	1.7
Ireland	46.5	115.2	150.7	66.6	120.4	143.8	2.7%	3.8%	3.4%	8.3	2.7	5.7
Denmark	55.4	94.5	158.1	88.2	98.2	139.3	3.2%	3.1%	3.6%	1.5	5.3	3.3
Spain	11.8	55.8	210.8	23.2	65.9	222.1	0.7%	1.8%	4.8%	19.8	19.1	19.5
Greece	16.1	24.5	68.0	22.3	24.1	57.0	0.9%	0.8%	1.5%	4.9	16.4	10.3
Portugal	8.4	17.7	90.1	20.5	21.7	66.3	0.5%	0.6%	2.1%	2.8	20.9	11.3
Total EUR-12	1720.5	3027.2	4393.1	2601.6	3112.3	4036.9	100.0%	100.0%	100.0%	2.6	3.9	3.2

Table D.3.13. Intra-EU imports (million ECU)

Country	Actual			Deflated			Country share (%)			Real average annual change (%)		
	1978	1986	1993	1978	1986	1993	1978	1986	1993	78/86	86/93	78/93
FRG	356.7	450.6	758.5	466.9	440.9	687.0	28.1%	19.1%	20.2%	0.2	7.8	3.8
France	226.5	486.6	793.5	360.7	505.8	699.1	17.8%	20.6%	21.2%	4.6	4.8	4.7
Italy	61.3	195.7	258.5	98.3	204.7	277.4	4.8%	8.3%	6.9%	10.6	4.5	7.8
Netherlands	160.2	272.7	412.9	233.2	288.0	369.3	12.6%	11.6%	11.0%	3.5	5.0	4.2
Bel. & Lux.	171.4	260.2	376.9	239.3	259.9	329.5	13.5%	11.0%	10.1%	1.3	3.5	2.3
UK	184.3	435.3	557.1	316.7	453.0	534.1	14.5%	18.5%	14.9%	5.5	2.5	4.1
Ireland	45.2	113.8	144.8	64.7	118.9	138.2	3.6%	4.8%	3.9%	8.7	2.3	5.7
Denmark	38.3	64.7	114.5	61.0	67.3	100.9	3.0%	2.7%	3.1%	1.6	6.3	3.8
Spain	8.8	39.3	180.9	17.3	46.4	190.6	0.7%	1.7%	4.8%	24.1	22.5	23.4
Greece	15.3	23.9	64.9	21.2	23.5	54.4	1.2%	1.0%	1.7%	5.4	15.7	10.2
Portugal	1.7	13.7	86.7	4.1	16.8	63.8	0.1%	0.6%	2.3%	30.5	26.7	28.7
Intra-EUR-12	1269.6	2356.5	3749.2	1883.4	2425.2	3444.3	100.0%	100.0%	100.0%	3.5	5.4	4.4

Table D.3.14. Extra-EU imports (million ECU)

Country	Actual			Deflated			Country share (%)			Real average annual change (%)		
	1978	1986	1993	1978	1986	1993	1978	1986	1993	78/86	86/93	78/93
FRG	51.6	96.3	187.4	67.5	94.2	169.7	11.4%	17.8%	29.1%	6.1	9.6	7.7
France	157.0	131.5	97.8	250.0	136.7	86.2	34.8%	24.3%	15.2%	-6.3	-5.5	-5.9
Italy	16.2	30.5	34.2	26.0	31.9	36.7	3.6%	5.6%	5.3%	3.4	2.1	2.8
Netherlands	56.3	69.2	124.1	82.0	73.1	111.0	12.5%	12.8%	19.3%	4.5	7.5	5.9
Bel. & Lux.	5.3	13.4	17.0	7.4	13.4	14.9	1.2%	2.5%	2.6%	9.6	4.6	7.3
UK	135.5	149.0	97.4	232.8	155.0	93.4	30.1%	27.5%	15.1%	-2.6	-5.6	-4.0
Ireland	1.3	1.3	5.9	1.9	1.4	5.6	0.3%	0.2%	0.9%	24.6	26.3	25.4
Denmark	17.2	29.8	43.6	27.4	31.0	38.4	3.8%	5.5%	6.8%	1.7	3.6	2.5
Spain	3.0	16.4	30.0	5.9	19.4	31.6	0.7%	3.0%	4.7%	20.0	7.8	14.3
Greece	0.8	0.5	3.1	1.0	0.5	2.6	0.2%	0.1%	0.5%	-3.5	51.1	22.0
Portugal	6.6	3.9	3.4	16.3	4.8	2.5	1.5%	0.7%	0.5%	-11.7	-6.8	-9.4
Extra-EUR-12	450.8	541.8	643.9	718.2	561.3	592.6	100.0%	100.0%	100.0%	-2.1	1.1	-0.6

Table D.3.15. Total exports (million ECU)

Country	Actual			Deflated			Country share (%)			Real average annual change (%)		
	1978	1986	1993	1978	1986	1993	1978	1986	1993	78/86	86/93	78/93
FRG	327.5	768.0	1056.4	428.7	751.5	956.9	16.1%	20.5%	17.6%	7.9	3.8	6.0
France	206.5	376.8	819.9	328.8	391.7	392.9	10.1%	10.0%	13.6%	2.6	9.5	5.8
Italy	108.4	230.2	448.8	173.9	240.8	382.8	5.3%	6.1%	7.5%	5.5	10.7	7.9
Netherlands	674.6	1099.7	1314.8	982.0	1161.2	409.7	33.1%	29.3%	21.9%	2.6	0.4	1.6
Bel. & Lux.	147.8	428.9	879.2	206.4	428.5	342.5	7.2%	11.4%	14.6%	9.6	8.8	9.3
UK	340.3	413.0	691.8	584.7	429.8	432.7	16.7%	11.0%	11.5%	-3.4	6.4	1.2
Ireland	99.9	168.9	218.4	143.1	176.5	44.5	4.9%	4.5%	3.6%	3.1	2.8	2.9
Denmark	55.1	122.6	243.9	87.7	127.4	210.4	2.7%	3.3%	4.1%	4.9	8.3	6.5
Spain	73.6	127.3	293.9	144.9	150.3	117.3	3.6%	3.4%	4.9%	5.5	10.9	8.1
Greece	4.9	11.1	42.3	6.8	10.9	18.3	0.2%	0.3%	0.7%	17.5	22.1	19.6
Portugal	0.8	2.6	4.9	2.0	3.2	9.2	0.0%	0.1%	0.1%	13.5	8.5	11.1
Total EUR-12	2039.5	3749.6	6014.1	3089.0	3871.8	2929.7	100.0%	100.0%	100.0%	3.1	5.3	4.1

Table D.3.16. Intra-EU exports (million ECU)

Country	Actual			Deflated			Country share (%)			Real average annual change (%)		
	1978	1986	1993	1978	1986	1993	1978	1986	1993	78/86	86/93	78/93
FRG	186.3	476.1	581.9	243.8	465.9	527.1	14.8%	19.3%	14.7%	9.1	2.1	5.8
France	153.9	277.9	618.3	245.1	288.9	544.8	12.3%	11.3%	15.6%	2.4	9.9	5.9
Italy	82.5	169.6	303.9	132.3	177.4	326.1	6.6%	6.9%	7.7%	4.7	9.3	6.9
Netherlands	425.1	773.0	873.0	618.8	816.3	780.9	33.9%	31.3%	22.1%	3.9	-0.5	1.9
Bel. & Lux.	138.3	373.3	770.5	193.1	372.9	673.5	11.0%	15.1%	19.5%	8.7	8.9	8.8
UK	145.4	179.0	343.2	249.8	186.3	329.1	11.6%	7.3%	8.7%	-3.2	8.6	2.3
Ireland	90.4	150.7	196.2	129.5	157.5	187.2	7.2%	6.1%	5.0%	3.0	3.0	3.0
Denmark	6.4	29.2	116.5	10.2	30.4	102.6	0.5%	1.2%	2.9%	15.5	20.2	17.7
Spain	26.3	34.7	129.1	51.8	41.0	136.0	2.1%	1.4%	3.3%	-1.9	19.3	8.0
Greece	0.9	4.2	17.5	1.2	4.1	14.7	0.1%	0.2%	0.4%	144.7	25.1	88.9
Portugal	0.1	0.5	2.0	0.2	0.6	1.5	0.0%	0.0%	0.1%	58.1	31.9	45.8
Intra-EUR-12	1255.6	2468.6	3952.0	1875.9	2541.1	3623.4	100.0%	100.0%	100.0%	4.1	5.3	4.6

Table D.3.17. Extra-EU exports (million ECU)

Country	Actual			Deflated			Country share (%)			Real average annual change (%)		
	1978	1986	1993	1978	1986	1993	1978	1986	1993	78/86	86/93	78/93
FRG	141.2	291.9	474.5	184.8	285.6	429.8	18.6%	23.7%	23.0%	6.6	6.7	6.7
France	52.6	98.8	201.6	83.8	102.7	177.6	6.9%	8.0%	9.8%	3.3	8.7	5.8
Italy	26.0	59.8	144.8	41.7	62.6	155.4	3.4%	4.9%	7.0%	9.2	16.2	12.5
Netherlands	249.5	305.6	441.8	363.2	322.7	395.2	32.8%	24.8%	21.4%	-0.1	3.8	1.7
Bel. & Lux.	9.5	55.5	108.7	13.3	55.4	95.0	1.2%	4.5%	5.3%	20.8	8.4	15.0
UK	194.9	233.9	348.5	334.9	243.4	334.1	25.6%	19.0%	16.9%	-3.4	4.8	0.5
Ireland	9.5	18.1	22.2	13.6	18.9	21.2	1.2%	1.5%	1.1%	4.9	2.8	3.9
Denmark	27.8	65.8	127.3	44.3	68.4	112.2	3.7%	5.3%	6.2%	5.8	8.5	7.1
Spain	45.1	91.3	164.8	88.8	107.8	173.7	5.9%	7.4%	8.0%	18.8	7.3	13.5
Greece	4.0	6.8	24.7	5.5	6.7	20.7	0.5%	0.6%	1.2%	10.6	24.7	17.2
Portugal	0.7	2.1	2.9	1.7	2.6	2.1	0.1%	0.2%	0.1%	12.5	3.5	8.3
Extra-EUR-12	760.7	1230.2	2062.0	1175.4	1276.8	1917.0	100.0%	100.0%	100.0%	1.7	6.3	3.9

Table D.3.18. Trade ratios (extra-EU)

Country	1978	1979	1980	1981	1982	1983	1984	1985	1986	1987	1988	1989	1990	1991	1992	1993
FRG	0.46	0.26	0.19	0.31	0.36	0.34	0.32	0.40	0.50	0.45	0.47	0.50	0.47	0.41	0.51	0.43
France	-0.50	-0.39	-0.41	-0.28	-0.16	-0.15	-0.17	-0.13	-0.14	-0.20	-0.01	0.12	0.27	0.20	0.29	0.35
Italy	0.23	0.37	0.19	0.44	0.40	0.41	0.42	0.36	0.32	0.31	0.32	0.34	0.50	0.42	0.47	0.62
Netherlands	0.63	0.46	0.51	0.59	0.54	0.58	0.51	0.51	0.63	0.62	0.57	0.59	0.47	0.52	0.55	0.56
Bel. & Lux.	0.28	0.25	0.45	0.55	0.57	0.61	0.72	0.64	0.61	0.65	0.72	0.69	0.74	0.69	0.64	0.73
UK	0.18	0.17	0.30	0.43	0.39	0.36	0.39	0.35	0.22	0.39	0.38	0.43	0.45	0.55	0.57	0.56
Ireland	0.76	0.58	0.88	0.80	0.63	0.54	0.57	0.87	0.87	0.79	0.77	0.52	0.48	0.48	0.62	0.58
Denmark	0.24	0.23	0.22	0.24	0.30	0.33	0.37	0.37	0.38	0.41	0.27	0.33	0.41	0.36	0.39	0.49
Spain	0.88	0.88	0.81	0.90	0.88	0.84	0.71	0.67	0.70	0.65	0.63	0.65	0.63	0.69	0.65	0.69
Greece	0.68	0.74	0.52	0.71	0.87	0.91	0.86	0.86	0.86	0.74	0.56	0.31	0.68	0.52	0.72	0.78
Portugal	-0.81	-0.77	-0.84	-0.83	-0.65	-0.66	-0.48	-0.50	-0.30	-0.45	-0.60	-0.23	-0.15	-0.12	-0.14	-0.08
EUR-12	0.26	0.21	0.21	0.36	0.38	0.38	0.37	0.37	0.39	0.40	0.42	0.46	0.47	0.47	0.51	0.52

Table D.3.19. Trade ratios (intra-EU)

Country	1978	1979	1980	1981	1982	1983	1984	1985	1986	1987	1988	1989	1990	1991	1992	1993
FRG	-0.31	-0.29	-0.20	-0.15	-0.13	0.01	0.01	0.04	0.03	0.00	-0.02	-0.11	-0.18	-0.21	-0.17	-0.13
France	-0.19	-0.17	-0.22	-0.23	-0.27	-0.24	-0.26	-0.25	-0.27	-0.25	-0.30	-0.26	-0.18	-0.19	-0.20	-0.12
Italy	0.15	0.18	0.06	0.10	0.15	0.08	0.00	-0.16	-0.07	-0.02	-0.05	-0.06	-0.03	0.03	0.05	0.08
Netherlands	0.45	0.46	0.41	0.44	0.42	0.42	0.44	0.45	0.48	0.44	0.45	0.38	0.32	0.30	0.20	0.36
Bel. & Lux.	-0.11	0.00	0.02	0.07	0.08	0.13	0.13	0.12	0.18	0.20	0.25	0.30	0.35	0.35	0.32	0.34
UK	-0.12	-0.18	-0.11	-0.16	-0.30	-0.36	-0.39	-0.42	-0.42	-0.37	-0.33	-0.36	-0.35	-0.29	-0.29	-0.24
Ireland	0.33	0.24	0.07	-0.01	0.04	0.16	0.17	0.10	0.14	0.21	0.17	0.24	0.29	0.20	0.20	0.15
Denmark	-0.71	-0.68	-0.66	-0.51	-0.49	-0.44	-0.38	-0.41	-0.38	-0.35	-0.28	-0.24	-0.12	0.00	0.01	0.01
Spain	0.50	0.46	0.59	0.46	0.34	0.19	0.50	0.42	-0.06	0.00	0.04	-0.09	-0.14	-0.11	-0.14	-0.17
Greece	-0.89	-0.88	-0.98	-0.85	-0.84	-0.72	-0.85	-0.79	-0.70	-0.69	-0.75	-0.76	-0.74	-0.69	-0.57	-0.58
Portugal	-0.90	-0.93	-0.86	-0.90	-1.00	-0.94	-0.61	-0.72	-0.93	-0.96	-0.95	-0.97	-0.95	-0.87	-0.92	-0.95
EUR-12	-0.01	0.01	0.01	0.01	0.01	0.01	0.01	0.01	0.01	0.01	0.01	0.01	0.01	0.01	0.01	0.01

Table D.3.20. Intra-EU imports as % of total

Country	1978	1979	1980	1981	1982	1983	1984	1985	1986	1987	1988	1989	1990	1991	1992	1993
FRG	87.4	83.8	71.1	70.7	72.2	59.9	60.6	65.3	66.8	68.0	67.2	87.1	87.2	86.5	86.7	80.2
France	59.1	61.5	66.6	72.1	76.1	76.9	76.1	77.2	78.7	78.3	83.8	86.1	88.5	88.3	90.1	89.0
Italy	79.1	79.1	78.1	80.3	80.7	82.8	84.0	86.3	86.5	86.1	86.5	86.0	86.3	87.4	87.7	88.3
Netherlands	74.0	67.4	77.2	78.3	76.1	77.8	69.9	72.0	79.7	80.3	78.3	81.2	79.3	83.1	85.8	76.9
Bel. & Lux.	96.9	96.5	97.7	97.3	96.9	96.0	96.4	95.6	95.1	95.7	96.5	95.3	95.6	95.4	94.4	95.7
UK	57.6	62.6	67.5	73.3	74.7	74.9	76.6	77.6	74.5	81.3	80.5	81.4	82.3	86.7	87.4	85.1
Ireland	97.2	95.0	99.0	98.4	96.2	94.2	95.1	98.7	98.8	98.1	97.8	96.1	95.4	95.7	96.8	96.1
Denmark	69.1	67.5	66.0	64.6	67.3	65.0	66.7	68.9	68.5	68.5	65.7	64.7	67.4	67.9	72.4	72.4
Spain	74.4	74.4	74.1	74.5	74.6	70.3	51.9	54.4	70.4	72.1	74.7	79.4	80.2	83.5	83.8	85.8
Greece	95.0	95.7	93.7	95.2	97.5	98.0	98.1	98.0	97.6	97.0	95.8	90.6	92.3	92.3	94.9	95.4
Portugal	20.1	21.8	18.1	20.0	27.1	31.5	29.5	38.6	77.4	91.2	92.2	95.1	95.6	95.2	95.2	96.2
EUR-12	73.8	73.6	74.4	76.6	77.7	74.9	74.2	76.5	77.8	79.6	80.2	85.4	85.9	87.1	88.1	85.3

Table D.3.21. Intra-EU exports as % of total

Country	1978	1979	1980	1981	1982	1983	1984	1985	1986	1987	1988	1989	1990	1991	1992	1993
FRG	56.9	62.6	66.7	62.5	62.5	63.5	63.1	64.9	62.0	65.9	65.1	64.7	63.2	63.4	60.0	55.1
France	74.5	72.2	75.6	74.6	71.9	73.5	72.6	72.8	73.8	76.2	74.3	74.0	75.2	77.4	76.8	75.4
Italy	76.1	71.3	73.0	65.8	70.3	70.1	68.4	68.3	73.7	75.9	74.7	73.1	66.8	75.0	74.0	67.7
Netherlands	63.0	67.3	72.0	69.9	70.2	69.9	65.8	68.4	70.3	69.8	69.7	68.9	70.3	71.8	72.7	66.4
Bel. & Lux.	93.6	94.3	94.3	92.7	91.2	88.2	85.1	85.7	87.0	87.9	88.4	87.6	87.1	88.7	87.8	87.6
UK	42.7	45.4	47.3	43.7	40.9	39.5	38.9	40.7	43.3	46.6	48.4	45.2	46.2	51.2	51.3	49.6
Ireland	90.5	89.3	88.5	87.4	86.7	86.9	88.4	86.3	89.2	91.0	89.0	92.6	92.9	92.3	91.3	89.8
Denmark	11.6	12.3	13.0	18.0	19.1	18.9	22.3	23.1	23.8	24.3	29.8	28.7	33.0	42.3	46.2	47.8
Spain	35.8	33.1	52.5	29.6	26.9	22.5	34.9	36.3	27.3	35.2	41.5	40.0	41.1	42.7	45.8	43.9
Greece	17.4	19.3	4.2	20.6	23.0	27.4	22.8	34.5	37.8	45.1	47.3	39.4	25.1	39.1	45.0	41.4
Portugal	10.8	6.9	16.7	11.1	0.0	5.9	21.6	22.9	19.2	38.9	50.0	33.3	40.5	61.5	52.1	40.8
EUR-12	61.6	64.3	67.9	63.9	63.8	63.8	63.0	64.8	65.8	67.6	67.8	67.1	67.2	69.3	68.6	65.7

Table D.3.22. Import penetration ratios (extra-EU)

Country	1978	1979	1980	1981	1982	1983	1984	1985	1986	1987	1988	1989	1990	1991	1992	1993
FRG	1.54	2.04	2.04	1.93	1.81	2.10	2.56	2.30	1.91	1.62	1.63	1.69	1.79	1.90	2.02	2.67
France	7.00	5.59	4.33	3.32	3.02	2.93	3.48	3.67	3.49	3.70	2.66	2.27	1.93	1.93	1.82	2.09
Italy	1.39	1.57	1.60	1.41	1.39	7.00	7.75	8.35	7.37	4.50	3.18	3.55	5.95	5.63	4.17	3.87
Netherlands	12.30	16.98	11.87	9.50	11.06	10.80	17.75	16.47	9.12	9.15	9.63	9.25	11.64	9.05	7.61	13.00
Bel. & Lux.	1.13	1.29	0.87	0.96	1.17	1.28	1.24	1.61	1.77	1.68	1.53	2.72	2.18	2.60	3.40	2.73
UK	6.15	5.03	3.72	2.66	2.91	3.34	3.37	3.45	3.88	2.89	2.84	2.81	2.28	1.77	1.83	2.02
Ireland	0.51	0.88	0.20	0.35	0.81	1.22	1.14	0.33	0.31	0.48	0.59	1.05	1.55	1.34	1.02	1.15
Denmark	8.48	8.26	8.98	8.64	8.01	8.20	8.25	7.34	5.61	5.67	5.83	6.23	5.53	6.57	6.09	6.05
Spain	0.53	0.55	0.30	0.51	0.53	0.81	1.19	1.40	1.66	2.16	2.03	1.92	1.95	1.70	2.20	1.97
Greece	0.97	0.63	0.62	0.73	0.30	0.29	0.43	0.33	0.29	0.56	0.65	1.98	1.48	1.87	1.31	1.06
Portugal	9.81	9.42	10.19	9.60	8.28	8.62	10.14	9.44	3.92	2.61	3.06	2.14	2.10	2.67	2.61	1.98
EUR-12	4.08	3.95	3.16	2.61	2.64	3.09	3.69	3.63	3.23	2.90	2.66	2.67	2.61	2.43	2.47	2.90

Table D.3.23. Import penetration ratios (intra-EU)

Country	1978	1979	1980	1981	1982	1983	1984	1985	1986	1987	1988	1989	1990	1991	1992	1993
FRG	10.67	10.57	9.07	8.36	8.37	7.21	8.31	9.10	8.92	8.21	8.73	11.49	12.24	12.14	13.13	10.80
France	10.10	8.93	8.69	8.61	9.66	9.81	11.12	12.47	12.93	13.34	13.79	14.12	14.92	14.67	16.67	16.92
Italy	5.27	5.93	5.70	5.77	5.87	33.75	40.84	52.74	47.29	28.02	20.43	21.90	38.16	39.20	29.68	29.29
Netherlands	35.00	35.16	40.31	34.25	35.13	37.98	41.28	42.49	35.92	37.20	34.87	40.10	44.47	44.36	45.83	43.26
Bel. & Lux.	36.59	35.62	36.42	35.49	37.27	30.92	33.78	35.02	34.40	38.12	44.27	55.48	47.35	53.92	56.88	60.45
UK	8.36	8.40	7.74	7.31	8.58	9.96	11.01	11.96	11.35	12.59	11.72	12.32	10.61	11.55	12.72	11.57
Ireland	17.80	16.80	20.24	22.08	21.27	19.74	22.74	25.72	27.05	26.73	25.89	25.64	31.92	30.35	30.76	28.26
Denmark	18.89	17.14	17.46	15.74	16.57	15.27	16.60	16.29	12.18	12.33	11.22	11.42	11.44	13.87	15.99	15.89
Spain	1.56	1.60	0.90	1.48	1.55	1.96	1.28	1.67	3.98	5.57	5.99	7.44	7.92	8.65	11.38	11.89
Greece	19.68	15.35	10.37	14.28	14.69	14.06	22.04	19.20	13.78	18.28	16.02	19.44	18.28	22.28	24.51	22.29
Portugal	2.48	2.64	2.25	2.43	3.07	4.01	4.24	5.93	13.78	28.11	36.99	43.19	45.80	51.54	51.43	50.55
EUR-12	11.50	11.02	10.55	9.99	10.62	11.72	13.14	14.43	14.03	14.18	14.04	15.67	15.92	16.45	18.28	16.89

Table D.3.24. Intra-EU exports as a % of production

Country	1978	1979	1980	1981	1982	1983	1984	1985	1986	1987	1988	1989	1990	1991	1992	1993
FRG	5.7	6.0	6.2	6.3	6.5	7.4	8.5	9.8	9.3	8.2	8.5	9.1	8.6	8.1	9.3	8.2
France	7.4	6.7	5.9	5.7	5.9	6.3	7.0	8.0	7.9	8.5	8.0	8.8	10.6	10.3	11.5	13.4
Italy	6.9	8.1	6.3	6.8	7.6	34.1	36.9	40.4	40.6	26.2	18.2	19.3	32.8	37.7	29.8	29.3
Netherlands	46.4	50.3	53.0	48.2	48.9	50.5	52.4	54.6	51.0	50.2	48.9	49.7	51.8	51.2	48.9	50.4
Bel. & Lux.	31.5	35.1	36.8	38.1	40.0	35.3	37.5	38.6	40.9	45.6	53.5	64.7	60.0	66.1	66.8	69.5
UK	6.5	5.9	6.1	5.1	4.6	4.7	5.0	5.1	4.9	6.0	6.1	5.9	5.2	6.5	7.1	7.1
Ireland	29.4	24.4	22.1	21.3	22.1	24.6	28.6	28.3	31.8	34.8	31.9	35.4	45.1	38.8	38.7	33.8
Denmark	3.2	3.2	3.6	4.9	5.4	5.5	6.8	6.4	5.2	5.6	6.0	6.6	8.1	12.4	14.4	14.4
Spain	4.2	3.9	3.4	3.6	2.9	2.6	3.5	3.8	3.3	5.1	6.0	5.8	5.7	6.6	8.2	8.0
Greece	1.3	1.1	0.1	1.2	1.4	2.5	2.0	2.6	2.6	3.8	2.6	3.1	3.0	4.8	7.6	6.6
Portugal	0.1	0.1	0.2	0.1	0.0	0.1	1.1	1.1	0.6	0.9	1.5	1.3	2.1	6.8	4.4	2.3
EUR-12	11.0	10.9	10.6	10.0	10.4	12.0	13.3	14.3	14.1	14.1	13.8	14.7	14.8	15.3	16.5	16.6

Table D.3.25. Extra-EU exports as a % of production

Country	1978	1979	1980	1981	1982	1983	1984	1985	1986	1987	1988	1989	1990	1991	1992	1993
FRG	4.3	3.6	3.1	3.8	3.9	4.3	5.0	5.3	5.7	4.3	4.5	5.0	5.0	4.6	6.2	6.7
France	2.5	2.6	1.9	1.9	2.3	2.3	2.6	3.0	2.8	2.7	2.8	3.1	3.5	3.0	3.5	4.4
Italy	2.2	3.3	2.3	3.5	3.2	14.4	16.8	18.5	14.3	8.2	6.1	7.1	16.3	12.5	10.4	13.9
Netherlands	27.2	24.4	20.3	20.4	20.8	21.8	27.0	25.0	20.1	20.2	19.0	20.0	19.5	17.5	18.3	25.5
Bel. & Lux.	2.2	2.1	2.2	3.0	3.9	4.7	6.6	6.4	6.1	6.3	7.0	9.1	8.9	8.4	9.2	9.8
UK	8.8	7.1	6.8	6.6	6.7	7.3	7.8	7.4	6.4	6.8	6.5	7.2	6.1	6.2	6.8	7.2
Ireland	3.1	2.9	2.8	3.0	3.4	3.7	3.8	4.5	3.8	3.4	3.9	2.8	3.4	3.3	3.7	3.8
Denmark	13.7	13.1	13.9	13.6	14.1	15.0	16.4	15.2	11.8	12.7	9.7	11.5	12.0	12.5	12.3	15.8
Spain	7.2	7.5	2.7	8.3	7.6	8.7	6.5	6.6	8.6	9.3	8.2	8.6	8.1	8.7	9.7	10.3
Greece	5.9	4.6	2.1	4.7	4.6	6.5	6.8	4.9	4.3	4.3	2.6	4.4	8.5	6.9	8.8	9.3
Portugal	1.1	1.3	1.0	1.0	1.9	2.0	4.0	3.5	2.5	1.4	1.2	2.4	2.8	4.1	3.9	3.4
EUR-12	6.7	5.9	4.8	5.4	5.7	6.7	7.6	7.6	7.1	6.5	6.3	6.8	6.9	6.4	7.4	8.7

Figure D.3.1. Intra/extra-EU exports

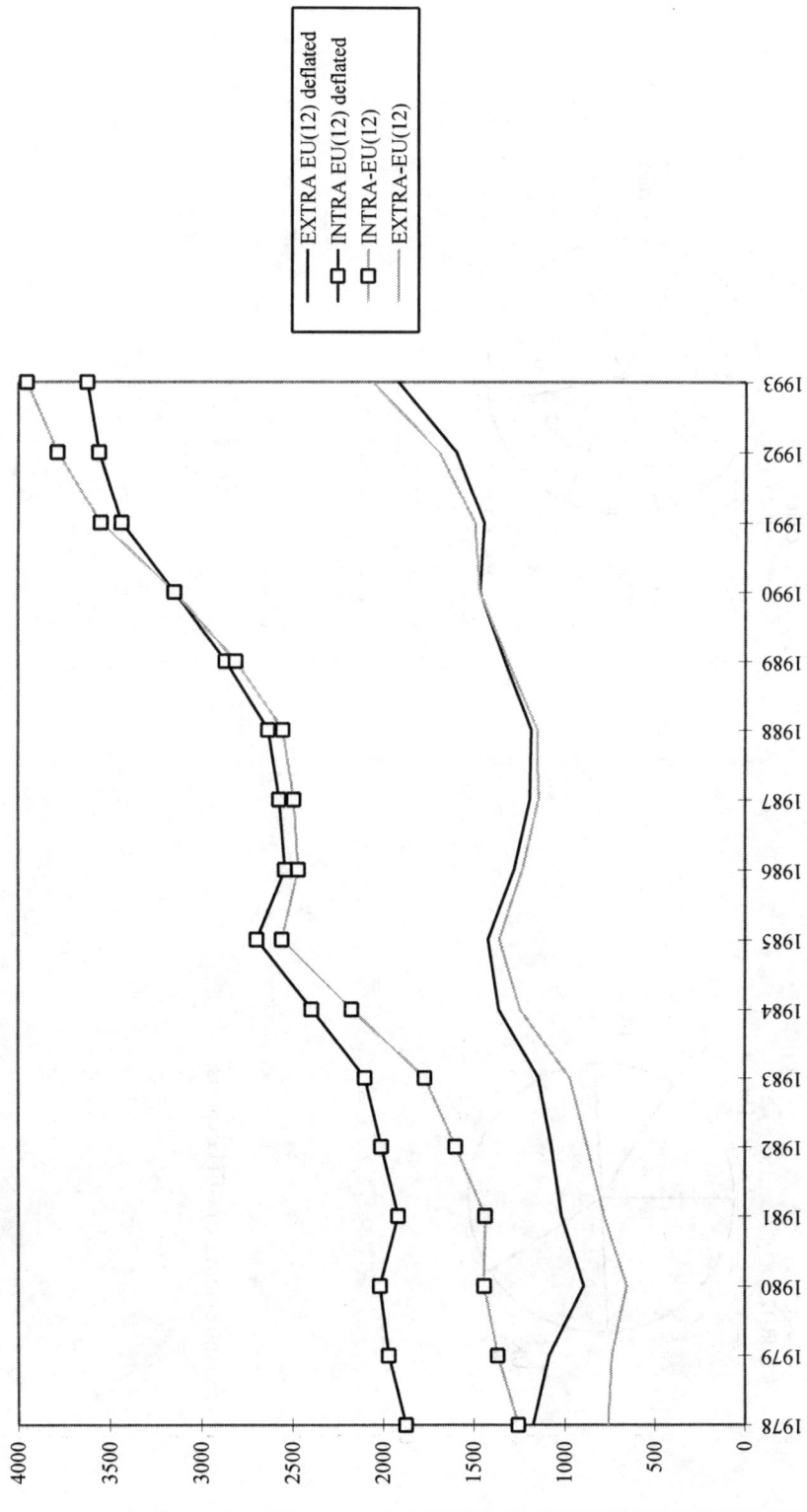

Note: 1978, 1979 are estimated figures (estimates for Spain, Portugal and Greece).

Figure D.3.2. EU exports 1978

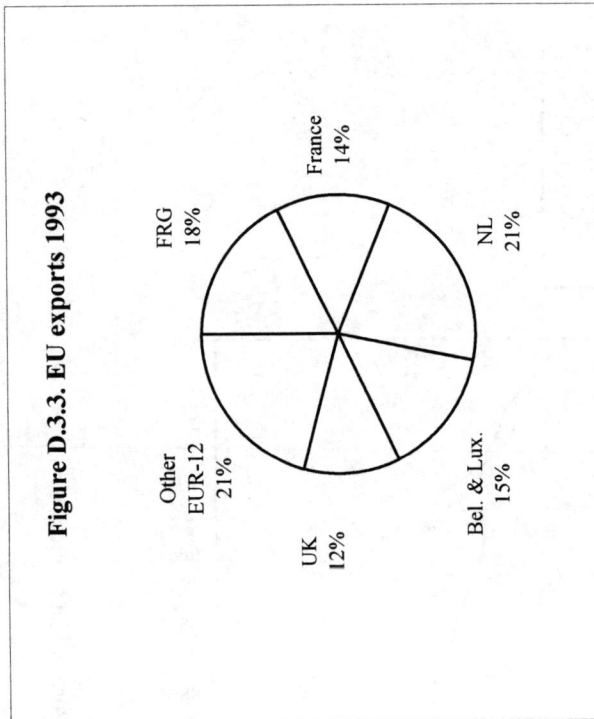

FRG
16%

France
10%

NL
33%

Other
EUR-12
24%

UK
17%

Figure D.3.3. EU exports 1993

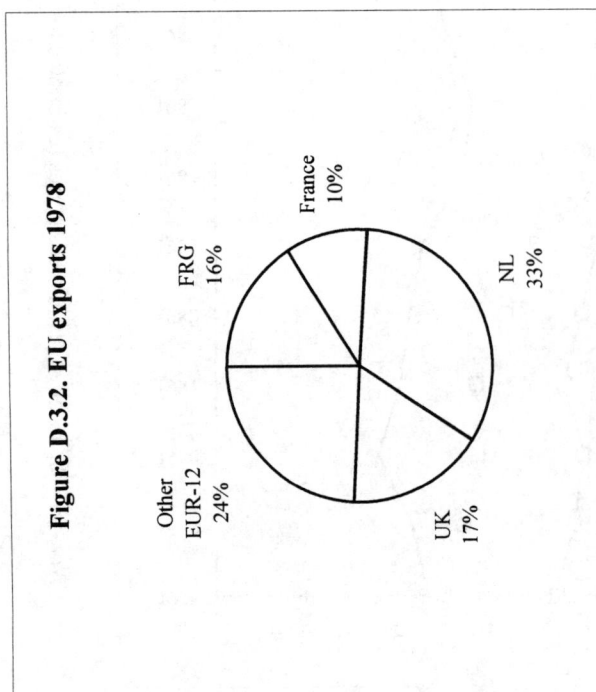

FRG
18%

France
14%

NL
21%

Other
EUR-12
21%

Bel. & Lux.
15%

UK
12%

Note: Intra- and extra-EU exports.

D.4. NACE 423

4230 Manufacture of other food products

Table D.4.1. Number of enterprises

Country	1978	1986	1993	Country share (%)			Total change (%)		
				1978	1986	1993	78/86	86/93	78/93
FRG	194	187	199	9.3%	8.5%	9.0%	-3.6%	6.2%	2.3%
France	120	128	160	5.8%	5.8%	7.3%	6.7%	25.1%	33.4%
Italy	92	110	127	4.4%	5.0%	5.7%	19.6%	15.0%	37.5%
Netherlands	71	55	50	3.4%	2.5%	2.2%	-22.2%	-10.3%	-30.2%
Belgium	40	39	36	1.9%	1.8%	1.6%	-2.5%	-6.8%	-9.1%
UK	154	177	161	7.4%	8.1%	7.3%	14.9%	-8.9%	4.8%
Ireland	14	18	24	0.7%	0.8%	1.1%	28.6%	31.9%	69.5%
Denmark	22	20	20	1.1%	0.9%	0.9%	-9.1%	1.5%	-7.7%
Spain	1245	1370	1349	59.7%	62.6%	61.2%	10.0%	-1.5%	8.4%
Greece			43			1.9%			
Portugal	135	85	36	6.5%	3.9%	1.6%	-36.9%	-57.3%	-73.0%
EUR-12	2087	2189	2205	100.0%	100.0%	100.0%	4.9%	0.7%	5.6%

Table D.4.2. Number of persons employed, excluding home workers

Country	1978	1986	1993	Country share (%)			Total change (%)		
				1978	1986	1993	78/86	86/93	78/93
FRG	50777	44531	52483	28.7%	26.0%	29.0%	-12.3%	17.9%	3.4%
France	14719	16340	17037	8.3%	9.5%	9.4%	11.0%	4.3%	15.8%
Italy	12720	13419	13531	7.2%	7.8%	7.5%	5.5%	0.8%	6.4%
Netherlands	9789	9241	7814	5.5%	5.4%	4.3%	-5.6%	-15.4%	-20.2%
Belgium	3942	4105	3525	2.2%	2.4%	1.9%	4.1%	-14.1%	-10.6%
UK	62671	57708	51804	35.4%	33.7%	28.6%	-7.9%	-10.2%	-17.3%
Ireland	1603	1789	2115	0.9%	1.0%	1.2%	11.6%	18.2%	31.9%
Denmark	4250	4186	5350	2.4%	2.4%	3.0%	-1.5%	27.8%	25.9%
Spain	14591	18025	21590	8.2%	10.5%	11.9%	23.5%	19.8%	48.0%
Greece			3937			2.2%			
Portugal	1864	1969	2017	1.1%	1.1%	1.1%	5.6%	2.4%	8.2%
EUR-12	176926	171313	181204	100.0%	100.0%	100.0%	-3.2%	5.8%	2.4%
USA	211975	198286	195918				-6.5%	-1.2%	-7.6%

Table D.4.3. Production value, excluding VAT

Country	Actual			Deflated			Country share (%)			Real average annual change (%)		
	1978	1986	1993	1978	1986	1993	1978	1986	1993	78/86	86/93	78/93
FRG	4684	7906	11198	6229	7280	10189	41.7%	30.7%	31.7%	2.3	5.2	3.6
France	1252	3146	4181	1365	2668	3878	11.1%	12.2%	11.8%	8.8	5.6	7.3
Italy	949	2642	3589	1293	2391	3835	8.4%	10.3%	10.2%	8.3	7.1	7.8
Netherlands	863	1539	1761	1094	1352	1629	7.7%	6.0%	5.0%	3.1	3.6	3.3
Belgium	389	771	888	367	549	820	3.5%	3.0%	2.5%	5.8	6.8	6.3
UK	1628	6242	8025	3186	6837	7600	14.5%	24.3%	22.7%	12.5	1.7	7.5
Ireland	147	601	1372	160	509	1273	1.3%	2.3%	3.9%	16.3	15.4	15.8
Denmark	353	593	929	385	503	862	3.1%	2.3%	2.6%	6.0	9.2	7.5
Spain	736	1962	2964	953	1876	3232	6.5%	7.6%	8.4%	9.6	8.3	9.0
Greece	153	154	229	172	123	189	1.4%	0.6%	0.6%	-4.0	7.4	1.3
Portugal	91	160	227	376	143	103	0.8%	0.6%	0.6%	-10.4	-4.3	-7.6
EUR-12	11245	25716	35363	15581	24231	33611	100.0%	100.0%	100.0%	6.0	4.9	5.5
USA	27406	56568	61281		49664	53195				2.6	1.0	1.4

Table D.4.4. Production value per enterprise

Country	Actual			Deflated		
	1978	1986	1993	1978	1986	1993
FRG	24.1	42.3	56.4	32.1	38.9	51.3
France	10.4	24.6	26.1	11.4	20.8	24.2
Italy	10.3	24.0	28.4	14.1	21.7	30.3
Netherlands	12.2	27.9	35.5	15.4	24.5	32.9
Belgium	9.7	19.8	24.4	9.2	14.1	22.6
UK	10.6	35.3	49.8	20.7	38.6	47.1
Ireland	10.5	33.4	57.8	11.4	28.3	53.6
Denmark	16.1	29.6	45.8	17.5	25.1	42.5
Spain	0.6	1.4	2.2	0.8	1.4	2.4
Greece			5.4			4.5
Portugal	0.7	1.9	6.2	2.8	1.7	2.8
EUR-12	5.4	11.7	16.0	7.5	11.1	15.2

Table D.4.5. Consumption value

Country	Actual			Deflated			Country share (%)			Real average annual change (%)		
	1978	1986	1993	1978	1986	1993	1978	1986	1993	78/86	86/93	78/93
FRG	4602	7259	10909	6111	7269	9102	41.4%	29.2%	32.4%	2.7	3.5	3.1
France	1229	3265	3696	2443	3181	2944	11.1%	13.1%	11.0%	3.7	-1.0	1.5
Italy	987	2683	3683	2614	2534	2394	8.9%	10.8%	10.9%	0.2	-0.5	-0.1
Netherlands	672	1054	902	917	1052	787	6.0%	4.2%	2.7%	3.7	-0.1	1.9
Bel. & Lux.	406	777	848	635	767	703	3.7%	3.1%	2.5%	154.2	-0.2	82.1
UK	1841	6733	8636	3486	6511	5808	16.6%	27.1%	25.7%	10.1	-1.5	4.7
Ireland	77	203	376	184	195	296	0.7%	0.8%	1.1%	1.8	7.7	4.6
Denmark	329	593	741	593	572	578	3.0%	2.4%	2.2%	2.5	2.9	2.7
Spain	672	1869	3136	1585	1718	1953	6.1%	7.5%	9.3%	1.4	2.2	1.8
Greece	193	261	402	734	212	114	1.7%	1.1%	1.2%	-14.2	-8.3	-11.4
Portugal	95	175	305	392	156	139	0.9%	0.7%	0.9%	-9.8	-1.4	-5.9
EUR-12	11102	24872	33634	19694	24168	24817	100.0%	100.0%	100.0%	2.9	0.5	1.8

Table D.4.6. Labour costs

Country	Actual			Deflated			Country share (%)		
	1978	1986	1993	1978	1986	1993	1978	1986	1993
FRG	689	1030	1683	916	948	1531	19.6%	19.2%	23.4%
France	181	434	573	197	368	531	5.1%	8.1%	8.0%
Italy	137	340	494	186	308	528	3.9%	6.3%	6.9%
Netherlands	149	221	255	188	194	236	4.2%	4.1%	3.6%
Belgium	62	105	122	59	75	112	1.8%	1.9%	1.7%
UK	166	895	1330	325	980	1259	4.7%	16.6%	18.5%
Ireland	11	35	61	12	30	56	0.3%	0.7%	0.8%
Denmark	60	94	157	66	80	146	1.7%	1.8%	2.2%
Spain	81	230	423	106	220	461	2.3%	4.3%	5.9%
Greece			55			46			0.8%
Portugal	2	7	34	10	6	16	0.1%	0.1%	0.5%
EUR-12	3516	5377	7180	2065	3209	4923	100.0%	100.0%	100.0%

Table D.4.7. Gross value added at factor cost

Country	Actual			Deflated			Country share (%)			Real average annual change (%)		
	1978	1986	1993	1978	1986	1993	1978	1986	1993	78/86	86/93	78/93
FRG	1040	1690	2664	1382	1556	2424	10.7%	6.8%	8.7%	2.6	7.4	4.8
France	281	710	1031	306	602	957	2.9%	2.9%	3.4%	9.2	7.2	8.3
Italy	217	676	1020	296	611	1090	2.2%	2.7%	3.3%	10.1	8.8	9.5
Netherlands	207	322	420	262	282	389	2.1%	1.3%	1.4%	2.5	5.2	3.8
Belgium	87	160	211	82	114	195	0.9%	0.6%	0.7%	5.8	8.7	7.2
UK	409	1981	2686	801	2170	2543	4.2%	8.0%	8.8%	18.4	2.5	11.0
Ireland			1027			953			3.4%		8.3	8.3
Denmark	103	176	355	112	149	330	1.1%	0.7%	1.2%	5.5	14.1	9.5
Spain	164	593	973	213	567	1061	1.7%	2.4%	3.2%	14.3	9.5	12.1
Greece			108			90			0.4%		12.9	12.9
EUR-12	2507	6306	10495	3454	6051	10030	100.0%	100.0%	100.0%	8.3	7.6	7.9
USA	9711	24776	30610	3454	21753	26571				6.3	3.0	3.7

Table D.4.8. Gross value added per person employed (in 000 ECU)

Country	Actual			Deflated		
	1978	1986	1993	1978	1986	1993
FRG	20.5	38.0	50.7	27.2	34.9	46.2
France	19.1	43.4	60.5	20.8	36.8	56.1
Italy	17.1	50.4	75.4	23.3	45.6	80.6
Netherlands	21.1	34.8	53.8	26.7	30.5	49.7
Belgium	22.0	38.9	59.9	20.7	27.7	55.3
UK	6.5	34.3	51.8	12.8	37.6	49.1
Ireland			485.7			450.6
Denmark	24.2	42.0	66.4	26.4	35.6	61.6
Spain	11.2	32.9	45.1	14.6	31.5	49.1
Greece			27.5			22.8
EUR-12	14.2	36.8	57.9	19.5	35.3	55.4
USA	45.8	125.0	156.2	16.3	109.7	135.6

Table D.4.9. Investment

Country	Actual 1978	Actual 1986	Actual 1993	Deflated 1978	Deflated 1986	Deflated 1993	Country share (%) 1978	Country share (%) 1986	Country share (%) 1993
FRG	128	216	474	170	199	432	38.8%	24.6%	29.4%
France	36	108	167	39	91	155	11.0%	12.2%	10.4%
Italy	20	69	147	28	62	157	6.2%	7.8%	9.1%
Netherlands	79	154	192	100	135	177	23.9%	17.5%	11.9%
Belgium	9	27	34	9	19	32	2.9%	3.1%	2.1%
UK	42	279	490	83	306	464	12.8%	31.8%	30.4%
Ireland	6	17	24	6	14	22	1.7%	1.9%	1.5%
Denmark	9	9	67	10	8	63	2.8%	1.0%	4.2%
Greece			18			15			1.1%
EUR-12	329	878	1613	444	834	1516	100.0%	100.0%	100.0%
EU (average)	41	110	179	56	104	168			
USA	505	1373			1205				

Table D.4.10. Proportion of investments in gross value added at factor cost (in %)

Country	1978	1979	1980	1981	1982	1983	1984	1985	1986	1987	1988	1989	1990	1991	1992	1993
FRG	12.3	11.6	17.4	18.7	12.6	14.9	18.1	14.4	12.8	16.2	20.1	21.1	15.3	17.5	17.3	17.8
France	12.9	12.4	14.7	13.3	14.6	12.7	15.4	15.9	15.2	15.1	15.7	18.0	16.9	17.2	13.8	16.2
Italy	9.4	9.9	12.8	11.0	12.0	25.0	11.9	10.8	10.2	13.8	12.2	17.9	13.9	14.1	14.3	14.4
Netherlands	38.0	44.3	44.2	53.5	50.7	58.0	59.0	38.1	47.9	50.1	52.5	32.4	48.7	45.7	45.7	45.6
Belgium	10.9	15.6	15.6	18.9	17.9	20.5	20.9	13.5	16.9	17.7	18.5	11.5	17.2	16.3	16.3	16.3
UK	10.3	11.5	10.1	10.2	11.3	11.2	16.8	17.9	14.1	19.0	20.0	17.7	16.3	16.9	17.4	18.2
Ireland				2.7	1.8	4.2	8.7	4.5	5.2	5.6	2.4	3.8	1.9	2.4	2.4	2.3
Denmark	9.0	10.5	7.0								16.3	20.7	19.5	17.9	22.1	19.0
Greece										10.4	17.9	17.8	34.8	19.2	9.0	16.6
EU (average)	12.9	12.9	14.1	14.1	12.7	14.3	16.3	15.2	13.8	16.6	16.6	16.3	14.7	15.1	14.8	15.1
USA	5.2	5.4	6.2	5.6	6.0	5.0	5.4	5.5	5.5	5.4	5.1	5.7	5.4	5.1	5.5	

Table D.4.11. Producer price index

Country	1978	1979	1980	1981	1982	1983	1984	1985	1986	1987	1988	1989	1990	1991	1992	1993
FRG	75.2	72.2	74.0	74.8	83.6	88.1	94.6	98.9	108.6	101.5	101.6	102.3	100.0	101.7	105.3	109.9
France	91.7	92.8	85.4	86.0	90.8	96.4	107.2	112.9	117.9	105.8	102.1	103.1	100.0	100.2	102.3	107.8
Italy	73.4	75.7	78.1	69.7	74.9	82.2	91.0	96.7	110.5	100.1	94.9	99.4	100.0	107.5	108.1	93.6
Netherlands	78.9	77.9	79.5	77.2	87.6	92.3	106.5	105.8	113.9	101.5	100.4	102.6	100.0	101.0	103.1	108.1
Bel. & Lux.	106.0	106.2	98.3	91.8	96.9	104.0	120.5	127.0	140.5	105.5	105.4	106.7	100.0	100.6	103.4	108.3
UK	51.1	54.6	64.7	74.4	77.6	81.9	93.8	100.2	91.3	88.8	96.4	99.4	100.0	109.1	108.3	105.6
Ireland	91.7	92.8	85.4	86.0	90.8	96.4	107.2	112.9	117.9	105.8	102.1	103.1	100.0	100.2	102.3	107.8
Denmark	91.7	92.8	85.4	86.0	90.8	96.4	107.2	112.9	117.9	105.8	102.1	103.1	100.0	100.2	102.3	107.8
Spain	77.2	77.9	74.9	76.4	83.6	81.4	95.6	103.6	104.6	92.8	90.7	97.0	100.0	103.1	101.3	91.7
Greece	89.1	85.0	86.7	90.5	99.0	99.9	107.4	109.5	125.0	102.1	99.9	101.1	100.0	109.4	115.3	120.7
Portugal	24.2	30.1	35.2	42.2	51.7	64.8	83.8	100.0	111.7	122.2	133.9	151.0	170.9	189.6	206.7	220.0
USA							137.1	142.6	113.9	97.7	97.9	111.5	100.0	105.1	102.1	115.2

Table D.4.12. Total imports (million ECU)

Country	Actual			Deflated			Country share (%)			Real average annual change (%)		
	1978	1986	1993	1978	1986	1993	1978	1986	1993	78/86	86/93	78/93
FRG	320.1	620.6	1570.8	425.7	571.5	1429.3	18.8%	16.1%	22.9%	4.3	14.4	9.0
France	233.9	634.7	1013.6	255.2	538.3	940.3	13.8%	16.5%	14.8%	10.2	8.4	9.3
Italy	83.0	216.3	504.5	113.1	195.7	539.0	4.9%	5.6%	7.4%	7.7	15.8	11.5
Netherlands	160.7	364.4	495.5	203.7	319.9	458.4	9.4%	9.5%	7.2%	6.5	5.5	6.0
Bel. & Lux.	163.2	455.7	638.3	153.9	324.3	589.4	9.6%	11.8%	9.3%	9.9	9.1	9.5
UK	526.6	1029.8	1539.6	1030.5	1127.9	1458.0	31.0%	26.8%	22.5%	2.8	4.0	3.4
Ireland	66.5	164.0	191.2	72.6	139.1	177.4	3.9%	4.3%	2.8%	9.2	4.3	6.9
Denmark	58.7	151.1	181.3	64.0	128.2	168.2	3.5%	3.9%	2.6%	9.2	4.9	7.2
Spain	33.8	67.1	427.2	43.8	64.1	465.9	2.0%	1.7%	6.2%	12.5	35.4	23.2
Greece	46.4	123.2	192.6	52.0	98.6	159.6	2.7%	3.2%	2.8%	9.0	7.5	8.3
Portugal	7.8	22.1	100.3	32.2	19.8	45.6	0.5%	0.6%	1.5%	-3.2	13.2	4.5
Total EUR-12	1700.7	3849.5	6855.0	2446.8	3527.5	6430.8	100.0%	100.0%	100.0%	5.0	9.0	6.9

Table D.4.13. Intra-EU imports (million ECU)

Country	Actual			Deflated			Country share (%)			Real average annual change (%)		
	1978	1986	1993	1978	1986	1993	1978	1986	1993	78/86	86/93	78/93
FRG	163.8	427.4	1216.5	217.8	393.6	1106.9	17.2%	15.7%	22.3%	7.9	16.8	12.0
France	173.8	499.8	826.5	189.6	423.9	766.7	18.2%	18.3%	15.1%	11.1	9.0	10.1
Italy	66.1	179.1	436.1	90.1	162.1	465.9	6.9%	6.6%	8.0%	8.1	16.5	12.0
Netherlands	118.3	298.8	364.7	149.9	262.3	337.4	12.4%	11.0%	6.7%	7.9	4.0	6.1
Bel. & Lux.	154.1	436.6	600.0	145.3	310.7	554.0	16.2%	16.0%	11.0%	10.1	8.8	9.5
UK	128.7	454.8	1064.7	251.9	498.1	1008.2	13.5%	16.7%	19.5%	9.6	10.9	10.2
Ireland	44.9	133.1	168.9	49.0	112.9	156.7	4.7%	4.9%	3.1%	11.7	5.8	8.9
Denmark	45.4	121.2	135.6	49.5	102.8	125.8	4.8%	4.4%	2.5%	9.8	4.2	7.2
Spain	24.4	50.8	372.7	31.6	48.6	406.4	2.6%	1.9%	6.8%	16.3	39.0	26.9
Greece	29.3	104.6	181.6	32.9	83.7	150.5	3.1%	3.8%	3.3%	14.0	9.6	12.0
Portugal	4.2	18.4	91.8	17.5	16.5	41.7	0.4%	0.7%	1.7%	5.5	14.8	9.8
Intra-EUR-12	953.0	2725.0	5459.2	1225.2	2415.2	5120.3	100.0%	100.0%	100.0%	8.9	11.4	10.1

Table D.4.14. Extra-EU imports (million ECU)

Country	Actual			Deflated			Country share (%)			Real average annual change (%)		
	1978	1986	1993	1978	1986	1993	1978	1986	1993	78/86	86/93	78/93
FRG	156.2	192.4	354.4	207.7	177.2	322.5	20.9%	17.1%	25.4%	0.1	9.5	4.5
France	60.1	134.5	187.1	65.6	114.1	173.6	8.0%	12.0%	13.4%	8.0	6.2	7.2
Italy	16.9	36.9	68.4	23.0	33.4	73.1	2.3%	3.3%	4.9%	8.7	14.0	11.2
Netherlands	42.4	65.5	130.8	53.7	57.5	121.0	5.7%	5.8%	9.4%	2.9	11.4	6.9
Bel. & Lux.	9.1	18.7	38.2	8.6	13.3	35.3	1.2%	1.7%	2.7%	6.3	15.8	10.7
UK	397.9	575.0	474.9	778.7	629.8	449.7	53.3%	51.2%	34.0%	0.8	-4.0	-1.4
Ireland	21.6	30.8	22.3	23.6	26.1	20.7	2.9%	2.7%	1.6%	3.7	-2.6	0.8
Denmark	13.3	29.8	45.7	14.5	25.3	42.4	1.8%	2.7%	3.3%	8.0	8.0	8.0
Spain	9.3	16.3	54.5	12.1	15.6	59.4	1.2%	1.5%	3.9%	7.8	25.1	15.8
Greece	17.0	18.6	11.0	19.1	14.9	9.1	2.3%	1.7%	0.8%	2.6	14.6	8.2
Portugal	3.4	3.7	8.5	14.0	3.3	3.9	0.5%	0.3%	0.6%	-14.5	7.2	-4.4
Extra-EUR-12	747.2	1122.5	1395.8	1220.6	1110.4	1310.6	100.0%	100.0%	100.0%	0.4	2.6	1.4

Table D.4.15. Total exports (million ECU)

Country	Actual			Deflated			Country share (%)			Real average annual change (%)		
	1978	1986	1993	1978	1986	1993	1978	1986	1993	78/86	86/93	78/93
FRG	402.7	1267.3	1860.0	535.5	1166.9	1692.4	21.8%	27.0%	20.8%	10.4	5.6	8.2
France	256.3	514.9	1497.9	279.6	436.7	1389.5	13.9%	11.0%	16.7%	6.3	18.7	12.1
Italy	45.0	175.4	411.2	61.3	158.7	439.3	2.4%	3.7%	4.6%	13.5	16.0	14.7
Netherlands	352.1	850.1	1354.3	446.3	746.4	1252.8	19.1%	18.1%	15.1%	7.0	7.8	7.4
Bel. & Lux.	146.4	449.8	678.1	138.1	320.1	626.1	7.9%	9.6%	7.6%	13.0	10.3	11.7
UK	313.7	539.1	929.1	613.9	590.5	879.8	17.0%	11.5%	10.4%	-0.2	6.0	2.7
Ireland	136.1	561.8	1557.5	148.5	476.5	1444.8	7.4%	12.0%	17.4%	16.1	18.8	17.3
Denmark	83.0	151.1	369.2	90.6	128.2	342.5	4.5%	3.2%	4.1%	6.6	16.7	11.3
Spain	97.5	160.3	255.1	126.3	153.3	278.2	5.3%	3.4%	2.8%	3.4	9.6	6.3
Greece	6.6	15.6	19.6	7.4	12.5	16.2	0.4%	0.3%	0.2%	14.8	13.3	14.1
Portugal	3.9	7.5	22.0	16.0	6.7	10.0	0.2%	0.2%	0.2%	-4.5	14.0	4.2
Total EUR-12	1843.3	4693.2	8954.1	2463.4	4196.5	8371.8	100.0%	100.0%	100.0%	7.1	10.4	8.6

Table D.4.16. Intra-EU exports (million ECU)

Country	Actual			Deflated			Country share (%)			Real average annual change (%)		
	1978	1986	1993	1978	1986	1993	1978	1986	1993	78/86	86/93	78/93
FRG	235.9	722.2	1029.2	313.7	665.0	936.5	24.6%	27.3%	18.0%	9.9	5.3	7.8
France	139.7	304.0	1085.1	152.4	257.8	1006.6	14.5%	11.5%	19.0%	7.5	22.8	14.6
Italy	31.6	108.5	297.1	43.1	98.2	317.4	3.3%	4.1%	5.2%	12.0	18.7	15.1
Netherlands	236.7	518.3	857.7	300.0	455.0	793.4	24.6%	19.6%	15.0%	5.4	8.4	6.8
Bel. & Lux.	110.7	386.3	559.2	104.4	274.9	516.3	11.5%	14.6%	9.8%	13.6	9.6	11.8
UK	110.7	257.4	552.1	216.6	281.9	522.8	11.5%	9.7%	9.7%	3.4	9.3	6.2
Ireland	56.1	270.8	1052.8	61.2	229.7	976.6	5.8%	10.3%	18.4%	19.1	26.8	22.7
Denmark	17.3	33.4	179.0	18.9	28.3	166.0	1.8%	1.3%	3.1%	10.7	32.0	20.6
Spain	18.6	32.7	82.4	24.1	31.3	89.9	1.9%	1.2%	1.4%	4.3	20.4	11.8
Greece	2.3	4.4	7.4	2.5	3.5	6.1	0.2%	0.2%	0.1%	4.9	25.9	14.7
Portugal	0.8	3.4	12.0	3.2	3.0	5.5	0.1%	0.1%	0.2%	23.1	9.6	16.8
Intra-EUR-12	960.3	2641.8	5714.0	1240.2	2328.8	5337.2	100.0%	100.0%	100.0%	8.3	12.6	10.3

Table D.4.17. Extra-EU exports (million ECU)

Country	Actual			Deflated			Country share (%)			Real average annual change (%)		
	1978	1986	1993	1978	1986	1993	1978	1986	1993	78/86	86/93	78/93
FRG	166.7	534.5	830.8	221.7	492.2	756.0	19.2%	27.5%	25.6%	11.0	6.5	8.9
France	116.5	210.8	412.9	127.1	178.8	383.0	13.4%	10.9%	12.7%	5.4	11.8	8.4
Italy	13.4	62.7	114.1	18.3	56.7	121.9	1.5%	3.2%	3.5%	16.8	12.6	14.8
Netherlands	114.1	280.2	496.6	144.6	246.0	459.4	13.1%	14.4%	15.3%	8.3	9.4	8.8
Bel. & Lux.	35.7	63.4	118.9	33.7	45.1	109.8	4.1%	3.3%	3.7%	15.8	13.9	14.9
UK	203.1	281.7	377.0	397.5	308.5	357.0	23.3%	14.5%	11.6%	-2.5	2.3	-0.3
Ireland	80.0	291.0	504.7	87.3	246.8	468.2	9.2%	15.0%	15.6%	15.9	10.0	13.1
Denmark	65.8	90.5	190.2	71.8	76.8	176.4	7.6%	4.7%	5.9%	2.5	13.8	7.8
Spain	67.8	110.5	172.7	87.8	105.6	188.3	7.8%	5.7%	5.3%	3.9	9.0	6.3
Greece	4.3	11.0	12.2	4.8	8.8	10.1	0.5%	0.6%	0.4%	25.9	11.1	19.0
Portugal	2.9	4.0	10.1	12.0	3.6	4.6	0.3%	0.2%	0.3%	-3.7	19.4	7.1
Extra-EUR-12	870.3	1940.6	3240.1	1206.5	1769.0	3034.7	100.0%	100.0%	100.0%	5.4	8.1	6.6

Table D.4.18. Trade ratio (extra-EU)

Country	1978	1979	1980	1981	1982	1983	1984	1985	1986	1987	1988	1989	1990	1991	1992	1993
FRG	0.03	0.01	0.27	0.31	0.29	0.27	0.33	0.37	0.47	0.49	0.51	0.50	0.43	0.39	0.40	0.40
France	0.32	0.29	0.31	0.25	0.23	0.16	0.21	0.28	0.22	0.20	0.26	0.30	0.34	0.32	0.36	0.38
Italy	-0.12	-0.07	-0.02	0.15	0.30	0.20	0.14	0.14	0.26	0.30	0.27	0.34	0.28	0.23	0.41	0.25
Netherlands	0.46	0.43	0.48	0.53	0.55	0.53	0.49	0.58	0.62	0.65	0.65	0.63	0.60	0.61	0.58	0.58
Bel. & Lux.	0.59	0.54	0.58	0.81	0.62	0.67	0.60	0.57	0.54	0.54	0.58	0.51	0.50	0.49	0.53	0.51
UK	-0.32	-0.46	-0.40	-0.24	-0.34	-0.33	-0.50	-0.34	-0.34	-0.23	-0.25	-0.22	-0.16	-0.12	-0.09	-0.11
Ireland	0.57	0.67	0.59	0.71	0.80	0.84	0.81	0.84	0.81	0.87	0.88	0.89	0.87	0.88	0.90	0.92
Denmark	0.66	0.71	0.75	0.73	0.75	0.75	0.55	0.53	0.50	0.58	0.66	0.61	0.55	0.51	0.50	0.61
Spain	0.76	0.78	0.68	0.81	0.83	0.80	0.75	0.80	0.74	0.82	0.80	0.71	0.64	0.46	0.48	0.52
Greece	-0.59	-0.62	-0.73	-0.47	-0.69	-0.56	-0.49	-0.56	-0.26	-0.64	-0.82	-0.72	-0.61	-0.53	-0.58	0.05
Portugal	-0.08	-0.19	-0.14	0.07	-0.49	-0.12	0.12	-0.02	0.04	0.30	0.34	0.53	0.56	0.58	0.68	0.09
EUR-12	0.08	0.04	0.12	0.25	0.20	0.20	0.07	0.22	0.27	0.34	0.35	0.36	0.36	0.36	0.39	0.40

Table D.4.19. Trade ratio (intra-EU)

Country	1978	1979	1980	1981	1982	1983	1984	1985	1986	1987	1988	1989	1990	1991	1992	1993
FRG	0.18	0.16	0.16	0.15	0.19	0.22	0.24	0.25	0.26	0.03	0.11	0.13	0.05	0.01	0.01	-0.08
France	-0.11	-0.09	-0.09	-0.08	-0.20	-0.23	-0.31	-0.32	-0.24	-0.23	-0.22	-0.13	0.06	0.11	0.14	0.14
Italy	-0.35	-0.29	-0.31	-0.28	-0.29	-0.34	-0.27	-0.29	-0.25	-0.26	-0.25	-0.25	-0.22	-0.24	-0.25	-0.19
Netherlands	0.33	0.25	0.34	0.34	0.35	0.34	0.30	0.26	0.27	0.29	0.30	0.28	0.31	0.34	0.32	0.40
Bel. & Lux.	-0.16	-0.14	-0.11	-0.08	-0.07	-0.01	0.01	0.08	-0.06	-0.06	-0.08	-0.05	-0.02	-0.02	-0.02	-0.04
UK	-0.08	-0.12	-0.08	-0.11	-0.10	-0.10	-0.12	-0.14	-0.28	-0.33	-0.35	-0.35	-0.29	-0.30	-0.28	-0.32
Ireland	0.11	0.06	-0.01	-0.08	-0.11	-0.09	0.03	0.11	0.34	0.59	0.59	0.62	0.55	0.56	0.57	0.72
Denmark	-0.45	-0.23	-0.08	0.01	-0.13	-0.37	-0.59	-0.56	-0.57	-0.36	-0.05	-0.16	-0.08	-0.04	-0.08	0.14
Spain	-0.14	-0.14	-0.08	-0.19	-0.16	-0.08	0.15	0.22	-0.22	-0.26	-0.52	-0.51	-0.60	-0.57	-0.47	-0.64
Greece	-0.86	-0.87	-0.85	-0.85	-0.89	-0.89	-0.89	-0.90	-0.92	-0.92	-0.97	-0.93	-0.93	-0.93	-0.89	-0.92
Portugal	-0.69	-0.69	0.00	-0.79	-0.68	-0.85	-0.88	-0.84	-0.69	-0.73	-0.75	-0.70	-0.70	-0.77	-0.75	-0.77
EUR-12	0.00	-0.01	0.02	0.01	0.00	0.01	0.00	0.00	-0.02	-0.01	0.00	0.00	0.00	0.01	0.01	0.02

Table D.4.20. Intra-EU imports as % of total

Country	1978	1979	1980	1981	1982	1983	1984	1985	1986	1987	1988	1989	1990	1991	1992	1993
FRG	51.2	48.0	61.8	61.3	61.6	62.2	63.3	63.9	68.9	78.2	78.2	77.4	77.5	77.2	78.1	77.4
France	74.3	69.0	70.8	69.0	69.7	71.7	75.4	79.2	78.7	79.7	81.9	82.7	82.9	82.9	82.5	81.5
Italy	79.6	79.6	82.1	86.0	88.1	82.8	80.7	77.2	82.8	86.1	86.1	88.2	88.4	89.1	90.3	86.4
Netherlands	73.6	76.5	74.1	72.3	73.2	71.1	69.1	74.3	82.0	82.6	81.8	81.3	78.2	78.2	77.1	73.6
Bel. & Lux.	94.4	94.2	94.7	94.8	94.1	95.4	94.5	94.7	95.8	95.6	96.0	94.7	94.9	94.5	94.4	94.0
UK	24.4	25.8	26.6	35.2	29.8	31.5	24.1	32.7	44.2	55.5	56.3	60.4	61.4	66.3	68.2	69.2
Ireland	67.5	73.1	69.5	76.9	81.3	81.2	79.3	79.7	81.2	84.6	86.9	85.8	84.8	88.1	90.8	88.3
Denmark	77.3	77.5	77.6	74.7	79.6	82.2	78.7	78.5	80.2	75.5	76.4	76.3	75.8	75.9	77.8	74.8
Spain	72.2	74.0	67.1	75.6	79.2	75.8	63.9	66.9	75.7	82.9	87.9	86.0	90.8	84.6	85.8	87.2
Greece	63.2	63.9	63.1	62.5	65.6	60.9	62.5	58.3	84.9	60.8	60.8	59.5	67.3	76.6	79.7	94.3
Portugal	54.4	53.1	48.4	60.0	50.5	62.6	65.2	64.5	83.3	91.6	92.3	94.8	94.2	94.4	92.7	91.5
EUR-12	56.0	55.4	58.7	62.2	60.9	61.5	56.5	63.1	70.8	75.3	76.1	77.1	78.2	79.4	80.4	79.6

Table D.4.21. Intra-EU exports as % of total

Country	1978	1979	1980	1981	1982	1983	1984	1985	1986	1987	1988	1989	1990	1991	1992	1993
FRG	58.6	55.9	56.1	53.0	56.3	59.6	58.3	56.6	57.0	56.3	58.0	58.6	59.6	59.8	60.4	55.3
France	54.5	50.5	51.8	53.0	49.0	53.3	51.5	52.3	59.0	62.5	62.8	66.2	73.0	75.6	74.3	72.4
Italy	70.2	71.3	71.1	71.0	67.9	60.4	63.7	57.5	61.9	65.1	67.5	68.1	73.2	74.9	69.9	72.3
Netherlands	67.2	68.3	67.2	58.9	59.1	57.2	55.5	54.3	61.0	61.5	61.8	63.0	62.8	64.3	64.8	63.3
Bel. & Lux.	75.6	78.7	79.2	62.3	76.5	80.0	82.1	85.4	85.9	85.5	84.7	84.1	85.7	85.2	83.0	82.5
UK	35.3	42.5	41.9	41.4	41.1	42.9	42.8	42.6	47.7	50.1	51.1	53.1	54.7	57.2	58.8	59.4
Ireland	41.2	37.5	36.6	32.6	28.1	24.4	30.4	30.1	48.2	60.2	61.7	60.9	57.4	63.4	64.4	67.6
Denmark	20.8	26.6	30.1	32.3	30.3	22.1	12.3	13.6	22.1	23.5	27.7	26.2	32.9	37.7	38.5	48.5
Spain	19.1	19.0	22.0	16.6	18.7	20.9	22.6	23.1	20.4	21.1	20.9	25.5	35.2	35.9	43.2	32.3
Greece	34.1	35.1	47.7	26.7	38.3	24.0	22.1	21.1	28.2	22.0	19.7	25.2	24.0	28.1	44.3	37.8
Portugal	20.1	23.1	25.7	13.3	35.7	15.0	8.9	14.8	45.3	47.6	46.7	48.6	45.2	37.2	26.4	54.5
EUR-12	52.1	52.7	53.3	49.5	50.3	50.9	50.8	50.4	56.3	58.2	59.0	60.2	62.1	64.3	64.3	63.8

Table D.4.22. Import penetration ratios (extra-EU)

Country	1978	1979	1980	1981	1982	1983	1984	1985	1986	1987	1988	1989	1990	1991	1992	1993
FRG	3.39	3.88	2.54	3.19	3.23	3.77	3.56	3.67	2.65	2.16	2.17	2.07	2.29	2.60	2.67	3.25
France	4.89	6.43	6.76	7.27	6.83	5.94	5.50	4.83	4.12	3.74	3.73	3.90	4.39	4.59	4.74	5.06
Italy	1.71	1.74	1.45	1.21	0.94	1.31	1.58	2.40	1.38	1.25	1.50	1.39	1.51	1.48	1.26	1.86
Netherlands	6.31	6.45	6.39	8.54	8.48	12.73	13.16	12.28	6.22	7.75	10.59	6.96	10.00	10.70	11.59	14.50
Bel. & Lux.	2.24	2.18	2.11	2.73	2.68	2.81	2.80	3.39	2.41	2.76	2.97	3.20	3.39	3.85	4.17	4.50
UK	21.61	12.85	10.89	8.26	9.66	9.52	14.74	10.41	8.54	6.62	7.22	6.64	6.25	5.70	5.30	5.50
Ireland	27.98	23.39	21.34	15.54	13.15	11.24	17.66	19.14	15.19	12.74	9.69	8.46	6.85	6.38	6.12	5.94
Denmark	4.04	4.49	4.53	3.34	2.50	3.80	6.39	6.40	5.03	5.04	6.41	5.49	4.36	4.37	4.99	6.16
Spain	1.39	1.09	1.02	0.65	0.61	0.69	0.66	0.54	0.87	0.74	0.68	1.00	1.08	2.05	2.08	1.74
Greece	8.79	9.14	8.07	9.69	10.01	12.83	14.82	17.91	7.11	17.42	17.07	19.66	14.19	9.65	8.32	2.74
Portugal	3.58	3.64	3.87	2.89	3.63	3.16	3.30	2.95	2.12	1.34	1.46	0.99	1.32	1.68	2.72	2.78
EUR-12	6.73	6.34	5.52	5.20	5.49	5.83	7.59	6.28	4.51	3.86	4.09	3.84	3.83	3.85	3.79	4.15

Table D.4.23. Import penetration ratios (intra-EU)

Country	1978	1979	1980	1981	1982	1983	1984	1985	1986	1987	1988	1989	1990	1991	1992	1993
FRG	3.56	3.58	4.14	5.06	5.19	6.20	6.14	6.53	5.89	7.74	7.80	7.09	7.89	8.83	9.53	11.15
France	14.14	14.30	16.42	16.19	15.74	15.09	16.96	18.49	15.31	14.76	16.83	18.68	21.26	22.33	22.32	22.36
Italy	6.70	6.79	6.72	7.39	7.02	6.35	6.62	8.14	6.68	7.78	9.27	10.39	11.54	12.08	11.74	11.84
Netherlands	17.62	20.91	18.29	22.31	23.13	31.27	29.45	35.50	28.36	36.84	47.93	30.91	37.13	39.88	40.78	40.43
Bel. & Lux.	37.98	36.11	37.48	49.28	43.32	57.81	50.50	63.06	56.18	61.18	72.00	57.83	63.39	67.47	70.15	70.74
UK	6.99	4.46	3.95	4.49	4.10	4.39	4.69	5.06	6.75	8.25	9.32	10.13	9.95	11.20	11.35	12.33
Ireland	58.16	63.59	48.55	51.97	57.48	48.55	67.82	75.56	65.66	69.84	64.38	51.00	38.40	47.32	60.20	44.95
Denmark	13.80	15.44	15.70	9.89	9.85	17.69	23.74	23.39	20.44	15.56	20.81	17.72	13.66	13.78	17.43	18.29
Spain	3.63	3.14	2.07	2.07	2.37	2.22	1.16	1.09	2.72	3.59	4.92	6.15	10.77	11.26	12.59	11.88
Greece	15.16	16.25	13.88	16.23	19.17	20.05	24.82	25.07	40.00	27.09	26.44	28.93	29.24	31.57	32.86	45.21
Portugal	4.46	4.32	3.75	4.61	3.85	5.42	6.18	5.47	10.54	14.70	18.28	17.90	22.04	28.47	34.80	30.08
EUR-12	8.58	7.89	7.85	8.57	8.53	9.33	9.86	10.77	10.96	11.80	13.03	12.98	13.84	14.91	15.59	16.23

Table D.4.24. Intra-EU exports as a % of production

Country	1978	1979	1980	1981	1982	1983	1984	1985	1986	1987	1988	1989	1990	1991	1992	1993
FRG	5.0	4.9	5.5	6.5	7.2	9.2	9.3	9.9	9.1	7.9	9.1	8.6	8.4	8.7	9.3	9.2
France	11.2	11.6	13.4	13.4	10.7	9.8	9.4	10.0	9.7	9.6	11.1	14.5	22.3	25.2	26.2	26.0
Italy	3.3	3.9	3.7	4.3	4.0	3.2	3.9	4.6	4.1	4.6	5.7	6.4	7.7	7.6	7.2	8.3
Netherlands	27.4	28.3	28.6	31.1	32.2	38.0	35.2	37.1	33.7	40.9	48.0	36.7	42.8	46.3	46.8	48.7
Bel. & Lux.	28.5	28.1	30.5	36.4	36.4	51.3	47.2	61.5	50.1	54.4	62.9	51.8	58.3	62.0	63.1	63.0
UK	6.8	3.8	3.6	3.7	3.6	3.8	4.1	4.1	4.1	4.4	4.9	5.2	5.8	6.4	6.7	6.9
Ireland	38.2	35.1	29.8	26.3	23.9	19.6	28.6	29.6	45.1	58.0	58.0	54.7	46.5	54.1	58.5	76.7
Denmark	4.9	8.3	10.8	8.6	6.7	7.1	5.1	5.6	5.6	6.7	13.3	10.2	9.9	11.0	12.8	19.3
Spain	2.5	2.2	1.7	1.3	1.6	1.8	1.5	1.6	1.7	2.0	1.5	2.0	2.8	3.2	4.7	2.8
Greece	1.5	1.5	1.4	1.6	1.6	1.6	2.2	2.1	2.9	1.9	0.7	2.0	1.9	1.9	3.0	3.2
Portugal	0.9	0.8	1.1	0.6	0.8	0.5	0.4	0.5	2.1	2.6	3.1	3.5	4.6	4.7	6.2	5.3
EUR-12	8.5	7.7	8.0	8.5	8.4	9.1	9.6	10.3	10.3	11.0	12.3	12.3	13.3	14.4	15.2	16.2

Table D.4.25. Extra-EU exports as a % of production

Country	1978	1979	1980	1981	1982	1983	1984	1985	1986	1987	1988	1989	1990	1991	1992	1993
FRG	3.6	3.9	4.3	5.8	5.6	6.2	6.6	7.4	6.8	5.9	6.3	5.9	5.5	5.8	6.0	7.4
France	9.3	11.3	12.5	11.9	11.1	8.6	8.9	9.1	6.7	5.8	6.6	7.4	8.2	8.2	9.0	9.9
Italy	1.4	1.5	1.4	1.7	1.8	2.0	2.2	3.3	2.4	2.4	2.7	2.9	2.8	2.4	3.1	3.2
Netherlands	13.2	12.9	13.7	19.1	19.7	25.0	24.5	27.9	18.2	22.2	27.2	20.6	24.5	25.2	25.4	28.2
Bel. & Lux.	9.2	7.6	8.0	22.0	11.2	12.8	10.1	10.5	8.2	9.2	11.4	9.7	9.7	10.7	12.8	13.4
UK	12.5	5.2	5.0	5.3	5.1	5.1	5.5	5.5	4.5	4.4	4.7	4.6	4.8	4.8	4.7	4.7
Ireland	54.5	58.5	51.5	54.5	61.0	60.8	65.5	68.8	48.5	38.3	35.9	35.1	34.5	31.2	32.4	36.8
Denmark	18.6	22.9	25.1	18.0	15.4	23.1	18.4	17.3	15.3	17.0	22.0	18.1	13.0	11.7	12.7	20.5
Spain	9.2	8.1	5.1	5.8	6.2	5.9	4.3	4.6	5.6	6.9	5.9	5.8	5.2	5.8	6.2	5.8
Greece	2.8	2.7	1.5	4.4	2.4	5.1	7.5	7.9	7.1	6.4	2.9	5.6	5.7	4.7	3.5	5.3
Portugal	3.2	2.6	3.0	3.5	1.3	2.6	4.4	3.0	2.5	2.8	3.5	3.7	5.5	7.9	17.2	4.5
EUR-12	7.7	6.3	6.6	8.1	7.7	8.2	8.3	9.1	7.3	7.4	8.0	7.8	7.8	7.8	8.2	9.0

Figure D.4.1. Intra/extra-EU exports

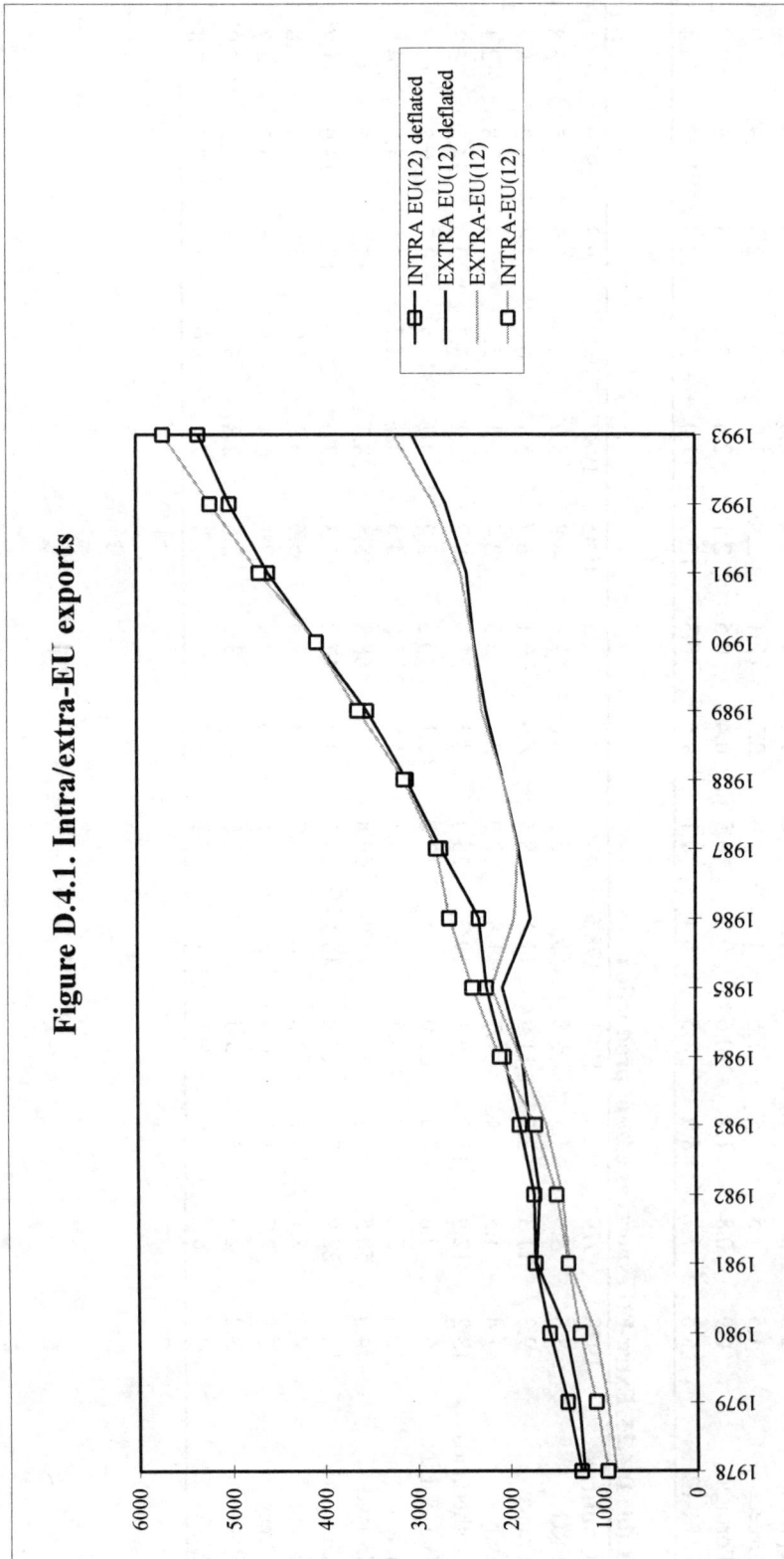

Legend:
- INTRA EU(12) deflated
- EXTRA EU(12) deflated
- EXTRA-EU(12)
- INTRA-EU(12)

Note: 1978, 1979 are estimated figures (estimates for Spain, Portugal and Greece).

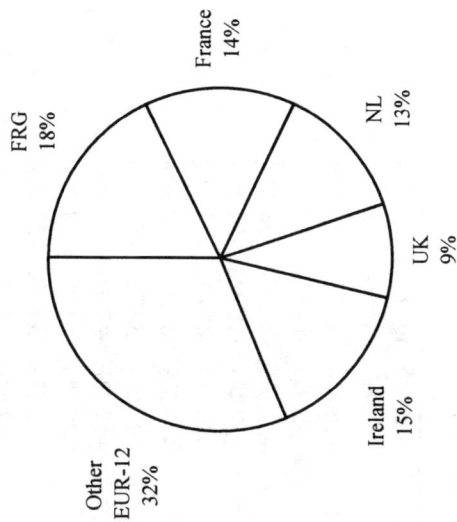

Figure D.4.3. EU exports 1993

FRG 18%
France 14%
NL 13%
UK 9%
Ireland 15%
Other EUR-12 32%

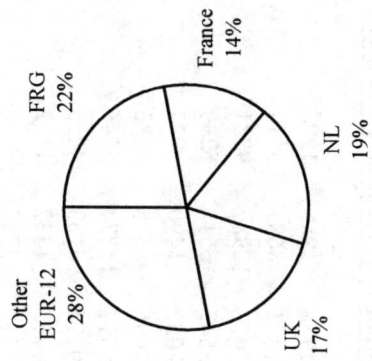

Figure D.4.2. EU exports 1978

FRG 22%
France 14%
NL 19%
UK 17%
Other EUR-12 28%

Note: Intra- and extra-EU exports.

D.5. NACE 424

4240   Distilling of ethyl alcohol from fermented materials; spirit distilling and compounding

Table D.5.1. Number of enterprises

Country	1978	1986	1993	Country share (%)			Total change (%)		
				1978	1986	1993	78/86	86/93	78/93
FRG	105	65	54	8.4%	8.5%	11.6%	-38.1%	-17.6%	-49.0%
France	99	90	79	7.9%	11.8%	17.1%	-9.1%	-12.3%	-20.2%
Italy	112	75	54	8.9%	9.8%	11.8%	-33.0%	-27.4%	-51.4%
Netherlands	22	14	9	1.8%	1.8%	1.9%	-36.4%	-37.2%	-60.0%
Belgium	11	8	9	0.9%	1.0%	2.0%	-27.3%	16.9%	-15.0%
UK	72	52	30	5.7%	6.8%	6.5%	-27.8%	-42.1%	-58.2%
Spain	687	347	148	54.7%	45.5%	32.1%	-49.5%	-57.4%	-78.5%
Greece	19	21	22	1.5%	2.8%	4.9%	8.2%	6.7%	15.5%
Portugal	130	91	56	10.3%	11.9%	12.1%	-29.8%	-38.9%	-57.1%
EUR-12	1257	763	461	100.0%	100.0%	100.0%	-39.3%	-39.6%	-63.3%

Table D.5.2. Number of persons employed, excluding home workers

Country	1978	1986	1993	Country share (%)			Total change (%)		
				1978	1986	1993	78/86	86/93	78/93
FRG	11873	8687	5414	16.0%	16.6%	16.9%	-26.8%	-37.7%	-54.4%
France	11672	10982	9381	15.7%	20.9%	29.4%	-5.9%	-14.6%	-19.6%
Italy	8547	6614	5230	11.5%	12.6%	16.4%	-22.6%	-20.9%	-38.8%
Netherlands	2052	1490	977	2.8%	2.8%	3.1%	-27.4%	-34.4%	-52.4%
Belgium	1096	538	283	1.5%	1.0%	0.9%	-50.9%	-47.4%	-74.2%
UK	26517	15774	5146	35.6%	30.1%	16.1%	-40.5%	-67.4%	-80.6%
Spain	9775	6163	4025	13.1%	11.7%	12.6%	-37.0%	-34.7%	-58.8%
Greece	1775	1432	1132	2.4%	2.7%	3.5%	-19.3%	-21.0%	-36.3%
Portugal	1119	794	358	1.5%	1.5%	1.1%	-29.0%	-54.9%	-68.0%
EUR-12	74426	52474	31946	100.0%	100.0%	100.0%	-29.5%	-39.1%	-57.1%
USA	8570	10160	10580				18.6%	4.1%	23.5%

Table D.5.3. Production value, excluding VAT

Country	Actual			Deflated			Country share (%)			Real average annual change (%)		
	1978	1986	1993	1978	1986	1993	1978	1986	1993	78/86	86/93	78/93
FRG	1795	2069	2553	2778	2126	2278	24.4%	19.8%	19.4%	-3.2	1.9	-0.8
France	1352	2443	3320	2140	2751	2818	18.4%	23.4%	25.2%	3.6	0.5	2.2
Italy	596	1415	2201	985	1655	2154	8.1%	13.6%	16.7%	7.8	4.2	6.1
Netherlands	368	327	270	669	353	232	5.0%	3.1%	2.1%	-6.3	-5.6	-6.0
Belgium	110	77	53	175	91	48	1.5%	0.7%	0.4%	-5.7	-8.0	-6.8
UK	2453	3105	3350	3940	3593	2970	33.3%	29.7%	25.5%	-0.5	-2.6	-1.5
Spain	567	879	1286	918	1171	1227	7.7%	8.4%	9.8%	3.6	1.1	2.4
Greece	100	95	91	134	125	52	1.4%	0.9%	0.7%	0.1	-11.3	-5.2
Portugal	25	26	26	61	32	19	0.3%	0.3%	0.2%	-4.3	-5.8	-5.0
EUR-12	7367	10436	13150	11800	11898	11798	100.0%	100.0%	100.0%	0.3	0.0	0.2
USA	1067	2606	2821		2280	2426				6.6	1.1	2.3

Table D.5.4. Production value per enterprise

Country	Actual			Deflated		
	1978	1986	1993	1978	1986	1993
FRG	17.1	31.8	47.7	26.5	32.7	42.5
France	13.7	27.1	42.0	21.6	30.6	35.7
Italy	5.3	18.9	40.4	8.8	22.1	39.6
Netherlands	16.7	23.4	30.7	30.4	25.2	26.4
Belgium	10.0	9.6	5.6	15.9	11.4	5.2
UK	34.1	59.7	111.3	54.7	69.1	98.7
Spain	0.8	2.5	8.7	1.3	3.4	8.3
Greece	5.1	4.5	4.1	6.9	6.0	2.3
Portugal	0.2	0.3	0.5	0.5	0.4	0.3
EUR-12	5.9	13.7	28.5	9.4	15.6	25.6

Table D.5.5. Consumption value

Country	Actual			Deflated			Country share (%)			Real average annual change (%)		
	1978	1986	1993	1978	1986	1993	1978	1986	1993	78/86	86/93	78/93
FRG	1945	2339	3001	2583	2342	2504	31.9%	27.3%	29.5%	-1.2	1.7	0.2
France	762	1603	1991	1515	1561	1586	12.5%	18.7%	19.6%	1.2	0.6	0.9
Italy	636	1470	2125	1686	1388	1381	10.4%	17.1%	20.9%	-1.6	0.0	-0.8
Netherlands	374	333	226	510	332	197	6.1%	3.9%	2.2%	-4.3	-6.6	-5.4
Bel. & Lux.	176	166	155	276	163	128	2.9%	1.9%	1.5%	73.1	-3.2	37.5
UK	1518	1534	660	2874	1483	444	24.9%	17.9%	6.5%	-7.6	-15.4	-11.2
Denmark	6	16	18	12	16	14	0.1%	0.2%	0.2%	6.7	0.1	3.6
Spain	554	969	1666	1306	890	1037	9.1%	11.3%	16.4%	-4.3	2.5	-1.2
Greece	93	110	254	353	89	72	1.5%	1.3%	2.5%	-15.6	-2.6	-9.6
Portugal	34	45	87	140	40	40	0.6%	0.5%	0.9%	-11.6	0.8	-5.8
EUR-12	6098	8583	10183	11254	8306	7404	100.0%	100.0%	100.0%	-3.6	-1.5	-2.6

Table D.5.6. Labour costs

Country	Actual			Deflated			Country share (%)		
	1978	1986	1993	1978	1986	1993	1978	1986	1993
FRG	169	223	223	261	230	199	22.3%	19.3%	16.1%
France	173	338	408	273	380	347	22.8%	29.2%	29.4%
Italy	94	175	267	155	205	261	12.4%	15.1%	19.3%
Netherlands	35	42	43	63	45	37	4.6%	3.6%	3.1%
Belgium	21	13	11	33	15	10	2.7%	1.1%	0.8%
UK	182	256	290	292	296	257	24.1%	22.1%	20.9%
Spain	76	95	124	123	127	118	10.1%	8.2%	8.9%
Greece	4	12	18	6	15	10	0.5%	1.0%	1.3%
Portugal	3	3	2	8	3	2	0.5%	0.2%	0.2%
EU (average)	141	219	266						
EUR-12	756	1156	1387	1215	1317	1242	100.0%	100.0%	100.0%

Table D.5.7.   Gross value added at factor cost

Country	Actual			Deflated			Country share (%)			Real average annual change (%)		
	1978	1986	1993	1978	1986	1993	1978	1986	1993	78/86	86/93	78/93
FRG	274	302	345	425	310	308	15.2%	10.5%	9.7%	-3.4	0.7	-1.5
France	319	723	950	504	814	807	17.6%	25.3%	26.5%	6.4	0.1	3.5
Italy	166	390	551	274	457	539	9.2%	13.6%	15.4%	7.8	3.1	5.6
Netherlands	80	69	66	146	75	56	4.4%	2.4%	1.8%	-7.0	-3.1	-5.2
Belgium	30			47			1.6%			3.6		
UK	748	1001	1166	1200	1158	1034	41.3%	35.0%	32.6%	0.0	-1.5	-0.7
Spain	194	376	488	313	501	466	10.7%	13.1%	13.6%	6.7	-0.7	3.2
Greece			13			7			0.3%		-21.1	-21.1
EUR-12	1810	2861	3579	3316	3284	3213	100.0%	100.0%	100.0%	1.7	-0.3	0.8
USA	410	1065	1342		932	1154				5.9	3.4	3.9

Table D.5.8.   Gross value added per person employed (in 000 ECU)

Country	Actual			Deflated		
	1978	1986	1993	1978	1986	1993
FRG	23.1	34.7	63.8	35.8	35.7	56.9
France	27.3	65.9	101.3	43.2	74.2	86.0
Italy	19.4	59.0	105.3	32.0	69.0	103.1
Netherlands	39.0	46.4	67.0	71.0	50.1	57.7
Belgium	27.1			43.0		
UK	28.2	63.4	226.6	45.3	73.4	200.9
Spain	19.8	61.0	121.3	32.1	81.2	115.8
Greece			11.1			6.4
EUR-12	24.3	54.5	112.0	44.6	62.6	100.6
USA	47.9	104.9	126.9		91.7	109.1

Table D.5.9. Investment

Country	Actual 1978	Actual 1986	Actual 1993	Deflated 1978	Deflated 1986	Deflated 1993	Country share (%) 1978	Country share (%) 1986	Country share (%) 1993
FRG	27	30	65	41	31	58	16.8%	14.4%	20.2%
France	36	75	107	57	84	91	22.5%	35.5%	33.4%
Italy	15	43	82	25	51	81	9.5%	20.6%	25.7%
Netherlands	17	8	7	31	9	6	10.8%	3.9%	2.1%
Belgium	1	3	8	2	4	7	0.7%	1.6%	2.4%
UK	56	43	41	90	50	36	35.1%	20.4%	12.8%
Denmark	7	8	9	11	8	8	4.5%	3.6%	2.8%
Greece			2			1			0.5%
EUR-12	159	210	320	258	237	287	100.0%	100.0%	100.0%
USA	43	84			73				

Table D.5.10. Proportion of investments in gross value added at factor cost (in %)

Country	1978	1979	1980	1981	1982	1983	1984	1985	1986	1987	1988	1989	1990	1991	1992	1993
FRG	9.8	9.9	11.0	11.2	13.9	13.6	13.1	11.1	10.0	13.9	18.5	25.0	12.4	18.4	18.3	18.8
France	11.3	8.8	11.2	10.5	11.3	8.2	9.6	8.5	10.3	9.2	9.4	9.7	11.0	12.3	11.1	11.3
Italy	9.2	9.4	11.4	13.9	14.2	10.4	16.2	18.7	11.1	15.5	16.1	14.8	14.1	12.6	14.9	14.9
Netherlands	21.5	19.7	9.4	5.3	5.1	6.1	6.8	8.0	11.7	26.1	12.7	13.3	11.0	9.2	10.6	10.4
Belgium	3.7	7.0	14.9	5.7	8.3	6.5										
UK	7.5	8.3	11.8	11.2	8.6	7.5	7.0	6.9	4.3	5.1	5.8	5.0	4.6	4.2	3.9	3.5
Greece										21.7	18.1	29.8	4.9	24.4	15.9	13.9
EU (average)	8.9	8.5	10.3	9.7	9.3	7.8	8.9	8.8	7.2	8.7	9.2	9.6	8.6	9.5	9.0	8.9
USA	10.6	8.5	6.2	8.0	12.4	8.6	7.6	9.0	7.9	6.5	5.5	6.2	5.4	5.0	5.5	

Table D.5.11. Producer price index

Country	1978	1979	1980	1981	1982	1983	1984	1985	1986	1987	1988	1989	1990	1991	1992	1993
FRG	64.6	65.8	66.7	72.7	84.4	90.4	91.7	92.5	97.3	99.7	99.3	98.9	100.0	101.2	106.2	112.1
France	63.2	65.8	65.6	72.5	76.1	78.3	82.4	86.7	88.8	88.9	89.9	93.5	100.0	104.0	110.9	117.8
Italy	60.5	62.1	64.8	72.5	73.7	76.3	79.7	82.4	85.5	86.6	90.4	95.8	100.0	111.0	113.9	102.2
Netherlands	55.0	55.6	66.2	67.9	73.9	76.9	85.0	87.2	92.6	96.2	96.5	97.1	100.0	103.3	109.2	116.1
Bel. & Lux.	63.0	65.3	61.6	77.2	79.6	78.6	78.6	80.5	84.6	86.1	86.5	96.0	100.0	102.5	106.3	109.6
UK	62.3	64.2	57.5	73.0	79.8	82.1	86.9	93.3	86.4	84.5	93.8	97.5	100.0	112.2	114.0	112.8
Ireland	63.2	65.8	65.6	72.5	76.1	78.3	82.4	86.7	88.8	88.9	89.9	93.5	100.0	104.0	110.9	117.8
Denmark	63.2	65.8	65.6	72.5	76.1	78.3	82.4	86.7	88.8	88.9	89.9	93.5	100.0	104.0	110.9	117.8
Spain	61.8	67.0	63.5	66.9	70.9	64.4	71.4	75.8	75.1	76.4	82.9	94.0	100.0	107.9	110.2	104.8
Greece	74.1	65.8	64.6	77.9	102.8	90.7	87.6	80.7	75.9	73.6	77.4	81.1	100.0	103.7	131.9	174.2
Portugal	40.8	42.1	47.3	57.6	65.2	63.7	70.0	82.0	81.5	82.0	80.1	86.3	100.0	121.5	140.3	136.0
USA							140.4	145.6	114.3	99.4	98.9	110.7	100.0	107.1	104.0	116.3

Table D.5.12. Total imports (million ECU)

Country	Actual			Deflated			Country share (%)			Real average annual change (%)		
	1978	1986	1993	1978	1986	1993	1978	1986	1993	78/86	86/93	78/93
FRG	171.1	319.2	685.5	264.9	328.1	611.5	23.6%	21.9%	24.5%	3.4	9.6	6.3
France	83.2	230.6	415.1	131.6	259.7	352.4	11.5%	15.8%	14.9%	9.0	4.9	7.1
Italy	74.6	173.1	184.2	123.2	202.5	180.2	10.3%	11.9%	6.6%	7.5	-1.3	3.4
Netherlands	62.0	108.3	162.7	112.7	117.0	140.1	8.5%	7.4%	5.8%	1.1	2.9	1.9
Bel. & Lux.	73.6	94.6	186.3	116.8	111.8	170.0	10.1%	6.5%	6.7%	0.4	7.4	3.7
UK	152.5	260.4	299.5	244.9	301.4	265.5	21.0%	17.8%	10.7%	3.3	-1.1	1.2
Ireland	21.9	31.0	37.3	34.7	34.9	31.7	3.0%	2.1%	1.3%	1.0	-0.9	0.1
Denmark	17.9	31.0	48.5	28.3	34.9	41.2	2.5%	2.1%	1.7%	2.8	2.5	2.6
Spain	46.9	152.0	504.5	75.9	202.4	481.4	6.5%	10.4%	18.1%	19.3	13.8	16.8
Greece	10.7	37.6	193.8	14.5	49.5	111.3	1.5%	2.6%	6.9%	22.1	14.6	18.6
Portugal	10.8	20.5	75.8	26.4	25.2	55.7	1.5%	1.4%	2.7%	19.1	14.7	17.1
Total EUR-12	725.2	1458.9	2793.1	1173.8	1667.3	2441.0	100.0%	100.0%	100.0%	4.7	5.7	5.2

Table D.5.13. Intra-EU imports (million ECU)

Country	Actual			Deflated			Country share (%)			Real average annual change (%)		
	1978	1986	1993	1978	1986	1993	1978	1986	1993	78/86	86/93	78/93
FRG	133.0	265.5	552.0	205.9	272.9	492.4	21.8%	20.7%	23.1%	4.5	9.2	6.7
France	61.8	194.2	347.3	97.8	218.7	294.8	10.1%	15.2%	14.5%	10.8	5.0	8.1
Italy	67.4	166.2	170.2	111.3	194.4	166.5	11.1%	13.0%	7.1%	8.4	-1.8	3.6
Netherlands	55.7	98.4	136.4	101.3	106.3	117.5	9.1%	7.7%	5.7%	1.2	2.0	1.5
Bel. & Lux.	71.3	90.2	176.2	113.2	106.6	160.8	11.7%	7.0%	7.4%	0.2	7.5	3.6
UK	118.1	210.7	208.6	189.6	243.9	184.9	19.4%	16.4%	8.7%	3.9	-3.5	0.4
Ireland	20.7	28.7	35.2	32.8	32.3	29.9	3.4%	2.2%	1.5%	0.8	-0.6	0.1
Denmark	16.3	28.4	43.1	25.8	32.0	36.6	2.7%	2.2%	1.8%	2.9	2.1	2.5
Spain	44.8	142.7	466.5	72.5	190.0	445.1	7.4%	11.1%	19.5%	18.8	13.6	16.4
Greece	10.3	35.7	181.6	13.9	47.0	104.2	1.7%	2.8%	7.6%	22.1	14.1	18.4
Portugal	9.7	20.1	73.8	23.7	24.7	54.3	1.6%	1.6%	3.1%	20.2	14.7	17.6
Intra-EUR-12	609.1	1281.3	2390.8	987.7	1468.7	2087.1	100.0%	100.0%	100.0%	5.3	5.2	5.3

Table D.5.14. Extra-EU imports (million ECU)

Country	Actual			Deflated			Country share (%)			Real average annual change (%)		
	1978	1986	1993	1978	1986	1993	1978	1986	1993	78/86	86/93	78/93
FRG	33.9	52.7	133.5	52.5	54.2	119.1	30.3%	29.9%	33.2%	1.1	12.5	6.5
France	21.4	36.3	67.8	33.9	40.9	57.6	19.1%	20.6%	16.9%	3.3	5.6	4.4
Italy	7.2	6.6	14.0	11.9	7.7	13.7	6.4%	3.7%	3.5%	2.6	13.1	7.5
Netherlands	6.3	9.8	26.3	11.5	10.6	22.7	5.6%	5.6%	6.5%	2.6	16.2	8.9
Bel. & Lux.	2.3	4.3	10.1	3.7	5.1	9.2	2.1%	2.4%	2.5%	7.2	10.1	8.5
UK	34.4	49.7	90.9	55.2	57.5	80.6	30.8%	28.2%	22.6%	1.7	8.9	5.0
Ireland	1.3	2.3	2.1	2.1	2.6	1.8	1.2%	1.3%	0.5%	5.4	3.4	4.5
Denmark	1.6	2.6	5.4	2.5	2.9	4.6	1.4%	1.5%	1.3%	2.9	7.0	4.8
Spain	2.0	9.2	37.9	3.3	12.3	36.2	1.8%	5.2%	9.4%	33.2	24.7	29.2
Greece	0.4	1.8	12.2	0.6	2.4	7.0	0.4%	1.0%	3.0%	35.8	26.8	31.6
Portugal	1.0	0.4	2.0	2.5	0.5	1.5	0.9%	0.2%	0.5%	190.3	19.9	110.8
Extra-EUR-12	111.8	176.2	402.2	179.4	196.6	353.8	100.0%	100.0%	100.0%	1.5	9.3	5.1

Table D.5.15. Total exports (million ECU)

Country	Actual			Deflated			Country share (%)			Real average annual change (%)		
	1978	1986	1993	1978	1986	1993	1978	1986	1993	78/86	86/93	78/93
FRG	21.0	48.7	237.6	32.5	50.1	212.0	1.1%	1.4%	3.9%	6.2	25.2	15.1
France	673.4	1070.7	1743.4	1065.5	1205.7	1480.0	33.7%	30.8%	28.7%	1.7	3.2	2.4
Italy	34.7	118.6	260.3	57.3	138.7	254.7	1.7%	3.4%	4.3%	13.7	9.7	11.9
Netherlands	56.1	102.9	206.4	102.0	111.1	177.8	2.8%	3.0%	3.4%	1.9	7.5	4.5
Bel. & Lux.	7.3	6.2	84.3	11.6	7.3	76.9	0.4%	0.2%	1.4%	-4.2	60.8	26.1
UK	1088.1	1831.2	2989.9	1747.2	2119.4	2650.6	54.5%	52.6%	49.2%	3.0	3.3	3.1
Ireland	26.1	199.6	355.0	41.3	224.8	301.4	1.3%	5.7%	5.8%	26.1	4.5	16.0
Denmark	11.5	14.9	30.3	18.2	16.8	25.7	0.6%	0.4%	0.5%	0.4	8.3	4.1
Spain	60.2	62.4	124.2	97.5	83.1	118.5	3.0%	1.8%	2.0%	0.4	5.9	3.0
Greece	17.4	23.1	31.6	23.5	30.4	18.1	0.9%	0.7%	0.5%	7.5	-3.7	2.2
Portugal	1.7	1.8	14.6	4.2	2.2	10.7	0.1%	0.1%	0.2%	-2.6	30.6	12.9
Total EUR-12	1997.5	3480.6	6077.6	3200.8	3989.7	5326.4	100.0%	100.0%	100.0%	3.0	4.3	3.6

Table D.5.16. Intra-EU exports (million ECU)

Country	Actual			Deflated			Country share (%)			Real average annual change (%)		
	1978	1986	1993	1978	1986	1993	1978	1986	1993	78/86	86/93	78/93
FRG	15.4	29.7	49.3	23.8	30.5	44.0	2.5%	2.3%	2.3%	4.3	6.1	5.1
France	296.0	397.2	484.2	468.4	447.3	411.0	47.1%	31.2%	22.4%	-0.5	-1.0	-0.7
Italy	13.5	57.5	136.0	22.3	67.3	133.1	2.1%	4.5%	6.3%	17.6	10.9	14.5
Netherlands	20.1	48.3	104.9	36.5	52.2	90.4	3.2%	3.8%	4.8%	6.3	8.8	7.5
Bel. & Lux.	6.0	5.1	31.8	9.5	6.0	29.0	1.0%	0.4%	1.5%	-3.4	34.6	14.3
UK	232.8	612.6	1075.4	373.8	709.0	953.4	37.1%	48.1%	49.7%	9.2	4.5	7.0
Ireland	15.4	87.3	195.9	24.4	98.3	166.3	2.5%	6.9%	9.1%	20.5	8.2	14.7
Denmark	4.0	5.4	16.1	6.3	6.1	13.7	0.6%	0.4%	0.7%	1.1	14.0	7.1
Spain	12.3	14.0	38.4	19.9	18.6	36.6	2.0%	1.1%	1.8%	1.8	17.4	9.1
Greece	12.6	16.0	22.5	16.9	21.1	12.9	2.0%	1.3%	1.0%	9.6	-3.9	3.3
Portugal	0.1	0.2	9.1	0.2	0.2	6.7	0.0%	0.0%	0.4%	2.6	66.4	32.4
Intra-EUR-12	628.1	1273.7	2163.3	1002.1	1456.6	1897.0	100.0%	100.0%	100.0%	5.0	4.0	4.5

Table D.5.17. Extra-EU exports (million ECU)

Country	Actual			Deflated			Country share (%)			Real average annual change (%)		
	1978	1986	1993	1978	1986	1993	1978	1986	1993	78/86	86/93	78/93
FRG	5.6	18.2	188.3	8.7	18.7	168.0	0.4%	0.8%	4.8%	10.3	47.1	27.5
France	377.5	673.3	1259.2	597.3	758.2	1068.9	28.0%	31.2%	32.2%	3.4	5.4	4.3
Italy	21.3	58.0	124.3	35.2	67.8	121.6	1.6%	2.7%	3.2%	11.5	10.4	11.0
Netherlands	17.6	20.6	101.6	32.0	22.2	87.5	1.3%	1.0%	2.6%	-1.4	25.4	11.1
Bel. & Lux.	1.3	1.0	52.5	2.1	1.2	47.9	0.1%	0.0%	1.3%	2.8	120.2	57.6
UK	855.2	1214.9	1914.6	1373.2	1406.1	1697.3	63.3%	56.2%	48.9%	0.8	2.9	1.8
Ireland	10.7	112.2	159.1	16.9	126.4	135.1	0.8%	5.2%	4.1%	35.4	1.3	19.5
Denmark	7.4	9.5	14.2	11.7	10.7	12.1	0.5%	0.4%	0.4%	0.7	5.0	2.7
Spain	47.4	44.5	85.8	76.6	59.3	81.9	3.5%	2.1%	2.2%	1.3	5.3	3.1
Greece	4.5	5.8	9.1	6.1	7.6	5.2	0.3%	0.3%	0.2%	5.4	2.2	3.9
Portugal	1.5	1.5	5.5	3.7	1.8	4.0	0.1%	0.1%	0.1%	-1.9	20.3	8.5
Extra-EUR-12	1350.0	2160.0	3914.3	2163.6	2480.1	3429.5	100.0%	100.0%	100.0%	2.0	4.9	3.3

Table D.5.18. Trade ratio (extra-EU)

Country	1978	1979	1980	1981	1982	1983	1984	1985	1986	1987	1988	1989	1990	1991	1992	1993
FRG	-0.72	-0.73	-0.67	-0.62	-0.54	-0.55	-0.50	-0.52	-0.49	-0.45	-0.45	-0.13	-0.20	-0.24	-0.05	0.17
France	0.89	0.87	0.87	0.90	0.91	0.91	0.92	0.92	0.90	0.91	0.92	0.92	0.91	0.92	0.91	0.90
Italy	0.49	0.53	0.78	0.79	0.85	0.82	0.82	0.79	0.80	0.75	0.69	0.56	0.71	0.69	0.75	0.80
Netherlands	0.47	0.34	0.60	0.67	0.60	0.49	0.52	0.49	0.36	0.32	0.49	0.37	0.18	0.13	0.49	0.59
Bel. & Lux.	-0.28	-0.39	-0.73	-0.56	-0.74	-0.53	-0.63	-0.59	-0.62	-0.69	-0.65	-0.38	-0.58	-0.32	-0.14	0.68
UK	0.92	0.91	0.91	0.92	0.92	0.92	0.91	0.93	0.92	0.89	0.92	0.91	0.89	0.90	0.93	0.91
Ireland	0.78	0.84	0.93	0.94	0.96	0.96	0.96	0.97	0.96	0.97	0.96	0.98	0.96	0.97	0.96	0.97
Denmark	0.64	0.65	0.65	0.58	0.66	0.65	0.64	0.69	0.57	0.55	0.37	0.46	0.26	0.24	0.34	0.45
Spain	0.92	0.91	0.91	0.93	0.90	0.79	0.85	0.77	0.66	0.80	0.74	0.55	0.39	0.27	0.31	0.39
Greece	0.83	0.80	0.93	0.76	0.70	0.61	0.73	0.46	0.53	0.47	0.03	-0.05	-0.42	-0.61	-0.33	-0.15
Portugal	0.21	0.32	0.88	-0.17	0.79	0.65	0.88	0.88	0.58	0.69	0.74	0.73	0.68	0.65	0.67	0.47
EUR-12	0.85	0.82	0.85	0.86	0.87	0.86	0.87	0.87	0.85	0.84	0.86	0.84	0.82	0.81	0.82	0.81

Table D.5.19. Trade ratio (intra-EU)

Country	1978	1979	1980	1981	1982	1983	1984	1985	1986	1987	1988	1989	1990	1991	1992	1993
FRG	-0.79	-0.78	-0.84	-0.85	-0.82	-0.80	-0.80	-0.78	-0.80	-0.78	-0.77	-0.74	-0.79	-0.82	-0.81	-0.84
France	0.65	0.61	0.57	0.50	0.41	0.37	0.38	0.35	0.34	0.36	0.29	0.27	0.20	0.18	0.13	0.16
Italy	-0.67	-0.52	-0.52	-0.46	-0.48	-0.50	-0.49	-0.55	-0.49	-0.45	-0.45	-0.39	-0.36	-0.24	-0.17	-0.11
Netherlands	-0.47	-0.43	-0.43	-0.46	-0.52	-0.38	-0.41	-0.42	-0.34	-0.28	-0.35	-0.31	-0.33	-0.30	-0.26	-0.13
Bel. & Lux.	-0.84	-0.86	-0.86	-0.88	-0.90	-0.91	-0.88	-0.89	-0.89	-0.90	-0.84	-0.81	-0.79	-0.80	-0.81	-0.69
UK	0.33	0.30	0.44	0.48	0.51	0.46	0.49	0.50	0.49	0.51	0.52	0.55	0.56	0.64	0.68	0.68
Ireland	-0.15	0.06	0.21	0.26	0.33	0.41	0.37	0.32	0.51	0.51	0.56	0.58	0.60	0.63	0.63	0.70
Denmark	-0.61	-0.60	-0.60	-0.67	-0.65	-0.58	-0.62	-0.59	-0.68	-0.65	-0.67	-0.65	-0.65	-0.63	-0.60	-0.46
Spain	-0.57	-0.60	-0.50	-0.60	-0.68	-0.73	-0.74	-0.62	-0.82	-0.78	-0.83	-0.83	-0.65	-0.76	-0.81	-0.85
Greece	0.10	-0.02	0.21	0.11	-0.33	-0.16	-0.25	-0.36	-0.38	-0.45	-0.67	-0.72	-0.76	-0.75	-0.71	-0.78
Portugal	-0.98	-0.98	0.00	-0.98	-0.99	-0.97	-0.97	-0.95	-0.98	-0.98	-0.98	-0.97	-0.95	-0.93	-0.84	-0.78
EUR-12	0.02	-0.01	0.01	0.02	0.02	0.01	0.03	0.02	0.00	0.02	0.00	0.02	0.02	0.01	0.00	-0.05

Table D.5.20. Intra-EU imports as % of total

Country	1978	1979	1980	1981	1982	1983	1984	1985	1986	1987	1988	1989	1990	1991	1992	1993
FRG	77.7	78.4	83.6	83.7	82.8	82.3	82.1	81.9	83.2	82.9	81.7	79.6	80.6	81.9	77.2	80.5
France	74.3	73.7	72.7	78.9	84.0	83.2	84.3	85.6	84.2	84.6	87.0	87.2	85.7	87.3	86.8	83.7
Italy	90.3	90.1	96.4	96.0	96.6	96.4	95.4	95.8	96.0	95.1	93.7	89.8	93.1	93.2	92.7	92.4
Netherlands	89.8	89.5	93.7	92.8	92.5	92.5	92.5	92.6	90.9	90.5	93.6	91.7	84.3	85.7	88.4	83.8
Bel. & Lux.	96.9	95.2	95.5	95.1	93.9	95.3	95.8	95.2	95.3	95.6	95.2	95.0	93.2	92.4	91.7	94.6
UK	77.4	77.6	73.9	74.4	73.7	77.9	76.1	79.7	80.9	74.6	80.3	77.8	73.0	74.1	75.9	69.6
Ireland	94.5	94.8	95.2	93.0	91.2	93.0	92.4	94.0	92.6	93.8	93.1	95.8	92.8	95.2	93.1	94.4
Denmark	91.1	91.2	91.3	89.0	90.3	90.8	90.0	91.1	91.6	90.9	90.6	89.0	87.0	86.2	86.8	88.9
Spain	95.6	95.6	95.3	95.8	95.6	94.6	96.8	95.2	93.9	96.5	95.8	93.1	90.1	89.7	89.6	92.5
Greece	95.8	95.6	97.2	94.1	95.4	95.0	95.4	94.1	94.9	94.7	92.8	91.2	86.5	87.4	89.9	93.7
Portugal	89.8	93.0	96.7	83.5	98.4	95.7	97.0	96.2	98.0	98.3	98.4	98.1	98.6	98.1	97.8	97.4
EUR-12	84.0	83.8	85.0	85.4	86.1	86.5	86.4	87.5	87.8	86.8	88.1	86.5	84.7	85.7	85.3	85.6

Table D.5.21 Intra-EU exports as % of total

Country	1978	1979	1980	1981	1982	1983	1984	1985	1986	1987	1988	1989	1990	1991	1992	1993
FRG	73.3	76.7	72.0	67.4	64.6	65.6	62.1	64.5	61.0	61.2	54.2	39.9	38.8	39.9	26.5	20.7
France	44.0	44.6	41.7	37.5	37.3	35.0	33.7	33.9	37.1	35.0	34.7	32.5	31.2	30.4	27.8	27.8
Italy	38.9	46.8	53.8	50.7	45.7	47.9	41.9	43.3	48.5	51.0	50.9	51.9	51.8	60.3	56.1	52.2
Netherlands	35.8	42.2	38.9	30.4	26.6	36.4	39.2	38.9	46.9	53.4	53.0	55.3	50.6	54.4	61.1	50.8
Bel. & Lux.	82.2	77.5	85.5	76.9	80.4	73.3	85.1	80.6	82.3	84.5	89.7	82.1	85.4	72.7	60.1	37.7
UK	21.4	23.3	25.8	26.6	27.0	29.3	29.5	31.2	33.5	35.2	35.5	36.3	36.2	39.3	38.7	36.0
Ireland	59.0	64.5	55.6	41.0	32.7	38.7	33.9	33.9	43.7	45.0	51.3	50.6	54.4	57.7	57.6	55.2
Denmark	34.8	35.9	36.8	30.2	29.7	35.3	32.2	32.8	36.2	38.7	46.9	39.3	45.6	47.0	45.1	53.1
Spain	20.4	20.0	24.3	17.4	18.6	24.7	26.4	36.1	22.4	25.2	21.7	24.7	43.5	39.2	32.4	30.9
Greece	72.2	69.8	75.1	70.7	61.4	72.9	65.2	69.4	69.3	63.8	61.1	55.1	54.7	66.5	66.0	71.2
Portugal	5.8	5.7	5.9	5.9	5.3	6.3	3.1	5.7	11.1	11.5	7.1	9.1	22.8	25.2	42.5	62.3
EUR-12	31.4	33.2	33.6	31.7	31.1	33.0	32.4	33.7	36.6	37.3	37.4	37.0	37.0	39.0	37.5	35.6

Table D.5.22. Import penetration ratios (extra-EU)

Country	1978	1979	1980	1981	1982	1983	1984	1985	1986	1987	1988	1989	1990	1991	1992	1993
FRG	1.74	2.05	1.62	1.69	1.66	1.86	2.05	2.38	2.25	2.53	2.31	3.11	2.71	2.67	4.22	4.45
France	2.81	2.72	2.38	2.43	2.11	2.48	2.41	2.23	2.26	2.34	2.53	2.68	3.10	2.51	2.95	3.40
Italy	1.13	1.22	0.36	0.43	0.38	0.31	0.36	0.51	0.45	0.50	0.69	1.13	0.65	0.68	0.61	0.66
Netherlands	1.69	1.85	1.45	1.98	1.84	1.74	2.07	2.16	2.95	3.81	2.93	4.04	7.25	6.90	6.54	11.63
Bel. & Lux.	1.30	2.03	1.91	1.90	2.13	1.61	1.88	2.09	2.60	2.44	3.04	2.95	4.29	5.14	6.18	6.52
UK	2.27	2.26	2.59	2.73	3.10	2.78	3.40	3.08	3.24	5.21	5.25	6.44	10.48	12.27	10.66	13.78
Denmark	25.00	23.29	21.95	25.71	26.88	28.41	27.52	31.52	16.15	17.76	14.69	20.77	21.36	23.89	25.34	29.67
Spain	0.36	0.36	0.28	0.25	0.35	0.52	0.26	0.38	0.95	0.46	0.66	1.32	2.08	2.43	2.96	2.27
Greece	0.44	0.56	0.23	0.54	0.89	1.12	1.01	2.01	1.64	2.09	3.01	5.31	8.43	8.60	7.45	4.81
Portugal	2.95	2.09	0.41	5.87	0.48	0.71	0.63	0.51	0.89	0.80	1.09	1.51	1.13	1.71	1.93	2.29
EUR-12	1.83	1.97	1.76	1.84	1.86	1.82	1.91	1.98	2.05	2.36	2.30	2.94	3.41	3.23	3.68	3.95

Table D.5.23. Import penetration ratios (intra-EU)

Country	1978	1979	1980	1981	1982	1983	1984	1985	1986	1987	1988	1989	1990	1991	1992	1993
FRG	6.84	8.29	9.91	10.37	9.31	9.23	9.79	11.03	11.35	12.46	11.97	13.72	12.73	13.51	15.63	18.39
France	8.11	7.61	6.43	9.09	11.15	12.35	12.90	13.21	12.12	12.89	16.94	18.35	18.86	17.37	19.57	17.44
Italy	10.59	11.20	11.12	11.31	12.11	8.70	7.89	12.23	11.31	10.20	10.65	10.35	9.14	9.50	7.95	8.01
Netherlands	14.91	15.78	21.91	25.60	22.50	21.35	25.87	27.20	29.58	36.31	43.06	44.70	39.19	41.22	50.09	60.34
Bel. & Lux.	40.44	40.68	40.26	37.30	33.28	34.99	43.15	42.63	54.50	54.00	63.02	57.19	59.71	64.48	69.39	113.82
UK	7.78	7.86	7.33	7.96	8.70	9.83	10.84	12.12	13.74	15.30	21.42	22.56	28.31	35.09	33.64	31.62
Denmark	254.69	247.95	242.68	215.24	260.22	280.68	256.88	323.91	176.40	183.55	145.50	173.22	145.91	149.56	166.97	236.81
Spain	8.09	8.01	6.03	5.74	7.84	9.45	7.91	7.43	14.73	12.66	15.16	17.89	19.11	21.82	25.87	28.00
Greece	11.06	12.98	11.94	8.66	18.24	21.14	22.84	31.93	32.56	37.06	40.03	55.40	54.08	59.67	66.15	71.64
Portugal	28.44	31.32	24.08	31.01	45.32	15.84	20.38	19.08	44.57	58.96	66.72	80.06	81.40	84.09	88.69	84.61
EUR-12	9.99	10.54	10.56	11.38	12.01	11.89	12.30	14.01	14.93	15.60	17.89	19.52	19.48	20.14	22.05	23.48

Note: In the case of Denmark, value of imports appears to exceed domestic consumption levels.

Table D.5.24. Intra-EU exports as a % of production

Country	1978	1979	1980	1981	1982	1983	1984	1985	1986	1987	1988	1989	1990	1991	1992	1993
FRG	0.9	1.2	0.9	0.9	1.0	1.1	1.2	1.6	1.4	1.8	1.8	2.3	1.7	1.6	1.9	1.9
France	21.9	19.8	16.0	16.8	16.8	16.7	16.9	16.6	16.3	16.9	18.2	18.0	16.8	15.5	15.1	14.6
Italy	2.3	3.7	3.7	4.3	4.4	3.0	2.8	3.7	4.1	4.0	4.2	4.7	4.3	5.9	5.6	6.2
Netherlands	5.5	6.5	8.9	9.2	7.0	9.3	10.8	11.2	14.8	20.8	22.3	25.0	21.3	23.9	32.3	38.9
Bel. & Lux.	5.5	5.0	4.9	3.9	2.7	2.6	4.6	4.2	6.6	5.9	14.1	12.8	16.0	18.1	20.0	60.2
UK	9.5	9.6	11.5	12.9	14.3	14.9	16.5	18.1	19.7	22.1	25.6	27.3	29.7	34.8	34.5	32.1
Spain	2.2	2.0	2.0	1.4	1.5	1.5	1.2	1.8	1.6	1.7	1.5	1.9	4.6	3.6	3.4	3.0
Greece	12.6	11.9	16.3	10.1	9.7	15.6	14.2	17.0	16.8	17.0	11.3	16.3	14.4	19.0	25.8	24.6
Portugal	0.4	0.4	0.5	0.4	0.4	0.3	0.4	0.6	0.8	1.3	1.5	3.5	8.0	11.5	28.4	35.0
EUR-12	8.5	8.7	9.1	9.6	10.0	10.0	10.5	11.7	12.2	13.1	14.3	15.6	15.6	16.3	16.9	16.5

Table D.5.25. Extra-EU exports as a % of production

Country	1978	1979	1980	1981	1982	1983	1984	1985	1986	1987	1988	1989	1990	1991	1992	1993
FRG	0.3	0.3	0.4	0.4	0.5	0.6	0.8	0.9	0.9	1.1	1.0	2.8	2.1	1.9	4.5	7.4
France	27.9	24.5	22.3	28.0	28.2	30.9	33.3	32.3	27.6	31.4	34.2	37.4	37.0	35.3	39.1	37.9
Italy	3.6	4.2	3.0	3.9	4.9	3.1	3.7	4.6	4.1	3.7	3.9	4.2	3.9	3.7	4.2	5.6
Netherlands	4.8	3.9	5.8	9.8	7.1	4.9	6.7	6.3	6.3	7.5	9.1	9.3	11.2	9.8	20.6	37.7
Bel. & Lux.	1.2	1.5	0.5	0.8	0.5	0.8	0.7	0.9	1.3	1.0	1.6	2.8	2.6	6.6	12.7	99.4
UK	34.9	31.6	33.0	35.7	38.6	35.9	39.4	39.9	39.1	40.6	46.5	47.9	52.3	53.6	54.6	57.1
Spain	8.3	7.8	6.0	6.5	6.6	4.6	3.4	3.0	5.1	4.5	5.0	5.2	5.4	5.1	7.0	6.7
Greece	4.6	4.7	5.3	3.8	5.3	4.8	6.5	6.2	6.1	6.9	4.6	8.7	6.8	4.7	8.7	10.0
Portugal	6.1	5.8	7.5	6.2	7.0	3.8	10.6	9.1	5.7	9.7	17.5	32.2	21.8	31.0	34.5	21.1
EUR-12	18.3	17.2	18.3	20.1	21.7	19.9	21.4	22.0	20.8	21.9	23.4	26.2	26.2	24.6	27.7	29.1

Figure D.5.1. Intra/extra-EU exports

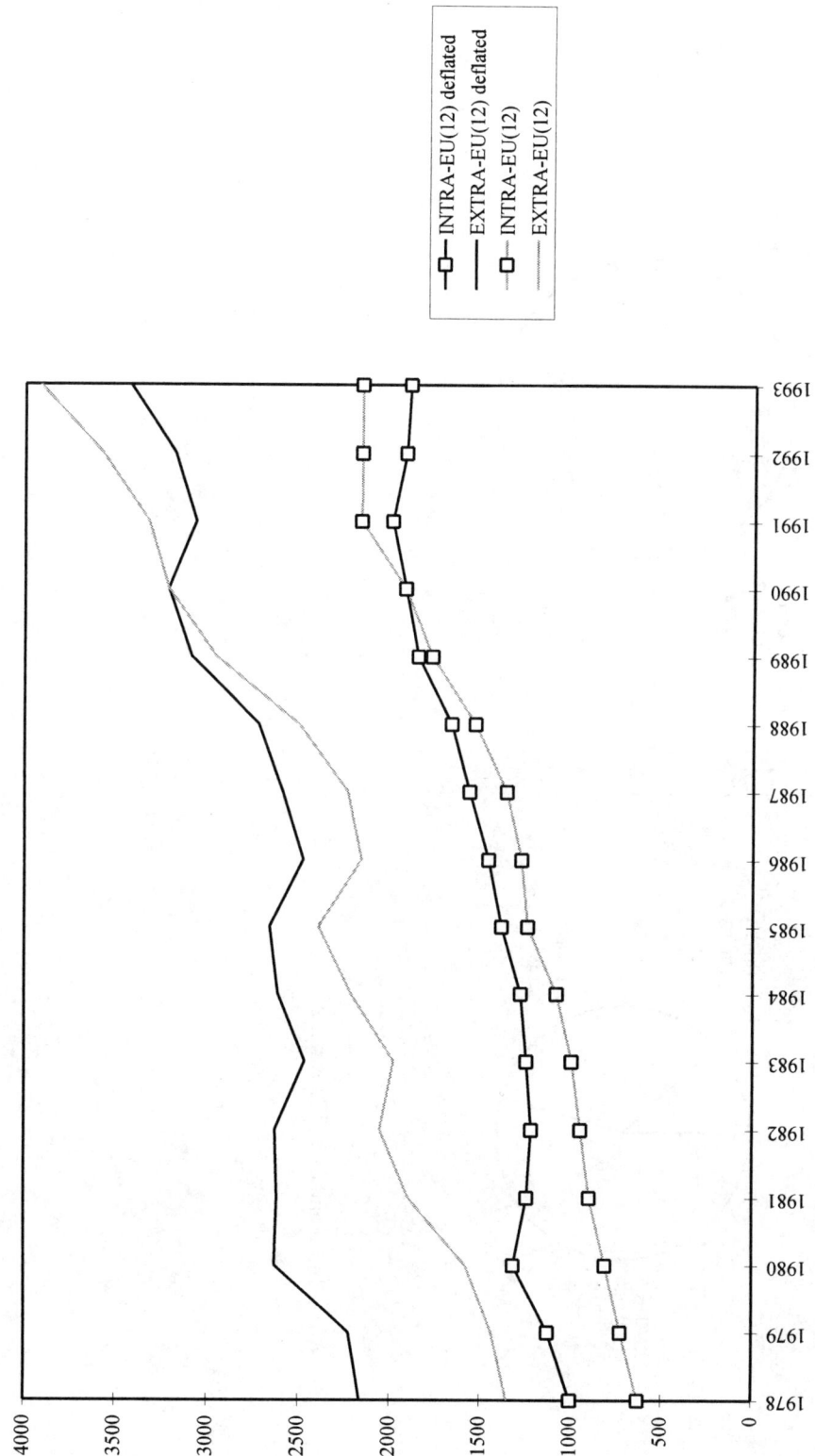

Note: 1978, 1979 are estimated figures (estimates for Spain, Portugal and Greece).

Figure D.5.2. EU exports 1978

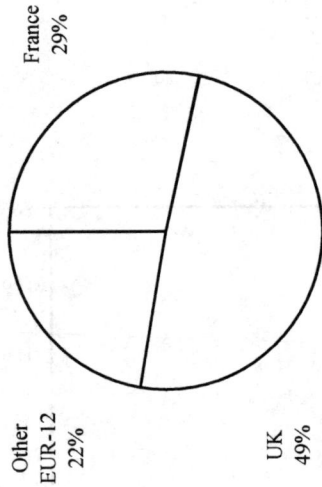

Figure D.5.3. EU exports 1993

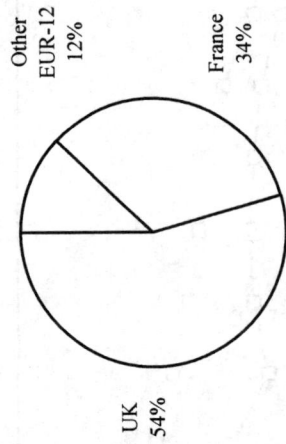

Note: Intra- and extra-EU exports.

D.6. NACE 427

4270 Brewing and malting

Table D.6.1. Number of enterprises

Country	1978	1986	1993	Country share (%) 1978	1986	1993	Total change (%) 78/86	86/93	78/93
FRG	595	456	379	59.8%	58.8%	61.6%	-23.4%	-16.8%	-36.2%
France	50	33	19	5.0%	4.3%	3.0%	-34.0%	-43.3%	-62.6%
Italy	27	17	6	2.7%	2.2%	1.0%	-37.0%	-65.3%	-78.2%
Netherlands	13	10	11	1.3%	1.3%	1.9%	-23.1%	14.1%	-12.2%
Belgium	71	46	28	7.1%	5.9%	4.6%	-35.2%	-38.1%	-59.9%
Luxembourg	6	5	4	0.6%	0.6%	0.7%	-16.7%	-18.0%	-31.7%
UK	129	110	81	13.0%	14.2%	13.2%	-14.7%	-26.2%	-37.1%
Ireland	14	13	14	1.4%	1.7%	2.3%	-7.1%	7.9%	0.2%
Denmark	20	25	22	2.0%	3.2%	3.6%	25.0%	-11.6%	10.5%
Spain	47	42	36	4.7%	5.4%	5.9%	-11.1%	-13.6%	-23.2%
Greece	15	11	6	1.5%	1.4%	1.0%	-31.2%	-39.6%	-58.4%
Portugal	8	8	8	0.8%	1.0%	1.3%	0.0%	0.0%	0.0%
EUR-12	996	776	616	100.0%	100.0%	100.0%	-22.1%	-20.6%	-38.1%

Table D.6.2. Number of persons employed, excluding home workers

Country	1978	1986	1993	Country share (%) 1978	1986	1993	Total change (%) 78/86	86/93	78/93
FRG	77100	58491	48342	35.2%	36.7%	41.0%	-24.1%	-17.4%	-37.3%
France	14698	9908	5730	6.7%	6.2%	4.9%	-32.6%	-42.2%	-61.0%
Italy	6045	5577	4530	2.8%	3.5%	3.8%	-7.7%	-18.8%	-25.1%
Netherlands	8867	8077	7621	4.0%	5.1%	6.5%	-8.9%	-5.6%	-14.0%
Belgium	13033	9548	5973	5.9%	6.0%	5.1%	-26.7%	-37.4%	-54.2%
Luxembourg	544	339	178	0.2%	0.2%	0.2%	-37.7%	-47.5%	-67.3%
UK	60670	34666	20544	27.7%	21.8%	17.4%	-42.9%	-40.7%	-66.1%
Ireland	5702	4448	3075	2.6%	2.8%	2.6%	-22.0%	-30.9%	-46.1%
Denmark	10724	9036	5278	4.9%	5.7%	4.5%	-15.7%	-41.6%	-50.8%
Spain	14456	13321	11884	6.6%	8.4%	10.1%	-7.9%	-10.8%	-17.8%
Greece	4003	2868	1875	1.8%	1.8%	1.6%	-28.4%	-34.6%	-53.2%
Portugal	3348	3085	2956	1.5%	1.9%	2.5%	-7.9%	-4.2%	-11.7%
EUR-12	219191	159364	117986	100.0%	100.0%	100.0%	-27.3%	-26.0%	-46.2%
USA	37670	28250	27710				-25.0%	-1.9%	-26.4%

Table D.6.3. Production value, excluding VAT

Country	Actual			Deflated			Country share (%)			Real average annual change (%)		
	1978	1986	1993	1978	1986	1993	1978	1986	1993	78/86	86/93	78/93
FRG	4500	6548	8612	7538	7324	7311	34.5%	30.4%	31.1%	-0.3	0.1	-0.1
France	977	1687	2152	1495	1854	1865	7.5%	7.8%	7.8%	3.0	0.1	1.6
Italy	353	924	1218	603	1012	1350	2.7%	4.3%	4.4%	8.4	5.5	7.0
Netherlands	784	1243	1616	1451	1396	1359	6.0%	5.8%	5.8%	-0.2	-0.3	-0.2
Belgium	753	900	932	1312	1042	756	5.8%	4.2%	3.4%	-2.6	-4.0	-3.2
Luxembourg	31	42	53	54	49	43	0.2%	0.2%	0.2%	-1.2	-1.0	-1.1
UK	3809	6438	7757	6246	7409	6889	29.2%	29.9%	28.0%	2.6	-0.9	1.0
Ireland	493	1047	1369	755	1151	1186	3.8%	4.9%	4.9%	5.7	0.7	3.4
Denmark	762	1252	1533	1166	1375	1329	5.8%	5.8%	5.5%	2.2	-0.4	1.0
Spain	361	1082	1921	1013	1497	1804	2.8%	5.0%	6.9%	5.3	2.8	4.2
Greece	147	206	257	165	218	215	1.1%	1.0%	0.9%	4.2	0.1	2.3
Portugal	61	184	294	151	226	216	0.5%	0.9%	1.1%	6.0	0.2	3.3
EUR-12	13031	21552	27713	21948	24553	24323	100.0%	100.0%	100.0%	1.5	-0.1	0.7
USA	4979	10689	11910		8456	10347				0.9	3.0	2.5

Table D.6.4. Production value per enterprise

Country	Actual			Deflated		
	1978	1986	1993	1978	1986	1993
FRG	7.6	14.4	22.7	12.7	16.1	19.3
France	19.5	51.1	114.9	29.9	56.2	99.6
Italy	13.1	54.3	206.6	22.3	59.5	229.0
Netherlands	60.3	124.3	141.7	111.7	139.6	119.1
Belgium	10.6	19.6	32.7	18.5	22.7	26.6
Luxembourg	5.2	8.4	12.9	9.0	9.7	10.5
UK	29.5	58.5	95.6	48.4	67.4	84.9
Ireland	35.2	80.5	97.6	53.9	88.5	84.6
Denmark	38.1	50.1	69.4	58.3	55.0	60.1
Spain	7.6	25.8	53.0	21.5	35.6	49.7
Greece	9.6	19.4	40.2	10.7	20.5	33.7
Portugal	7.7	23.0	36.7	18.8	28.3	27.0
EUR-12	13.1	27.8	45.0	22.0	31.7	39.5

Table D.6.5. Consumption value

Country	Actual 1978	Actual 1986	Actual 1993	Deflated 1978	Deflated 1986	Deflated 1993	Country share (%) 1978	Country share (%) 1986	Country share (%) 1993	Real avg annual change (%) 78/86	86/93	78/93
FRG	4409	6224	8210	5856	6232	6851	34.3%	29.2%	30.0%	0.8	1.5	1.1
France	904	1589	1986	1797	1548	1582	7.0%	7.5%	7.3%	-1.8	0.4	-0.8
Italy	335	952	1193	887	899	776	2.6%	4.5%	4.4%	1.5	-1.1	0.3
Netherlands	786	1261	1611	1072	1259	1405	6.1%	5.9%	5.9%	2.2	1.7	1.9
Bel. & Lux.	766	871	857	1199	859	710	6.0%	4.1%	3.1%	99.9	-2.0	52.3
UK	3843	6596	8059	7277	6379	5420	29.9%	30.9%	29.4%	-1.5	-2.0	-1.8
Ireland	494	1065	1404	1179	1026	1106	3.8%	5.0%	5.1%	-1.7	1.4	-0.3
Denmark	761	1250	1529	1371	1206	1192	5.9%	5.9%	5.6%	-1.5	0.0	-0.8
Spain	346	1111	1967	815	1021	1225	2.7%	5.2%	7.2%	3.4	2.7	3.1
Greece	153	213	273	580	173	78	1.2%	1.0%	1.0%	-14.0	-10.8	-12.5
Portugal	62	183	281	257	164	128	0.5%	0.9%	1.0%	-4.6	-3.1	-3.9
EUR-12	12858	21314	27370	22291	20766	20472	100.0%	100.0%	100.0%	-0.8	-0.2	-0.5

Table D.6.6. Labour costs

Country	Actual 1978	Actual 1986	Actual 1993	Deflated 1978	Deflated 1986	Deflated 1993	Country share (%) 1978	Country share (%) 1986	Country share (%) 1993
FRG	1235	1636	1987	2069	1830	1687	44.3%	41.2%	42.6%
France	210	315	303	321	346	263	7.5%	7.9%	6.5%
Italy	71	135	187	121	148	207	2.5%	3.4%	4.0%
Netherlands	159	260	325	295	292	273	5.7%	6.5%	7.0%
Belgium	206	242	252	359	280	205	7.4%	6.1%	5.4%
Luxembourg	8	8	9	14	10	7	0.3%	0.2%	0.2%
UK	481	666	744	789	766	661	17.3%	16.8%	15.9%
Ireland	66	153	165	100	168	143	2.4%	3.8%	3.5%
Denmark	194	234	197	296	257	171	7.0%	5.9%	4.2%
Spain	129	267	420	361	369	394	4.6%	6.7%	9.0%
Greece	14	33	49	16	35	41	0.5%	0.8%	1.1%
Portugal	14	23	31	34	28	23	0.5%	0.6%	0.7%
EU (average)	622	837	1056	398	377	339			
EUR-12	2785	3970	4668	4774	4528	4073	100.0%	100.0%	100.0%

Table D.6.7. Gross value added at factor cost

Country	Actual			Deflated			Country share (%)			Real average annual change (%)		
	1978	1986	1993	1978	1986	1993	1978	1986	1993	78/86	86/93	78/93
FRG	1850	2476	3081	3099	2769	2615	37.4%	35.1%	35.6%	-1.3	-0.7	-1.1
France	329	544	656	503	598	568	6.7%	7.7%	7.6%	2.5	-0.7	1.0
Italy	123	271	290	210	296	322	2.5%	3.8%	3.4%	6.3	4.8	5.6
Netherlands	285	471	586	528	530	493	5.8%	6.7%	6.8%	0.5	-0.6	0.0
Belgium	337	307	190	587	356	154	6.8%	4.4%	2.2%	-5.0	-10.8	-7.7
Luxembourg	15	23	30	26	27	24	0.3%	0.3%	0.3%	0.5	-0.6	0.0
UK	1349	1680	1807	2212	1933	1605	27.3%	23.8%	20.9%	-0.9	-2.5	-1.7
Ireland	296	338	375	453	371	325	6.0%	4.8%	4.3%	-2.3	-1.5	-2.0
Denmark	230	371	429	352	408	372	4.7%	5.3%	5.0%	2.0	0.1	1.1
Spain	127	577	1097	355	798	1030	2.6%	8.2%	12.7%	11.4	4.0	7.9
Greece			104			87			1.2%		5.4	5.4
EUR-12	4940	7058	8645	8326	8086	7595	100.0%	100.0%	100.0%	-0.2	-0.9	-0.5
USA	1935	5143	7145		4069	6207	100.0%	100.0%	100.0%	4.7	6.4	6.0

Table D.6.8. Gross value added per person employed (in 000 ECU)

Country	Actual			Deflated		
	1978	1986	1993	1978	1986	1993
FRG	24.0	42.3	63.7	40.2	47.3	54.1
France	22.4	54.9	114.5	34.2	60.4	99.2
Italy	20.3	48.5	64.1	34.7	53.1	71.1
Netherlands	32.2	58.4	76.9	59.5	65.6	64.7
Belgium	25.9	32.2	31.7	45.1	37.3	25.8
Luxembourg	27.6	67.8	168.5	48.0	78.6	136.8
UK	22.2	48.5	88.0	36.5	55.8	78.1
Ireland	51.9	75.9	121.8	79.4	83.5	105.6
Denmark	21.5	41.1	81.2	32.8	45.1	70.4
Spain	8.8	43.3	92.3	24.6	59.9	86.7
Greece			55.6			46.6
EUR-12	1475.5	2287.9	2924.6	2486.7	2621.2	2569.6
USA	8.8	32.3	60.6	8.8	25.5	52.6

Table D.6.9. Investment

Country	Actual 1978	Actual 1986	Actual 1993	Deflated 1978	Deflated 1986	Deflated 1993	Country share (%) 1978	Country share (%) 1986	Country share (%) 1993
FRG	439	658	1195	735	736	1014	42.0%	43.2%	50.8%
France	90	111	178	137	122	154	8.6%	7.3%	7.6%
Italy	26	84	85	45	92	94	2.5%	5.5%	3.6%
Netherlands	68	140	147	125	157	124	6.5%	9.2%	6.3%
Belgium	61	72	173	107	83	140	5.9%	4.7%	7.3%
Luxembourg	4	2	4	8	3	3	0.4%	0.2%	0.2%
UK	285	343	421	467	395	374	27.3%	22.5%	17.9%
Ireland	17	81	41	26	89	36	1.6%	5.3%	1.8%
Denmark	54	33	69	83	37	59	5.2%	2.2%	2.9%
Greece			38			32			1.6%
EUR-12	1044	1524	2350	1732	1713	2030	100.0%	100.0%	100.0%
EU (average)	116	169	235	192	190	203			
USA	320	480		380					

Table D.6.10. Proportion of investments in gross value added at factor cost (in %)

Country	1978	1979	1980	1981	1982	1983	1984	1985	1986	1987	1988	1989	1990	1991	1992	1993
FRG	23.7	24.6	26.1	25.9	25.4	25.8	27.4	23.9	26.6	30.8	30.8	32.8	36.3	42.0	43.8	38.8
France	27.3	25.9	29.6	24.2	19.0	20.4	37.3	33.2	20.3	24.9	27.1	29.2	30.4	23.1	27.0	27.1
Italy	21.4	23.6	36.2	36.1	27.1	34.5	41.2	35.5	30.9	23.1	23.0	27.9	26.5	33.5	29.3	29.2
Netherlands	23.7	32.7	26.0	23.9	9.9	10.6	19.2	25.0	29.7	28.7	25.4	24.0	23.0	26.5	25.0	25.1
Belgium	18.2	18.3	26.4	14.1	12.4	16.9	22.6	18.3	23.3	24.8	43.4	63.7	53.8	66.5	78.0	91.0
Luxembourg	29.3	16.7	19.4	20.8	13.9	15.7	17.6	19.5	10.4	16.2	33.0	17.6	9.1	14.8	14.3	13.8
UK	21.1	21.6	19.3	16.1	17.0	16.3	19.6	24.1	20.4	19.8	20.8	24.0	27.5	20.3	23.0	23.3
Ireland	5.8	9.8	12.6	12.1	14.0	10.5	18.0	18.9	24.1	17.1	11.1	16.3	16.2	13.1	12.1	11.0
Denmark	23.4	24.5	12.4	14.2	9.2	9.1	18.4	10.7	9.0	13.1	14.6	16.1	11.6	14.6	11.7	16.0
Greece										22.2	28.1	21.0	48.0	25.7	34.9	36.1
EU (average)	19.4	19.8	20.8	18.7	14.8	16.0	22.1	20.9	19.5	22.1	25.7	27.3	28.2	28.0	29.9	31.2
USA	16.6	21.0	18.0	17.2	14.8	11.9	11.1	6.8	9.3	6.5	7.8	7.7	6.7	7.2	5.5	

Table D.6.11. Producer price index

Country	1978	1979	1980	1981	1982	1983	1984	1985	1986	1987	1988	1989	1990	1991	1992	1993
FRG	59.7	62.3	63.9	67.9	75.5	81.0	83.4	83.1	89.4	93.3	94.1	96.8	100.0	103.9	109.3	117.8
France	65.3	68.3	65.4	75.4	79.2	81.7	85.0	88.8	91.0	92.8	92.6	95.3	100.0	103.4	108.6	115.4
Italy	58.5	62.1	65.6	60.0	68.1	80.1	86.9	88.6	91.3	90.9	93.1	97.8	100.0	104.0	104.4	90.2
Netherlands	54.0	55.0	56.5	59.1	75.5	79.7	82.9	85.1	89.0	92.0	93.5	95.3	100.0	103.8	108.5	118.9
Bel. & Lux.	57.4	61.0	64.9	73.8	71.6	75.5	76.9	82.0	86.3	87.5	87.8	91.8	100.0	108.2	113.5	123.2
UK	61.0	64.6	58.0	73.5	80.4	82.7	87.6	94.0	86.9	85.1	94.5	98.1	100.0	111.7	113.4	112.6
Ireland	65.3	68.3	65.4	75.4	79.2	81.7	85.0	88.8	91.0	92.8	92.6	95.3	100.0	103.4	108.6	115.4
Denmark	65.3	68.3	65.4	75.4	79.2	81.7	85.0	88.8	91.0	92.8	92.6	95.3	100.0	103.4	108.6	115.4
Spain	35.6	43.2	48.9	54.1	59.5	57.5	65.9	72.1	72.3	75.1	81.5	91.1	100.0	109.7	112.8	106.5
Greece	89.4	80.3	78.8	93.3	116.2	105.3	108.8	105.2	94.6	93.4	96.6	99.9	100.0	108.5	115.2	119.3
Portugal	40.8	42.1	47.3	57.6	65.2	63.7	70.0	82.0	81.5	82.0	80.1	86.3	100.0	121.5	140.3	136.0
USA							151.1	159.1	126.4	107.2	105.5	116.1	100.0	107.8	104.9	115.1

Table D.6.12. Total imports (million ECU)

Country	Actual			Deflated			Country share (%)			Real average annual change (%)		
	1978	1986	1993	1978	1986	1993	1978	1986	1993	78/86	86/93	78/93
FRG	69.6	154.6	264.4	116.6	172.9	224.4	20.9%	19.7%	19.5%	5.5	6.0	5.7
France	67.0	102.7	143.1	102.6	112.9	124.0	20.2%	13.1%	10.6%	1.7	1.6	1.7
Italy	36.7	166.4	248.0	62.7	182.3	274.9	11.0%	21.2%	18.3%	15.0	6.4	11.0
Netherlands	34.9	71.0	119.4	64.6	79.8	100.4	10.5%	9.1%	8.8%	4.4	3.9	4.2
Bel. & Lux.	50.6	48.8	46.1	88.1	56.5	37.4	15.2%	6.2%	3.4%	-3.9	-4.3	-4.1
UK	56.0	169.7	338.4	91.8	195.3	300.5	16.9%	21.7%	25.0%	10.5	6.5	8.6
Ireland	1.3	18.1	49.2	2.0	19.9	42.6	0.4%	2.3%	3.6%	35.2	13.7	25.2
Denmark	0.7	1.4	19.2	1.1	1.5	16.6	0.2%	0.2%	1.4%	327.1	95.4	219.0
Spain	7.3	39.9	83.0	20.5	55.2	77.9	2.2%	5.1%	6.1%	26.3	6.4	17.0
Greece	5.7	8.2	30.6	6.3	8.7	25.6	1.7%	1.0%	2.3%	8.5	19.2	13.5
Portugal	2.6	2.0	11.2	6.3	2.5	8.2	0.8%	0.3%	0.8%	54.2	32.6	44.1
Total EUR-12	332.3	783.3	1352.7	562.6	887.4	1232.9	100.0%	100.0%	100.0%	6.1	5.0	5.6

Table D.6.13. Intra-EU imports (million ECU)

Country	Actual			Deflated			Country share (%)			Real average annual change (%)		
	1978	1986	1993	1978	1986	1993	1978	1986	1993	78/86	86/93	78/93
FRG	62.8	144.3	239.7	105.2	161.4	203.5	20.1%	19.5%	19.3%	6.0	5.5	5.8
France	66.4	100.2	135.8	101.6	110.1	117.7	21.3%	13.6%	10.9%	1.5	1.2	1.4
Italy	33.8	154.8	229.4	57.8	169.6	254.3	10.8%	20.9%	18.4%	15.1	6.4	11.0
Netherlands	34.2	70.7	116.1	63.3	79.4	97.6	11.0%	9.6%	9.3%	4.7	3.6	4.2
Bel. & Lux.	48.8	46.3	37.5	85.0	53.7	30.4	15.6%	6.3%	3.0%	-4.0	-6.1	-5.0
UK	49.3	154.8	301.7	80.8	178.1	267.9	15.8%	20.9%	24.3%	10.8	6.2	8.7
Ireland	1.3	17.8	48.5	2.0	19.6	42.0	0.4%	2.4%	3.9%	35.6	13.6	25.4
Denmark	0.6	1.3	18.7	0.9	1.4	16.2	0.2%	0.2%	1.5%	325.3	101.4	220.9
Spain	6.9	38.8	78.4	19.4	53.7	73.6	2.2%	5.2%	6.3%	26.2	6.0	16.8
Greece	5.6	7.9	27.0	6.3	8.4	22.6	1.8%	1.1%	2.2%	7.9	18.1	12.7
Portugal	2.3	2.0	11.1	5.7	2.5	8.2	0.7%	0.3%	0.9%	67.9	32.0	51.1
Intra-EUR-12	312.1	739.4	1244.0	528.1	837.8	1134.1	100.0%	100.0%	100.0%	6.2	4.6	5.4

Table D.6.14. Extra-EU imports (million ECU)

Country	Actual			Deflated			Country share (%)			Real average annual change (%)		
	1978	1986	1993	1978	1986	1993	1978	1986	1993	78/86	86/93	78/93
FRG	6.8	10.2	24.8	11.4	11.4	21.1	33.4%	23.3%	22.8%	0.6	13.7	6.7
France	0.6	2.5	7.3	0.9	2.7	6.3	2.9%	5.7%	6.7%	24.0	16.1	20.3
Italy	2.9	11.5	18.6	5.0	12.6	20.6	14.2%	26.3%	17.1%	15.3	9.3	12.5
Netherlands	0.7	0.2	3.3	1.3	0.2	2.8	3.4%	0.5%	3.0%	-4.3	104.6	46.5
Bel. & Lux.	1.9	2.5	8.5	3.3	2.9	6.9	9.3%	5.7%	7.8%	1.9	26.7	13.5
UK	6.8	14.8	36.7	11.2	17.0	32.6	33.4%	33.8%	33.7%	10.5	12.3	11.3
Ireland	0.0	0.2	0.7	0.0	0.2	0.6	0.0%	0.5%	0.6%	0.0	156.1	72.8
Denmark	0.1	0.1	0.5	0.2	0.1	0.4	0.5%	0.2%	0.5%	-43.6	26.3	-11.0
Spain	0.4	1.0	4.6	1.0	1.4	4.3	1.8%	2.3%	4.2%	-25.6	70.9	19.4
Greece	0.0	0.3	3.7	0.0	0.3	3.1	0.0%	0.7%	3.4%	0.0	59.3	27.7
Portugal	0.2	0.0	0.1	0.5	0.0	0.1	1.1%	0.0%	0.1%	-28.4	-13.8	-21.6
Extra-EUR-12	20.4	43.8	108.8	34.7	48.9	98.8	100.0%	100.0%	100.0%	4.7	12.1	8.1

Table D.6.15. Total exports (million ECU)

Country	Actual			Deflated			Country share (%)			Real average annual change (%)		
	1978	1986	1993	1978	1986	1993	1978	1986	1993	78/86	86/93	78/93
FRG	146.7	369.4	537.7	245.7	413.2	456.5	18.8%	22.3%	21.2%	7.0	1.5	4.4
France	151.6	276.4	365.3	232.1	303.7	316.6	19.4%	16.7%	14.4%	4.1	1.1	2.7
Italy	1.1	6.7	15.6	1.9	7.3	17.3	0.1%	0.4%	0.6%	25.3	18.8	22.3
Netherlands	160.2	479.1	665.9	296.7	538.3	560.1	20.5%	28.9%	26.2%	7.8	0.7	4.5
Bel. & Lux.	139.4	200.7	308.9	242.8	232.6	250.7	17.9%	12.1%	12.2%	0.2	1.3	0.7
UK	54.8	138.0	272.5	89.9	158.8	242.0	7.0%	8.3%	10.7%	8.5	6.4	7.5
Ireland	33.0	52.7	124.9	50.5	57.9	108.2	4.2%	3.2%	4.9%	2.4	9.7	5.8
Denmark	68.8	119.7	174.4	105.3	131.5	151.1	8.8%	7.2%	6.9%	3.2	2.6	2.9
Spain	22.2	11.5	37.0	62.5	15.9	34.7	2.9%	0.7%	1.5%	51.6	12.4	33.3
Greece	0.2	0.6	14.2	0.3	0.6	11.9	0.0%	0.0%	0.6%	48.1	64.1	55.6
Portugal	1.8	3.2	23.3	4.4	3.9	17.1	0.2%	0.2%	0.9%	1.2	27.1	13.3
Total EUR-12	779.9	1658.5	2539.6	1331.9	1863.9	2166.2	100.0%	100.0%	100.0%	4.4	2.3	3.4

Table D.6.16. Intra-EU exports (million ECU)

Country	Actual			Deflated			Country share (%)			Real average annual change (%)		
	1978	1986	1993	1978	1986	1993	1978	1986	1993	78/86	86/93	78/93
FRG	60.8	154.3	287.4	101.8	172.6	244.0	19.9%	22.3%	22.6%	6.9	5.1	6.1
France	59.1	125.4	233.1	90.5	137.8	202.0	19.3%	18.2%	18.3%	6.9	5.9	6.4
Italy	0.1	1.5	7.2	0.2	1.6	8.0	0.0%	0.2%	0.6%	60.9	34.2	48.4
Netherlands	25.8	95.4	150.2	47.8	107.2	126.3	8.4%	13.8%	11.8%	12.3	3.2	8.1
Bel. & Lux.	77.5	151.1	230.0	135.0	175.1	186.7	25.3%	21.9%	18.1%	3.9	1.0	2.5
UK	14.2	52.8	107.0	23.3	60.8	95.0	4.6%	7.6%	8.4%	13.7	11.4	12.7
Ireland	24.1	35.8	105.6	36.9	39.3	91.5	7.9%	5.2%	8.3%	0.9	13.6	6.9
Denmark	34.9	69.2	133.9	53.4	76.0	116.0	11.4%	10.0%	10.5%	5.0	7.3	6.1
Spain	8.9	4.1	13.6	25.0	5.7	12.8	2.9%	0.6%	1.1%	65.2	18.3	43.3
Greece	0.0	0.0	0.5	0.0	0.0	0.4	0.0%	0.0%	0.0%	0.0	0.0	0.0
Portugal	0.4	0.7	5.5	0.9	0.9	4.0	0.1%	0.1%	0.4%	2.6	25.5	13.3
Intra-EUR-12	305.8	690.7	1274.0	514.7	777.0	1086.8	100.0%	100.0%	100.0%	5.4	5.1	5.2

Table D.6.17. Extra-EU exports (million ECU)

Country	Actual			Deflated			Country share (%)			Real average annual change (%)		
	1978	1986	1993	1978	1986	1993	1978	1986	1993	78/86	86/93	78/93
FRG	85.3	214.9	250.3	142.9	240.4	212.5	18.1%	22.4%	19.8%	7.3	-1.6	3.2
France	92.5	147.0	132.1	141.6	161.5	114.5	19.7%	15.4%	10.4%	2.9	-3.4	-0.1
Italy	1.1	3.9	8.3	1.9	4.3	9.2	0.2%	0.4%	0.7%	35.1	20.3	28.2
Netherlands	134.1	381.8	515.7	248.3	429.0	433.7	28.5%	39.9%	40.7%	7.3	0.3	4.0
Bel. & Lux.	61.9	48.4	78.9	107.8	56.1	64.0	13.2%	5.1%	6.2%	-4.2	3.5	-0.6
UK	40.7	84.3	165.5	66.7	97.0	147.0	8.6%	8.8%	13.1%	6.3	14.2	10.0
Ireland	8.9	16.8	19.4	13.6	18.5	16.8	1.9%	1.8%	1.5%	8.9	5.7	7.4
Denmark	33.9	50.5	40.5	51.9	55.5	35.1	7.2%	5.3%	3.2%	1.4	-5.7	-1.9
Spain	11.2	7.1	23.3	31.3	9.8	21.9	2.4%	0.7%	1.8%	45.9	12.6	30.4
Greece	0.2	0.4	13.7	0.3	0.4	11.5	0.1%	0.0%	1.1%	43.7	77.3	59.4
Portugal	0.8	2.0	17.8	1.9	2.5	13.1	0.2%	0.2%	1.4%	7.0	33.9	19.6
Extra-EUR-12	470.6	957.5	1265.6	808.3	1074.9	1079.3	100.0%	100.0%	100.0%	3.9	0.3	2.2

Table D.6.18. Trade ratio (extra-EU)

Country	1978	1979	1980	1981	1982	1983	1984	1985	1986	1987	1988	1989	1990	1991	1992	1993
FRG	0.85	0.40	0.38	0.41	0.37	0.40	0.42	0.41	0.41	0.36	0.37	0.37	0.33	0.15	0.19	0.34
France	0.39	0.32	0.37	0.47	0.49	0.53	0.53	0.52	0.46	0.42	0.43	0.46	0.43	0.45	0.45	0.44
Italy	-0.94	-0.90	-0.92	-0.92	-0.91	-0.93	-0.93	-0.94	-0.92	-0.94	-0.93	-0.92	-0.87	-0.88	-0.91	-0.88
Netherlands	0.64	0.65	0.56	0.67	0.64	0.66	0.67	0.70	0.74	0.71	0.68	0.68	0.68	0.64	0.64	0.70
Bel. & Lux.	0.47	0.51	0.46	0.53	0.51	0.56	0.55	0.64	0.61	0.57	0.53	0.60	0.61	0.61	0.67	0.74
UK	-0.01	-0.02	0.04	0.18	0.22	0.16	0.09	0.00	-0.10	-0.08	-0.14	-0.15	-0.15	-0.13	-0.11	-0.11
Ireland	0.92	0.90	0.89	0.90	0.87	0.82	0.72	0.72	0.49	0.36	0.30	0.34	0.35	0.26	0.28	0.43
Denmark	0.98	0.98	0.98	0.98	0.97	0.99	0.99	0.71	0.98	0.90	0.92	0.85	0.88	0.92	0.95	0.80
Spain	0.51	0.36	0.06	0.70	-0.41	-0.53	-0.52	-0.53	-0.55	-0.56	-0.40	-0.35	-0.32	-0.30	-0.37	-0.38
Greece	-0.92	-0.93	-0.95	-0.89	-0.95	-0.79	-0.85	-0.79	-0.86	-0.89	-0.90	-0.89	-0.91	-0.80	-0.78	-0.37
Portugal	-0.18	-0.19	-0.40	0.14	-0.23	0.82	0.71	0.09	0.23	0.02	-0.18	-0.09	-0.08	-0.07	0.24	0.35
EUR-12	0.40	0.38	0.35	0.44	0.40	0.40	0.41	0.38	0.36	0.32	0.31	0.31	0.29	0.25	0.25	0.30

Table D.6.19. Trade ratio (intra-EU)

Country	1978	1979	1980	1981	1982	1983	1984	1985	1986	1987	1988	1989	1990	1991	1992	1993
FRG	-0.02	0.06	0.03	0.03	-0.04	-0.02	-0.01	0.00	0.03	0.01	0.04	0.03	0.01	-0.15	-0.09	0.09
France	-0.06	-0.10	-0.03	-0.05	0.08	0.12	0.20	0.17	0.11	0.16	0.19	0.18	0.19	0.24	0.25	0.26
Italy	-0.99	-1.00	-0.99	-0.98	-0.96	-0.99	-0.99	-0.98	-0.98	-0.98	-0.98	-0.97	-0.94	-0.92	-0.96	-0.94
Netherlands	-0.14	-0.15	-0.14	-0.08	-0.13	0.02	-0.05	0.04	0.15	0.15	0.11	0.14	0.16	0.13	0.15	0.13
Bel. & Lux.	0.23	0.34	0.32	0.33	0.36	0.41	0.38	0.54	0.53	0.48	0.44	0.47	0.49	0.52	0.64	0.72
UK	-0.55	-0.57	-0.56	-0.43	-0.31	-0.36	-0.42	-0.45	-0.49	-0.64	-0.68	-0.71	-0.67	-0.43	-0.43	-0.48
Ireland	0.90	0.86	0.86	0.87	0.81	0.72	0.62	0.56	0.34	0.20	0.23	0.29	0.29	0.22	0.21	0.37
Denmark	0.97	0.97	0.97	0.97	0.95	0.98	0.98	0.57	0.96	0.84	0.90	0.80	0.84	0.91	0.94	0.75
Spain	0.12	-0.05	-0.46	0.42	-0.65	-0.71	-0.73	-0.73	-0.81	-0.87	-0.76	-0.66	-0.56	-0.57	-0.68	-0.70
Greece	-1.00	-1.00	-1.00	-1.00	-1.00	-1.00	-1.00	-1.00	-1.00	-1.00	-1.00	-1.00	-1.00	-1.00	-1.00	-0.96
Portugal	-0.73	-0.74	0.00	-0.43	-0.77	0.40	0.11	-0.63	-0.48	-0.75	-0.81	-0.84	-0.82	-0.75	-0.59	-0.34
EUR-12	-0.01	-0.03	-0.04	0.00	-0.03	-0.02	-0.01	-0.03	-0.03	-0.05	-0.03	-0.05	-0.04	-0.03	-0.03	0.01

Table D.6.20. Intra-EU imports as % of total

Country	1978	1979	1980	1981	1982	1983	1984	1985	1986	1987	1988	1989	1990	1991	1992	1993
FRG	90.2	89.6	91.9	91.7	93.1	93.0	92.4	93.0	93.3	94.7	94.6	94.5	94.6	92.6	92.3	90.7
France	99.1	99.0	99.5	99.1	98.4	98.7	98.4	98.3	97.6	98.1	97.0	97.0	97.3	97.0	95.8	94.9
Italy	92.1	91.7	92.2	90.1	89.8	92.4	93.2	92.5	93.0	93.4	94.0	93.7	94.0	90.8	92.6	92.5
Netherlands	98.0	99.8	99.8	99.8	99.9	99.7	99.6	99.6	99.6	99.6	98.6	95.8	94.3	96.6	98.9	97.2
Bel. & Lux.	96.4	97.1	98.0	97.9	97.5	96.2	97.4	95.9	94.9	94.8	95.5	97.2	96.2	89.5	83.0	81.3
UK	88.0	90.6	86.1	89.0	88.3	86.3	87.7	91.7	91.2	91.0	91.2	91.6	90.5	85.2	89.8	89.2
Ireland	100.0	100.0	100.0	87.0	100.0	100.0	100.0	100.0	98.3	98.3	98.4	97.9	99.5	97.8	97.5	98.6
Denmark	85.7	85.7	85.7	83.3	84.6	80.0	83.3	82.8	92.9	98.7	96.6	97.4	96.5	96.1	94.2	97.4
Spain	95.0	95.3	95.0	94.6	95.8	96.9	99.0	99.3	97.2	99.5	96.7	92.7	93.1	95.2	93.6	94.5
Greece	99.2	99.5	100.0	98.5	100.0	100.0	100.0	98.7	96.3	97.4	96.1	97.6	97.7	95.7	91.4	88.2
Portugal	91.3	94.2	100.0	66.7	100.0	100.0	100.0	100.0	100.0	100.0	94.9	100.0	99.5	100.0	99.4	99.1
EUR-12	93.9	94.5	94.5	94.0	94.0	93.6	94.0	94.2	94.4	95.0	94.7	94.5	94.2	91.8	92.7	92.0

Table D.6.21 Intra-EU exports as % of total

Country	1978	1979	1980	1981	1982	1983	1984	1985	1986	1987	1988	1989	1990	1991	1992	1993
FRG	41.4	44.0	43.9	41.0	39.5	38.0	36.9	38.6	41.8	45.3	47.0	45.5	48.7	50.5	52.6	53.4
France	39.0	41.7	42.4	32.1	39.7	39.2	45.1	43.2	45.4	55.2	56.8	51.9	56.6	59.4	60.4	63.8
Italy	9.1	3.6	14.8	18.8	34.7	17.0	16.7	23.1	22.4	28.6	29.7	40.6	41.3	56.4	37.3	46.2
Netherlands	16.1	15.8	21.4	17.1	16.6	21.3	17.4	18.9	19.9	22.7	23.0	24.3	25.3	27.0	29.4	22.6
Bel. & Lux.	55.6	64.5	69.9	59.7	66.8	63.6	62.7	71.2	75.3	75.4	75.7	67.7	67.4	68.6	74.7	74.5
UK	25.9	25.9	22.7	24.5	29.6	29.0	30.0	34.8	38.3	23.7	23.1	20.8	24.5	43.6	45.1	39.3
Ireland	73.0	69.7	73.9	65.2	64.9	61.0	68.4	57.1	67.9	69.5	85.3	87.1	88.0	90.4	83.2	84.5
Denmark	50.7	51.9	53.1	52.2	48.2	49.3	49.5	52.1	57.8	61.5	68.9	70.1	73.1	80.1	77.7	76.8
Spain	40.0	40.5	30.9	41.2	48.0	52.5	48.5	50.0	35.7	23.5	30.8	39.6	50.4	49.0	38.8	36.8
Greece	0.0	0.0	0.0	0.0	0.0	0.0	0.0	0.0	0.0	0.0	0.0	0.0	0.0	0.0	0.0	3.5
Portugal	20.6	20.7	21.4	20.0	20.8	22.6	20.8	19.4	21.9	14.0	14.5	10.7	11.5	16.2	15.6	23.6
EUR-12	39.2	40.3	41.8	36.8	38.1	37.9	38.6	39.9	41.6	44.1	46.7	44.9	47.3	51.5	52.5	50.2

Table D.6.22. Import penetration ratios (extra-EU)

Country	1978	1979	1980	1981	1982	1983	1984	1985	1986	1987	1988	1989	1990	1991	1992	1993
FRG	0.15	0.15	0.13	0.15	0.15	0.15	0.18	0.18	0.16	0.14	0.14	0.16	0.16	0.31	0.34	0.30
France	0.07	0.08	0.03	0.05	0.10	0.07	0.10	0.10	0.16	0.12	0.21	0.22	0.22	0.24	0.32	0.37
Italy	0.87	1.09	1.17	1.36	1.49	1.07	1.26	1.40	1.21	1.13	0.99	1.37	1.18	1.84	1.56	1.56
Netherlands	0.09	0.01	0.01	0.01	0.01	0.01	0.02	0.02	0.02	0.02	0.09	0.27	0.40	0.28	0.09	0.20
Bel. & Lux.	0.25	0.17	0.11	0.13	0.16	0.20	0.20	0.22	0.29	0.33	0.44	0.20	0.29	0.90	1.15	0.99
UK	0.18	0.16	0.22	0.15	0.19	0.26	0.25	0.20	0.22	0.25	0.26	0.30	0.41	0.67	0.44	0.46
Ireland	0.00	0.00	0.00	0.03	0.00	0.00	0.00	0.00	0.02	0.03	0.05	0.06	0.01	0.09	0.12	0.05
Denmark	0.01	0.01	0.00	0.00	0.01	0.00	0.01	0.25	0.01	0.01	0.01	0.02	0.02	0.02	0.02	0.03
Spain	0.11	0.09	0.05	0.06	0.06	0.05	0.00	0.00	0.09	0.02	0.07	0.19	0.22	0.17	0.30	0.23
Greece	0.00	0.00	0.00	0.00	0.00	0.00	0.00	0.00	0.14	0.09	0.25	0.17	0.23	0.44	1.11	1.35
Portugal	0.36	0.21	0.00	0.39	0.00	0.00	0.00	0.00	0.00	0.00	0.19	0.00	0.00	0.00	0.04	0.04
EUR-12	0.16	0.15	0.16	0.16	0.18	0.20	0.20	0.21	0.21	0.20	0.22	0.24	0.29	0.45	0.40	0.40

Table D.6.23. Import penetration ratios (intra-EU)

Country	1978	1979	1980	1981	1982	1983	1984	1985	1986	1987	1988	1989	1990	1991	1992	1993
FRG	1.42	1.32	1.43	1.63	2.04	2.05	2.14	2.40	2.32	2.59	2.52	2.67	2.86	3.86	4.02	2.92
France	7.34	7.93	7.69	6.62	6.27	6.00	6.34	6.27	6.30	6.63	7.06	7.29	7.79	7.60	7.22	6.84
Italy	10.10	12.05	14.08	12.72	13.45	13.13	17.56	17.57	16.26	16.10	15.51	20.56	18.49	18.16	19.61	19.23
Netherlands	4.35	4.78	7.23	5.27	7.19	6.95	6.78	6.32	5.61	5.97	6.65	6.37	6.58	7.62	8.51	7.21
Bel. & Lux.	6.37	5.64	5.72	5.95	6.19	5.19	7.44	5.52	5.32	6.28	9.36	7.13	7.77	7.70	5.65	4.38
UK	1.28	1.51	1.37	1.25	1.41	1.65	1.80	2.18	2.35	2.51	2.71	3.25	3.89	3.88	3.83	3.74
Ireland	0.26	0.34	0.31	0.25	0.34	0.52	0.78	0.96	1.67	2.41	2.89	2.71	2.93	4.04	4.51	3.45
Denmark	0.08	0.08	0.08	0.06	0.12	0.04	0.05	1.21	0.10	0.57	0.42	0.85	0.84	0.52	0.36	1.22
Spain	2.00	1.77	0.86	0.99	1.43	1.57	1.10	1.26	3.49	3.24	2.25	2.44	2.97	3.31	4.30	3.99
Greece	3.68	3.96	2.35	3.76	4.65	2.71	3.69	3.61	3.70	4.95	6.11	8.91	11.25	9.79	11.34	9.87
Portugal	3.75	3.47	3.64	0.77	2.88	0.00	0.28	1.72	1.09	2.53	4.51	5.47	7.65	7.76	6.63	3.94
EUR-12	2.43	2.60	2.72	2.49	2.88	2.94	3.12	3.38	3.47	3.76	3.85	4.16	4.62	4.96	5.14	4.55

Table D.6.24. Intra-EU exports as a % of production

Country	1978	1979	1980	1981	1982	1983	1984	1985	1986	1987	1988	1989	1990	1991	1992	1993
FRG	1.4	1.5	1.5	1.7	1.8	1.9	2.0	2.3	2.4	2.5	2.6	2.7	2.8	2.8	3.3	3.3
France	6.1	6.2	7.0	5.6	7.0	7.2	8.7	8.1	7.4	8.5	9.7	9.7	10.7	11.3	11.2	10.8
Italy	0.0	0.0	0.1	0.1	0.2	0.1	0.1	0.1	0.2	0.2	0.2	0.4	0.6	0.7	0.4	0.6
Netherlands	3.3	3.6	5.6	4.5	5.7	7.3	6.2	6.9	7.7	8.2	8.4	8.6	9.3	10.1	11.6	9.3
Bel. & Lux.	9.9	11.2	10.8	11.5	12.8	11.8	16.0	17.5	16.1	16.4	21.8	18.0	20.2	21.2	22.3	23.4
UK	0.4	0.4	0.4	0.5	0.7	0.8	0.7	0.8	0.8	0.6	0.5	0.6	0.8	1.6	1.6	1.4
Ireland	4.9	4.6	4.2	3.7	3.3	3.3	3.4	3.4	3.4	3.7	4.7	5.0	5.5	6.6	7.2	7.7
Denmark	4.6	4.5	4.5	4.4	4.6	4.6	4.8	4.5	5.5	6.7	7.6	7.8	9.7	11.1	11.2	8.7
Spain	2.5	1.6	0.3	2.3	0.3	0.3	0.2	0.2	0.4	0.2	0.3	0.5	0.8	0.9	0.8	0.7
Greece	0.0	0.0	0.0	0.0	0.0	0.0	0.0	0.0	0.0	0.0	0.0	0.0	0.0	0.0	0.0	0.2
Portugal	0.6	0.5	0.3	0.3	0.4	0.5	0.3	0.4	0.4	0.4	0.5	0.5	0.8	1.1	1.6	1.9
EUR-12	2.3	2.4	2.5	2.4	2.7	2.8	3.0	3.2	3.2	3.4	3.6	3.8	4.2	4.6	4.9	4.6

Table D.6.25. Extra-EU exports as a % of production

Country	1978	1979	1980	1981	1982	1983	1984	1985	1986	1987	1988	1989	1990	1991	1992	1993
FRG	1.9	1.8	1.9	2.4	2.7	3.1	3.4	3.7	3.3	3.1	2.9	3.2	2.9	2.7	2.9	2.9
France	9.5	8.6	9.2	11.8	10.2	11.2	10.5	10.5	8.7	6.9	7.3	9.0	8.2	7.8	7.3	6.1
Italy	0.3	0.7	0.2	0.1	0.2	0.1	0.3	0.2	0.4	0.3	0.4	0.4	0.7	0.5	0.6	0.7
Netherlands	17.1	19.0	20.7	22.0	28.4	27.1	29.3	29.6	30.7	27.8	27.9	26.7	27.4	27.1	27.9	31.9
Bel. & Lux.	7.9	6.1	4.6	7.7	6.3	6.6	9.4	7.0	5.1	5.1	6.4	7.7	9.2	8.7	7.2	8.0
UK	1.1	1.2	1.3	1.5	1.8	1.9	1.7	1.6	1.3	0.6	0.6	0.8	0.9	2.1	1.9	2.1
Ireland	1.8	2.0	1.5	2.0	1.8	2.1	1.6	2.6	1.6	1.6	0.8	0.7	0.7	0.7	1.5	1.4
Denmark	4.5	4.2	4.0	4.0	5.0	4.8	4.9	4.1	4.0	4.2	3.4	3.3	3.6	2.8	3.2	2.6
Spain	3.1	1.9	0.7	2.7	0.3	0.2	0.2	0.2	0.7	0.7	0.7	0.7	0.8	1.0	1.3	1.2
Greece	0.2	0.2	0.1	0.2	0.1	0.2	0.2	0.5	0.2	0.2	0.2	0.3	0.4	1.2	1.6	5.3
Portugal	1.3	1.1	0.7	0.7	0.8	1.2	0.8	1.2	1.1	2.1	2.5	4.0	5.7	5.6	8.6	6.1
EUR-12	3.7	3.7	3.4	4.2	4.3	4.5	4.8	4.7	4.4	3.8	3.7	4.2	4.2	4.3	4.4	4.4

Figure D.6.1. Intra/extra-EU exports

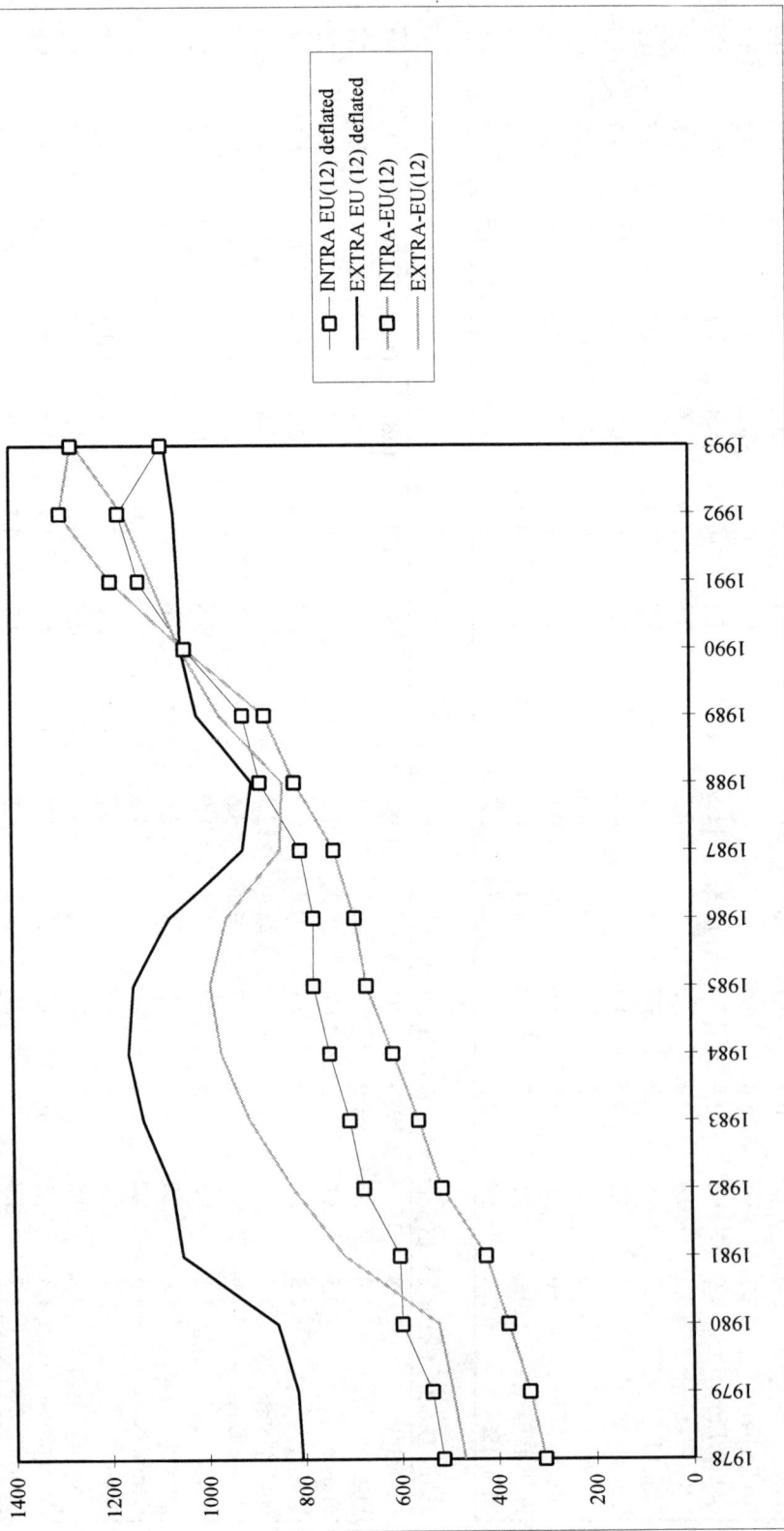

Note: 1978, 1979 are estimated figures (estimates for Spain, Portugal and Greece).

Figure D.6.2. EU exports 1978

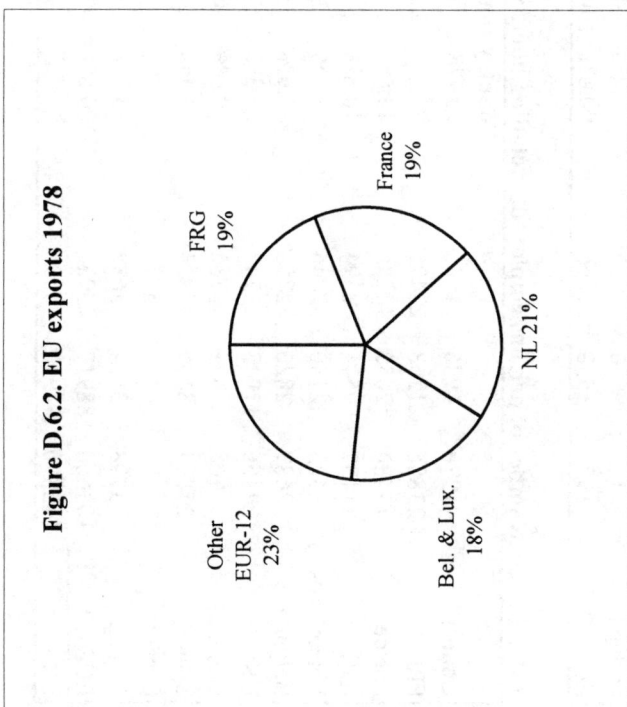

Figure D.6.3. EU exports 1993

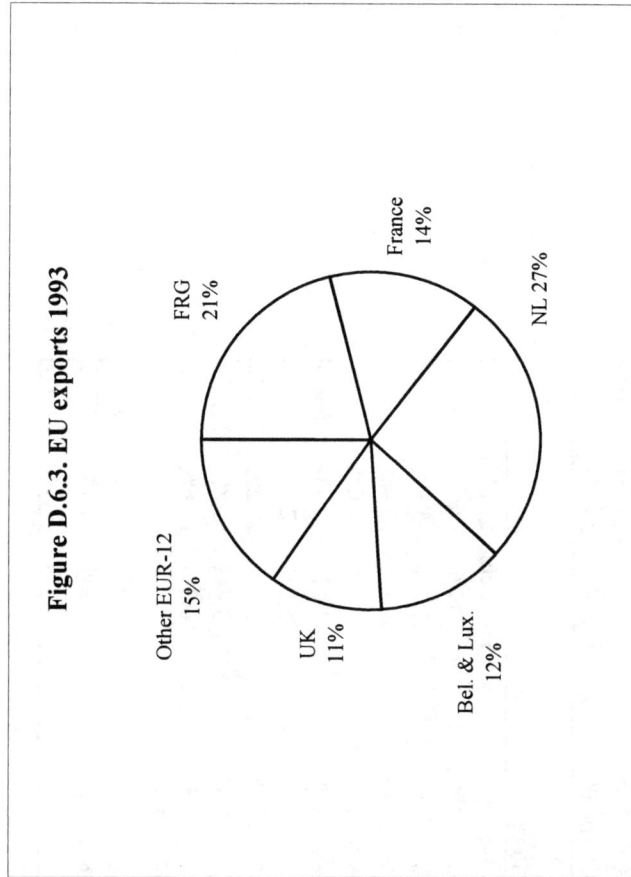

Note: Intra- and extra-EU exports.

D.7.   NACE 428

4280   **Manufacture of soft drinks, including the bottling of natural spa waters**

Table D.7.1.   Number of enterprises

Country	1978	1986	1993	Country share (%) 1978	1986	1993	Total change (%) 78/86	86/93	78/93
FRG	241	192	148	12.2%	12.5%	12.7%	-20.3%	-23.0%	-38.6%
France	62	61	57	3.1%	4.0%	4.9%	-1.6%	-7.2%	-8.7%
Italy	123	115	96	6.2%	7.5%	8.2%	-6.5%	-16.4%	-21.8%
Netherlands	16	14	12	0.8%	0.9%	1.1%	-12.5%	-11.8%	-22.8%
Belgium	27	24	20	1.4%	1.6%	1.7%	-11.1%	-16.5%	-25.8%
UK	153	108	60	7.8%	7.0%	5.2%	-29.4%	-44.4%	-60.7%
Denmark	7	4	4	0.4%	0.3%	0.3%	-42.9%	0.0%	-42.9%
Spain	1207	908	670	61.3%	59.0%	57.5%	-24.8%	-26.2%	-44.5%
Greece	29	36	42	1.5%	2.3%	3.6%	24.9%	17.5%	46.7%
Portugal	102	76	56	5.2%	4.9%	4.8%	-25.5%	-25.7%	-44.6%
EUR-12	1970	1538	1166	100.0%	100.0%	100.0%	-21.9%	-24.2%	-40.8%

Table D.7.2.   Number of persons employed, excluding home workers

Country	1978	1986	1993	Country share (%) 1978	1986	1993	Total change (%) 78/86	86/93	78/93
FRG	23886	21268	22495	23.1%	23.9%	25.0%	-11.0%	5.8%	-5.8%
France	13484	12655	14285	13.0%	14.2%	15.9%	-6.1%	12.9%	5.9%
Italy	11137	9541	8394	10.8%	10.7%	9.3%	-14.3%	-12.0%	-24.6%
Netherlands	1525	2150	2446	1.5%	2.4%	2.7%	41.0%	13.8%	60.4%
Belgium	2687	2826	2758	2.6%	3.2%	3.1%	5.2%	-2.4%	2.6%
UK	24166	17943	15747	23.3%	20.2%	17.5%	-25.8%	-12.2%	-34.8%
Denmark	668	691	786	0.6%	0.8%	0.9%	3.4%	13.8%	17.7%
Spain	21864	18309	15824	21.1%	20.6%	17.6%	-16.3%	-13.6%	-27.6%
Greece			3533			3.9%			
Portugal	3798	3534	3652	3.7%	4.0%	4.1%	-6.9%	3.3%	-3.8%
EUR-12	103600	88917	89921	100.0%	100.0%	100.0%	-14.2%	1.1%	-13.2%
USA	112890	98940	77595				-12.4%	-21.6%	-31.3%

Table D.7.3. Production value, excluding VAT

Country	Actual			Deflated			Country share (%)			Real average annual change (%)		
	1978	1986	1993	1978	1986	1993	1978	1986	1993	78/86	86/93	78/93
FRG	1391	2580	4113	2177	2938	3462	34.2%	24.8%	23.0%	4.0	2.8	3.4
France	710	1770	3381	1235	1982	2958	17.4%	17.0%	18.9%	6.2	6.6	6.4
Italy	409	1412	2329	634	1521	2470	10.1%	13.6%	13.0%	12.1	7.3	9.9
Netherlands	169	424	707	289	467	605	4.2%	4.1%	3.9%	6.9	4.0	5.5
Belgium	167	330	493	246	347	432	4.1%	3.2%	2.8%	5.3	3.8	4.6
Luxembourg	37	37	37	54	39	32	0.9%	0.4%	0.2%	-4.1	-2.5	-3.4
UK	921	2092	3163	1511	2407	2809	22.6%	20.1%	17.7%	7.3	2.5	5.0
Denmark	28	57	86	49	64	75	0.7%	0.6%	0.5%	4.2	2.3	3.3
Spain	196	1367	2907	613	2004	2828	4.8%	13.2%	16.2%	20.2	5.2	13.2
Greece	6	211	502	8	213	455	0.2%	2.0%	2.8%	94.3	11.9	55.9
Portugal	34	104	199	82	127	147	0.8%	1.0%	1.1%	6.5	3.6	5.1
EUR-12	4068	10383	17917	6899	12111	16274	100.0%	100.0%	100.0%	7.6	4.5	6.2
USA	9212	20896	22146		18014	19598				4.9	1.2	2.1

Table D.7.4. Production value per enterprise

Country	Actual			Deflated		
	1978	1986	1993	1978	1986	1993
FRG	5.8	13.4	27.8	9.0	15.3	23.4
France	11.4	29.0	59.7	19.9	32.5	52.3
Italy	3.3	12.3	24.2	5.2	13.2	25.7
Netherlands	10.6	30.3	57.2	18.0	33.4	49.0
Belgium	6.2	13.7	24.6	9.1	14.5	21.6
UK	6.0	19.4	52.6	9.9	22.3	46.7
Denmark	4.1	14.4	21.5	7.1	16.1	18.8
Spain	0.2	1.5	4.3	0.5	2.2	4.2
Greece	0.2	5.9	11.8	0.3	5.9	10.7
Portugal	0.3	1.4	3.5	0.8	1.7	2.6
EUR-12	2.1	6.8	15.4	3.5	7.9	14.0

Table D.7.5. Consumption value

Country	Actual			Deflated			Country share (%)			Real average annual change (%)		
	1978	1986	1993	1978	1986	1993	1978	1986	1993	78/86	86/93	78/93
FRG	1379	2544	4085	1832	2548	3409	35.8%	25.8%	24.3%	4.4	4.6	4.5
France	701	1745	3314	1393	1699	2639	18.2%	17.7%	19.7%	2.7	7.2	4.8
Italy	371	1391	2252	983	1314	1464	9.6%	14.1%	13.4%	4.1	1.6	3.0
Netherlands	184	473	832	251	473	726	4.8%	4.8%	4.9%	8.8	6.6	7.7
Bel. & Lux.	234	452	739	366	446	613	6.1%	4.6%	4.4%	97.0	4.9	54.0
UK	923	2135	3228	1749	2064	2171	24.0%	21.6%	19.2%	2.3	1.0	1.7
Ireland	2	7	19	5	6	15	0.1%	0.1%	0.1%	40.4	24.0	32.8
Denmark	29	60	89	53	58	69	0.8%	0.6%	0.5%	1.9	2.7	2.3
Spain	533	746	1513	1256	686	942	13.8%	7.6%	9.0%	-6.7	5.2	-1.1
Greece	25	212	518	95	172	147	0.6%	2.1%	3.1%	9.9	-1.8	4.4
Portugal	34	105	229	139	94	104	0.9%	1.1%	1.4%	-3.5	2.1	-0.9
EUR-12	3856	9870	16819	8122	9561	12300	100.0%	100.0%	100.0%	2.2	3.8	2.9

Table D.7.6. Labour costs

Country	Actual			Deflated			Country share (%)		
	1978	1986	1993	1978	1986	1993	1978	1986	1993
FRG	320	509	751	501	580	632	31.5%	28.5%	27.6%
France	175	344	528	304	385	462	17.2%	19.2%	19.4%
Italy	116	227	330	180	245	350	11.4%	12.7%	12.1%
Netherlands	23	56	78	40	62	67	2.3%	3.1%	2.9%
Belgium	39	63	83	57	67	73	3.8%	3.5%	3.0%
UK	138	253	408	226	292	363	13.6%	14.2%	15.0%
Denmark	10	12	15	17	13	13	1.0%	0.7%	0.6%
Spain	185	307	448	322	344	392	18.2%	17.2%	16.5%
Greece			57			52			2.1%
Portugal	11	16	25	26	20	19	1.1%	0.9%	0.9%
EU (average)	182	313	461	167	201	242			
EUR-12	1016	1788	2725	1673	2007	2423	100.0%	100.0%	100.0%

Table D.7.7. Gross value added at factor cost

Country	Actual			Deflated			Country share (%)			Real average annual change (%)		
	1978	1986	1993	1978	1986	1993	1978	1986	1993	78/86	86/93	78/93
FRG	544	824	1326	851	938	1116	32.2%	24.6%	25.0%	1.4	3.0	2.1
France	256	596	1025	445	667	897	15.1%	17.8%	19.3%	5.5	5.0	5.2
Italy	180	469	679	279	505	720	10.7%	14.0%	12.8%	8.2	5.9	7.1
Netherlands	40	88	162	68	97	139	2.3%	2.6%	3.1%	30.6	5.4	18.9
Belgium	61	57	47	89	60	41	3.6%	1.7%	0.9%	-1.6	-4.6	-3.0
UK	365	634	851	598	730	756	21.6%	19.0%	16.1%	4.8	0.6	2.8
Denmark	11	22	33	18	25	29	0.6%	0.7%	0.6%	4.4	2.6	3.5
Spain	235	655	1069	733	960	1040	13.9%	19.6%	20.2%	3.9	1.4	2.7
Greece			107			97			2.0%		15.5	15.5
EUR-12	1690	3345	5299	3083	3983	4835	100.0%	100.0%	100.0%	3.5	2.9	3.2
USA	3529	8040	8124		6931	7189				5.8	0.6	1.7

Table D.7.8. Gross value added per person employed (in 000 ECU)

Country	Actual			Deflated		
	1978	1986	1993	1978	1986	1993
FRG	22.8	38.7	58.9	35.6	44.1	49.6
France	19.0	47.1	71.8	33.0	52.7	62.8
Italy	16.2	49.1	80.9	25.1	52.9	85.7
Netherlands	26.0	41.1	66.2	44.3	45.3	56.7
Belgium	22.5	20.3	17.0	33.3	21.3	14.9
UK	15.1	35.4	54.0	24.7	40.7	48.0
Denmark	15.9	31.7	42.5	27.6	35.5	37.2
Spain			67.6			65.7
EUR-12	16.3	37.6	58.9	29.8	44.8	53.8
USA	31.3	81.3	104.7		70.1	92.7

Table D.7.9. Investment

Country	Actual			Deflated			Country share (%)		
	1978	1986	1993	1978	1986	1993	1978	1986	1993
FRG	118	207	410	184	236	345	45.5%	38.0%	32.9%
France	27	125	306	47	140	268	10.4%	23.0%	24.6%
Italy	29	101	164	45	109	174	11.2%	18.5%	13.1%
Netherlands	22	20	57	37	22	49	8.3%	3.7%	4.6%
Belgium	20	17	80	30	18	70	7.8%	3.1%	6.4%
UK	41	68	189	67	78	168	15.8%	12.5%	15.2%
Denmark	3	6	6	5	7	5	1.0%	1.2%	0.5%
Greece			33			30			2.6%
EUR-12	259	544	1246	414	610	1110	100.0%	100.0%	100.0%
EU (average)	37	78	156	103	152	247			
USA	366	543			468				

Table D.7.10. Proportion of investments in gross value added at factor cost (in %)

Country	1978	1979	1980	1981	1982	1983	1984	1985	1986	1987	1988	1989	1990	1991	1992	1993
FRG	35.7	36.7	35.7	39.0	38.4	41.8	42.0	42.2	44.1	43.0	47.3	50.7	52.1	51.1	48.4	48.4
France	33.1	40.8	41.2	47.0	49.8	50.3	47.2	46.2	52.7	55.3	55.0	63.5	70.8	59.0	62.9	63.2
Italy	25.1	28.1	30.1	35.3	37.1	37.6	44.0	53.9	52.9	63.5	69.6	55.4	58.8	58.4	67.8	80.0
Netherlands	44.4	18.5	22.0	27.8	29.3	33.6	38.4	43.1	45.3	49.7	51.8	58.6	62.8	59.1	59.7	59.9
Belgium	33.2	37.3	40.6	36.7	42.9	36.6	18.4	20.4	21.4	23.5	22.3	23.0	23.0	23.2	22.6	22.2
UK	24.8	31.9	46.9	44.4	41.3	45.6	39.0	37.1	40.7	42.2	40.1	41.9	44.4	42.3	42.4	44.4
Denmark	27.7	26.2	39.7	49.6	43.2	37.4	41.4	43.7	44.3	46.6	48.6	49.9	50.5	50.9	51.2	51.3
Spain	24.4	30.3	42.3	41.7	42.1	44.2	45.0	47.6	52.5	54.1	50.8	54.8	53.1	56.1	54.0	61.5
Greece										15.9	25.9	22.5	20.9	26.0	26.5	28.4
EU (average)	29.8	33.3	38.1	39.3	39.4	41.8	40.4	41.7	44.8	45.9	46.4	47.8	50.5	48.6	50.3	53.8
USA							57.9	63.6	70.1	75.8	79.8	81.4	84.7	88.0	92.7	92.7

Table D.7.11. Producer price index

Country	1978	1979	1980	1981	1982	1983	1984	1985	1986	1987	1988	1989	1990	1991	1992	1993
FRG	63.9	66.2	66.7	68.5	74.8	79.7	81.9	82.9	87.8	93.0	94.1	96.3	100.0	105.8	113.5	118.8
France	57.5	61.1	65.0	68.9	71.3	73.2	77.3	84.5	89.3	90.8	92.6	95.8	100.0	104.5	109.3	114.3
Italy	64.5	67.7	70.8	69.7	75.2	82.4	86.0	87.9	92.8	95.1	95.3	99.0	100.0	104.3	105.4	94.3
Netherlands	58.6	59.3	62.9	66.4	78.8	82.4	84.0	85.5	90.7	93.6	94.0	97.4	100.0	104.8	110.4	116.7
Bel. & Lux.	67.7	70.4	70.7	77.1	78.3	80.4	82.6	88.1	95.0	94.9	93.3	94.2	100.0	102.7	108.6	114.1
UK	61.0	64.6	58.0	73.5	80.4	82.7	87.6	94.0	86.9	85.1	94.5	98.1	100.0	111.7	113.4	112.6
Ireland	57.5	61.1	65.0	68.9	71.3	73.2	77.3	84.5	89.3	90.8	92.6	95.8	100.0	104.5	109.3	114.3
Denmark	57.5	61.1	65.0	68.9	71.3	73.2	77.3	84.5	89.3	90.8	92.6	95.8	100.0	104.5	109.3	114.3
Spain	32.0	37.9	44.2	50.4	55.6	54.1	61.5	67.9	68.2	71.3	79.9	92.1	100.0	107.5	110.1	102.8
Greece	80.2	57.2	67.5	84.0	97.5	98.3	95.3	95.7	99.4	89.5	89.9	93.0	100.0	106.9	108.9	110.3
Portugal	40.8	42.1	47.3	57.6	65.2	63.7	70.0	82.0	81.5	82.0	80.1	86.3	100.0	121.5	140.3	136.0
USA							140.8	147.1	116.0	101.2	100.7	111.0	100.0	105.0	100.9	113.0

Table D.7.12. Total imports (million ECU)

Country	Actual			Deflated			Country share (%)			Real average annual change (%)		
	1978	1986	1993	1978	1986	1993	1978	1986	1993	78/86	86/93	78/93
FRG	47.6	84.4	240.3	74.5	96.1	202.3	38.3%	19.8%	24.4%	3.8	12.9	8.1
France	8.4	84.5	112.6	14.6	94.6	98.5	6.8%	19.8%	11.4%	27.6	2.4	15.8
Italy	2.1	10.9	33.4	3.3	11.7	35.4	1.7%	2.6%	3.4%	29.9	17.4	24.1
Netherlands	18.6	68.6	146.8	31.7	75.6	125.8	15.0%	16.1%	14.9%	13.7	10.8	12.3
Bel. & Lux.	35.5	100.7	221.2	52.4	106.0	193.9	28.6%	23.6%	22.5%	10.0	9.1	9.6
UK	8.3	57.7	105.7	13.6	66.4	93.9	6.7%	13.5%	10.7%	26.6	8.9	18.4
Ireland	1.2	8.6	43.2	2.1	9.6	37.8	1.0%	2.0%	4.4%	27.6	25.0	26.4
Denmark	1.5	4.3	9.2	2.6	4.8	8.0	1.2%	1.0%	0.9%	8.3	12.4	10.2
Spain	1.1	4.3	25.7	3.3	6.3	25.0	0.8%	1.0%	2.6%	89.5	27.6	60.6
Greece	0.0	0.7	15.5	0.0	0.7	14.1	0.0%	0.2%	1.6%	35.3	87.2	75.6
Portugal	0.0	1.5	29.9	0.0	1.8	22.0	0.0%	0.4%	3.0%	0.0	55.6	55.6
Total EUR-12	124.3	426.6	983.5	198.1	473.8	856.6	100.0%	100.0%	100.0%	11.8	9.5	10.8

Table D.7.13. Intra-EU imports (million ECU)

Country	Actual			Deflated			Country share (%)			Real average annual change (%)		
	1978	1986	1993	1978	1986	1993	1978	1986	1993	78/86	86/93	78/93
FRG	44.3	62.0	189.6	69.3	70.6	159.6	37.6%	15.7%	21.2%	1.1	15.8	7.9
France	8.2	83.4	106.4	14.3	93.4	93.1	7.0%	21.1%	11.9%	27.7	1.7	15.6
Italy	1.8	9.8	24.8	2.8	10.6	26.3	1.5%	2.5%	2.8%	33.6	14.6	24.7
Netherlands	18.5	68.0	145.2	31.6	75.0	124.4	15.7%	17.2%	16.3%	13.7	10.7	12.3
Bel. & Lux.	35.3	100.3	217.7	52.1	105.6	190.8	30.0%	25.4%	24.4%	10.0	8.9	9.5
UK	7.6	55.6	93.3	12.5	64.0	82.9	6.5%	14.1%	10.5%	28.2	7.6	18.6
Ireland	1.2	8.6	42.9	2.1	9.6	37.5	1.0%	2.2%	4.8%	27.8	24.9	26.5
Denmark	0.1	1.8	4.7	0.2	2.0	4.1	0.1%	0.5%	0.5%	39.7	26.8	33.7
Spain	0.8	3.1	24.4	2.5	4.5	23.7	0.7%	0.8%	2.7%	89.4	31.3	62.3
Greece	0.0	0.7	13.8	0.0	0.7	12.5	0.0%	0.2%	1.5%	8.8	83.6	43.7
Portugal	0.0	1.4	29.7	0.0	1.7	21.8	0.0%	0.4%	3.3%	0.0	58.1	27.1
Intra-EUR-12	117.8	395.4	892.4	187.3	437.7	776.8	100.0%	100.0%	100.0%	11.5	9.3	10.5

Table D.7.14. Extra-EU imports (million ECU)

Country	Actual			Deflated			Country share (%)			Real average annual change (%)		
	1978	1986	1993	1978	1986	1993	1978	1986	1993	78/86	86/93	78/93
FRG	3.3	22.3	50.6	5.2	25.4	42.6	49.9%	71.5%	55.5%	22.4	9.8	16.5
France	0.1	1.0	6.2	0.2	1.1	5.4	1.5%	3.2%	6.8%	53.7	43.5	48.9
Italy	0.4	1.0	8.7	0.6	1.1	9.2	6.1%	3.2%	9.5%	11.2	37.6	23.5
Netherlands	0.2	0.5	1.6	0.3	0.6	1.4	3.0%	1.6%	1.8%	15.1	25.8	20.1
Bel. & Lux.	0.2	0.3	3.4	0.3	0.3	3.0	3.0%	1.0%	3.7%	10.9	54.9	31.5
UK	0.8	2.1	12.4	1.3	2.4	11.0	12.1%	6.7%	13.6%	13.8	30.8	21.7
Ireland	0.0	0.0	0.3	0.0	0.0	0.3	0.0%	0.0%	0.3%	21.7	58.5	40.1
Denmark	1.4	2.4	4.5	2.4	2.7	3.9	21.2%	7.7%	4.9%	1.7	7.6	4.4
Spain	0.2	1.1	1.3	0.7	1.6	1.3	3.2%	3.5%	1.4%	-14.8	18.7	0.8
Greece	0.0	0.0	1.7	0.0	0.0	1.5	0.0%	0.0%	1.9%	0.0	79.0	36.9
Portugal	0.0	0.0	0.2	0.0	0.0	0.1	0.0%	0.0%	0.2%	0.0	-1.0	-0.5
Extra-EUR-12	6.6	31.2	91.1	11.0	35.2	79.6	100.0%	100.0%	100.0%	15.9	13.9	14.9

Table D.7.15. Total exports (million ECU)

Country	Actual			Deflated			Country share (%)			Real average annual change (%)		
	1978	1986	1993	1978	1986	1993	1978	1986	1993	78/86	86/93	78/93
FRG	21.5	83.8	144.2	33.6	95.4	121.4	8.4%	13.4%	10.2%	15.5	4.8	10.5
France	75.4	205.8	541.3	131.2	230.5	473.6	29.6%	32.9%	38.1%	7.8	11.2	9.4
Italy	24.0	19.6	72.4	37.2	21.1	76.8	9.4%	3.1%	5.1%	-2.7	26.3	10.9
Netherlands	59.7	120.3	267.6	101.9	132.6	229.3	23.4%	19.3%	18.8%	6.0	9.7	7.7
Bel. & Lux.	17.0	110.0	179.8	25.1	115.8	157.6	6.7%	17.6%	12.7%	21.8	6.3	14.6
UK	40.2	32.2	110.5	65.9	37.1	98.1	15.8%	5.2%	7.8%	-5.5	15.6	4.4
Ireland	3.7	19.2	21.6	6.4	21.5	18.9	1.5%	3.1%	1.5%	18.2	-1.6	8.9
Denmark	5.2	14.7	12.0	9.0	16.5	10.5	2.0%	2.4%	0.8%	9.0	-5.0	2.5
Spain	6.0	15.1	40.4	18.9	22.1	39.3	2.4%	2.4%	2.8%	38.5	12.2	26.2
Greece	1.3	2.0	23.8	1.6	2.0	21.6	0.5%	0.3%	1.7%	26.8	72.6	48.2
Portugal	0.6	1.5	6.2	1.4	1.8	4.6	0.2%	0.2%	0.4%	15.9	23.3	19.4
Total EUR-12	254.6	624.7	1419.9	432.3	696.5	1251.6	100.0%	100.0%	100.0%	6.6	8.9	7.7

Table D.7.16. Intra-EU exports (million ECU)

Country	Actual			Deflated			Country share (%)			Real average annual change (%)		
	1978	1986	1993	1978	1986	1993	1978	1986	1993	78/86	86/93	78/93
FRG	7.6	58.7	79.3	11.9	66.9	66.8	6.2%	14.9%	8.2%	27.0	2.2	15.4
France	32.7	106.7	359.7	56.9	119.5	314.7	26.7%	27.2%	37.1%	9.9	15.8	12.7
Italy	5.1	9.5	40.9	7.9	10.2	43.4	4.2%	2.4%	4.2%	5.8	31.4	17.8
Netherlands	49.5	77.1	219.4	84.5	85.0	188.0	40.5%	19.6%	22.6%	1.3	13.3	6.9
Bel. & Lux.	16.7	104.8	164.8	24.7	110.3	144.4	13.6%	26.7%	17.0%	21.4	6.0	14.2
UK	4.6	13.9	63.5	7.5	16.0	56.4	3.8%	3.5%	6.5%	15.0	20.3	17.5
Ireland	3.6	18.3	20.1	6.3	20.5	17.6	2.9%	4.7%	2.1%	18.0	-1.8	8.7
Denmark	0.9	2.1	2.9	1.6	2.4	2.5	0.7%	0.5%	0.3%	10.6	7.0	8.9
Spain	1.7	1.4	18.7	5.2	2.1	18.2	1.4%	0.4%	1.9%	165.9	101.4	135.8
Greece	0.0	0.0	0.3	0.0	0.0	0.3	0.0%	0.0%	0.0%	0.0	-3.7	-1.7
Portugal	0.0	0.1	0.6	0.0	0.1	0.4	0.0%	0.0%	0.1%	0.1	96.6	45.1
Intra-EUR-12	122.4	393.0	970.2	206.4	432.9	852.7	100.0%	100.0%	100.0%	9.9	10.4	10.1

Table D.7.17. Extra-EU exports (million ECU)

Country	Actual			Deflated			Country share (%)			Real average annual change (%)		
	1978	1986	1993	1978	1986	1993	1978	1986	1993	78/86	86/93	78/93
FRG	13.9	25.0	64.9	21.8	28.5	54.6	10.6%	10.9%	14.4%	5.4	11.2	8.1
France	42.6	98.6	181.6	74.1	110.4	158.9	32.3%	42.9%	40.4%	6.7	6.0	6.4
Italy	18.9	9.6	31.5	29.3	10.3	33.4	14.3%	4.2%	7.0%	-4.4	27.1	10.3
Netherlands	10.2	43.1	48.2	17.4	47.5	41.3	7.7%	18.8%	10.7%	22.4	7.4	15.4
Bel. & Lux.	0.4	4.8	15.0	0.6	5.1	13.1	0.3%	2.1%	3.3%	50.1	31.1	41.2
UK	35.5	18.2	47.0	58.2	20.9	41.7	27.0%	7.9%	10.5%	-10.1	11.8	0.1
Ireland	0.1	0.8	1.5	0.2	0.9	1.3	0.1%	0.3%	0.3%	71.9	11.1	43.5
Denmark	4.3	12.5	9.2	7.5	14.0	8.0	3.3%	5.4%	2.0%	9.3	-5.8	2.3
Spain	4.2	13.4	21.7	13.3	19.6	21.1	3.2%	5.8%	4.8%	40.2	1.9	22.3
Greece	1.3	1.8	23.6	1.6	1.8	21.4	1.0%	0.8%	5.2%	25.1	74.2	48.0
Portugal	0.3	1.2	5.6	0.7	1.5	4.1	0.2%	0.5%	1.2%	29.8	26.8	28.4
Extra-EUR-12	131.7	229.7	449.7	224.6	260.6	399.1	100.0%	100.0%	100.0%	3.1	6.8	4.8

Table D.7.18. Trade ratio (extra-EU)

Country	1978	1979	1980	1981	1982	1983	1984	1985	1986	1987	1988	1989	1990	1991	1992	1993
FRG	0.62	0.65	0.56	0.44	0.33	0.20	0.13	0.22	0.06	0.05	0.01	-0.10	0.15	0.21	0.14	0.12
France	1.00	0.99	0.99	0.98	0.97	0.98	0.95	0.98	0.98	0.98	0.97	0.95	0.89	0.95	0.94	0.93
Italy	0.96	0.97	0.93	0.94	0.93	0.85	0.84	0.83	0.81	0.82	0.76	0.74	0.75	0.69	0.39	0.57
Netherlands	0.96	0.94	0.95	0.97	0.97	0.98	0.99	0.97	0.98	0.97	0.95	0.95	0.95	0.98	0.94	0.94
Bel. & Lux.	0.33	0.14	0.50	0.33	0.78	0.83	0.90	0.85	0.88	0.92	0.89	0.90	0.88	0.96	0.75	0.63
UK	0.96	0.95	0.88	0.93	0.92	0.83	0.79	0.78	0.79	0.66	0.55	0.38	0.41	0.59	0.60	0.58
Ireland	1.00	1.00	1.00	0.00	0.25	-0.67	1.00	1.00	1.00	1.00	1.00	1.00	0.80	0.37	0.38	0.67
Denmark	0.51	0.55	0.58	0.61	0.57	0.61	0.71	0.71	0.68	0.63	0.43	0.35	0.34	0.12	0.25	0.34
Spain	0.91	0.91	0.89	0.91	0.91	0.92	0.79	1.00	0.85	0.84	0.48	0.52	0.70	0.74	0.87	0.89
Greece	1.00	1.00	1.00	1.00	1.00	1.00	1.00	1.00	1.00	0.75	0.33	0.18	0.77	0.93	0.59	0.87
Portugal	1.00	1.00	1.00	1.00	1.00	1.00	1.00	1.00	1.00	1.00	1.00	0.97	1.00	0.97	0.98	0.93
EUR-12	0.90	0.90	0.85	0.86	0.84	0.82	0.81	0.79	0.76	0.75	0.69	0.63	0.66	0.72	0.67	0.66

Table D.7.19. Trade ratio (intra-EU)

Country	1978	1979	1980	1981	1982	1983	1984	1985	1986	1987	1988	1989	1990	1991	1992	1993
FRG	-0.71	-0.54	-0.38	-0.25	-0.20	-0.09	-0.10	0.03	-0.03	-0.10	-0.08	0.03	-0.27	-0.33	-0.36	-0.41
France	0.60	0.54	0.47	0.36	0.21	0.10	0.00	0.06	0.12	0.25	0.21	0.11	0.36	0.48	0.50	0.54
Italy	0.48	0.47	-0.06	0.25	0.19	0.12	0.34	-0.13	-0.02	-0.22	-0.16	0.10	-0.08	-0.10	-0.12	0.25
Netherlands	0.46	0.34	0.13	0.12	0.10	0.11	0.16	0.04	0.06	0.20	0.12	0.13	0.05	0.11	-0.12	0.20
Bel. & Lux.	-0.36	-0.28	-0.21	-0.10	-0.04	0.06	-0.05	0.04	0.02	-0.03	0.04	0.10	-0.11	-0.18	-0.19	-0.14
UK	-0.25	-0.21	-0.24	-0.66	-0.74	-0.82	-0.61	-0.53	-0.60	-0.70	-0.57	-0.64	-0.52	-0.36	-0.35	-0.19
Ireland	0.50	0.19	0.20	0.30	0.36	0.55	0.38	0.22	0.36	0.29	-0.07	-0.18	-0.23	-0.29	-0.40	-0.35
Denmark	0.80	0.67	0.50	0.54	0.00	0.22	0.21	0.12	0.08	-0.28	-0.14	0.19	0.21	-0.01	0.38	-0.24
Spain	0.35	0.35	-0.13	0.58	0.36	0.07	0.76	-0.60	-0.38	-0.25	-0.38	-0.72	-0.05	-0.73	-0.57	-0.13
Greece	0.00	0.00	0.00	0.00	0.00	0.00	-1.00	-1.00	-1.00	-1.00	-1.00	-0.79	-0.95	-0.90	-0.87	-0.96
Portugal	0.00	0.00	0.00	0.00	0.00	0.00	0.00	1.00	-0.87	-0.67	-0.92	-0.96	-0.96	-0.92	-0.94	-0.96
EUR-12	0.02	0.03	-0.01	-0.01	-0.03	-0.02	0.00	-0.01	0.00	0.00	-0.01	-0.02	-0.03	-0.02	-0.08	0.04

Table D.7.20. Intra-EU imports as % of total

Country	1978	1979	1980	1981	1982	1983	1984	1985	1986	1987	1988	1989	1990	1991	1992	1993
FRG	93.1	91.4	89.4	88.3	84.6	78.1	70.9	71.7	73.5	78.4	75.8	68.2	81.8	84.4	85.3	78.9
France	97.6	97.4	97.5	97.9	97.7	98.6	96.8	98.8	98.7	98.3	98.2	96.7	92.8	96.6	96.0	94.5
Italy	85.7	88.6	94.0	89.4	91.8	91.4	84.0	91.7	89.9	92.5	91.9	91.7	88.7	82.9	78.7	74.3
Netherlands	99.5	98.0	98.8	98.7	98.8	99.0	98.8	98.8	99.1	99.5	99.2	99.4	99.4	99.5	99.3	98.9
Bel. & Lux.	99.4	99.1	99.6	99.7	99.6	99.5	99.8	99.6	99.6	99.7	99.7	99.7	99.7	99.7	99.0	98.4
UK	91.6	92.0	88.9	96.3	97.1	96.6	95.7	95.1	96.4	95.9	94.3	92.9	89.7	91.3	91.5	88.3
Ireland	100.0	100.0	100.0	97.6	93.1	90.6	100.0	99.0	100.0	100.0	100.0	100.0	99.7	98.5	99.2	99.3
Denmark	6.7	9.1	11.1	12.5	25.0	25.0	34.4	41.7	41.9	54.8	49.2	42.1	43.3	54.0	32.9	51.1
Spain	75.8	75.0	81.8	70.0	72.7	87.0	42.9	80.0	72.1	79.7	68.8	78.1	87.5	89.8	95.2	94.9
Greece	0.0	0.0	0.0	0.0	0.0	0.0	100.0	100.0	100.0	84.2	90.5	93.4	93.9	94.8	83.1	89.0
Portugal	0.0	0.0	0.0	0.0	0.0	0.0	0.0	0.0	93.3	100.0	99.0	98.9	100.0	99.3	99.5	99.3
EUR-12	94.8	94.4	94.6	94.9	94.2	93.4	92.4	92.4	92.7	93.5	92.4	91.0	91.8	92.5	93.1	90.7

Table D.7.21 Intra-EU exports as % of total

Country	1978	1979	1980	1981	1982	1983	1984	1985	1986	1987	1988	1989	1990	1991	1992	1993
FRG	35.3	39.6	52.1	63.4	64.9	66.4	60.9	63.5	70.0	72.9	72.2	73.5	65.4	64.2	67.2	55.0
France	43.4	39.8	50.4	51.0	50.0	47.9	46.1	43.6	51.8	55.4	53.5	51.2	62.4	66.9	68.4	66.5
Italy	21.3	26.6	42.4	34.5	39.5	49.3	49.4	43.0	48.5	44.4	53.5	65.6	47.7	41.3	55.9	56.5
Netherlands	82.9	74.5	73.9	61.3	59.0	53.5	47.6	57.5	64.1	78.3	81.7	82.7	81.6	70.9	75.9	82.0
Bel. & Lux.	98.2	98.8	98.5	99.0	96.6	95.9	95.1	95.9	95.3	93.7	95.2	96.5	94.1	83.7	91.1	91.7
UK	11.4	15.5	24.4	18.1	16.7	21.1	40.1	43.3	43.2	46.6	57.6	56.0	53.7	56.6	56.8	57.5
Ireland	97.3	100.0	98.1	98.7	95.8	98.8	98.8	96.1	95.3	93.4	91.9	95.2	95.8	93.8	96.0	93.1
Denmark	17.3	12.7	9.1	10.3	8.3	11.2	12.7	13.5	14.3	13.4	22.4	33.7	37.4	47.6	39.5	24.2
Spain	27.4	25.5	15.9	36.1	21.3	22.8	44.0	3.2	9.3	17.5	25.5	15.0	52.2	16.9	27.2	46.3
Greece	0.0	0.0	0.0	0.0	0.0	0.0	0.0	0.0	0.0	0.0	0.0	54.8	4.8	3.4	6.8	1.3
Portugal	0.0	0.0	0.0	0.0	0.0	0.0	0.0	3.8	6.7	27.6	11.4	2.7	3.2	7.5	7.2	9.7
EUR-12	48.1	47.9	58.3	57.0	56.5	57.8	55.7	58.2	62.9	66.7	68.3	68.4	68.0	66.2	69.4	68.3

Table D.7.22. Import penetration ratios (extra-EU)

Country	1978	1979	1980	1981	1982	1983	1984	1985	1986	1987	1988	1989	1990	1991	1992	1993
FRG	0.24	0.27	0.31	0.37	0.45	0.52	0.81	0.86	0.88	0.83	0.98	1.27	0.94	1.00	1.09	1.24
France	0.01	0.03	0.03	0.04	0.07	0.05	0.15	0.05	0.06	0.06	0.08	0.18	0.29	0.13	0.16	0.19
Italy	0.11	0.08	0.05	0.06	0.04	0.06	0.07	0.07	0.07	0.06	0.09	0.11	0.16	0.25	0.34	0.39
Netherlands	0.11	0.23	0.16	0.20	0.19	0.13	0.14	0.14	0.11	0.08	0.11	0.11	0.11	0.07	0.19	0.19
Bel. & Lux.	0.09	0.12	0.03	0.06	0.05	0.04	0.05	0.06	0.07	0.06	0.08	0.05	0.08	0.08	0.26	0.46
UK	0.09	0.06	0.09	0.07	0.08	0.09	0.10	0.12	0.10	0.16	0.19	0.31	0.40	0.26	0.29	0.38
Ireland	0.00	0.00	0.00	4.35	6.67	62.50	0.00	0.00	0.00	0.00	0.00	0.00	0.35	1.97	0.91	1.55
Denmark	4.77	4.68	5.84	5.69	4.86	4.29	3.75	3.86	3.98	4.32	4.81	4.86	4.68	6.41	6.84	5.06
Spain	0.04	0.04	0.04	0.03	0.06	0.05	0.05	0.00	0.15	0.15	0.46	0.39	0.17	0.18	0.11	0.09
Greece	0.00	0.00	0.00	0.00	0.00	0.00	0.00	0.00	0.00	0.09	0.14	0.25	0.13	0.07	0.34	0.33
Portugal	0.00	0.00	0.00	0.00	0.00	0.00	0.00	0.00	0.00	0.00	0.00	0.05	0.00	0.05	0.05	0.09
EUR-12	0.17	0.17	0.17	0.19	0.21	0.23	0.31	0.30	0.32	0.31	0.39	0.50	0.44	0.43	0.48	0.54

Table D.7.23. Import penetration ratios (intra-EU)

Country	1978	1979	1980	1981	1982	1983	1984	1985	1986	1987	1988	1989	1990	1991	1992	1993
FRG	3.21	2.76	2.66	2.75	2.45	1.85	1.98	2.19	2.44	3.02	3.08	2.72	4.22	5.41	6.36	4.64
France	1.17	1.31	1.68	2.30	2.84	3.76	4.97	4.68	4.78	4.18	4.73	5.58	3.77	3.64	3.76	3.21
Italy	0.49	0.65	1.43	0.65	0.55	0.66	0.41	0.78	0.70	0.87	1.09	1.21	1.29	1.22	1.28	1.10
Netherlands	10.05	11.39	13.39	14.90	15.12	12.71	13.54	13.07	14.36	14.54	16.07	16.66	16.43	18.00	25.96	17.46
Bel. & Lux.	15.10	16.43	16.92	18.51	13.54	13.62	19.18	17.75	22.18	23.30	26.62	23.70	25.54	27.01	28.64	29.45
UK	0.82	0.67	0.75	1.95	2.49	2.71	2.35	2.34	2.60	3.86	3.28	4.09	3.54	2.78	3.17	2.89
Ireland	60.00	172.22	130.77	173.91	120.00	600.00	240.00	128.38	130.30	123.38	105.17	113.90	114.44	126.89	115.68	221.13
Denmark	0.34	0.47	0.73	0.81	1.62	1.43	2.06	2.76	2.99	5.24	4.66	3.54	3.69	7.52	3.36	5.28
Spain	0.15	0.15	0.16	0.12	0.15	0.34	0.05	0.06	0.42	0.65	1.04	1.41	1.26	1.61	2.29	1.61
Greece	0.00	0.00	0.00	0.00	0.00	0.00	0.22	0.35	0.33	0.73	1.29	4.01	2.00	1.37	1.59	2.67
Portugal	0.00	0.00	0.00	0.00	0.00	0.00	0.00	0.00	1.33	3.31	6.06	4.41	7.67	7.75	10.46	12.96
EUR-12	3.06	2.91	2.95	3.44	3.41	3.32	3.81	3.69	4.01	4.45	4.74	5.05	4.94	5.33	6.42	5.31

Note: In the case of Ireland, the value of imports appears to exceed domestic consumption in most years.

Processed foodstuffs

Table D.7.24. Intra-EU exports as a % of production

Country	1978	1979	1980	1981	1982	1983	1984	1985	1986	1987	1988	1989	1990	1991	1992	1993
FRG	0.5	0.8	1.2	1.6	1.6	1.5	1.6	2.3	2.3	2.4	2.6	2.9	2.4	2.8	3.0	1.9
France	4.6	4.3	4.6	4.8	4.3	4.5	4.9	5.2	6.0	6.9	7.1	6.8	8.1	10.2	11.1	10.6
Italy	1.2	1.7	1.2	1.0	0.8	0.8	0.8	0.6	0.7	0.6	0.8	1.5	1.1	1.0	1.0	1.8
Netherlands	29.3	25.7	19.7	22.0	21.1	17.3	20.7	15.6	18.2	24.6	23.7	25.0	20.8	26.6	26.6	31.1
Bel. & Lux.	8.2	10.9	12.9	17.8	14.2	17.2	20.9	22.6	28.6	27.6	38.3	37.3	26.7	24.9	26.8	31.1
UK	0.5	0.4	0.5	0.4	0.4	0.3	0.6	0.7	0.7	0.7	0.9	0.9	1.1	1.4	1.6	2.0
Denmark	3.2	2.4	2.3	2.8	1.7	2.3	3.3	3.6	3.7	3.1	3.7	5.0	5.4	7.7	7.3	3.4
Spain	0.8	0.4	0.1	0.3	0.2	0.2	0.2	0.0	0.1	0.2	0.3	0.1	0.7	0.1	0.3	0.6
Greece	0.0	0.0	0.0	0.0	0.0	0.0	0.0	0.0	0.0	0.0	0.0	0.5	0.1	0.1	0.1	0.1
Portugal	0.0	0.0	0.0	0.0	0.0	0.0	0.0	0.1	0.1	0.7	0.3	0.1	0.2	0.3	0.4	0.3
EUR-12	3.0	2.9	2.8	3.2	3.0	3.0	3.4	3.5	3.8	4.2	4.4	4.6	4.4	4.9	5.3	5.4

Table D.7.25. Extra-EU exports as a % of production

Country	1978	1979	1980	1981	1982	1983	1984	1985	1986	1987	1988	1989	1990	1991	1992	1993
FRG	1.0	1.2	1.1	0.9	0.9	0.8	1.0	1.3	1.0	0.9	1.0	1.0	1.3	1.5	1.5	1.6
France	6.0	6.5	4.5	4.6	4.3	4.9	5.7	6.7	5.6	5.5	6.2	6.5	4.9	5.0	5.1	5.4
Italy	4.6	4.6	1.5	1.8	1.0	0.7	0.8	0.7	0.7	0.7	0.6	0.7	1.1	1.3	0.8	1.4
Netherlands	6.0	8.8	7.0	13.9	14.6	15.0	22.8	11.5	10.2	6.8	5.3	5.2	4.7	10.9	8.5	6.8
Bel. & Lux.	0.2	0.2	0.1	0.1	0.4	0.6	1.0	0.9	1.3	1.8	1.8	1.2	1.6	4.8	2.5	2.8
UK	3.9	2.4	1.4	1.8	1.9	1.1	0.9	1.0	0.9	0.8	0.7	0.7	1.0	1.0	1.2	1.5
Ireland	0.4	0.3	0.4	0.3	1.2	0.2	0.4	1.1	1.4	1.8	2.0	1.3	1.2	1.7	1.1	1.7
Denmark	15.1	16.6	23.0	24.8	18.8	18.3	23.0	22.9	21.8	20.0	12.5	9.9	9.1	8.5	11.2	10.7
Spain	2.2	1.3	0.4	0.5	0.7	0.7	0.2	0.2	1.0	1.0	0.8	0.7	0.6	0.7	0.9	0.7
Greece	20.8	4.2	1.2	2.0	1.1	3.0	2.2	1.1	0.9	0.6	0.3	0.4	1.0	2.1	1.4	4.7
Portugal	0.8	0.7	0.3	0.3	0.5	0.7	0.7	2.4	1.2	1.6	1.9	3.8	5.2	4.2	4.7	2.8
EUR-12	3.3	3.1	1.9	2.3	2.2	2.2	2.7	2.4	2.2	2.0	2.0	2.1	2.1	2.5	2.3	2.5

Figure D.7.1. Intra/extra-EU exports

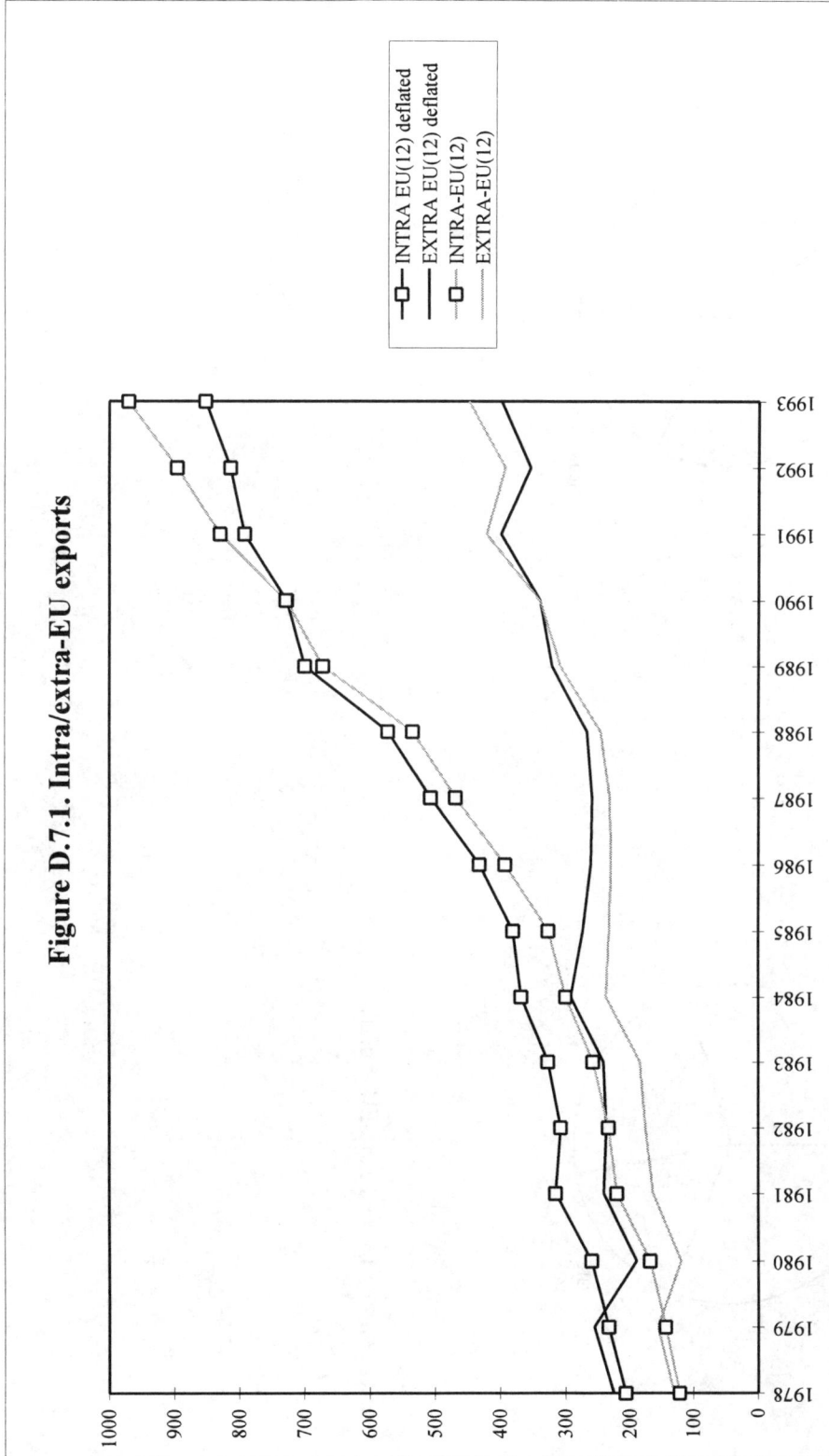

Legend:
- INTRA EU(12) deflated
- EXTRA EU(12) deflated
- INTRA-EU(12)
- EXTRA-EU(12)

Note: 1978, 1979 are estimated figures (estimates for Greece, Spain and Portugal).

Figure D.7.2. EU exports 1978

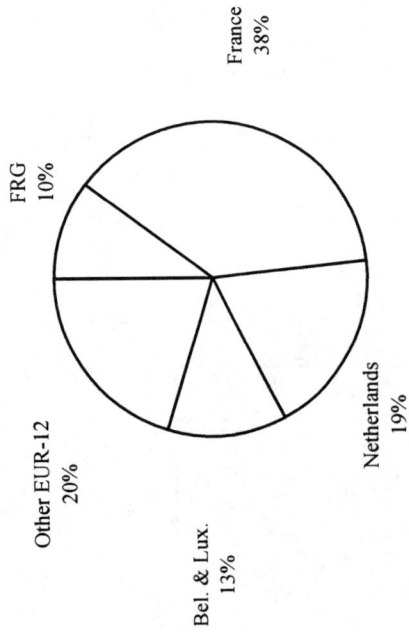

France
30%

Netherlands
23%

UK
16%

Other
EUR-12
31%

Figure D.7.3. EU exports 1993

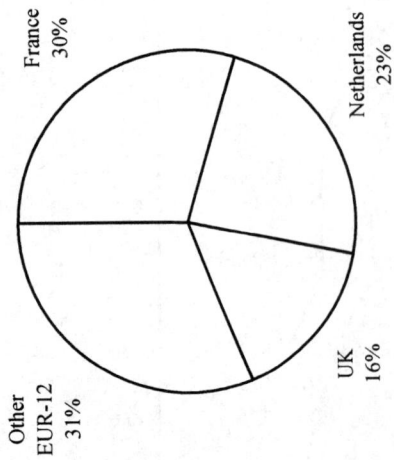

France
38%

FRG
10%

Other EUR-12
20%

Bel. & Lux.
13%

Netherlands
19%

Note: Intra- and extra-EU exports.

APPENDIX E

Results of microanalysis (industry survey)

Results are summarized in Figures E.1 to E.14.

Sample profile

Total number of companies interviewed = 78. However, there were 113 responses when comparing impacts by sector, as some of the companies are involved in more than one of the sectors examined. A summary profile of the participating companies is provided in Figures E.0. to E.3. and Table E.0.

Firm size

50 of the firms were large (more than 500 employees).
28 of the firms were SMEs (fewer than 500 employees).

Production outside headquarters country

Just over half of the companies interviewed had production units in other EU countries. The companies interviewed in Spain, Portugal and Ireland were less likely to have production units outside the headquarters country, whereas the British, Dutch, French and Belgian companies were more likely to. We also interviewed the EU operations of one US holding company with significant activity in the EU soft drinks sector. This explains the inclusion of 'USA' in a number of tables and figures, as a holding company origin rather than an operations location.

Activities/levels of integration

Two-fifths of the companies interviewed were neither backward nor forward integrated in that they only manufactured their products. A further two-fifths were involved in distribution as well as manufacturing. There was no significant variation noted in the level of integration by Member State, although in Spain seven out of the nine firms interviewed only manufactured. Also, certain sectors are more likely to move into forward integration in terms of product distribution, for instance soft drinks.

EU trade

Four-fifths of the companies interviewed were involved in EU trade. Companies in Italy, Portugal and Greece were less likely to be involved in EU trade.

EU trade a priority

Three-fifths of the companies interviewed saw the EU as a trading priority.

Market share

This information, where available, is indicated on a national basis. As the data supplied by companies on market share and overall market size are incomplete, it has not been possible to present an aggregate EU market share figure for each product category. However, the national market share information indicates that the larger companies interviewed in most cases account for a substantial share of their markets.

TABLE E.O.	Pasta	Industrial baking	Cocoa and sugar confectionery products	Other food products	Spirits	Brewing and malting	Soft drinks	Total number of firms
EU	No of firms - 9 Large - 5 SME - 4 EU trade priority - 7	No of firms - 19 Large - 12 SME - 7 EU trade priority - 14	No of firms - 22 Large - 15 SME - 6 EU trade priority - 14 mkt share- 58% (chocolate) 50+% (ice cream)	No of firms - 19 Large - 13 SME - 3 EU trade priority - 13	No of firms - 8 Large - 5 SME - 3 EU trade priority - 3 mkt leader - No 2 in the world	No of firms - 15 Large - 12 SME - 3 EU trade priority - 7	No of firms - 21 Large - 18 SME - 2 EU trade priority - 13 mkt leader - Top 2 companies (soft drinks) Top 3 companies (mineral water)	78
Belgium	No of firms - 2	No of firms - 2 mkt share - 19%	No of firms - 2 mkt leader - chewing gum	No of firms - 1 mkt leader - coffee		No of firms - 1 mkt share - 56%	No of firms - 2 mkt share - 56%	7
Denmark		No of firms - 2 mkt share - 70%	No of firms - 1 mkt share - 23% (chocolate) mkt leader - chewing gum		No of firms - 1 mkt share - 60%	No of firms - 1		5
France	No of firms - 1	No of firms - 3 mkt share - 10% (bakery)	No of firms - 1 mkt share - 27% (chocolate) 30% (bagged sweets)	No of firms - 1 mkt leader - coffee	No of firms - 1 mkt share - 22%	No of firms - 3 mkt share - 30% (malting) 43% (beer)	No of firms - 4 mkt share - 41+% mkt leader - No 2 (carbonates sector)	7
Germany		No of firms - 3 mkt share - high	No of firms - 2 mkt leader - sugar confectionery	No of firms - 2 mkt leader - coffee	No of firms - 1 mkt share - 10+%	No of firms - 1 mkt share - 8%	No of firms - 3 mkt share - 16+% mkt leader - mineral water	9
Greece		No of firms - 1 mkt share - 60% (bread rolls)	No of firms - 2 mkt share - 19% (chocolate) 40% (ice cream)	No of firms - 1 mkt leader - coffee			No of firms - 3 mkt share - 30% (min. water) 70% (soft drinks) 55% (fruit juices)	4
Ireland			No of firms - 3 mkt share - 8% (ice cream)	No of firms - 1				4

Italy	No of firms - 2 mkt share - 38%	No of firms - 3 mkt share - 31% (bakery)	No of firms - 2 mkt leader	No of firms - 4 mkt leaders mkt share - (30%) condimenti	No of firms - 2	No of firms - 2 mkt share - 5%	No of firms - 3 mkt share - 20% (water) 11% (bibite)	10
NL	No of firms - 1	No of firms - 1	No of firms - 3	No of firms - 4 mkt share - 50+% (coffee) 30% (infant food)	No of firms - 1	No of firms - 1 mkt share - 16%	No of firms - 1	7
Portugal	No of firms - 1 mkt share - 38%	No of firms - 1 mkt share - 30%		No of firms - 2 mkt share - 47%		No of firms - 1	No of firms - 1	4
Spain	No of firms - 1	No of firms - 1 mkt share - 5%	No of firms - 2 mkt share - 64% (chocolate)	No of firms - 1	No of firms - 1	No of firms - 1 mkt share - 17%	No of firms - 2 mkt share - 13% (soft drinks) 6% (min. water)	9
United Kingdom	No of firms - 1	No of firms - 2 mkt share - 40% (biscuits) 30% (bread)	No of firms - 4 mkt share - 58% (chocolate)	No of firms - 2 mkt share - 40% (soups) 60% (infant food)	No of firms - 1	No of firms - 4 mkt share - 23%	No of firms - 1	11
USA							No of firms - 1	1

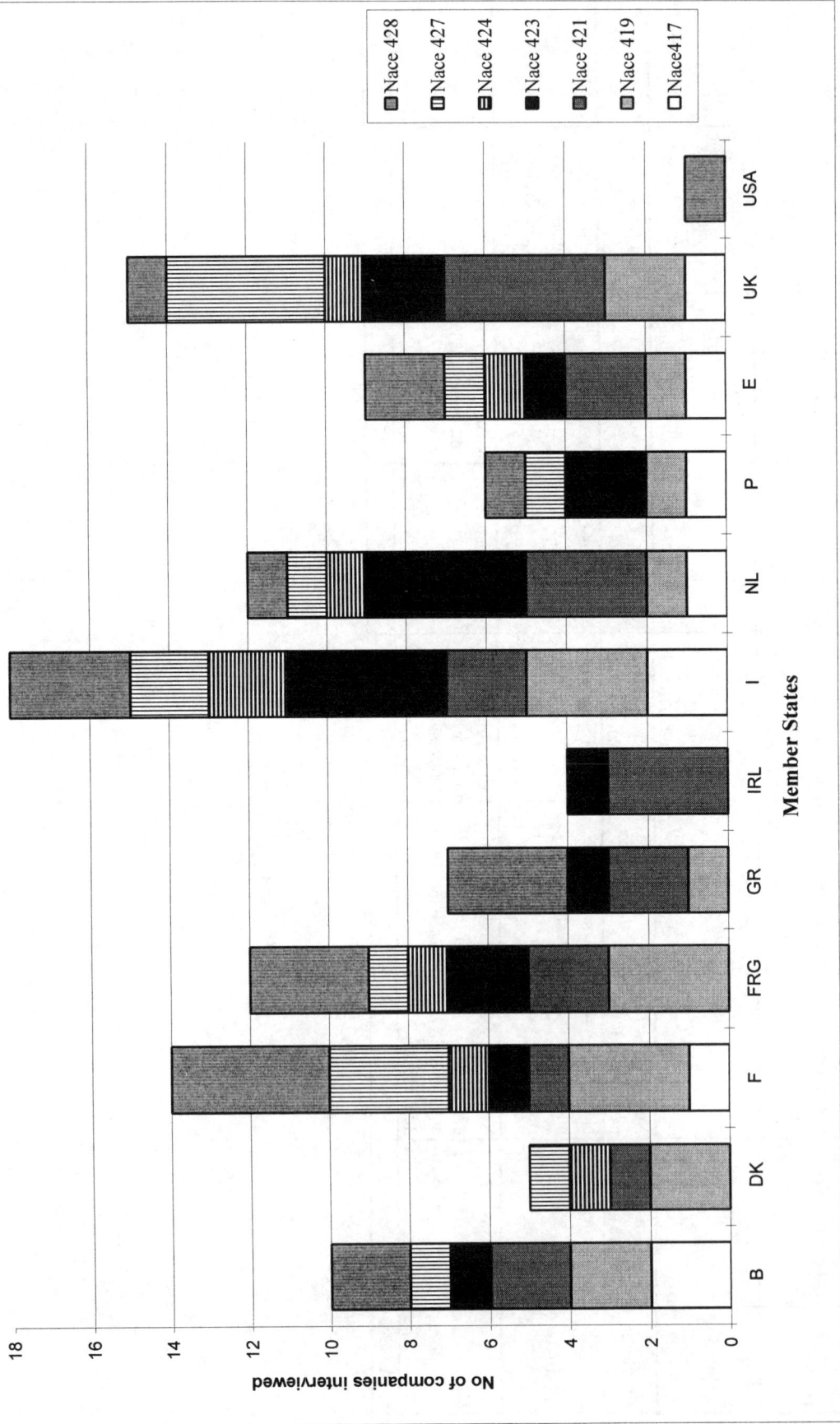

Figure E.0. Companies interviewed by food/drink sector and Member State

Figure E.1. Sample profile - size of companies interviewed by Member State

	Large (>500 employees)	SME (< 500 employees)
B	3	3
DK	3	2
F	7	0
FRG	8	0
GR	3	1
IRL	0	3
I	3	6
NL	7	0
P	1	3
E	3	6
UK	11	0
USA	1	0
Total	50	24

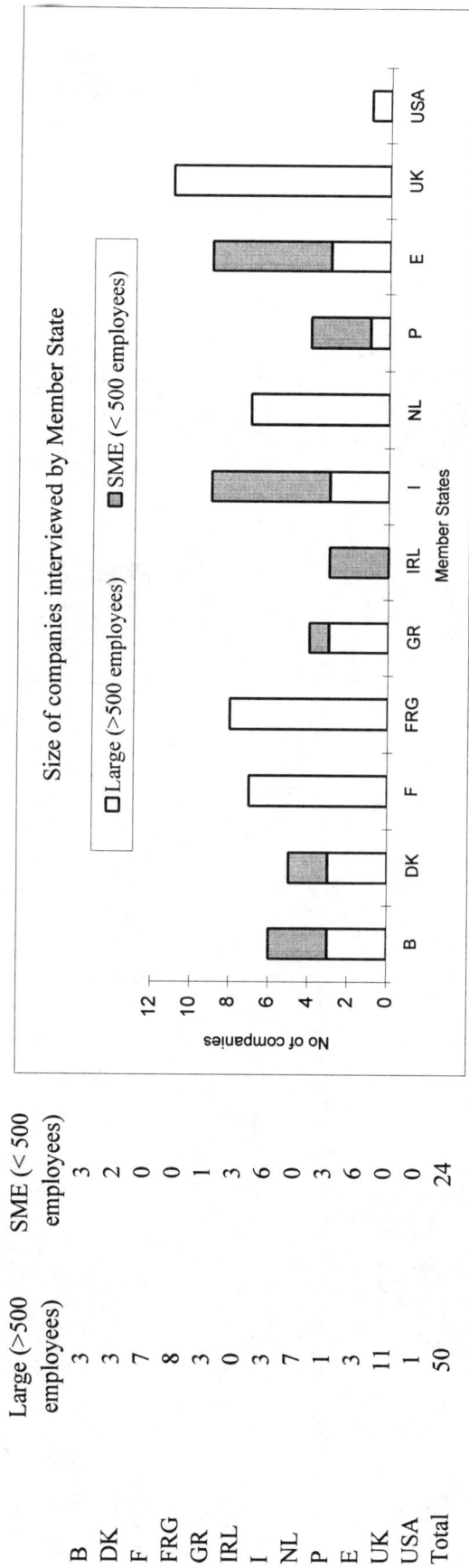

Size of companies interviewed by Member State

Figure E.2. Sample profile - size of companies interviewed by food/drink sector

	Large (>500 employees)	SME (< 500 employees)
NACE 417	5	4
NACE 419	12	7
NACE 421	15	6
NACE 424	13	3
NACE 425	5	3
NACE 427	12	3
NACE 428	18	2
Total	80	28

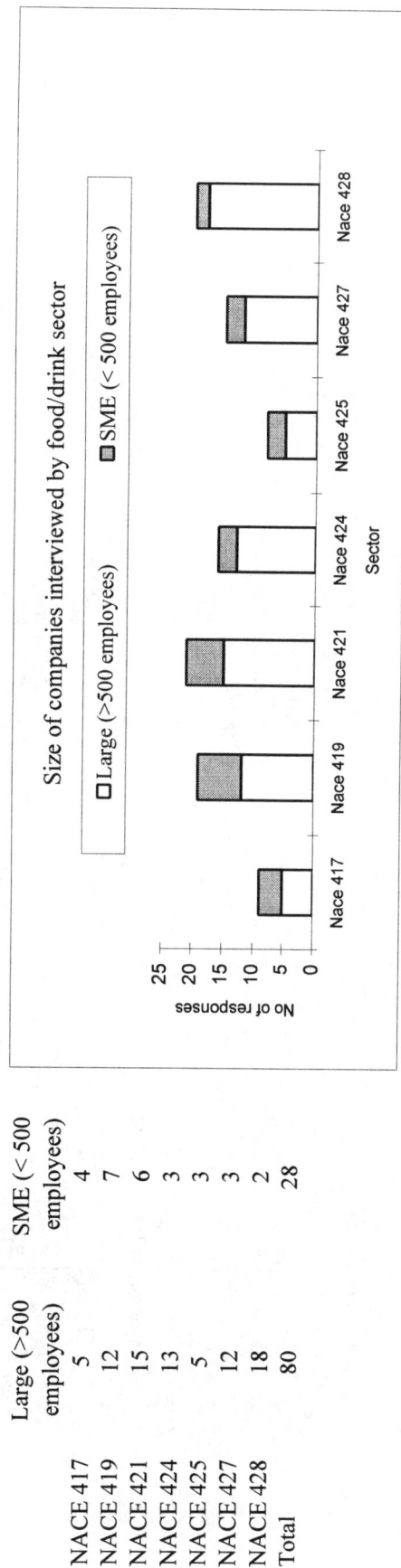

Size of companies interviewed by food/drink sector

Figure E.3. Sample profile - proportion of companies interviewed involved in EU trade and who consider the EU a trading priority

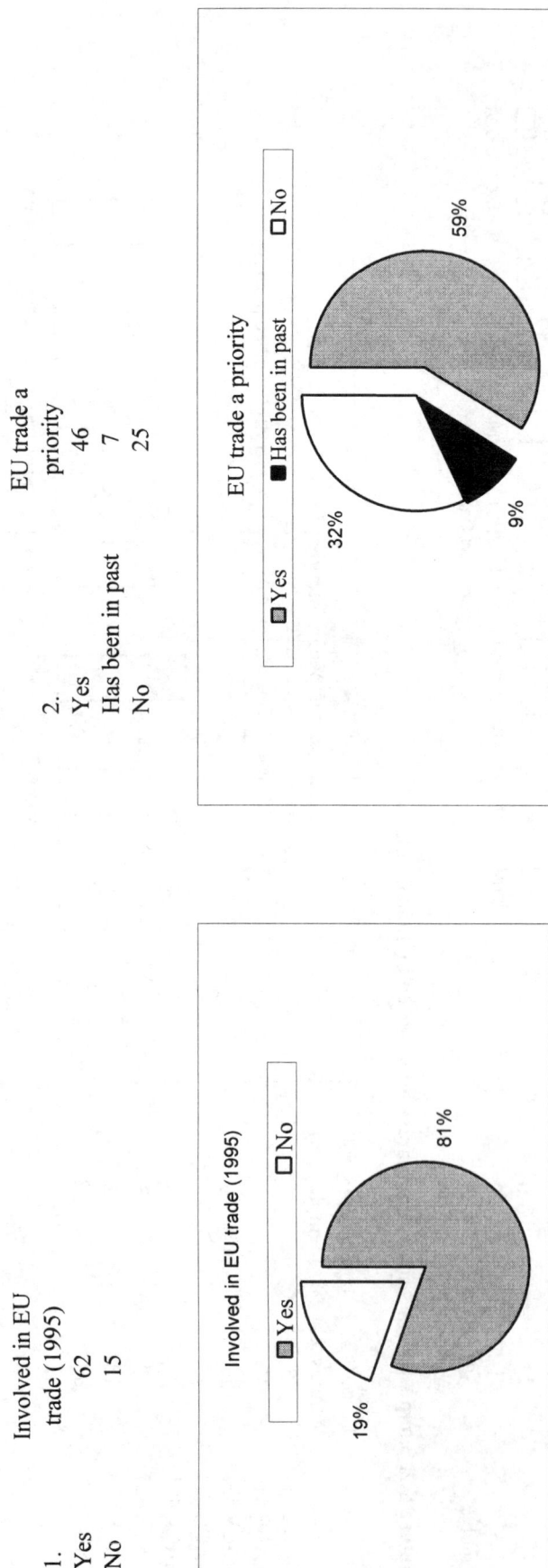

1.	Involved in EU trade (1995)
Yes	62
No	15

2.	EU trade a priority
Yes	46
Has been in past	7
No	25

Involved in EU trade (1995)

■ Yes □ No

81%

19%

EU trade a priority

■ Yes ■ Has been in past □ No

59%

9%

32%

Figure E.4. Importance of SMP in the food/drink sectors

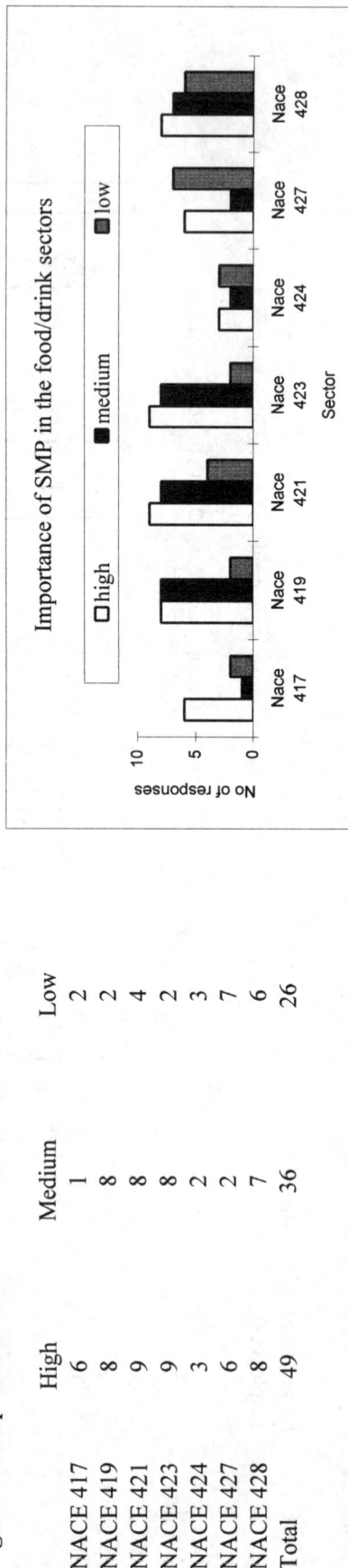

	High	Medium	Low
NACE 417	6	1	2
NACE 419	8	8	2
NACE 421	9	8	4
NACE 423	9	8	2
NACE 424	3	2	3
NACE 427	6	2	7
NACE 428	8	7	6
Total	49	36	26

Importance of SMP in the food/drink sectors

□ high ■ medium ■ low

Figure E.5. Removal of trade barriers in the food/drink sectors

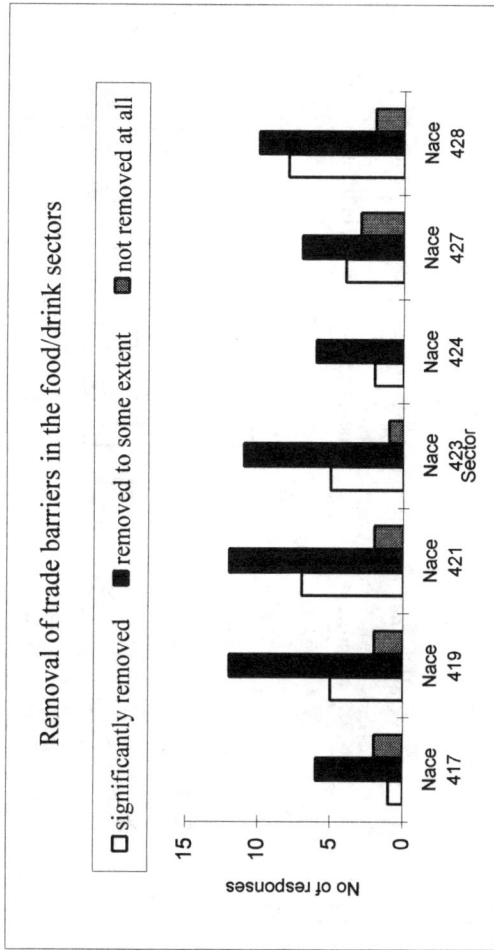

Removal of trade barriers in the food/drink sectors

	Significantly removed	Removed to some extent	Not removed at all
NACE 417	1	6	2
NACE 419	5	12	2
NACE 421	7	12	2
NACE 423	5	11	1
NACE 424	2	6	0
NACE 427	4	7	3
NACE 428	8	10	2
Total	32	64	12

Figure E.6. Overall impact of SMP on the food/drink sectors

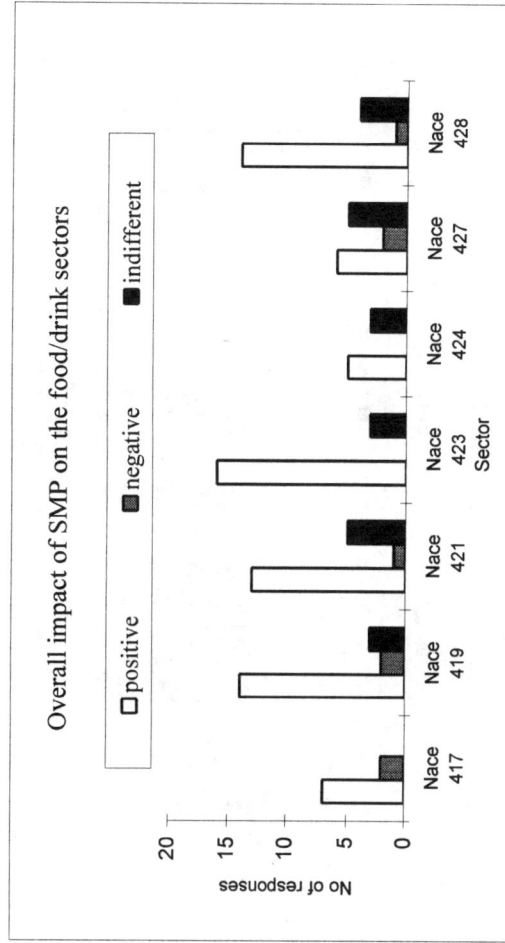

Overall impact of SMP on the food/drink sectors

	Positive	Negative	Indifferent
NACE 417	7	2	0
NACE 419	14	2	3
NACE 421	13	1	5
NACE 423	16	0	3
NACE 424	5	0	3
NACE 427	6	2	5
NACE 428	14	1	4
Total	75	8	23

Figure E.7. Importance of SMP to consumers by food/drink sector

	High	Medium	Low
NACE 417	5	2	2
NACE 419	8	3	7
NACE 421	8	6	5
NACE 423	8	5	6
NACE 424	4	3	1
NACE 427	7	3	5
NACE 428	13	5	3
Total	53	27	29

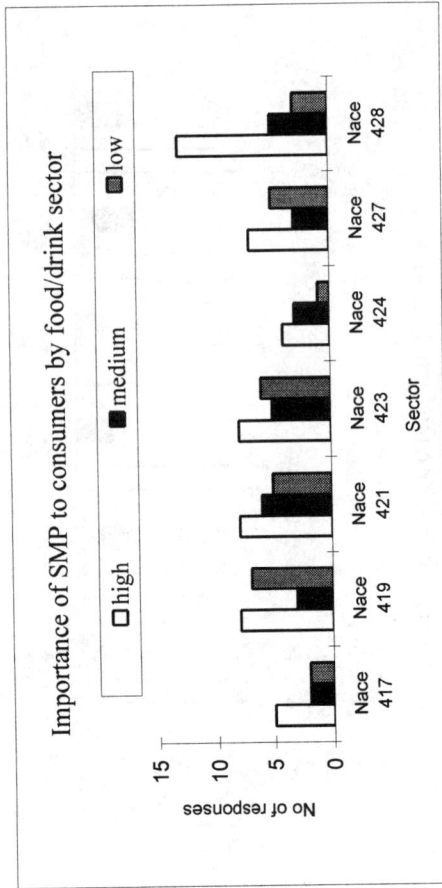

Importance of SMP to consumers by food/drink sector

Figure E.8. Overall impact of SMP on consumers by food/drink sector

	Positive	Negative	Indifferent
NACE 417	7	2	0
NACE 419	14	2	3
NACE 421	13	1	5
NACE 423	16	0	3
NACE 424	5	0	3
NACE 427	6	2	5
NACE 428	14	1	4
Total	75	8	23

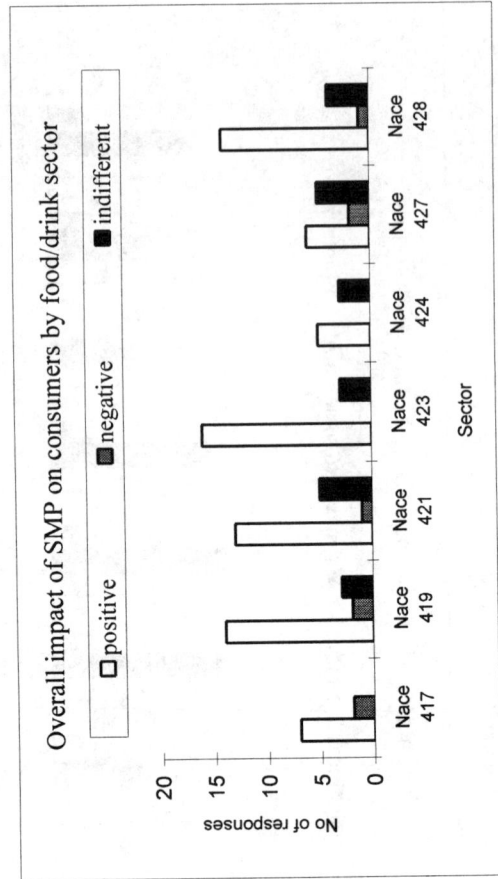

Overall impact of SMP on consumers by food/drink sector

Figure E.9. Impact of SMP on food/drink sector market growth

	Yes	No
NACE 417	5	4
NACE 419	6	12
NACE 421	8	12
NACE 423	7	11
NACE 424	6	2
NACE 427	4	11
NACE 428	9	12
Total	45	64

The impact of the SMP on food/drink sector market growth

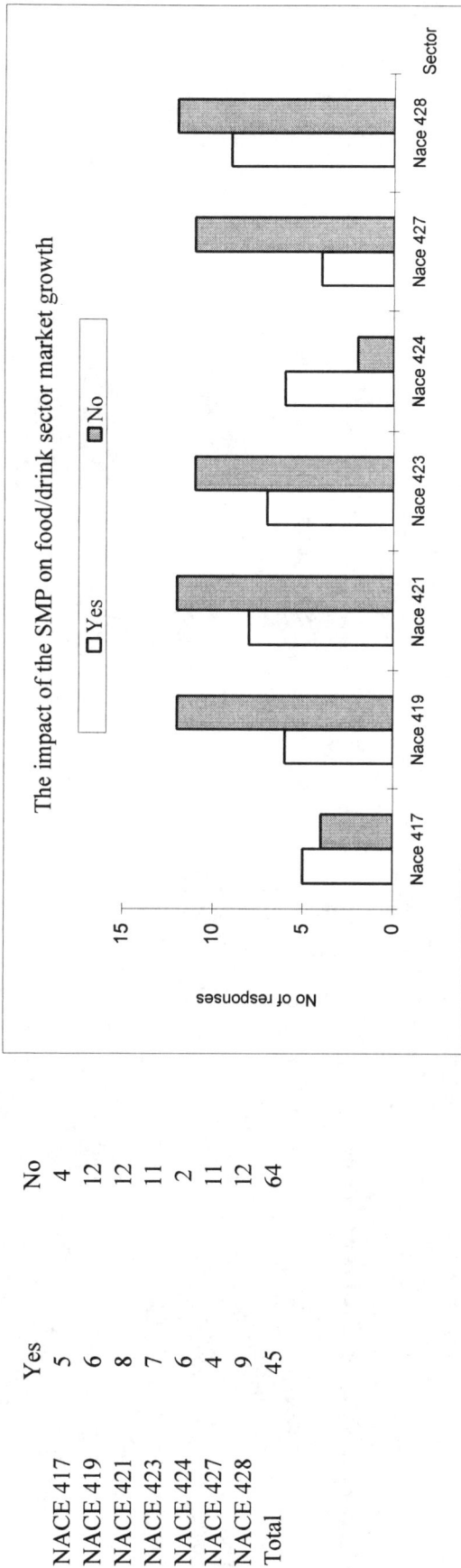

Figure E.10. Impact of SMP on market entry conditions by Member State

	Easier	Harder	No change
B	1	1	4
DK	4	1	0
F	4	0	3
FRG	3	1	5
GR	3	0	1
IRL	4	0	0
I	3	0	7
NL	5	1	1
P	2	2	0
E	5	1	2
UK	5	0	4
USA	1	0	0
Total	40	7	27

Impact of SMP on market entry conditions by Member State

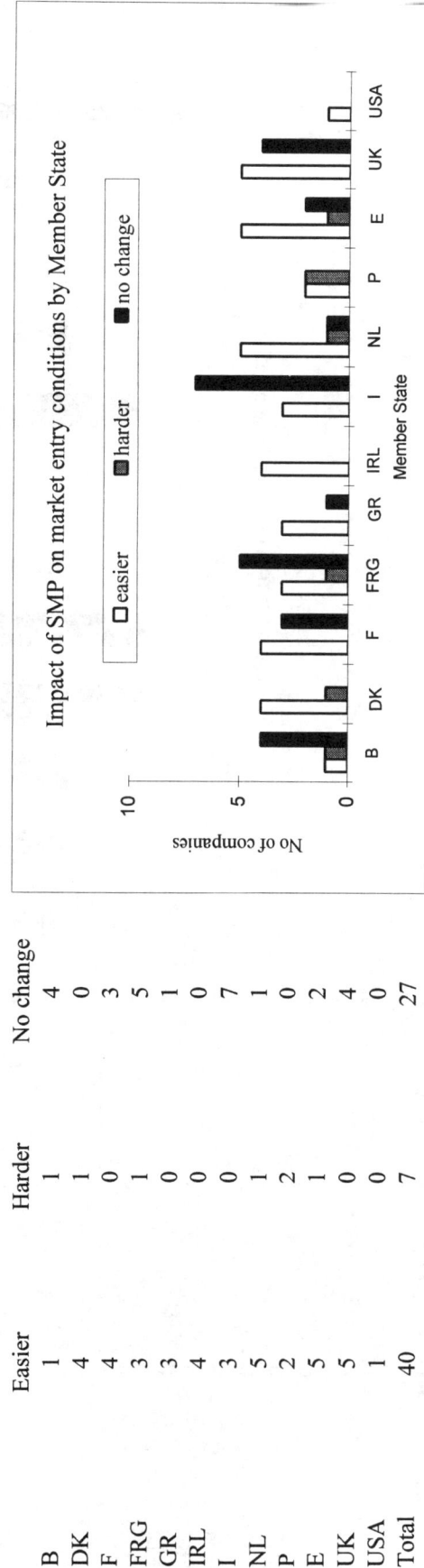

Figure E.11. Impact of SMP on market price by Member State

	Price increased	Price decreased	No change in price
B	0	2	4
DK	0	3	2
F	0	2	5
FRG	0	5	4
GR	0	3	1
IRL	1	2	1
I	0	4	5
NL	1	3	3
P	0	3	1
E	1	2	4
UK	3	0	6
USA	0	1	0
Total	6	30	36

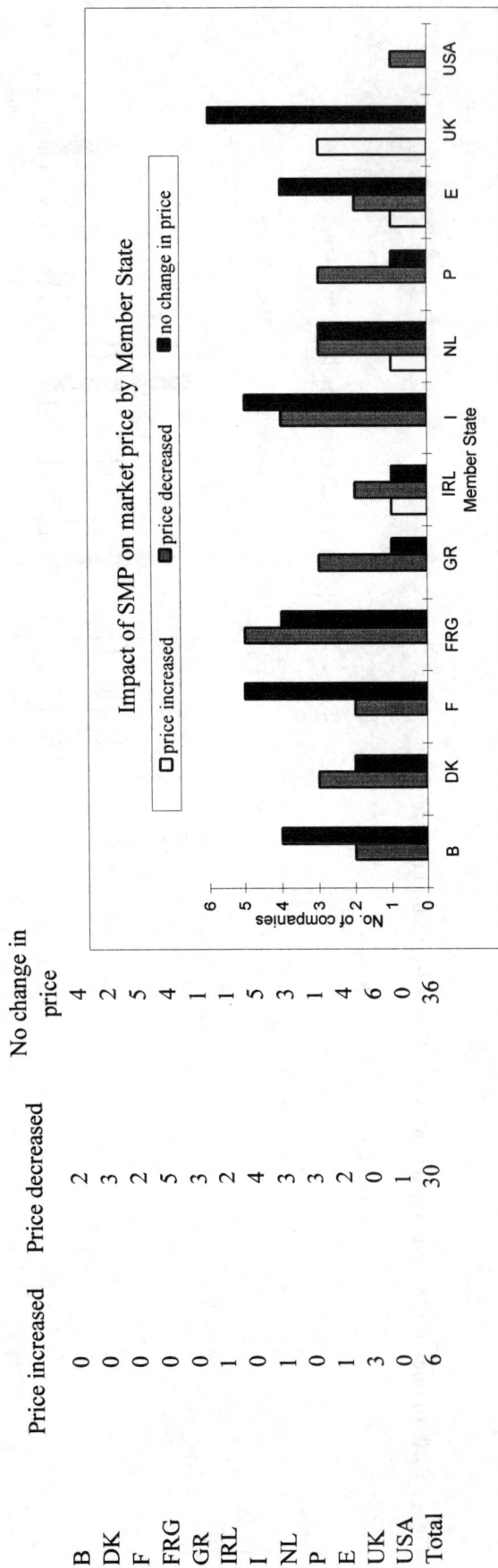

Impact of SMP on market price by Member State

Figure E.12. SMP perceived as a challenge

	Perceived as a challenge
Yes	42
No	35

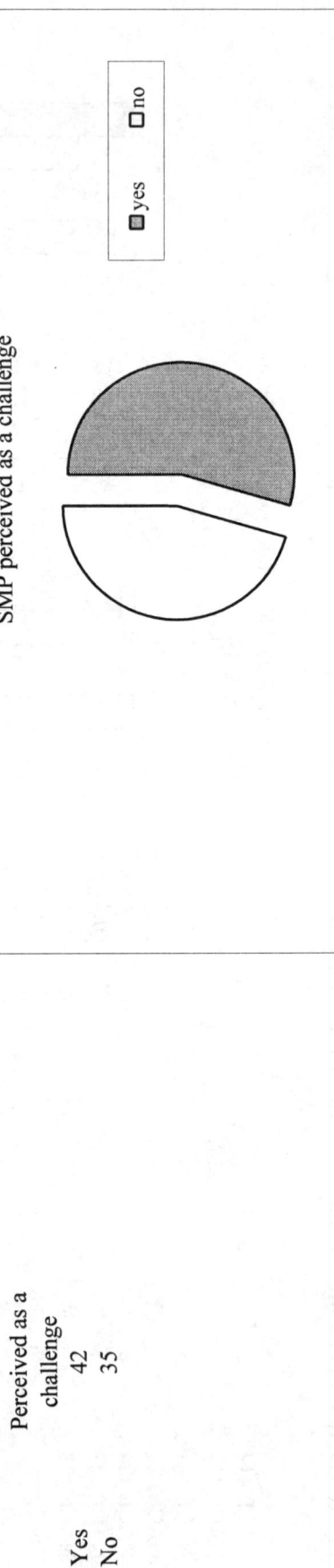

SMP perceived as a challenge

Figure E.13. Changes in companies

	Changes as direct result of SMP	Changes	No changes
Number and size of plants	5	28	44
Forward/backward integration	5	16	55
Structure	4	29	44
Internal organization	17	26	34
Production locations	6	17	54
Trading activities	4	24	49
Employment/training	7	26	44
Transport/logistics	15	25	36
Sourcing/procurement patterns	5	20	51
R&D/product development	9	30	37
Product lines	13	41	23
Marketing strategies	7	32	37
Total	97	314	508

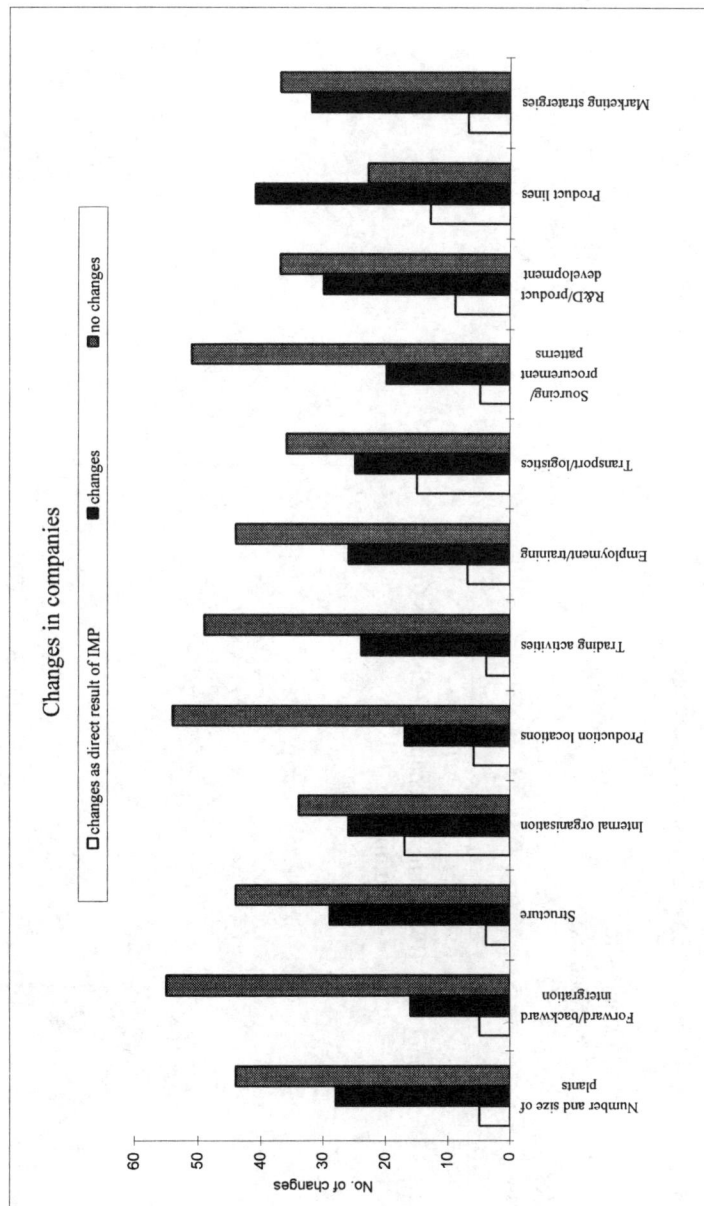

Changes in companies

Figure E.14. Impact of SMP in company changes

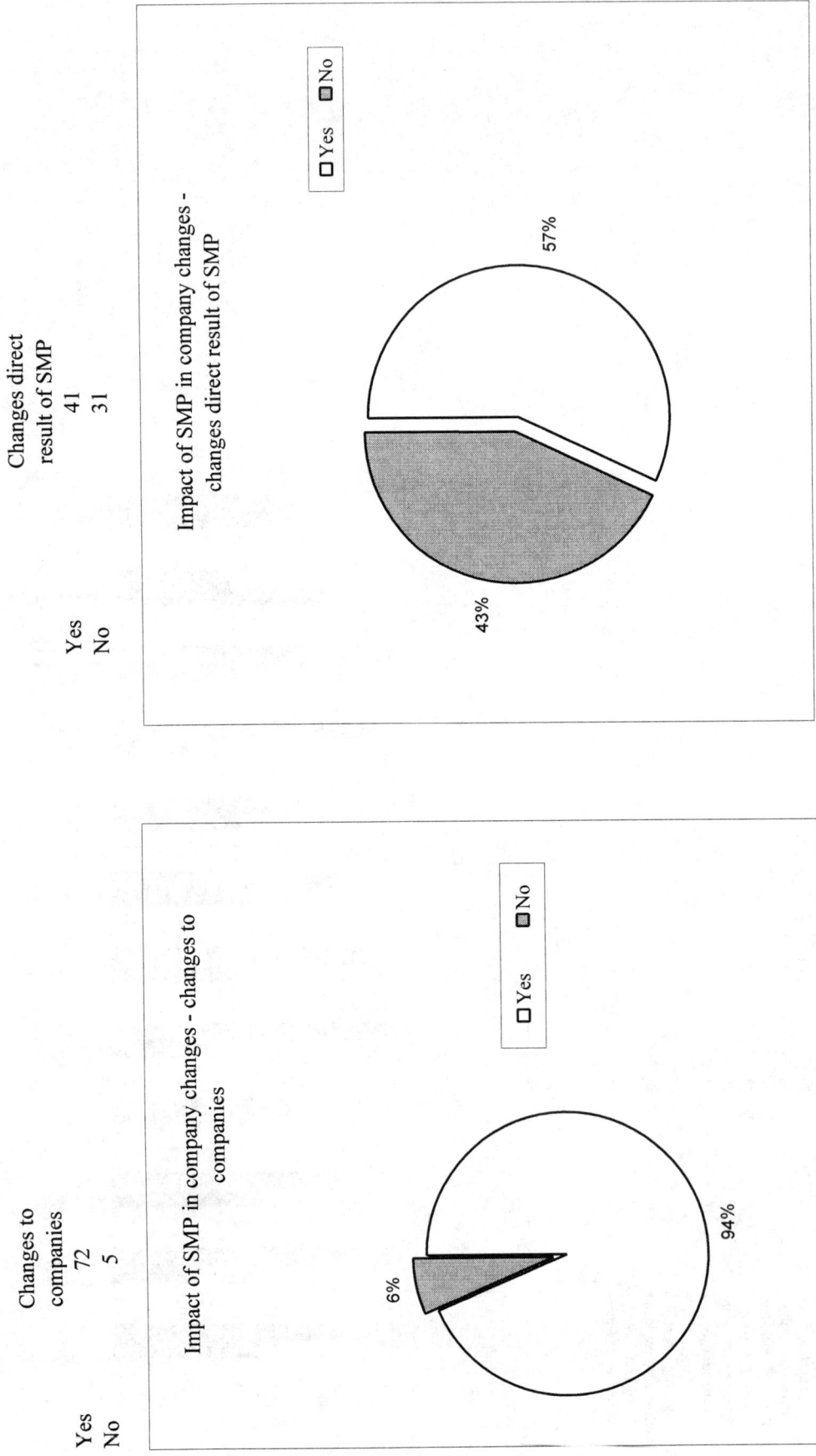

	Changes to companies
Yes	72
No	5

Impact of SMP in company changes - changes to companies

	Changes direct result of SMP
Yes	41
No	31

Impact of SMP in company changes - changes direct result of SMP

APPENDIX F

Case studies

In total five case studies were carried out, across a spectrum of countries, sectors, products and sizes. The five companies include Whitbread plc, Danone Group, Schöller GmbH & Co KG, Van Melle BV and Grupo Gallo. Table F.1. gives the broad specifications of the case studies.

Table F.1.   Case study specifications

Company	Sector (NACE)	Product	Country (HQ)
Whitbread plc	427	Brewing	UK
Danone Group	419	Biscuits	France
Schöller GmbH & Co KG	423	Ice cream	Germany
Van Melle BV	421	Chocolate/confectionery	Netherlands
Grupo Gallo s.a.	417	Pasta	Spain

F.1. Case study: Whitbread plc (UK)

F.1.1. Background

Whitbread plc is a leading UK food, drinks and leisure company. It owns and operates some of the country's most popular pubs, restaurants, hotels, shops and leisure clubs as well as brewing some of the UK's most famous brands of beer. Whitbread's activities in the hotel and catering sector have been incorporated in this case study because they are studied as part of Whitbread's corporate identity and strategy to respond to the SMP.

Whitbread employs around 65,000 people and has a turnover of some UKL 2.5 billion and net assets of over UKL 2.3 billion.

F.1.2. Whitbread development and current strategy

At the heart of Whitbread's strategy is its professed drive to provide experiences which its customers enjoy, appreciate and consider good value for money.

It is this strategy that has taken the company from its historic base in brewing into pubs, pub food, restaurants, hotels and leisure and also into high street retailing. Whitbread's future, it believes, depends on broadening the appeal of these businesses to an ever-widening range of consumers, in growing their scale both organically and through well-chosen acquisitions and in expanding into new areas which build on its existing skills and experience.

Whitbread's strategic objectives are:

(a) to be the pre-eminent retailer in drinks and eating out in the UK;
(b) to develop a strong, profitable brands-oriented beer business;
(c) continually to reduce its cost of doing business;
(d) to provide better customer service than its competitors;
(e) to manage the cash flow as though it were its own;
(f) to strengthen a distinctive culture through collaboration, shared values and effective communication.

Whitbread is managed by four operating divisions depending on the line of business (Whitbread Inns, Whitbread Restaurants and Leisure, Whitbread Beer Company, Whitbread Pub Partnerships).

F.1.3. Financial history

Whitbread's most recent financial performance has been as follows:

Whitbread plc profit & loss account - million UKL	1990/91	1991/92	1992/93	1993/94	1994/95
Turnover	2,059.8	2,191.2	2,346.4	2,360.4	2,471.8
Operating profit before exceptional items	275.7	256.6	264.4	257.9	264.6
Operating profit before exceptional items as % of turnover	13.4%	11.7%	11.3%	10.9%	10.7%
Profit before exceptional items and tax	248.4	179.8	219.0	231.7	255.1
Profit before tax	161.5	118.6	177.0	234.0	275.4
Average number of employees:					
Full-time	32,168	33,585	33,177	31,9091	33,374
Part-time	33,480	30,168	30,716	30,480	31,864

Whitbread's turnover in the last five years has increased by 20%. Its operating profit has declined slightly. As a result its operating profitability has declined as a percentage of turnover. A strong balance sheet, however, has enabled the company to increase its dividend over the same period by 25%.

Whitbread as a company is highly conscious of the need to provide shareholder return rather than looking for growth *per se*. Instinctively, therefore, it would be cautious about pursuing any long-term growth opportunities thrown up by the impact of the SMP. At the same time, Whitbread has maintained its employment levels over the past five years unlike most UK companies which have heavily 'downsized' over the same period.

F.1.4. Whitbread in its competitive environment

The impact of the SMP on Whitbread should be viewed in the context of the company's historic roots and conservative approach. The UK beer industry (like Germany's today) was, until the 1960s, highly fragmented with hundreds of local brewers servicing their local markets via their own tied outlets and the non-tied (free) trade. The two decades to 1980 saw a spate of mergers and takeovers in UK brewing such that five companies (including Whitbread) dominated the market.

These same companies were the subject of a Monopolies and Mergers Commission (MMC) report (1988) which resulted in their having to 'loosen' the extent of the tie. In practice, this meant that they could no longer depend on their own pubs to take the majority of their beer volume. In Whitbread's case, the formation of the 'Whitbread Beer Company' was a natural consequence of the MMC report.

In summary, Whitbread and the UK beer industry were undergoing a period of unparalleled upheaval even before one considers the impact of the SMP.

Furthermore, the brewer had to face the change in social and economic conditions in which it operates and which has occurred over the past decade. Socially, the pub as a venue for social drinking has lost popularity to the take-home trade and the impact of sales through grocery multiples has severely impacted on the viability of specialist off-licences such as Thresher

(Whitbread's Off-Licences) which controls about a quarter of the total UK specialist off-licence trade.

Economically, the recession and lack of inflation in the UK has hit the food and drinks market generally. While volumes may have held up, this has been at the expense of price increases. Price pressure has been further intensified by the growing power of the grocery multiples as outlets for drink. The result of these effects can be seen in Whitbread's margins in its financial statement above. These effects would have been apparent before any impacts of cross-border purchase described below. The effects of cross-border shopping and the SMP were to make the situation that much worse for the company.

F.1.5. SMP and cross-border shopping

In the context of cross-border shopping, the opening of the single market meant the abolition of routine border controls and the replacement of strictly defined limits on the quantities of goods imported for personal consumption with far more liberal 'indicative levels'. The Council of Ministers set guidance levels for personal imports by travellers within the EU. Below these levels (110 litres in the case of beer), the goods are presumed to be for the traveller's personal consumption. Above this level the onus is on the traveller to demonstrate that he has no intention of selling on the goods involved.

Whitbread, as a leading UK retailer, cites the cumulative effect of the SMP on the trade as follows.

Cross-Channel shopping for duty-paid plus duty-free drinks are direct substitutes for UK purchases. Valued conservatively at take-home prices, the loss has increased from UKL 0.4 billion in 1992 to just under UKL 1.25 billion in 1994. The loss of revenue in 1994 is equivalent to over 15% of the UK take-home liquor market. This is the same as transferring all the alcohol sales of Tesco plus Thresher to Calais or taking UKL 24,000 per annum for every off-licence till in the UK. Adding on the value of cross-Channel tobacco sales would add another UKL 500 million to the deficit and take the total loss to the UK retailer to over UKL 1.7 billion – not counting the spend lost on other items bought during the visit, such as French cheese and meat.

Much of the pain being felt by UK retailers falls on the independent shopkeeper who has limited opportunities to reposition his business and whose margins are easily affected. Their long-term survival is threatened by the current situation.

F.1.6. Principal changes as a result of the SMP

New market opportunities

The SMP has certainly put the thought of cross-border mergers or alliances into the mind of Whitbread.

> 'I wouldn't be giving too much away if I said that these thoughts have crossed our minds.'

These opportunities potentially lie on both the purchasing and the sales sides, although nothing as yet has materialized.

The principal change in market opportunities for Whitbread has occurred in the evolution of the leisure and eating-out market in the UK. The increase in eating-out (forecast to grow by 45% before 2000) has fuelled the growth of Whitbread in the food and leisure sector.

The SMP was not considered to have had any other direct effects. Indirectly, however, Whitbread acknowledges that the UK consumer has become increasingly European as a result of a greater exposure to Europe. Also, the ease with which Continental products are entering the UK means a greater acceptance of them by consumers.

New market structures

The size of plant in the brewing industry has been driven ever-upwards by the efficiencies to be found in the economies of scale.

> 'Our biggest is up to about 2 million barrels. The biggest, Bass brewery, is about 15% bigger than that. On the Continent, Heineken or Interbrew might have over 3 million barrels. So they are slightly larger but there is no one out there with 5 million barrels or anything.'

However, the structure of the market will not change significantly because breweries have lower costs and greater efficiencies when they produce a single product rather than a range of products. Heineken produces more because it concentrates on one product (Whitbread has 57!).

Rivalry among European brewers is historically low since many have agreements to distribute one another's beer. Whitbread has agreements with both Heineken and Interbrew. Whitbread has done particularly well with importing the products of European brewers but these tend to be premium products.

Beer's cross-border market opportunities will always be limited by the cost structure. The ingredients of beer (water particularly) means that it is difficult to transport economically over long distances as a low cost product. Even the impact of cross-border shopping in northern France has been markedly higher in south-east England and diminishes in proportion to the distance from the Channel ports.

F.1.7.   Whitbread's evolution 1985–95: SMP impact

Internationalization and expansion

In the 1980s Whitbread had a 'substantial' wine and spirit business in the USA which it has since divested.

> 'What we have today is a smaller restaurant business in Germany (Maredo and Churrasco) plus a German hotel.'

Total investment requirements to compete

While the stakes required to compete in the US wine and spirits business were too high for the company to sustain, its European business has been constructed on a more modest investment level with the acquisition of two relatively small chains of German steak-house restaurants. This cross-border activity has not, however, impacted significantly since both operations are allowed a large degree of independence.

'They both stand alone. We have a slight degree of "hands on" in Germany because of their proximity - it's just a matter of practicality.'

While there would be potential economies of scale in beer, the preference of German customers for local products rules out cross-border sourcing. For food products (meat specifically), the German operation is not of a sufficient size to benefit from UK sourcing power.

Capacity adjustments

The most significant capacity adjustment at Whitbread has been the reduction in brewery members from 13 to 5 in the period 1985–95.

'The big change for us has been in the relative importance of the beer business to Whitbread. Today it represents less than 15% of the company's revenue and profit flow. If I went back to the mid-1980s that would be more like 30%.'

The SMP contribution to this adjustment would appear to be negligible.

'It was a strategic manoeuvre or series of manoeuvres that we felt had to happen in a UK context alone, whether or not there was to be a single market. These changes would have been demanded by the consumer's behaviour and by the UK competitive structure.'

Location decisions

In response to the SMP, Whitbread has not adapted its location decisions in any measurable way. Most decision-making on strategic issues is taken at its London HQ although certain restaurant location issues and selection of sites are locally based.

The location of sourcing has not been influenced by the SMP directly and no sales offices for Whitbread beer have been established on the Continent.

The high bulk to value ratio of beer and its low sales on the Continent mean that no change in production location of its products is anticipated.

Cost-cutting/rationalization

Although Whitbread has cut its brewing locations from 13 to 5 in the decade to 1995, its manpower levels have not diminished significantly.

Cost-cutting has occurred in distribution efficiency and logistics since this forms such a large part of the brewery cost structure. Similarly, energy costs have been cut (UKL 6 million in 1994/95).

An indirect cost increase has been the need (following the SMP) to conform to efficient discharge levels and energy efficiency.

Adaptation of product range

Whitbread has seen a fundamental change in the product range in a shift in emphasis from beer to food. The credit for this can indirectly be laid at the door of the SMP since it has aided a general Europeanization of UK taste.

'It would be right to say that our product range has become more European - more Continental dishes and more Continental beers.'

To some extent there has even been some synergy across border since successful UK dishes in the restaurant chains are tried on German customers.

Marketing strategies

The above (mostly indirect) effect of the SMP has clear implications on marketing strategies.

'Our strategies for beers such as Stella Artois are heavily reliant on their Continental heritage to justify their price premium over the standard UK-made product.'

No pan-European strategy has taken place, however, with no real attempt to create 'Euro-brands' out of home-grown successes like Boddingtons.

Vertical integration

Vertical integration of manufacturing and beer retailing is still vital to the financial health of a company like Whitbread.

'Whereas the majority of the output would have gone to Whitbread-owned and -tied pubs in 1985, today this figure is less than a quarter'.

Therefore, the effect of the SMP, via a freer market, has been to force breweries like Whitbread to abandon their historic strategy of vertical integration. Since beer is so expensive to distribute, it is highly unlikely that cross-border upstream integration will play any more than a peripheral role in the future.

Managerial reorganization

The impact of the SMP on Whitbread has been sufficient for it to create a new sub-function within the company.

'Well, it's created my job for a start.'

The volume of EC legislation that impacts on the company now, or will do so in the future, is such that a permanent Brussels representative is becoming desirable. The SMP has clearly created work in administration at the managerial level rather than simplifying any procedures.

Management is considered far more efficient in the company now, but this has been due to technology and communication solely. The impact of the SMP has clearly been to hamper this efficiency by inputting more bureaucracy.

Innovation

As a direct result of the SMP, innovation in new products has been biased towards more European products. This has significantly impacted on Whitbread retailer operations (not on brewing, however). For instance, the Europeanization of the UK consumer has driven more sophisticated and innovative ways to display wine and a more adventurous approach to wine sourcing from new areas in France, Spain, Portugal and Italy. At the same time, however, it has encouraged innovation in non-EU wines which are increasingly seen to be better presented, better packaged and to have more consistent quality.

Competition avoidance

The issue of competition avoidance is central to the impact of the SMP on Whitbread. While the single market was recognized, back in 1985, to be an opportunity, the threat posed by cross-border shopping was never fully appreciated by the company. The effect, when it came, was all the more disturbing.

> 'We weren't able to forecast any profound effects. On the one hand, there was some anxiety that our beer manufacturing stood to be at risk from cheaper manufacturing on the Continent but that has largely not materialized.'

There was some catching up in efficiency prior to 1992 by UK brewers, which was inspired by anxiety about the single market but in reality had more to do with cost-efficiency generally.

Other strategic responses

On the positive side, the forecasts that were made before the advent of the single market were that it would not benefit Whitbread a great deal and that it might prove a threat.

> 'We realized the fact of the single market in itself was not going to change market and consumer preferences.'

Whitbread viewed its ability to succeed on the Continent to be a function of getting products into those markets that people were likely to want. This ability is clearly constrained by the practicality of a UK company opening restaurants that the people on the Continent would want to patronize.

> 'We didn't come up with much on the positive side about the single market.'

F.1.8. Consequences of adjustments for company performance

Growth in turnover

Beer is a national product and as such is probably less likely to benefit from any cross-border initiatives than most other food and drink products. There are still structural barriers but the fundamental non-tariff barrier in beer is consumer taste.

> 'The single largest impediment to selling beer to the Germans is that they don't like any beer other than German beer.'

Overall, the impact of the SMP on growth in turnover has been low.

Profitability and competitiveness

The impact of the SMP has been felt more by Whitbread in beer cross-border trade. This is a function of differential duty rates between the UK and France/Belgium.

> 'It has removed barriers but the effect has been detrimental.'

'I am fairly clear the effect has been negative because of this one issue and all other SMP effects have been peripheral.'

The effect can be measured quite readily and Whitbread estimate that the equivalent of over a million pints of beer a day are coming onto the UK market from this cross-border trade, resulting in a direct loss of trade to the company. The UK government, in the period 1985 to 1992, acted to raise duty on beer in the run-up to the single market. This made matters worse by creating a larger retail price differential which inevitably encouraged cross-border trade even more.

The fact that most of this trade is duty-driven and price-based (rather than SMP- or taste-based) is firmly proven by the lack of traffic in food.

R&D

The long-term effects of the SMP on Whitbread are a gradual reorientation of its beer and food products towards a more Europeanized taste.

'There is one side-effect of the cross-Channel traffic that is having fundamental impacts on our business ... people are being exposed to a new packaging form: the 25 cl bottle.'

This is the predominant packaging type for Continental and higher strength beer. People like the format and over the past year or so British brewers like Whitbread have had to lay down capacity to pack in the 25 cl bottle form.

'Whitbread has invested in plant to generate this ... "dumpy" bottle for the market, which we would not otherwise have done.'

Across the industry, the effect of this could be an investment of more than UKL 10 million per year additional to normal expenditure.

As a corollary, the traditional packaging form of beer in the UK, the can, is seeing a steady decline in consumer popularity. This, plus the fact that the can is difficult to justify within new EC environmental legislation, means that packaging R&D has switched emphatically to the glass bottle.

F.1.9. Production costs and breakdown

Analysis of cost changes

For Whitbread, the financial drivers to improved profitability have been efficiency and cost reductions. This can be broken down as below since the start of the SMP.

	1992/93	1993/94	1994/95
Sales (UKL)	2,319	2,360	2,471
Cost of sales:			
Processing	1,819	1,840	1,915
Distribution	37	34	39
Administration	265	262	253

This can be further analysed by changes as below.

	Change in costs 1992–95	
	Cost change	As % of sales
Processing	+5%	−1%
Distribution	+5%	No change
Administration	−4%	−1%

There is absolutely no doubt from the above analysis that Whitbread has had to become more efficient in terms of its production costs.

The biggest single factor in its cost structure is the processing itself, which occurs in the brewery. While costs for Whitbread have increased by 5% for processing, the latter has declined by one percentage point in importance in the cost structure.

Distribution and logistics costs may have been expected to rise if the SMP had resulted in Whitbread having a greater cross-border trade. This would be because beer has such a high volume to value ratio. However, since Whitbread's business did not shift markedly to the Continent following the inception of the single market, it is apparent that distribution economies and scale efficiencies drove the company and not any specific effects of the SMP. The final proof of this lies in the fact that most distribution, as a percentage of sales, did not move at all over the period 1992–95.

Further proof of the lack of impact on Whitbread of the SMP specifically comes in the movement of administration costs over the same period. These actually declined in total (by 4%) and as a function of the total cost structure in relation to sales (by 1%). This confirms the fact that administrative cost savings were made as a result of margin pressure and greater competitiveness in the industry.

Clearly, however, the impact of cross-border shopping has been to put pressure on Whitbread's margins which in turn will force it to try to cut production, processing or any other costs it can in order to maintain profitability. The fact that the overall operating margin for the company has declined over the period merely exaggerates this margin pressure still further.

> 'Price pressure has meant that price reductions (in real terms) have often exceeded cost reductions.'

As well as the vertical integration of the beer business which produces cost economies, there is a horizontal cost saving linkage between the various Whitbread restaurant chains.

> 'This horizontal linkage is apparent, for example, in procurement – so the buying of food for all those businesses is an integrated operation. We are not vertically integrated with our (food) manufacturers.'

The buying of food for all concepts is an integrated process which optimizes the purchasing power – it is irrelevant in the short term where the supplier is based. The company concedes, however, it is more likely that in future a supplier of pasta, for example, could come from another EU country following the SMP.

Cost structure: consumer pressure and cross-Channel shopping

Further cost effects on Whitbread's retail business are caused by cross-Channel shopping and its increase following the SMP. The inability of most outlets which retail beer in the UK to compete with cheap beer from Calais affects their operating economics. However, the outlets most affected tend to be the smaller, family-owned and -operated units rather than larger chains such as Whitbread.

Cost structure: duty and stronger beer

The other major effect of the SMP on cost structures emanates from the difference of the basis of duty between Britain and France. In the UK, duty has always been calculated according to strength not volume. This has encouraged the production of weaker beer.

> 'UK people buying beer in France are buying stronger beer and acquiring a taste for it.'

This convergence is inspired by the lack of duty harmonization, and not by the SMP. It is largely viewed as a government failure in the UK.

F.1.10. Productivity and competitiveness

Labour productivity and capital productivity

The productivity of labour and capital in Whitbread's business is a function of cost and margin against price obtained. The largest element of cost is still duty on beer for Whitbread. The lack of harmonization of duty has been crucial in forming the actual effects of the SMP on Whitbread. As wine is untaxed throughout most of Europe, it is very difficult to tax beer or spirits at a high rate.

> 'There was nothing the Commission could do to bring about a political will, that is a matter for UK ministers. They didn't want to confront the fact that, in much of Europe, alcohol was and still is almost untaxed.'

The effects of the SMP are completely overshadowed by the UK government's intervention and taxation policies on alcohol. When the current government came to office in 1979, the difference in duty between Britain and France was 7p per pint of beer – today this stands at 30p.

> 'The Brits get no sympathy in Brussels on this matter and deservedly so.'

Capital productivity and legislation

The long-term effects on productivity of technology and economic advances is to reduce unit costs considerably. The effect of legislation, however, is to create work and more bureaucracy which in turn reduces productivity of labour and capital.

Of the many facets of SMP legislation, those that impact Whitbread day to day concern hygiene, additives, ingredients and labelling.

> 'It is fair to say we have felt no cost implications because we have pushed the impact on to our suppliers.'

The future effects of SMP legislation for Whitbread could actually be seen to hinder cross-border trade rather than enhance it. Legislation on purity of beer in Germany, for example, has not been removed and will act to prevent foreign companies entering what is Europe's largest market for beer. Advertising restrictions on alcohol effectively distort competition by preventing new concepts or brands being communicated adequately to the consumer.

The impact of the SMP on capital productivity in beer will be further complicated by its possible relationship with and substitution for wine. Wine is seen (particularly by the French) as an agricultural product, not an industrial one (like beer and spirits). This means it may be more subject to common agricultural policy (CAP) legislation, which is interventionist, than to the SMP which aims to free up the market. It is difficult for the UK government to lobby with any credibility on this issue. The UK government would have to lobby other countries not to tax beer and spirits as highly when it itself has imposed among the highest duties in the EU.

> 'The UK government has moderated its duty increase over the past three years, which has clearly been forced upon it by alcohol price disparity with the Continent'.

This would tend to suggest that equalization of duty is occurring, but in fact there is no political will to achieve anything other than broad parity within bands.

> 'Harmonization has given way to approximation and now they don't talk about it at all'.

Labour productivity and legislation

As a retailer Whitbread employs a large number of people (65,000 in 1995) over a large number of relatively small retail outlets. Labour productivity is a key issue which is addressed all the time. For instance, EC restrictions on maximum working hours per retail employee can have severe repercussions, particularly on small retail businesses.

F.1.11. Conclusions: Whitbread's experience with the SMP

When faced with the prospect of the single market in 1985, Whitbread feared foreign competition from larger firms.

> 'We feared foreign brewers dumping beer on us from the duty-paid route. We did not anticipate cross-border shopping.'

The main implications for Whitbread concern the various pieces of legislation and the difficulties of coping with it.

> 'You have to employ people like me to undo the complications and simplify the effects.'

Rationalization and the drive for efficiency in Whitbread's operation are undoubtedly dynamics that would have happened anyway - driven by a greater competitiveness within the UK brewing and food industries.

Cost-cutting and margin reduction have mostly been in response to market forces but the single market and the advent of cross-border shopping have meant this rationalization has, of necessity, had to be more draconian.

Access to the principal EU beer market (Germany) is effectively denied to Whitbread by continued local protectionism by German brewers and consumer preferences. The benefit of a wider vista of market opportunity which was envisaged by the creators of the SMP is therefore a practical impossibility for beer and food companies like Whitbread. The Germans have actually used the plethora of legislation and Directives (e.g. on sweeteners) to increase their protectionism and maintain their fragmentation.

This in summary is the exact opposite to the objective of the EU when the SMP and single market were first agreed in 1985. Whitbread has seen no obvious benefits of new market opportunities and has only suffered the margin pressure consequent on cross-border sales of beer from France. The impact of the many pieces of legislation enacted as part of the SMP has been to create bureaucracy in the beer industry rather than a freer market where all companies may compete on an equal footing and invest accordingly.

F.2.   Case study: Danone Group - Biscuit Division (France)

F.2.1. Background

Danone is a leading French multinational group in the food processing sector. A public company, Danone organized the diversification of the BSN Group which, back in the 1970s, had its activities centred on bottle glass. BSN entirely reoriented its activities towards the food processing industry, retaining glass packaging from its original activities.

Danone is currently present in several sub-sectors including dairy products, mineral waters, biscuits, pastes, condiments, packaging, beer. Total group turnover, world-wide, was FF 76.8 bn in 1994, equivalent to some ECU 12 bn. Out of this figure, FF 70.7 bn or 92% are European sales. All of Danone's activities are international but highly Europe-centred. Biscuit sales in Europe amount to FF 12.8 bn (or some ECU 2 bn), representing 18% of total group turnover in 1994 (Europe only).

F.2.2. Danone-Biscuits development and current strategy

Danone's activities in the biscuit sector started in 1985 with the acquisition of General Biscuits. At the time of this acquisition, General Biscuits was already a major player with a solid market share of 20% over Europe, 30 production sites in 8 countries and production totalling some 345,000 t annually. General Biscuits also possessed a portfolio of well-known national brands such as 'L'Alsacienne', 'LU', 'Heudebert', 'De Beukelaer', 'Mother's', and 'Salerno'. Full integration of General Biscuits into the BSN Group followed in 1987.

At the time of its acquisition, General Biscuits was present in the sugar biscuits and rusks segments. Since this initial acquisition, further growth has largely been achieved by acquisition. The group has expanded into other segments of the biscuit sector such as salt biscuits, dry pastries and chocolate biscuits.

With output of 570,000 t in 1994, Danone is now the largest European producer and the second largest world-wide. The BSN-Danone corporate philosophy is based on a few key strategic operations:

(a)   the diversification from bottle glass into food processing;
(b)   the construction of a diversified portfolio;

(c)   internationalization, with a strong European focus;
(d)   maintaining the group as a federation of SMEs.

'It was essential to construct a European market position because of the competition.'

The idea of a federation of SMEs is worth a word of explanation. The group is indeed being structured as a federation of companies grouped into product-oriented branches. These companies operate largely on a national basis. They enjoy a large degree of autonomy under the group's stewardship and financial guidelines. Central administration is light, when compared with other multinational groups. The emphasis is on autonomy, initiative and entrepreneurship. Danone sets a high priority on developing a group SME culture and in fostering the development of its people. Under Antoine Riboud, the President, the group has sought to develop a strong culture of autonomy, entrepreneurship, and professional development of its staff.

The overall corporate objective is to create value for the shareholders by positioning Danone as a growth value on the stock exchange. Given that the food market in Europe is rather stable, achieving this objective requires:
(a)   a dynamic acquisition strategy;
(b)   value creation or, to use Danone's wording, 'global productivity'.

The biscuit business of Danone is operated through a multi-level organization:
(a)   at group level, the 'Branche Biscuits', a small corporate structure;
(b)   a network of national companies, generally operating under the name of General
        Biscuits: these local companies have production and distribution activities;
(c)   a number of local companies such as Heudebert (I) or Chokoladovny (CZ).

Behind this, the group provides the classical functions of a holding company, such as financial consolidation, investment screening and treasury management.

F.2.3. Financial history

Danone-Biscuits' more recent financial performance is as follows:

Danone-Biscuits (mn FF)	1986	1988	1990	1992	1994
Net sales	9992	11065	12776	13457	12837
Operating result	641	841	1231	1126	807
Operating result/sales (%)	6.4	7.6	10	8.4	6.2
Operational cash flow	776	777	914	1191	964
Total assets (2)	3488	4362	15054	15518	16800
Average number of employees	11628	10879	13956	13801	12051

The above data suggest that between 1986 and 1994:

(a) turnover has increased by 28% – this must be viewed in the light of the active policy of
    acquisitions pursued during this period;
(b) the average operational result amounts to 7.7% of sales, which is in line with averages for
    this sector;
(c) annual cash flow averages 7.6% of turnover;
(d) productivity, measured by turnover/employee, has increased by 23% in nominal terms, i.e.
    it has practically stagnated in real terms;

(e) total assets have grown substantially, largely as a result of the group investing heavily in the biscuit branch via acquisitions.

F.2.4. Danone-Biscuits in its competitive environment

In order to appreciate the position acquired by Danone in the biscuit sector, it is interesting to examine the sector's structure and evolution since 1986.

Biscuits, a sub-sector of industrial baking (NACE 419) and sub-divided into segments such as sugar-based, savoury, or chocolate-covered biscuits and dry pastries (e.g. wafers), remains in some respects a labour-intensive operation. In particular, because of the fragile nature of the product and despite technological progress, the packaging of biscuits still largely resists automation. Complex products (e.g. chocolate-covered biscuits) require multi-stage processes sometimes involving inter-plant transfers.

On the input side, since wheat is a basic ingredient, biscuit making is very sensitive to fluctuations in agricultural product prices, which in turn are highly dependent on the evolution of the common agricultural policy.

Consumer tastes still tend to be national and sometimes even regional. However, pan-European brands are increasingly well accepted for some products. In several sub-segments, sales even have a seasonal character and biscuit consumption is often linked to specific events.

Total production of biscuits and rusks in the EU amounted to about 3.9 million tonnes in 1991. The largest producing country is the UK, with 950,000 t, followed by France, Italy and Germany, with 600,000 to 650,000 t each. Production tends to be almost entirely absorbed by national consumption with exports representing only some 5% of global production. This is linked to the keeping qualities of biscuits and the relatively high logistics costs.

The market is very concentrated. Three main players together hold some 50% of the European market (United Biscuits (UK), BSN (F) and Barilla (I)). BSN-Danone currently holds a 19% share of the European market (some 720,000 tonnes of production).

F.2.5. Principal changes as a result of the SMP

New market opportunities

The biscuit market is basically stable, with a growth rate of some 2-3% over the 1985-95 period. The only national markets with fast growth have been Germany after unification and Denmark. The main market developments during this period have been:

(a) stable or slow growing consumption in Western Europe, with the exception of Germany after unification;
(b) the growing importance of the retail chains because of both their buying power and the growth of private labels;
(c) consumer tastes remaining largely national but increasingly accepting Euro-products when supported by a strong brand.

The single main opportunity for growth has resulted from the opening of the Eastern European market.

New market structures

In the context of the single market, the objective for large firms has been to become geographically present everywhere in Europe. This has happened largely through acquisitions of production units and local distribution companies or by means of strategic alliances. Bought-out production units have subsequently been modernized. By acting in this way, large international groups have been able both to diversify their product portfolios and to promote products adapted to local tastes as well as Euro-branded products.

During this period, substantial consolidation has been achieved by acquisitions by the major groups eager to acquire market share and build up muscle to face the large retail chains. This situation left niche strategy and supply of retailers as the main options left for small and local producers. As an example of moves followed by Danone competitors, United Biscuits (UK) has recently strengthened its position in Continental Europe with purchases in Denmark (Oxford Biscuits), Hungary and Finland.

The key SMP legislative developments with an influence on the biscuit sector have been:

(a) the Additives and Labelling Directives, which have allowed more uniform formulations to be promoted across European countries;
(b) the removal of border controls.

The Hygiene Directives have also played a concrete, although minor, role. To some extent they have contributed to preventing the erection of new barriers by Member States. However, this impact would have been mostly felt in sectors other than biscuits. As biscuit products do not contain water and are less subject to microbiological problems, the impact of the Hygiene Directives has been less significant in this sector.

The pending Directive on fortification and specific labelling issues still appears to be a source of uncertainty.

> 'The industry expects a position from the Commission. Also at this time, there is still a need for country-specific labelling for specific claims.'

Overall, it would appear that benefits to the consumer have been positive, if not spectacular. Consumer prices have remained stable, if not declining. The product range on offer has not, however, been substantially widened.

F.2.6. Danone-Biscuits evolution 1985–95: SMP impact

Danone entered the biscuit sector at the time of the SMP announcement. The prospect of a unified European market was immediately perceived as an opportunity to create a strong international activity supported by Euro-branding and by a network of local companies with production and distribution activities. Accordingly, Danone has sought to achieve a European leader position by:

(a) consolidating its geographical positions through continuous acquisition of local companies in all European countries. By 1994, Danone had acquired companies in France, Belgium, the Netherlands, Germany, the UK, Spain as well as participations in Greece, Ireland, the Czech Republic and Russia;
(b) promoting its leading brands to achieve European status (primarily LU (sugar biscuits));

(c) creating a network of plants, mostly by modernizing acquired ones;
(d) setting up a strong network of local sales companies with financial responsibility for their objectives and a large degree of autonomy for marketing, product development, and related functions;
(e) creating a presence in all biscuit segments (sugar, salt, dry confectionery) and in rusks.

International expansion

Through the acquisition of General Biscuits in 1985, BSN immediately achieved an international operational presence in the main EU markets: France, UK, Germany, Benelux.

Since that date, the group has continuously increased its geographical presence, mostly by acquisition. In Central and Eastern Europe, the main platform has been the Czech firm Chokoladovny, acquired in 1990 with Nestlé and modernized since then. This is to become the platform for exports to other Central and Eastern European countries. Danone has recently acquired a Russian company in line with the above strategy.

Year	Company	Link	Country
1987	Siro	acquisition	Spain
1989	Jacobs	acquisition	UK
	Belin (ex Nabisco)	acquisition	France
	Saiwa	acquisition	France
1990	Belin Surgelés	divestment	France
1991	W&R Jacobs	acquisition	Ireland
	Chokoladovny	acquisition	Czech Republic
	Papadopoulos	participation	Greece
1992	Henninger	association	Greece
1994	Bolshevick	acquisition	Russia

Partially as a result of this international expansion, there has been a real mentality change in the group which, from being a company with a largely 'French' outlook, has become very internationally driven. The SMP has been instrumental in promoting this change of mentality.

'Before (the SMP), we were more afraid to move (cross-border), because of the local barriers. Now, we know that we have the EC regulations available as a tool to unlock the doors.'

'The recourse procedures (of the Commission) are simple and effective ... only a bit slow.'

Total investment requirements to compete

During the period, two main kinds of investment were undertaken by the group in the biscuit branch:

(a) financial investments to acquire more businesses. These were mostly made by the group. As a result, the branch assets grew from some FF 3.5 bn to over FF 16 bn. Over this period, total operational cash flow amounted to some FF 8 bn. It is clear that only massive funding by the group made this investment possible. This was the price paid to acquire a leading European market position;
(b) industrial investment, mostly in plant modernization. Over the 1987-90 period, this represented FF 1,906 bn against a cash flow (*marge brute d'autofinancement*) of

FF 1,620 bn. It is clear from these figures that 1987-90 was a period of investment undertaken with the prospect of a longer-term return.

Capacity adjustments

Production of the group increased from 345,000 t (1986) to some 570,000 t (1994). Most of this capacity increase has resulted from acquisitions. Some old plants have also been modernized and, in specific cases (Nantes in 1988), closed to be replaced by larger and more modern ones.

Location decisions

The Danone biscuit branch has its headquarters in Paris (France). It consists of a network of local companies, which usually have production and operational functions. Since the emphasis of the group policy has been on a pan-European presence, and since local production has been considered necessary, no major relocation decision has been taken.

Cost-cutting/rationalization

The group is conscious of the need to be cost-competitive. Usually plants acquired have been modernized, particularly when destined to produce products sold under Euro-brands like LU or Belin. The effort has been focused on maintaining uniform standards and quality.

The cost emphasis of BSN-Danone is based on a global view of productivity. This means that productivity is seen not only as cost-cutting, but also as quality improvement and performance (e.g. reduction of cycle time) improvement.

Programmes for productivity improvement (based on the company's 'global productivity' philosophy) have been implemented across the group. The corporate department produces benchmarks for performance of the group's units. These are circulated between units. It is requested that lagging units develop an action plan in order to adjust to best practices in the group. Corporate assistance is provided to individual units to develop their plans.

Adaptation of product range

The product range has been consolidated from the portfolio of acquired companies. These were initially very diverse and consisted of two types of product: some fitting local tastes (e.g. 'Bastogne' spekuloos); some with a more international and classic appeal (e.g. the 'Petit Beurre'). Since the main thrust of BSN-Danone has been to go for strong positions in international segments, the tendency has been:

(a) to reduce the product range;
(b) to focus on products to be promoted under Euro-brands.

Marketing strategies

The main thrust of Danone's efforts has been in building a Europe-wide position and consolidating power vis-à-vis larger retail chains who control volume buying. This has mainly involved the development of a product portfolio under Euro-brands (e.g. LU for sugar biscuits and Belin for savoury biscuits). Most of the products with an international appeal are increasingly promoted under Euro-brands.

Vertical integration

Danone's philosophy is to manage product portfolios rather than create industry clusters. Thus the group has focused on biscuit making (including packaging), and is not further integrated upstream (milling) or downstream (distribution).

Managerial reorganization

As already indicated, within each branch the BSN-Danone structure relies on a network of SMEs enjoying a large degree of autonomy and responsible for their own management and performance within group guidelines.

In 1990, all the French companies were reorganized as far as their logistics and purchasing were concerned. Inter-plant logistics were rationalized and the number of suppliers has been gradually decreased. Pan-European purchasing intensity has also increased. This has largely been possible as a result of EC horizontal Directives (mostly the Labelling and Additives Directives) which have allowed more uniform formulations. Finally, central coordination and information functions were created and developed (e.g. on legislation).

Innovation

A continuous effort has been made on both process improvement and product development. The emphasis is on food processing research which allows the introduction of Euro-products at a uniform level of quality and low cost across Europe.

Packaging is an important issue, because of the legal constraints and the logistic issues involved. Intensive research programmes are examining this issue, particularly to avoid or limit the use of packaging.

Competition avoidance

Even though local producers are competitors in specific local markets, Danone is mostly competing against:

(a) large international competitors such as United Biscuits;
(b) private labels.

Brand support is therefore a very important component of the company's activities.

F.2.7. Consequences of adjustments for company performance

Growth in turnover

As is apparent from the financial performance table, group turnover has grown from FF 9.2 bn to FF 12.8 bn since 1986. This reflects a dynamic acquisition policy more than real market growth. This slow growth also conceals variations between product segments and countries.

Profitability and competitiveness

Inspection of the financial results shows that the position of the group is stable but has not grown naturally. The financial figures are not complete and do not provide the full profitability picture of the biscuit branch, since this information is confidential. Inspection of the figures available suggests that the levels of profitability achieved are acceptable, in the perspective of longer-term developments. This is because of:

(a) the efforts required until now to acquire and sustain market position in a slow-growth market with active private labels;

(b) the influence of fluctuations in the price of wheat and the increased price of this raw material since the reform of the CAP in a context of stable end-product prices.

It must be emphasized that the 1986–96 period has been a period of portfolio construction (hence investment) for Danone. The challenge now is to see whether the group will be able to use the European position it has acquired to generate profits from this established portfolio.

R&D

See 'Innovation' above.

F.2.8. Production costs and breakdown

Over the 1986–94 period, the structure of costs and value has changed in roughly the following order of magnitude:

Value chain (%)	1986	1994
Raw material	30	33
Production	40	33
Marketing, administration and margin	30	33

Costs of raw materials have increased, mostly due to increases in the price of wheat. A slight reduction in the cost of additives, which has been allowed by the horizontal Directives, has not offset this effect.

> 'Our costs are most sensitive to fluctuations in the price of wheat: the CAP has had a much more profound effect (than the SMP).'

> 'No measurable productivity change can be directly attributed to the SMP.'

Production costs have decreased, due to modernization and, in certain cases, plant size increases. However:

(a) no major scale effects have been achieved, since production remains largely national;

(b) packaging, due to the nature of the product, remains very labour-intensive.

F.2.9. Productivity and competitiveness

Labour and capital productivity

At branch level, turnover per employee increased from FF 860,000 in 1986 to FF 1 million in 1994, an increase of 16% in nominal terms. An explanation of this is that within the Danone Group productivity is a global concept incorporating not only cost elements but also quality and performance, generally more qualitative elements of a productivity enhancement. This has allowed the company to construct a European position based on image and quality rather than exclusively on low cost.

Capital productivity, as measured by cash flow/assets, is medium and stable. It should be remembered that Danone is a portfolio company and that the biscuits branch represents a stable and low risk activity, as opposed to more rapidly growing and evolving segments like fresh products.

Productivity and legislation

It is clear that EC legislation has to some extent contributed to productivity and operational improvements. However, this effect has been rather marginal in quantitative terms.

The Additives and Labelling Directives have contributed to the increasing use of uniform formulations. This has certainly reduced production costs, but not to a significant (or even measurable) degree, since no large scale benefit has been derived from it.

F.2.10. Conclusions: Danone's (biscuit) experience with the SMP

Overall, the SMP has had a positive but moderate impact on the biscuit branch of Danone.

The key areas have been:

(a) productivity and operational performance: facilitating the use of uniform formulations and hence inter-plant transfers with some scale economies;
(b) on the qualitative side: stimulating an international spirit, in particular the drive to export, and creating the feeling of 'being a European company'.

F.3. Case study: Schöller Lebensmittel GmbH & Co KG (Germany)

F.3.1. Background

Schöller Lebensmittel GmbH & Co KG is a leading German food manufacturer. The company is the second largest producer of ice cream in Germany, has a turnover of some DM 1.5 bn and employs some 3,200 persons (full-time) in the EU and around 800 persons outside the EU. The company is 65% owned by Südzucker, a leading German sugar processor. Apart from manufacturing some leading ice cream brands, the company also manufactures a limited range of specialist bakery goods (biscuits) and a range of deep-frozen food products.

F.3.2. Schöller development and current strategy

The company was established in Nürnberg in 1937 and has gradually expanded its activities since then, taking on bakery products in the 1950s, establishing a plant in Vienna, Austria, in 1971, a new plant in northern Germany in 1980, taking over a plant in Belgium in 1984 and establishing/acquiring production units in eastern Germany (Potsdam), Hungary and Poland in the 1990s. Since 1984, the company has operated a joint venture with the large German restaurant chain 'Mövenpick'.

Schöller's main strategic objectives are:

(a) to maintain high quality products by purchasing high quality, high value raw materials and using the most modern technology efficiently;

(b) to maximize service provided to customers via its own distribution network;

(c) to work as a team with well-trained personnel;

(d) to maintain sound financial management.

F.3.3. Financial history

Although Schöller publishes no accounts, the company has indicated that for the period from 1985 to 1994 turnover has more or less doubled. This has been due to a 20% growth in German sales of ice cream, strong growth in bakery products and more importantly substantial growth in sales from the Belgian plant (serving Benelux, France, the UK) during the 1980s.

	Schöller turnover (mn DM)					
Germany	1985^1	1990^1	1991^1	1992^1	1993^2	1994^2
Ice cream	490	881	998	1141	685	696
Bakery goods	54	88	233	250	185	166

[1] Gross prices.
[2] Net prices.

During the 1990s, however, after a one-off sharp and temporary rise in consumption due to German unification, turnover has tended to stagnate and margins have deteriorated. This deterioration is attributed to a number of external factors including:

(a) increasing pressure as a result of the rise in retailer concentration and the rise in own-label products;

(b) flat consumption levels;

(c) increased competition;

(d) Austrian accession to the EU.

These pressures have resulted in the closure of a number of plants, rationalization of the company's distribution network and a substantial reduction in the number of persons employed.

F.3.4. Schöller's competitive environment

From the 1960s and up to the end of the 1980s Schöller was able to establish a strong position in the German ice cream market through a mixture of internal growth (new plant in northern Germany in 1980); acquisitions and joint ventures/acquisition of brands (Motta brand for Germany and Austria). This approach was reinforced by the establishment of a distribution network covering both transport to the end-user and product storage.

Since the 1980s the company's position has been weakened by the growing strength of the multiple retailers, the emergence of European buying groups and the rise of own labels. Multiple retailers account for a larger share of overall purchases than during the mid-1980s but more importantly they purchase on a European basis on their own terms and to their own specification. They therefore bypass the long-established distribution networks controlled by the two market leaders in the German ice cream market and allow new entrants into the market. In addition, the share of multiples' own brands of ice cream on the German market is estimated to have doubled (to 10%) since 1990.

In Austria, accession to the European Union on 1 January 1995 meant that the hitherto protected Austrian ice cream market was for the first time opened to competition and this forced the closure of Schöller's Vienna plant in 1995.

More generally it should be noted that Schöller operates in a market dominated by a small number of multinational companies operating on an EU-wide or indeed a global scale. The fact that these companies already held dominant market positions in most EU countries prior to the launch of the SMP means that market entry for relatively smaller players has become extremely difficult. This is particularly the case since ice cream is a strongly branded sector which relies heavily on manufacturers' in-house distribution and requires very substantial brand support in the form of advertising expenditure to maintain a market presence.

Finally, low levels of income growth and high levels of unemployment in Germany have reduced overall consumer spending on ice cream during the 1990s.

F.3.5. Principal changes as a result of the SMP

New market opportunities

As is indicated above, Schöller expanded its operations in the EU prior to the launch of the SMP. The company has experienced some increase in exports since the launch of the SMP in 1985 but these are relatively insignificant in terms of overall turnover (under 10%).

While the SMP was felt to have facilitated cross-border trade (e.g. by not having to produce veterinary certificates at the Belgium/France border, by allowing uniform labelling, more uniform recipes, reducing border crossing costs), the overall impact on cross-border trade was felt to be limited due to the continued existence of varying consumer preferences in the different Member States (e.g. French consumers prefer sorbet type ice cream whereas German consumers prefer creamy ice cream with a higher fat content).

The main new market opportunities found by Schöller have been in Central and Eastern Europe since 1990.

New market structures

There are significant constraints to the economies of scale to be achieved in the ice cream sector due to the wide range of product lines which need to be produced (173) and the need to adjust these constantly to maintain consumer interest. Nevertheless Schöller has clearly decided to rationalize its operations and concentrate EU production in two main sites.

F.3.6. Schöller's evolution 1985–95: SMP impact

Internationalization and expansion

As indicated above, Schöller's main expansion within the EU took place prior to 1985, with the exception of the acquisition of a small manufacturing unit and some French distribution in the late 1980s. Since 1985, Schöller's main investments outside Germany have taken place in Central Europe where, since 1990, the company has invested to obtain the market growth (and margins) no longer generally available in Germany and the other EU markets in which the company operates.

Investment requirements to compete

In order to maintain its market share Schöller has had to considerably expand expenditure on marketing, particularly on advertising directed at the final consumer, which is designed to support its premium brands. While it has not invested significantly in new plant in the EU outside Germany (apart from a new plant in the new German *Länder* which is now closed), it has invested substantially in new machinery/production lines to allow it to produce innovative products.

Capacity adjustments

Within the EU during the past five years Schöller has closed four of its manufacturing plants and concentrated production in two sites. This represents a reduction of some 40% of previously existing capacity. At the same time, the company has reduced its own distribution and deep-frozen storage points within Germany by half (from 70 to 36). Both these changes and a more streamlined central administration have resulted in a cut in employment of between 10–15%.

Location decisions

Schöller's EU strategy predates the SMP and as a consequence the most significant expansion in production locations took place pre-1985. The decision to open a new plant in the new east German *Länder* was a direct result of unification, while the decision to close the Austrian plant was a direct result of EU accession. More generally, within the EU the company has concentrated on consolidating its position in the German/Benelux markets while expansion has been sought in Central Europe.

Cost-cutting/rationalization

As indicated above, Schöller has sought to reduce costs by cutting capacity. It has also reduced the number of employees, although it points out that this has not significantly reduced overall labour costs due to rises in wage costs for the work-force remaining in employment. While it has cut the costs of its distribution network, most of the savings generated in this manner have had to be put into higher marketing (advertising and product development) expenditure to maintain market share. Schöller indicated it had achieved savings on its packaging costs, by reducing the volume of packaging used and thus incurring lower charges under the German 'Green Dot' packaging waste recovery and recycling system, as well as reducing transport costs.

Adaptation of product range

As one of the branded ice cream market leaders in Germany operating in a market where constant product innovation is central to marketing strategy, Schöller is continuously updating and adapting its product range by introducing new and innovative products. While differing consumer preferences between Member States inhibit the development of Europe-wide product lines (Euro-brands), efforts in this direction have been started.

Marketing strategies

While historically Schöller operated in a relatively secure domestic market, the influx of competition in the form of other manufacturers, the increased concentration in the retail sector and the growth of private labels have all meant that Schöller has had to start to spend heavily on advertising and promotion to defend its brands and ensure access to retailers' shelf space. This essentially represents a shift away from a strategy which was geared to maintaining market share by controlling the distribution network.

Vertical integration

Due to the fact that it is majority-owned by Südzucker, a major raw material supplier of sugar, Schöller is in effect part of a company which is forward integrated. Schöller in turn has historically maintained market share through its strong presence in transport (own fleet of trucks), storage (freezer depots) and distribution (over 100,000 'tied' deep-freezers in retail outlets such as kiosks, garages, restaurants, etc. as well as its own sales force). Due to increased competition on the German market both in the traditionally 'tied' market and from retailers' own brands, the focus of the marketing effort has partially shifted toward creating and maintaining brand awareness amongst consumers.

Managerial reorganization

The impact of the SMP has been such as to require a major effort on the part of Schöller to monitor EC food and related legislation. The company employed four persons full-time to monitor SMP and related issues and had to provide language training for those involved. While in some respects production processes have been simplified by the introduction of more uniform recipes, the effort involved in labelling and following national legislation on ice cream composition has been substantial.

Innovation

As indicated above, the ice cream market is essentially driven by innovation both in terms of the product itself and around the product, e.g. packaging. Thus Schöller, as one of the leading brands in Germany, has had to invest heavily in product development as well as machinery to provide innovative products. This could be said to be an indirect result of the SMP since the presence of more competition on Schöller's domestic market has resulted in a stronger need to maintain its market presence through rapid changes in its product range. The company is seeking to generate 'Euro' products but rapid development of these is inhibited by continuing differences in national product preferences.

Competition avoidance

Even though the company faces competition from local producers in specific local/regional markets, Schöller is primarily competing against the large multinational players, such as Unilever, Mars, Nestlé, and against private labels. While as part of the large Südzucker Group it is relatively well protected from takeover, it has sought to meet the competitive challenge in the market by increasing brand support, maintaining high quality products, entering into alliances (e.g. Mövenpick) and new markets (Central and Eastern Europe).

F.3.7. Consequences of adjustments for company performance

Growth in turnover

As is shown in Section F.1.4, between 1985 and 1992 Schöller turnover for ice cream more than doubled while for bakery goods it rose almost five-fold, albeit from a much lower base. This reflects the growth in Schöller's German ice cream market (in part due to German unification) as well as increased sales in France and the Benelux countries. Since 1992 sales have, however, tended to stagnate indicating both a stabilization in consumption and an increase in competition in the market.

Profitability and competitiveness

Schöller publishes no separate accounts, so it is not possible to comment directly on the impact of the company's strategy on profitability except to say that it is clear that increased retailer concentration and the growth of private labels have put increasing pressure on margins. This in turn has resulted in a major effort by the company to reduce costs where it can in terms of production and distribution of its products.

R&D

See 'Innovation' above.

F.3.8. Production costs

Broadly speaking the structure of costs is as follows:

	Cost share (%)
Raw materials and packaging	25
Production	25
Administration	10
Finance, marketing, distribution and margin	40

Over the period since 1985 there has been a marginal reduction in packaging costs (due to lightweighting etc.) but no significant reduction in the cost of the principal raw material used, which is sugar. The price of sugar is largely determined by the EU's common agricultural policy and the reforms introduced here have not had any significant impact on the sugar price.

Beyond this, the only major change in costs has resulted from a shift in the balance between marketing and distribution costs with strong growth in marketing expenditure occurring due to increased advertising.

F.3.9. Productivity and competitiveness

Labour and capital productivity

It is clear that in the last few years Schöller has engaged in a substantial rationalization programme, closing a number of plants and reducing employment within the EU by an estimated 10 to 15%. While it is not possible to calculate the precise impact of these changes on output per unit of labour/unit of capital, it seems clear that for both of these measures there will have been a considerable improvement as a result of the rationalization programme undertaken.

Productivity and legislation

While the SMP (particularly additives and labelling legislation) has allowed more uniform use of recipes and this has contributed to operational improvements, these gains have been too marginal to measure in purely quantitative terms. At the same time it was noted that the cost of monitoring and complying with SMP legislation as well as seeking to influence it tended to offset gains derived from the production side.

F.3.10. Conclusions: Schöller's experience with the SMP

Overall the SMP has had a relatively modest but positive impact for Schöller which has tended to be considerably outweighed by the broader 'environmental' issues affecting the company. The latter issues are listed below:

(a) growing strength of multiple retailers/own labels;
(b) increased competition from large multinational players in the home market;
(c) German unification;
(d) changes in Central and Eastern Europe;
(e) operation in high labour cost/strong DM zone.

Many of the steps towards operating on a more EU-wide scale were taken prior to 1985 and this means that there have been no significant changes in EU presence/trade since then. Indeed, it was pointed out that the fact that pre-1985 the market was already dominated by a few large multinational or even global players with strong brands meant that the cost of entry into new markets was in any case likely to be high.

F.4. Case study: Van Melle BV (Netherlands)

F.4.1. Background

Van Melle BV is a leading Dutch manufacturer of confectionery products, mainly of sugar-based confectionery with a strong focus on fruit-flavoured sweets. The company is active on both the home and export markets. It has a network of affiliated sales companies throughout Western Europe and is also present in other parts of the world, including Eastern and Central Europe, North and South America, and East Asia.

Founded in 1912, Van Melle is still largely a family company, although it is quoted on the Dutch stock exchange. It currently employs about 2,500 people world-wide, has a turnover of some HFL 705 million (1995) and total assets of some HFL 492 million.[23]

F.4.2. Van Melle's development and current position

Van Melle's basic values are reflected in its 'mission' statement:

(a) care for its people, motivate, develop and involve them;
(b) delight consumers with high quality confectionery products;
(c) care for the environment and reduce the company's impact on it to a sustainable level;
(d) ensure a meaningful and profitable future as an independent company.

In terms of concrete objectives, Van Melle aims to:

(a) serve the upper segment of the market with high quality products, backed by a strong environmentally caring position;

---

[23] 1 Dutch Guilder (HFL) = ECU 0.52.

(b) consolidate its existing position and market share in stable growth countries;

(c) expand internationally in countries with growing markets where the political and economic climates are such that expected returns equal the risk connected with making investments.

Van Melle also places a high priority on environmental care. The company's goal is to make all activities sustainable within a period of 10 years. This means the company intends to create a position in which its activities will have – on balance – no harmful effect on the environment, or to remain within the limits of what the environment can endure without lasting damage.

The encouragement of autonomy and the management of human resources play a key role in the corporate strategy. In 1995, Van Melle's activities were managed by the following structure:

(a) Van Melle Nederland BV: European production and home market activities;

(b) Van Melle International Holding BV: a financial holding consolidating all international (i.e. non-Dutch) activities;

(c) Van Melle International Trust BV: a network of sales and production companies, 14 in 1995, located in Western Europe (Belgium, France, Germany, Switzerland), Eastern and Central Europe, the USA and Latin America, East Asia.

Van Melle can be described as a public company with a strong family influence. The founding family, Van Melle, is still the majority shareholder and some of its members maintain a leading role in the management of the company.

F.4.3. Financial history

Van Melle's financial performance over the last 10 years is presented below.

Van Melle NV (mn HFL)	1985	1988	1990	1992	1995
Net sales	273	376	424	558	706
Operating result	22	33	27	51	70
Net profit	19	14	13	32	48
Operating result/sales (%)	8	9	6	9	10
Operational cash flow	20	7	40	57	63
Net assets (2)	n.a.	128	148	198	324
Average number of employees:					
- in the Netherlands	n.a.	890	1070	1135	1100
- abroad	n.a.	1130	1240	1150	1430
Total	n.a.	2020	2310	2285	2530

Van Melle's overall turnover in this period has increased by some 260% in nominal terms, which represents an annual growth rate of some 10%. During the same period, its operating profit/sales ratio has fluctuated between 8% and 10%. Over the 1989-95 period (at 31.12), Van Melle's share value has increased by 90% from HFL 31 to HFL 57.

As a corporate policy, Van Melle seeks to achieve long-term value and growth for its shareholders while maintaining its independence. It is therefore:

(a) pursuing growth opportunities thrown up by the internationalization of markets and by the SMP, which requires substantial financial resources;

(b) building and consolidating protection mechanisms to avoid hostile takeovers: these mechanisms include alliances and the establishment of a Foundation ('Stichting') with preferred voting shares.

F.4.4. Van Melle in its competitive environment

The confectionery market consists of four main segments: sugar confectionery, chocolate confectionery, bulk and chocolate biscuits. Van Melle is currently present only in the sugar confectionery segment. The EU market for sugar confectionery amounted to some 1.4 million tonnes in 1994 and demand is generally flat (with the exception of Denmark, a small market). Germany and the UK are the largest markets, representing over 50% of total consumption. The Netherlands represents only a small volume of some 85,000 t.

For a relatively large company like Van Melle with in-house production of some 70,000 t/year, exports are absolutely essential. Traditionally, the main export markets in the EU for Dutch produced sugar confectionery are, in decreasing order of importance, Germany, Belgium, the UK and, to a lesser extent, France. In all these markets demand, both in terms of global consumption and in consumption per head, has been flat since 1990.

Largely because of the influence of local tastes in consumption patterns, sugar-based confectionery markets tend to remain nationally oriented. Indeed in 1994 intra-EU trade represented only some 270,000 t, or 19% of total consumption. This is in contrast with chocolate and chocolate biscuits, the production of which is now much more international largely as a result of increased concentration in this sector during the late 1980s.

The main producers of sugar confectionery in the EU which compete with Van Melle in export markets are large international firms: Nestlé (Rowntree), Lamy-Lutti, Kraft-Jacobs-Suchard, and Mars. All these firms expanded considerably in the EU via acquisitions during the late 1980s. Since 1992, relatively little significant movement has occurred in industry structures.

Since sugar confectionery aims largely at a young customer base, product appeal is often based on packaging and displays tend to change rapidly, resulting in short product life cycles and the need for constant product innovation and R&D. New products are being launched on the market at short intervals and are constantly replaced by new versions. At present, the recession, which adversely affects all sectors, particularly penalizes impulse buying and related products.

The increasing power of retailers in the EU has put extra pressure on producers of fast moving consumer goods. This has affected sugar confectionery and has resulted in an increased requirement for expenditure on branding and logistics. The situation has been accentuated by the launch of distributors' own labels in these markets.

Another major development has been the opening of Eastern European markets, which was immediately perceived by the industry as a major opportunity. Some producers have reacted by installing or acquiring local production capacity. Others have preferred to trade.

A key issue in this product sector is the price of sugar. As a result of the common agricultural policy reforms and the current sugar regime, sugar producers are said not to receive adequate compensation for exports ('refunds') and find it accordingly more difficult to export. There is also a strong concentration of sugar suppliers which reduces flexibility on sugar supply prices.

Thus some of the main challenges Van Melle has faced during the last years have been:

(a) maintaining and consolidating market share in the EU and exploiting the new growth opportunities in the export markets;

(b) extending the product life cycle;

(c) protecting itself from the power of the retailers.

Broadly speaking, Van Melle has pursued these aims over the 1985–95 period by:

(a) expanding its geographical presence;
(b) focusing on efficient production of its core product lines;
(c) offering basic, high quality products, concentrating on their intrinsic qualities rather than on packaging or the display of short-lived features to achieve a long life cycle;
(d) progressively creating global branding;
(e) achieving production cost-efficiency via scale economies and automation.

The SMP has undoubtedly provided a favourable context for this reorientation.

F.4.5. SMP and cross-border trading

The direct importance of the SMP for Van Melle's business is not generally considered to be very high. The main SMP provisions affecting Van Melle's activities in Europe have been as follows:

(a) the removal of border controls (all products sold in the EU are exported from the Netherlands) has considerably improved the movement of goods between EU countries;
(b) taxation and VAT are still a problem, particularly in the perspective of uniform prices across the EU. VAT rates, in particular, still vary widely across the EU, ranging from 6% (Netherlands) to 25% (Denmark);
(c) the Fruit Juice Directive has definitely enabled the use of more uniform product formulations across the EU.

In future, the Directive on fortification will be the single most important legislative issue for Van Melle. In addition, the company felt that the introduction of the European Monetary Union (EMU) would help to eliminate currency fluctuations. Waste packaging is not regarded as a problem, since practically no returnable/reusable packaging is used, implying no reverse logistics issue.

F.4.6. Principal changes as a result of the SMP

New market opportunities

Against a context of increased internationalization in the industry yet persistence of national tastes, stable consumption patterns within Western Europe and the opening of Eastern European markets, Van Melle – which was already present on the main EU markets before 1985 - has responded thus:

(a) geographical expansion, mainly exporting to the growing markets in Eastern and Central Europe. Commercial penetration has been pursued through local sales and distribution companies, which Van Melle has either created or acquired;
(b) a product policy aimed at penetrating the international market, particularly via large retail chains. This has required efficient production (made possible by exploitation of scale economies, automation and the use of uniform formulations), and a product focus on basic qualities (quality, 'natural' products taking into account local tastes and aiming at a long life cycle).

New market structures

During the late 1980s, intensive concentration occurred in the confectionery sector, largely via acquisitions by a few large multinational companies like Nestlé, Kraft-Jacobs-Suchard, Lamy-Lutti, Cadbury Schweppes (UK), Ferrero (I), Wrigley (DK), and Mars (USA), etc. All EU national confectionery markets are now dominated by these multinational companies.

Country	Supplier
Germany	Kraft-Jacobs-Suchard (KJS); Ferrero; Nestlé; Mars
UK	Cadbury Schweppes; Nestlé; Mars
France	KJS; Nestlé; Mars
Spain	KJS; Nestlé; Cadbury Schweppes
Netherlands	Mars; Nestlé; KJS
Belgium	KJS; Mars

Source: Caobisco.

To some extent this concentration activity was made more attractive by the announcement of the SMP in 1986. The SMP has subsequently allowed all major players to achieve: harmonization of formulations and packaging, additives, colours, labelling; more efficient logistics; and Euro-branding.

F.4.7. Van Melle's evolution 1985–95: SMP impact

Internationalization and expansion (EU)

Before 1986, Van Melle was producing 90% of its volume in the Netherlands and had trade or production activities in Belgium, France, Germany, the UK, Ireland and Denmark. Over the 1985-95 period, Van Melle undertook a considerable expansion of its international activities, mostly outside the EU. As a result, the Netherlands (and the EU) currently accounts for only some 50% of Van Melle's total volume. Trade activities have expanded to all EU countries. Inside the EU, the main problems encountered were:

(a) in France, largely due to the increased cost of distribution;
(b) in the UK and Germany, due to difficulties with the products adopted;
(c) in the UK and Italy, due to currency fluctuations.

Van Melle has concentrated on consolidating its position in the EU markets. This has been achieved by concentrating production geographically and developing a network of local sales companies with a large degree of autonomy in terms of their strategy and activities.

Total investment requirements to compete

Over the 1985–95 period, Van Melle invested some HFL 308 million (or about ECU 160 million), predominantly from its own funds (there is basically no long-term debt). This has represented some 70% of the operational cash flow over the same period (10% of it went into shareholders' dividends). Most of this investment was devoted to:

(a) modernization, expansion and automation of production units (e.g. Breda (NL));
(b) rationalization of operations by cutting off non-performing production units, particularly in the UK and Germany.

Over the same period, substantial efforts and investment were also made in environmental management. A full multi-annual environmental action and investment plan was launched in 1992.

Maintaining independence in the context of a high takeover activity (Van Melle is a public company) led to the introduction of a number of defence mechanisms, including the establishment of a Foundation (*Stichting*) holding preferred voting shares alliances, the most important being formalized in 1991 with Perfetti Spa, an Italian manufacturer with products and a geographical presence complementary to those of Van Melle. Both companies had previously collaborated for more than 10 years. This alliance bears mostly on cooperative distribution arrangements. Perfetti has become a minority shareholder of Van Melle.

Capacity adjustments

With the increase of international sales, the production requirements have increased substantially. Over the period 1985–95, total production for European markets has evolved from roughly 45,000 t/year to some 70,000 t/year (all plants). As indicated above, in order to increase efficiency in terms of productivity, quality control and product homogeneity, the company invested heavily to concentrate production in one main plant and one country (Breda, NL) while enlarging and automating this operation.

Back in 1986 this approach was not considered practical, largely because of the diversity of national legislation and standards across the EU. Following the SMP it has been made possible by a combination of the following:

(a) Van Melle's international strategy to achieve a large horizontal presence by focusing on products that can be efficiently produced and uniformly marketed across the EU;
(b) the SMP, which has been instrumental in the implementation of this strategy. EC Directives on additives, fruit juices and labelling have particularly enabled the marketing of uniform formulations throughout the EU.

Location decisions

As outlined above the entire company strategy has been to build a position based on products that could override differences in local tastes and of a high and consistent quality. This has been achieved by the relocation of activities in Breda (NL). Over the same period, a network of national sales companies has been developed and consolidated to adjust to specific local market conditions, such as cultural differences (publicity, advertising) and customer/retailer relations.

Cost-cutting/rationalization

Cost-cutting was and still is a necessity in a marketplace dominated by multinational companies (with large product ranges and scale economies) and distributors' aggressive entry into large and mature segments (private labels and price undercutting). The main features of the cost-cutting and rationalization programmes implemented by Van Melle have been described in the previous section.

Adaptation of product range and marketing strategies

Until 1985, Van Melle's growth allowed the development of a diversified portfolio of products sold under different brand names and packaging in the various countries. There was a fair degree of national diversification in this product range.

The emergence of the single market and the strengthening of the distribution sector indicated a need for strong price proposals and Euro-branding. In this context, it was felt that Van Melle would strengthen its position by focusing its product range and offering Europe-wide quality, pricing and branding. Over time, Van Melle's product range was gradually reorganized into three groups:

(a) Van Melle brands, including: two global brands, to spearhead the development of internationalization (Mentos and Fruitella); additional local brands, better suited to local tastes, particularly in the Benelux, Germany and France;
(b) trading brands, whereby the Van Melle network of sales companies distributes products of affiliated companies (Verduijn, Smith's and Peco), all of which are traded in the Netherlands;
(c) Look-o-Look which emphasizes display and 'help yourself' purchasing and is mostly distributed on the Dutch market.

Vertical integration

Since 1986, Van Melle has not further integrated upstream or downstream. In order to do so, it would have to acquire firms much larger than itself (producers of glucose syrup). In order to maximize its contribution in the value-added chain, the firm has concentrated on its core business: producing high quality products at competitive prices.

Managerial reorganization

Internationalization in Van Melle's sector carries the double requirement to offer Europe-wide pricing, branding and quality uniformity, while adjusting locally for cultural differences. In order to achieve both consistency and flexibility, in 1988 it was felt appropriate to launch a new organization structure. This structure is called 'Management Cooperation System' and has resulted in a very flat organization, based on:

(a) local decentralized operational units: independent companies largely responsible for their own policies and results;
(b) strong central strategy and support functions.

Innovation

After the SMP, the innovation effort has largely centred on process improvement, notably automation. In terms of product innovation, efforts have centred on stabilizing quality and formulations, all requirements for internationalization. Substantial efforts have also been devoted to using natural raw materials and to environmental performance, a priority objective for Van Melle.

Competition avoidance

From the above, it is clear that Van Melle faces three types of competitor:

(a) local producers;
(b) large multinationals (Kraft-Jacobs-Suchard, Tobler (Sugus), etc.);
(c) private labels (Carrefour, Sainsbury, etc.).

The last two categories represent the strongest challenge. Consequently, Van Melle's strategy has focused on achieving the following two main objectives:

(a) European leadership, in selected products (Mentos, Fruitella), as it could not competitively match the full range of the multinationals. This is pursued through maintenance of high quality, tight management of logistics and Euro-branding;

(b) cost-competitiveness through scale economies and automation, to defend its position from local suppliers of private labels.

Other strategic responses

Van Melle is putting a strong emphasis on environmental performance. This has resulted in a long-term action plan.

F.4.8. Consequences of adjustments for company performance

Growth in turnover

Overall Van Melle turnover has grown by 233% in nominal terms (some 170% in real terms) over the period 1986–95. In the EU the growth has been much slower: some 160% in nominal terms and some 18% in real terms. Given overall market stagnation, this increase largely resulted from:

(a) entry into new markets, such as Spain, Greece and Portugal, which was facilitated by the SMP and by accession;

(b) market share consolidation, particularly in Germany;

(c) market expansion in the new German *Länder*.

In summary, the SMP coupled with the company's strategic choices has enabled Van Melle to build a solid European base for its international expansion.

Profitability and competitiveness

Over the period under review, Van Melle's profitability has evolved as follows.

Ratios (%)	1986	1988	1990	1992	1994
Operating results/net sales	9.7	8.0	6.3	9.1	10.0
Net profit/sales	5.4	3.8	3.1	5.7	6.8

It appears that although operating results as a proportion of sales are in the same range in 1995 as in 1986, the net profit/sales ratio has improved markedly. Since the data are consolidated, it is difficult to isolate the effect of EU operations. It should be remembered that:

(a) as a corporate policy, Van Melle looks after the long-term independence and interests of its shareholders rather than short-term share value;

(b) profits have been consistently reinvested in the company's development.

R&D

Over the 1985–95 period, the share of R&D has been increased from some 4–5% of total costs to some 6–8%.

F.4.9. Production costs and breakdown

As a result of the production rationalization, the structure of costs has been dramatically improved. The relative share of sourcing and processing has declined from some 80% of total costs in 1985 to some 65% in 1995. This has allowed the company to throw more resources into marketing and Euro-branding.

Also, total production costs were reduced by 15–20% during this period.

F.4.10. Productivity and competitiveness

Labour and capital productivity

Over the period under review, mainly as a result of automation and scale build up, the share of labour costs in total production costs was reduced from some 50% to 35%. The following table gives an indication of increases in manpower and capital productivity, at group level.

Ratios	1986	1988	1990	1992	1994
Turnover/employee[1]	169	175	163	206	208
Turnover/fixed assets (%)	3.7	3.3	3.1	3.1	2.9
Turnover/current assets (%)	2.8	2.8	2.7	2.6	1.7

[1] In '000 HFL. Turnover in nominal terms deflated by 3% per year.

It is apparent from the above table that, over the period 1985–95, at group level overall manpower productivity has constantly improved while capital productivity has been hard to maintain.

Productivity and legislation

The SMP legislation has had an indirect effect on Van Melle's productivity programme, because it created conditions where large scale, uniform and automated production made sense. It must be stressed that the productivity programme was also the consequence of a deliberate choice in marketing strategy and product range offering.

F.4.11. Conclusions: Van Melle's experience with the SMP

Overall, Van Melle's experience with the SMP has definitely been positive. Contrary to many other companies in the food processing sector, especially large and diversified ones, Van Melle did not immediately see the SMP as an opportunity to expand geographically in the EU. Indeed, they were already present in most countries. It can rather be said that the main SMP contribution to Van Melle's development was:

(a) the implementation of uniform packaging and labelling, allowing Euro-branding;
(b) the creation of conditions for large scale production and uniform formulations, hence drastically reducing unit production cost and liberating resources for market development (it should be stressed that Van Melle's aptitude actually to benefit from these cost reduction possibilities eventually depended on a successfully focused product range).

To this, Van Melle reacted by:

(a) geographically concentrating its production while increasing its productivity and scale;

(b) developing Euro-branding around a few core products, with basic attributes largely independent of local tastes and a long life cycle.

In conclusion, the SMP impact on Van Melle's development has been large and indirect. It has boosted an internationalization policy that had been anticipated by Van Melle at the eve of the single market launch. But within a mature EU confectionery market it was external developments especially in Central and Eastern Europe that have made scale and efficiency improvements really worthwhile.

'You may say that the EU legislation has helped us but has not been the most significant influence factor.'

F.5. Case study: Grupo Gallo s.a. (Spain)

F.5.1. Background

Grupo Gallo was founded by its current General Manager, who started flour production in 1946 with a single factory, located outside Barcelona, and an initial capital of PTA 15,000. From 1946 to the present the group has grown gradually. In 1994 it recorded sales of over PTA 20 bn and a 40% market share, and became the undisputed market leader in the Spanish pasta market. It milled some 163,100 t of hard wheat producing nearly 99,400 t of semolina and 66,500 t of pasta. The company has 497 employees and exports pasta with a value of more than PTA 2.6 bn. Grupo Gallo remains family-owned.

F.5.2. Gallo development and current strategy

The growth strategy of Grupo Gallo has been historically centred on two pillars: the acquisition of regional pasta factories and brands, and investment in production systems aimed at achieving vertical integration. Parallel to this, Comercial Gallo s.a. was founded in 1978 to provide central marketing for all group products.

Grupo Gallo now has a completely integrated structure that covers all stages of the production process, from semolina production to pasta manufacturing, and its own distribution system for its products which enables these to move directly to the sales points. The company's head office, national and international marketing divisions and central technical services are located in Barcelona. The company has four factories (Barcelona, La Coruña, Badajoz and Cordoba) specializing in semolina and pasta production, two flour mills (Málaga, Lerida) and one plant producing specialities (Barcelona). In addition, it has some investment in Portugal and the United States.

Currently almost all production is marketed under the 'Gallo' brand name. Although product diversification is low compared to other sectors, Grupo Gallo has a relatively wide range of products, particularly of pasta specialities, pasta sauces (a market leader), flour and breadcrumbs. The company exports semolina directly, mainly to third countries.

During the last decade the company continued to invest heavily (in excess of PTA 10 bn), modernizing its plants, increasing production capacity, and improving distribution structures. The key changes in strategy occurred in 1986 when an international division was created, and for the first time a public relations company was hired to launch a significant promotional campaign.

'Company philosophy changed from product selling to image selling.'

The accession of Spain and Portugal to the EU and the resulting opening of foreign markets strongly stimulated exports and thereby greatly increased sales. In 1995, Grupo Gallo exported pasta with a value of PTA 2.6 bn, mainly through its commercial subsidiaries in Portugal (Pagal Lusitania) and the USA (Pagal Intl). Exports to other EU countries are not significant. The company plans to expand export sales so that these account for 20% of production.

F.5.3. Financial history

Grupo Gallo sales, in current values, increased from PTA 7.347 bn in 1985 to PTA 20.347 bn in 1994. This represents a 177% increase over the decade under review. Investment has also steadily increased, but the rate of increase has slowed down in the last two years. As indicated above, these investments went into plant rationalization and cost reduction, particularly in terms of labour since the number of employees fell from 645 in 1989 to 497 in 1995.

Key statistics, Grupo Gallo (in million PTA)					
	Turnover	Investment	Exports	Profitability	Employment
1985	7,347	58	40	62	282
1987	10,957	54	-	15	288
1989	14,097	542	771	683	645
1990	14,438	500	840	204	598
1991	15,969	1,258	1,085	596	557
1992	18,191	1,056	1,965	472	521
1993	19,903	869	2,508	541	492
1994	20,347	894	2,074	597	497

F.5.4. Gallo in its competitive environment

The Spanish pasta sector employs some 1,400 persons and is characterized by the presence of a large number of small companies (26 in total) with an aggregate output of 225,000 t/year. Pasta consumption per capita in Spain is very low, around 4-4.5 kg/year. Grupo Gallo currently holds a 30–35% market share and is thus the largest pasta supplier in Spain. The second largest presence in the pasta market is held by Productos Alimenticios la Familia (15%) and seven other companies share between them the remaining 50%.

In anticipation of a growing demand, many of the larger companies invested heavily in the last few years to improve and increase their plant capacity and obtain economies of scale and improved competitiveness. However, the forecast growth in consumption did not occur and the pasta sector is now characterized by considerable excess capacity.

In addition, the retail sector is becoming ever more concentrated and powerful, introducing private labels which have already gained substantial market share. Manufacturers increasingly rely on retailers to gain access to shelf space and this in turn is leading to intense price competition.

In this environment, after a period of heavy advertising on the brand image, the company has had to cut back in order to maintain profitability. Up to a few years ago the market was characterized by heavily branded products (including 'Gallo') with smaller manufacturers producing mainly for retailers' own brands. The increasing strength of retailers has accentuated this trend and, consequently, Grupo Gallo now supplies some 30% of its output to retailers' own brands.

F.5.5. Principal changes as a result of the SMP

The company indicated that it considered Spanish and Portuguese accession to have had a considerably greater impact than the SMP. In particular it was noted that prior to accession Portugal operated an import ban for pasta and the removal of the ban had greatly expanded the market for Grupo Gallo. It was also noted that when the SMP became operative, Spain was still in the transition period. More generally, while the significance of exports has increased, it was noted that these are primarily to non-EU countries (except for Portugal) and the scale of exports to other EU countries remains very modest.

New market opportunities

Since 1985 exports have grown strongly (from PTA 40 million in 1985 to PTA 2.6 bn in 1995), but, as indicated above, this growth has primarily taken place in non-EU markets. It was, however, noted that intra-EU export procedures had become relatively easier.

Market structure

After Spanish accession to the EU there was concern about a potential invasion of Italian and/or French products owing to the perceived image and competitiveness of these countries' production. This invasion has not, however, taken place and imported pasta has only a very small market share (3-4%, compared to a 40% Italian market share in the French market).

However, Grupo Gallo highlighted the fact that the single market 'mutual recognition' principle brought about an increasingly 'unfair' competition from northern European manufacturers as southern European countries have stricter internal rules for pasta production (confined to the use of hard wheat semolina). Northern European countries thus market at lower prices pasta products made of soft wheat or potato starch. For Mediterranean producers (Italy, Spain, Greece and France) this situation has created a situation of 'unfair' competition. To some extent the problem has now been resolved by adding the 'superior quality pasta' denomination for pasta produced exclusively from durum wheat.

In 1980 Grupo Gallo had a portfolio of 135,000 active customers that were supplied from 27 warehouses served by 400 salesmen. In 1995 80% of sales went to 65 key customers, and exports were also destined for large customers. The company does not consider the SMP to have been directly responsible for this change in customer/supplier relationship:

(a) Up-stream: Grupo Gallo has three semolina factories and these arrange supply contracts with producers. It has commercial links with the main cereals cooperatives, but in general the price for its main raw material, durum wheat, is primarily CAP-determined.
(b) Down-stream: Grupo Gallo relies on Comercial Gallo, founded before Spain joined the EU, for domestic and other international marketing. Any changes in the role of Comercial Gallo, especially *vis-à-vis* retailers, are not attributed to the SMP but to general economic trends.

F.5.6. Grupo Gallo's evolution 1985–95: SMP impact

The company considers that the changes in organization that have taken place have resulted from accession rather than the SMP.

Internationalization

In 1986 Comercial Gallo set up an international division to access foreign markets, especially the USA and Canada.

Total investment requirements to compete

As indicated above, the company spent heavily on promotion to build up its brand as well as on plant modernization and rationalization.

Capacity adjustment

Some significant changes have occurred since 1989, in particular a growth in output volumes from 59,000 tonnes (of pasta) in 1989 to 76,074 tonnes in 1995. However, the SMP was not perceived to have had any influence on this growth in the scale of production.

Location decisions

There have been no significant changes in production location.

Cost-cutting/rationalization

There have been substantial reductions in logistics costs owing to the evolution of the retailing structure and to the decrease in the number of customers. In 1980, the company had 135,000 active customers supplied from 27 warehouses served by 400 salesmen. In 1995, 80% of sales went to just 65 key customers.

Substantial investment was undertaken to reduce labour and other production costs. Consequently, significant reductions in staff have taken place. Personnel numbers have been reduced from 645 persons in 1989 to 497 in 1994. In Barcelona Grupo Gallo has a fully automated plant not requiring any personnel in the production process.

Adaptation of product range

The company strategy has focused on production and marketing of dry pasta with only a minimal degree of diversification and differentiation. This strategy has not changed since 1986.

Marketing strategies

There have been no strategic changes as a direct consequence of the SMP, although since the late 1980s Grupo Gallo began to have an important presence in AEFPA (Spanish Association of Pasta Producers) and to collaborate with ICEX (Spanish Institute for International Trade).

Vertical integration

The company did not make any changes in company structure in terms of vertical integration as a result of the SMP.

Managerial reorganization

Company reorganization took place in response to accession rather than the SMP (creation of an international division in 1986).

Innovation

There has been minimal product innovation although recently the company has launched a vitaminized pasta.

Competition avoidance

Grupo Gallo remains the Spanish market leader for pasta and to maintain this it has invested heavily in advertising and concentrated on maintaining a high quality product.

Other strategic responses

Company strategy depends entirely on Spanish domestic market characteristics. Transport costs are relatively high for this type of product and for this reason the Madrid plant was closed in 1985 to concentrate production in other factories and to achieve economies of scale. Due to the evolution of retail structures the company has started to produce own-label products for retailers which now account for 30% of output.

F.5.7. Consequences of adjustments for company performance

Growth in turnover

Between 1985 and 1994 turnover grew from some PTA 7.5 bn to PTA 20 bn and the export share of this turnover went from virtually zero to over 10%. This growth in exports is not attributable to the SMP as most exports go to third countries. More important has been the fact of Spain's accession in 1986 and the creation of the international division in that same year.

Productivity and competitiveness

The company considers that the improvements in productivity and competitiveness achieved over the last decade enable it to compete efficiently in domestic and international markets.

Profitability

In general, sector profitability is poor, but the company's investments have nevertheless performed due to Grupo Gallo's share in the volume growth in premium distributors' brands. This has meant that in spite of intense price competition in the sector, profitability has been more or less maintained during the 1990s.

R&D

The company undertakes minimal R&D.

F.5.8. Production costs and breakdown

There have been no major changes in production costs as a result of the SMP. Labour costs have increased but these increases have been offset by a reduction in numbers employed. Logistics costs have reduced through time due to the fact that the company is servicing a reduced number of customers.

Changes in processing costs

Raw material costs amount to around 50–60% of production costs. The SMP did not change this pattern since durum wheat prices depend on the common agricultural policy. Improvements in cost structure have only been achieved as a result of the economies of scale obtained.

The price of packaging varies between PTA 7 and PTA 45 per unit depending upon the product (pasta, sauces, flour, breadcrumbs). There have been no perceptible changes as a result of the SMP.

Changes in administrative costs

The most important cost reduction has been due to the use of information technology both in factories and in administrative work.

Changes in marketing costs

There has been a very substantial reduction in the sales force and substantial increases in advertising expenditure. In recent years, Grupo Gallo's advertising rose from just over PTA 200 million in 1991 to around over PTA 1,100 million in 1993 and PTA 900 million in 1994.

Changes in distribution costs

Transport costs are high in relation to the end-product price and this has stimulated investment in new plant (e.g. in Galicia) to minimize these costs.

Evolution in product prices

Price increases have been kept below the rate of inflation during the last years due to fierce sector competition.

F.5.9.   Productivity and competitiveness

Both labour and capital productivity have increased due to the investments carried out.

F.5.10.   Conclusions: Grupo Gallo's experience with the SMP

The extent to which the SMP has affected Grupo Gallo appears to have been very limited. This is partially because the company is still primarily a national player but also because contrary to expectation there has been little import penetration in the Spanish market. In part this is due to the relatively poor returns to be generated by shipping a low unit value product long distances. Even where foreign investment in Spanish plants has occurred (e.g. the Italian company Barilla acquired a Spanish plant and company), the market share captured has been relatively insignificant.

Overall the company's strategy and performance have clearly been far more affected by non-SMP factors (slow demand growth, increasing retailer concentration and, in particular, Spanish and Portuguese accession to the EU) and its orientation has tended to be defensive in its own market and focused on third-country exports. Part of the reason for this orientation could also lie in the fact that the barriers to entry in neighbouring countries, such as France and Italy, would be particularly high due to the presence of well-established market leaders.

Bibliography

Balassa, B. [1996], 'The Determinants of Intra-industry Specialization in United States Trades', *Oxford Economic Papers*, July 1966, pp. 220–256.

Bhaskara Rao, B. (ed.) [1994], *Co-integration for the Applied Economist*, London, St Martin's Press, 1994.

BIPE et al. [1989], *Europe in 1993: Economic Outlook by Sector*, BIPE (Paris)/Ifo-Institut (Munich)/ Prometeia (Bologna), 1989.

Blandford, D. [1984], 'Changes in Food Consumption in the OECD Area', *European Review of Agricultural Economics*, Vol. 11-1, Berlin-New York, Mouton De Gruyter,1984, pp. 43–65.

Buigues, P., Ilkowitz, F., Lebrun, J.F. [1990], 'The Impact of the Internal Market by Industrial Sector: the Challenge for the Member States', *European Economy*, Special Edition, 1990, Luxembourg, Office for Official Publications of the EC.

CIAA [1995], *Status Report on Food Legislation in the EU*, Confédération des Industries Agro-Alimentaires, 1 December 1995.

Connor, J. et al. [1985], *The Food Manufacturing Industry*, Massachusetts, Lexington Books, 1985.

DRI [1995], *The Emergence of Pan-European Markets*, Interim Report for the European Commission, September 1995.

DRI [1995a], *Survey of the Trade Associations' Perception of the Effects of the Single Market*, Final Report for the European Commission, November 1995.

European Commission [1985], *Completing the Internal Market*, White Paper from the Commission to the European Council, COM(85) 310 final, 14 June 1985, Luxembourg, Office for Official Publications of the EC.

European Commission [1985], *Completion of the Internal Market: Community Legislation on Foodstuffs*, Communication from the Commission to the Council and the European Parliament, COM(85) 603 final, 8 November 1985, Luxembourg, Office for Official Publications of the EC.

European Commission [1989], *The Free Movement of Foodstuffs within the Community*, second Communication on Food Law, COM(89) 256 final, Luxembourg, Office for Official Publications of the EC.

European Commission [1992], *The Implementation of the White Paper on the Completion of the Internal Market*, Seventh Report of the Commission to the Council and the European Parliament COM(92) 383 final, 2 September 1992, Luxembourg, Office for Official Publications of the EC.

European Commission [1992], *Dable Report 1: Synopsis of European Enterprises*, Brussels, 1992.

European Commission [1992], *The Geographical Dimension of Competition in the European Single Market*, December 1992.

European Commission [1993], *La Dimension Environnementale de '1992'*, Report of the European Commission's Task Force on the Environment and the Internal Market, Bonn, Economica Verlag, 1993.

European Commission [1994], *Internal Market – Current Status 1 July 1994*, Volumes 1 to 4, July 1994, Luxembourg, Office for Official Publications of the EC.

European Commission [1995], *The Single Market in 1994*, report from the Commission to the Council and the European Parliament, COM(95) 238 final, 15 June 1995, Luxembourg, Office for Official Publications of the EC.

European Commission [1995], *XXIVth Report on Competition Policy – 1994*, COM(95) 142 final, 28 April 1995, Luxembourg, Office for Official Publications of the EC.

European Commission [1995], *State of Community Law Concerning the Internal Market: Situation at 15 April 1995*, Doc. No XV/530/95.

European Commission [1995], *Twelfth Annual Report on Monitoring the Application of Community Law (1994)*, OJ C254, 29 September 1995, Luxembourg, Office for Official Publications of the EC.

European Commission [1996], *Cooperation between administrations for enforcement of internal market law — A progress report,* Report from the Commission to the Council and the European Parliament, COM(96) 20 final , 29 January 1996, Luxembourg, Office for Official Publications of the EC.

European Commission [1996], *The Single Market in 1995*, Report from the Commission to the Council and the European Parliament, COM(96) 51 final, 20 February 1996, Luxembourg, Office for Official Publications of the EC.

European Commission [1996], *Panorama of EU industry 1995/96,* 1996, Luxembourg, Office for Official Publications of the EC.

Galizzi, G. and Venturini, L. [1994], *Product Innovations in the Food Industry: Nature, characteristics and performance*, Piacenza Catholic University, 1994.

Group Mac [1988], *The 'Cost of Non-Europe' in the Foodstuffs Industry*, Volume 12, Parts A and B, European Commission, 1988, Luxembourg, Office for Official Publications of the EC.

Grunert, K.G., Hartvig Larsen, H., Madesn, T.K. and Baadsgaard, A. [1996], *Market Orientation in Food and Agriculture*, Boston, 1996.

Grunert, K.G., Harmsen, H., Meulenberg, M., Kuiper, E., Ottowitz, T., Declerck, F., Traill, B. and Goransson, G. [1995], *A Framework for Analysing Innovation in the Food Sector*, European Commission AAIR Programme, Discussion Paper No 10, December 1995.

Magner, J. [1989], 'The Environmental Issues in the Context of the Internal Market 1992 –The Situation in Denmark', in European Commission, *La Dimension Environnementale de '1992'*, Report of the European Commission's Task Force on the Environment and the Internal Market, Bonn, Economica Verlag, 1993.

OECD [1983], *The food industries in the 1980s*, OECD Conference Proceedings, Paris, OECD, 1983.

Oustapassidis, K. et al. [1995], *A Review of Some Preliminary Data Relating to Structural Change Within the European Food Industries and Factors Affecting It*, European Commission AAIR Programme, Discussion Paper No 9, December 1995.

Pitts, E. et al. [1995], *Measuring Food Industry Competitiveness*, European Commission AAIR programme, Discussion Paper No 7, July 1995.

Porter, M.E. [1980], *Competitive Strategy: Techniques for Analysing Industries and Competitors*, New York, The Free Press, 1980.

Porter, M.E. [1985], *Competitive Advantage: Creating and Sustaining Superior Performance*, New York, The Free Press, 1985.

Seymoor Cooke [1995], *Mergers and Acquisitions Worldwide*, London, 1995.

Seymoor Cooke [1995], *Alliances and Joint Ventures Worldwide*, London, 1995.

Stirling Univeristy [1990], *The Evolution of European Retailing*, Report by the Institute of Retail Studies, Stirling University, 1990.

Sutton, J. [1991], *Sunk Costs and Market Structure*, Boston, MIT Press, 1991.

Shaw, B. et al. [1989], 'Structural Change in the European Food Chain', in B. Traill (ed.), *Prospects for the European food system*, London, Elsevier, 1989.

Traill, B. et al. [1995], *Trade, FDI and Competitiveness in the European Food Industries*, European Commission AAIR Programme, Discussion Paper No 1, September 1995.

Uhl, J. N. [1991], 'Comparisons of Food Marketing Systems in the EU and US', in Buchholz, H.E. and Wendt, H. (ed) *Food Markets and the Food Industry in the Single European Market*, Proceedings of 25th EAAE Conference, Germany, Braunschweig (FAL), 1991.

Utterback, J.M. [1994], *Mastering the Dynamics of Innovation*, Boston, Harvard Business School Press, 1994.

Winkelmann, M., Pitts, E. and Matthews, A. [1995], *Revealed Comparative Advantage in the European Food Industry*, European Commission AAIR Programme, Discussion Paper No 6, March 1995.